D0209334

The Garden and the Workshop

The Garden and the Workshop

ESSAYS ON THE
CULTURAL HISTORY OF
VIENNA AND
BUDAPEST

Péter Hanák

PRINCETON UNIVERSITY PRESS

PRINCETON, NEW JERSEY

Copyright © 1998 by Princeton University Press
Published by Princeton University Press, 41 William Street,
Princeton, New Jersey 08540
In the United Kingdom: Princeton University Press,
Chichester, West Sussex

All Rights Reserved

Second printing, and first paperback printing, 1999
Paperback ISBN 0-691-00965-1

The Library of Congress has cataloged the cloth edition of this book as follows

Hanák, Péter.
The garden and the workshop : essays on the cultural
history of Vienna and Budapest / Péter Hanák.
p. cm.
Includes bibliographical references and index.
ISBN 0-691-01554-6 (cloth : alk. paper)
1. Vienna (Austria)—Civilization. 2. Budapest (Hungary)—
Civilization. 3. Vienna (Austria)—Intellectual life.
4. Budapest (Hungary)—Intellectual life. I. Title.
DB851.H34   1998
943.6'13—dc21   97-22688

This book has been composed in Sabon
by Wilsted & Taylor Publishing Services

The paper used in this publication meets the minimum requirements of
ANSI/NISO Z39.48-1992 (R1997) (*Permanence of Paper*)

http://pup.princeton.edu

Printed in the United States of America

2 4 6 8 10 9 7 5 3

CONTENTS

ILLUSTRATIONS

PÉTER HANÁK
1921–1997

WITH CHARACTERISTIC eagerness and almost boyish pride, Péter Hanák had awaited the appearance of this book, his first to be published in the America he had come to love so well. Just as the volume is going to press, death has intervened to rob him of his joy—and to deprive the historical profession of one of its most energetic and enthusiastic practitioners. Through fifty years of drastic historical change, Péter Hanák was among the most active Hungarian scholars: first in placing Hungary's history in transnational perspective; then in bringing newer Western methods to bear on Hungarian historical experience. In a world divided by the politics of the Cold War, Péter Hanák built bridges through historical scholarship, both in his writing and in his vigorous participation in the international conferences that have so strongly shaped contemporary academic culture.

For Péter Hanák history studied and history lived were inevitably allied. The cruelties of mid-century European politics were repeatedly visited upon him. Denied a university education under Hungarian anti-Jewish laws in 1939, he embarked on a career as a metal worker and trade unionist in Pécs. In 1942, he was "conscripted" into Jewish labor service in the Hungarian army. That fate, harsh though it was, enabled him to survive. His parents died in Auschwitz and his brother disappeared without a trace.

Like other young Jews who survived the Hungarian holocaust—one thinks of two outstanding modern European historians who became his valued colleagues, György Ránki and Ivan Berend—Hanák as a young man eagerly embraced Communism after the liberation of Hungary by the Red Army. His university education, possible at last, led him to history; his newfound politics, to the study of Hungarian radical movements in 1905. As a young assistant professor at Eötvös Loránd University (1953–1956), Hanák began to work on the nationality movements in 1848 and the restructuring of Hungary after the defeated revolution.

In 1956, contemporary history brusquely intervened once more in historian Hanák's life and work. As a sympathetic participant in the Hungarian movement for autonomy and reform in that year, Hanák was dismissed from his university teaching post. Yet for him as for some other outstanding scholars, the Academy of Science served as a refuge when the university was barred. In the painfully slow thaw in still-Stalinist Hungary, the Academy cautiously opened an intellectual window to the West. In the early sixties, Hanák and a few of his peers were allowed to travel to Western Europe and America, where a new world of scholarship entered their field of vision. They bought books and periodicals closed to them since the war's beginning, learned English, and began to consort with their Western colleagues—none more easily than the open, friendly Péter Hanák. By 1971, he was teaching as a visiting professor in Columbia and Yale, though he could not teach at home.

Hanák's major work in the sixties and early seventies recast our historical understanding of Hungary's political and social development in the mid-nineteenth century. In a multipronged attack on the Hungarian nationalist and traditional Austrian views of Hungary's place in the empire of the Habsburgs, Hanák brought the lights of international, social-structural, economic, and political analysis to bear, revealing in a new way the dynamics of the Austro-Hungarian political system in its wider European context. His undoctrinaire Marxism unquestionably enlarged the capaciousness of his grasp and enriched the density of his analysis.

By the 1970s, Péter Hanák's exposure to Western historical ideas became evident in his turn to a new kind of social history. The problem of *embourgeoisement* that preoccupied the younger generation of German historians, such as Jürgen Kocka, made its appearance in Hanák's *Ungarn in der Donaumonarchie* (Hungary in the Danubian [Habsburg] Monarchy). This German edition of 1984 explored the questions of Jewish and other minority assimilation as well as the demographic and social-structural transformation of Hungary before World War I.

Beyond these new concerns with social history, Péter Hanák became engaged with intellectual and cultural problems. Here, I suspect, his leadership in organizing colloquia between Hungarian and American historians for the exploration of comparative historical problems played its part. Several colloquia were devoted to Progressivism in both countries. This reflected current ideological interests in both the United States and Hungary. While young American historians were preoccupied with the reanimation of the legacy of pre–World War Progressivism and the New Deal in the conservative atmosphere of the Cold War, their Hungarian counterparts were reviving their own cosmopolitan and democratic intellectual tradition of the turn of the century. The latter, which included such national cultural heroes as Béla Bartók, the poet Endre Ady, and the later Communist philosopher-laureate, György Lukács, could be safely utilized in the development of a heightened liberal and democratic consciousness under the slowly softening Communist raj. In pursuit of this interest, Péter Hanák published a book on Oscar Jászi, an outstanding political and social analyst of the Austro-Hungarian empire who, fleeing his native Hungary in 1919, brought his great gifts to Oberlin College and the American political science profession.

Jászi's transnational ideal of a democratic comity of Hungary with its neighbors undoubtedly affected Hanák's historical as well as political outlook. In particular, he identified himself in the last years of Communism with the strengthening of Hungary's ties with Austria and the development of a multinational Central European community. His assumption in 1991 of a leading role in the Central European University founded by George Soros expressed in terms of professional commitment Hanák's cosmopolitan outlook, which was both Western-oriented and devoted to overcoming the ignorance and indifference of every Central European country to the culture and history of its neighbors.

As he had moved in his Marxist phase from the history of national movements to a densely textured political and institutional history of Hungary as a component of the larger empire, so Hanák moved from his Western-inspired social history of the 1970s to a fourth historical terrain in the 1980s; namely, that of cultural history. *The Garden and the Workshop* presents some of the fruits of that concern. Even more than his earlier work, these essays reflect Hanák's openness to the new perspectives and methods emerging in Western Europe and America. He brings to bear on problems of Hungarian cultural history the approaches of French explorers of *l'image de l'autre*, German students of *Wohnkultur*, American multidisciplinary historians of urban high culture, Austrian analysts of middle-brow theatrical and musical culture—to name but a few. If these individual efforts, so demanding in their scholarly variety, are not uniformly successful, they accomplish the major objective that informed the life's work of their author. A true citizen of the Republic of Letters throughout his long and often painful experience of history, Péter Hanák remained a teaching scholar, bringing to Hungary the lights of understanding generated in the world beyond its borders and, in exchange, projecting to those outside the profoundly enlightening experience of Hungary's rich history, culture and scholarship.

Péter Hanák's life and work bears eloquent witness to the intense relationship between history studied and history lived. He knew how to draw from the very terrors of history, of which he knew too many, its potential for enhancing our understanding of the human condition in its historical vicissitudes.

Carl E. Schorske
December 2, 1997

ACKNOWLEDGMENTS

MOST CHAPTERS of this volume were written in the 1980s and early 1990s, after I had finished writing and editing one of the volumes in the recent series of "The History of Hungary." This meant, first, that I was able—even induced—to explain problems, particularly those of cultural history that I could not do within the limited framework of a manual. Second, this occurred during the last stage of Communism in Hungary, the period of the "soft dictatorship," when the leadership of cultural administration tolerated discussions on such problems as decadence of the arts, existentialism as a humane philosophy, the eroticism of death, social marginality, and so on. At the same time I became acquainted with new questions and methods of French, German, and American cultural history.

I was very lucky that I could be a fellow of the Institute of History of the Hungarian Academy of Sciences for forty-five years, an institute that was a refuge of liberalism, creating and preserving the atmosphere of free scholarly thinking. I feel deep gratitude for the stimulating milieu, and particularly for the inestimable help of my late dear friend, György Ránki. Next to him, it was Professor Carl Schorske who offered the greatest support in my advancement. As a visiting professor in the United States in 1971, I had the privilege to take part in his faculty seminar at Princeton University. These meetings and discussions rendered me lasting experiences of how to approach problems of the history of ideas and artistic creation. I thank him for his beneficial influence, received through many common conferences and personal conversations during the last quarter century. He was helpful also in obtaining a fellowship for me at the Institute for Advanced Study in Princeton in 1986–1987. In the untroubled peace of the Institute I was able to complete this volume of my essays. The publication of my book is the suitable occasion to express my highest appreciation to the Institute and its professors for their advice and remarks.

As to the single articles, I am indebted to Dr. Gábor Gyáni for his valuable information relating to the materials of the Budapest City Archive, and to Dr. Ilona Sármány-Parsons for her contribution to my considerations on art history, and to the chapters on urbanization, and especially of Viennese and Budapest art nouveau. I recall with gratitude and sorrow the relevant remarks of the outstanding deceased poet, the late Ágnes Nemes Nagy, who corrected my views relating to fin-de-siècle decadence. I have to thank very much the informative advice given by the experts of the Archive of War History (Kriegsarchiv) in Vienna and in Budapest, where I collected the unknown people's letters for my article, "Vox Populi." I wish to express my sincere admiration for the devoted collaboration of my translators, particularly Professor Susan Gal, Professor Solomon Wank, Dr. Gloria Deak, Éva Pálmai, Brian Mclean, Nicholas Parsons, Christina Rozsnyai, and Peter Doherty.

Last but not least I have many thanks to give the editors of Princeton University Press for their laborious, careful, and accurate work.

I finished the introduction of this volume with the following words: "The workshop of Pest in a way was also a garden, sprouting flowers and fruits which, though frequently uprooted, could not be torn out by the blows and storms of history." I wrote these lines in Princeton, on October 23, 1986, the thirtieth anniversary of the 1956 Revolution in Hungary.

PUBLICATION HISTORY OF CHAPTERS

THE GREATEST PART of Chapter One, "Urbanization and Civilization: Vienna and Budapest in the Nineteenth Century," appeared in *Történelmi Szemle* (Historical Review) nos. 1–2 (Budapest, 1984). Translated by Brian Mclean.

Chapter Two, "The Image of the Germans and the Jews in the Hungarian Mirror of the Nineteenth Century," was published in *Századok* (Centuries) nos. 5–6 (Budapest, 1985). Translated by Peter Doherty and László Kontler.

Chapter Three, "The Garden and the Workshop: Reflections on Fin-de-Siècle Culture in Vienna and Budapest," appeared in *Ujhold Évkönyv* (Yearbook of the New Moon) (Budapest, 1986). Translated by Christina Rozsnyai.

Chapter Four, "The Alienation of Death in Budapest and Vienna at the Turn of the Century," was first published in my book *A kert és a műhely* (The Garden and the Workshop) (Budapest, 1988). Translated by Solomon Wank.

Chapter Five, "The Start of Endre Ady's Literary Career (1903–1905)," appeared under the title "A Szent Lélek lovagjától az Uj Versekig" (From the Knight of the Holy Spirit to the New Poems) in *Uj Irás* (New Poems) no. 8 (Budapest, 1978). Translated by Éva Pálmai.

Chapter Six, "The Cultural Role of the Vienna-Budapest Operetta," was published in *Budapest and New York. Studies in Metropolitan Transformation 1870–1930*, edited by Thomas Bender and Carl E. Schorske (New York, 1994). Translated by Gloria Deak.

Chapter Seven, "Social Marginality and Cultural Creativity in Vienna and Budapest (1890–1914)," first appeared in *Etudes Historiques Hongroises 1990. Vol. 4: European Intellectual Trends and Hungary*, edited by Ferenc Glatz (Budapest, 1990). Translated by Susan Gal. A revised version appeared in *Kreatives Milieu. Wien um 1900*, edited by Emil Brix and Allan Janik (Vienna–Munich, 1993).

Chapter Eight, "Vox Populi: Intercepted Letters in the First World War," was published under the title "Népi levelek az első világháborúból" (People's Letters from the First World War) in *Valóság* (Reality) no. 3 (Budapest, 1973). Translated by Nicholas Parsons.

INTRODUCTORY REFLECTIONS
ON CULTURAL HISTORY

THIS BOOK is about two famous, neighboring Central European cities: Vienna and Budapest. They are bound by a common destiny, tradition, and culture, yet divided by their history, character, tradition, and culture as well. Nothing can demonstrate the truth of this paradox more plainly than the way they were spliced together in the former Austro-Hungarian Monarchy, almost as complements of each other. For although they shared the same framework of state and enjoyed the same prosperity and cultural florescence under the Monarchy, their rivalry, mutual suspicion, social structure, and mentality drove a wedge between them.

The antagonism manifested itself more plainly in the last half century. The 1950s turned Vienna, the resurrected capital of *felix Austria*, into a border fortress of the West, the free world's shop window to the East, and a restored monument to the contented, peacetime years of old. Budapest, meanwhile, was featured on Western front pages, and in the minds of newspaper readers, in connection with the 1956 Revolution, and then with a loosening of the bonds of the Soviet system and hopes of liberal reforms. In the last few decades, Vienna has almost been made a star by art connoisseurs, the educated public, and tourists. Fin-de-siècle Vienna has been admired, researched, and explained in a succession of guidebooks, albums and specialist books, and several dozen monographs on cultural history.[1] Budapest, on the other hand, has been confined to one or two worthwhile books in Western languages.[2]

What lies behind Vienna's extraordinary present-day popularity, which greatly exceeds the recognition it received at the turn of the century? First, perhaps, comes the linguistic advantage. A knowledge of German is many times more common than a knowledge of Hungarian, and that also applies to translators, of course. Another factor may be emigration. Far more writers, artists, and men of letters, before and after the Second World War, migrated to America from Austria than from Hungary. Understandably, they glorified Vienna, with strong nostalgia and no little exaggeration. Laying aside partiality, it must be acknowledged that Vienna's time-honored culture, and the French and Italian-style culture grafted onto German in general, surpassed the culture of eastern Central Europe, notably in music, fine art, and drama, although Hungarian culture vied strongly with Vienna, mainly in poetry, romantic fiction, and twentieth-century music. This probably explains Vienna's popularity among the wider public, as a spectacle

and a civilization. It does not explain satisfactorily what aroused the scholarly interest of the American intellectual elite of outstanding thinkers, writers, and historians. Why have they seen in fin-de-siècle Vienna a paradigm
of the change of cultural epoch, comparable to Paris? Let me anticipate certain ideas in this book by mentioning briefly some characteristics of Viennese culture.

One obvious feature is that the national question plays a secondary role,
or is absent altogether. Austrians were almost wholly lacking in national romanticism. The occasional manifestations filtered in from outside. The
prime example here is the playwright Grillparzer. He did not regard himself
as a German, and only by citizenship as an Austrian; he was a veritable Viennese: "The best thing a man can be is a man," he remarked, "whether he
wears an *Attila* [hussar tunic] and speaks Hungarian, or, despite his German native language, dons an English frock coat and a French hat." I think
the best evidence here is that there was no expressly Austrian opera between
Beethoven's *Fidelio* and Richard Strauss's *Salome*. This great genre of national romanticism simply passed Vienna by.

What exercised the Austrian mind were not local dissensions or problems
of national destiny, but vital questions of universal human importance: the
nature of the world, life and death, illusion and reality, the soul, and sexuality. These are all attractive subjects, which have become more immediate
still in our day than they were at the end of the last century. Austrian high
culture was dominated by the problems of existence and nonexistence, the
finality of death, existential solitude, the place of the individual, and the secrets of love, in other words by Eros and Psyche, and the related embrace of
Eros and Thanatos. Imbuing all this was fin-de-siècle malaise, an uneasy
sense of nameless anxieties, a sinister inkling of imminent dangers. These
were motifs that only two cataclysmic wars, with fascist and communist
dictatorships, gas chambers and gulags, would endow with a horrifyingly
real significance, as a full historical and artistic vindication of Viennese
culture.

Vienna's brilliance long obscured the virtues and merits of its neighbors,
though these should not be underestimated. Budapest's last "peacetime" quarter century brought a cultural flowering of European significance. The liberalism of the nobility and the related national romanticism were in decline by that
time. The cultural regeneration at the beginning of this century embraced the
subject matter and forms of the European Sezession, modernism, and the
avant-garde. The Viennese themes—life, death, solitude, psyche, guilt, eroticism—appeared, along with a crisis of identity in poetry and pictures and on
stage. However, there are two essential differences dividing the cultural renewals of Budapest and Vienna. The Hungarian reform generation solved its
identity problems not by withdrawing from the national community but by re-
vising the concept and idea of a nation. It evolved an anti-feudal national

awareness based on the people and on critical self-knowledge, which chimed in with the program of transforming the whole society in a radical, democratic way. The other essential difference was that the national and universally human aspects were not severed or opposed to each other. Ady the poet, Lechner and Lajta the Sezession architects, and Bartók the musician discovered a submerged, forgotten realm of folk versification and folk forms and melodies, and built it into the new forms of twentieth-century modernism. Ady and his associates loved their people and worried about their fate for the same reasons and to the same extent as they worried about the catastrophes befalling mankind. They were neither chauvinistic nor cosmopolitan, but intellectuals who saw people and nation, nation and mankind, as one.

Although the studies in this book deal with cultural history at the turn of the century, it is worth recalling briefly, in a few introductory lines, some features of the region's history over the last 2,000 years. During its stormy history, this region (it has become acceptable again to call it Central Europe) was always an integral part of the Occident, as its eastern marches, Mediterranean culture and the Greco-Roman state, law, science, and art took permanent root. Pannonia was a northeastern border province of the Roman Empire for almost four centuries. The *limes* followed the Danube. Vindobona ("radiant city"), with its fine-sounding Celtic name, and Aquincum ("warm spring"), an Illyrian-Celtic foundation, became the two centers of the province, military strongholds and thriving civilian towns. Vienna and Buda-Pest rose again on the same sites at the beginning of the second millennium. The same region was crossed by the border of the Carolingian Empire, and later the Holy Roman Empire, which expanded in the direction of Hungary, Bohemia, and Poland after 1000. In the high Middle Ages, this was the limit of Western Christendom, with its culture-friendly, renewing Church. In early modern times, this marked the extent of Protestantism, and with it of Christian pluralism—the germ of hard-won religious toleration and slowly maturing political pluralism. The River Vistula and the Carpathian Mountains formed the eastern edge of the Renaissance, the Reformation, and early Humanist enlightenment and scholarship. An outstanding part was played in all this by Vienna, by its rival Buda, and by Prague, Krakow, and Warsaw, in conflict or alliance with them.

The Illyrians and Celts made an inspired choice when they picked the future sites of Vienna and Buda-Pest. They lie between the Alps and the plains, at the border between climatic zones, on the banks of the Danube, and at the junction of important trading routes running north-south and east-west. Both cities developed rapidly in the twelfth and thirteenth centuries, gaining the rank of royal free cities and then of princely seats. The growth and rivalry lasted until the end of the fifteenth century, culminating in a battle for Central European supremacy, between Frederic III of Habsburg and the Hungarian King Matthias Corvinus. The struggle, lasting a century, was won by the Habsburgs, who politicized more successfully and married more judiciously. Behind Vienna lay German support; behind Buda lurked the threat from the heathen Turks. For two long centuries, Habsburg rule brought the region misfortune rather than peace and prosperity. Their empire was scoured by religious wars and dynastic power struggles until the end of the seventeenth century. Then came a change, marked by three milestones: the relief of Vienna and reconquest of Buda from the Turks (1683–1686), the treaties of Utrecht and Rastatt ending the War of the Spanish Succession (1713–1714), and the Pragmatic Sanction that settled Hungary's status within the empire (1723). These three historical events shifted the Habsburg Empire's center of gravity from Western to Central Europe, and regained liberated Hungary its limited constitutionalism. This change of position continued under enlightened absolutism, with establishment of the "Danubian Monarchy," and culminated, under Emperor Francis Joseph, in the Austro-Hungarian Compromise (*Ausgleich*) of 1867. The resulting Dual Monarchy established an equilibrium between West and East, and within the Central European region, based on a manifold compromise between Vienna and Budapest. Fragile and vulnerable though the Dualist system may have been, Vienna and Budapest became for a long time an integral part of European culture and of the European equation.

The studies in this book do not form an editorially or thematically coherent whole. Readers may wonder what can link into some kind of coherence such distant subjects as the fin-de-siècle perception of death and popular letters of complaint, or artistic ferment and the worldwide success of operetta. The intrinsic connections between the studies derive not from uniformity of subject or narrative continuity but from a practical and theoretical concept of cultural history. This imposes on me, as author, a duty in the introduction to clarify how I define and employ the notion of "comparative cultural history." Beyond the conventional meaning, my definition involves three important theses. One looks beyond the peaks of high culture and its achievements, to embrace urban mass culture and the cultural products of peasants, traditionally relegated to folklore. I see as relevant to cultural history, instead of aesthetic worth or artistic excellence, the representative values and forces that shape the lifestyle and ideas of a community—in short, its normative behavior.

This leads to my second thesis: culture does not appear in itself, as the manifestation of an "absolute" spirit, but in constant interaction with society. In this sense, cultural history is akin to social and intellectual history, but goes beyond it, by embracing also a society's principal conventions (*Gewohnheitskultur*). This in turn brings cultural history close to the field of research dealing with everyday life, and at the same time expands its horizons to encompass the mentality and traditions that govern everyday life. My third thesis poses a link between cultural history and politics. This conclusion does not simply derive from the empirical observation that political events, especially a government's cultural policies, influence the free manifestation of culture. It reflects my realization that politics and culture are interpenetrating realms of human creativity and destructiveness. When investigated analytically they may appear to be separate, but in the synthetic analysis of cultural history they are intimately united.

Such were my tenets when writing and selecting the essays in this book. They explain why the chapters encompass different fields of cultural history. The book starts with a comprehensive theme: urbanization. The modern metropolis is a center of civilization and cultural elevation, the seat of education and high culture, spontaneous mass culture, and both organized and spontaneous counterculture. Modern urban studies deal with almost all major areas of cultural history: urban policy and planning, economy and ecology, sociology, housing and living (*Wohnkultur*), and the history of style. Historians may touch on everything from architecture and art history to social science, ethnography, and even medicine, to provide bonds for broad, interdisciplinary research. The opening essay revolves around three subjects: the relations between embourgeoisement and urbanization; the Central European model of middle-class living; and the causes behind the development of a new taste and style, affected by the cultural upheaval and generation revolt of the outgoing nineteenth century.

The second essay examines the development of prejudices against "other" groups. Social psychology is especially useful in dealing with this subject, and steers historiography into pioneering areas such as the study of national character and the psychology of noncognitive beliefs and stereotypes. The essay traces anti-German and anti-Semitic images, and how perception of them changed over time. The three extensive essays that follow were inspired by social and intellectual history, especially Carl E. Schorske's exquisite book entitled *Fin-de-Siècle Vienna*. The leitmotiv in all three essays is the interaction between politics and culture, specifically, how culture reflects and reacts to social and political challenges. The cultural upheaval at the end of the nineteenth century, the social milieu that favored stimulating intellectual battles, and the flight into creativity from ever more threatening, destructive trends and ideas are reflected in the comparison between Vienna and Budapest. The title of the third essay—and of the book—is not a metaphor formulated later, but two contemporary keywords. Fin-de-siècle artists in Vienna withdrew into their private *gardens*, to tend the gardens of their souls. Those in Budapest termed newspaper offices *workshops*—a phrase coined by the poet Endre Ady—where they found both a refuge and companions in arms. Fin-de-siècle modernism led to an awareness of existential dangers, in the case of the Viennese, and of the common fate of Hungarians and humanity, in Budapest.

The chapter on operetta in Vienna and Budapest investigates the causes of the success of this favorite theatrical genre, and its social and political role. In a state that contained more than a dozen nations, there was no other common language than music, either in politics or in culture. The famous operettas contributed to awakening some feeling of community, and at the same time, to finding the path to higher cultural levels. The subject of death and burial, inspired by French historical anthropology, draws on the adoration of death and its rituals, so central to everyday life, to throw light on the deep-rooted changes occurring in these societies' conventions and their perception of death. The importance of the seventh chapter lies in asking whether there was a significant correlation between social marginality and cultural creativity. The essay, based on a wide sample, finds evidence of such a correlation: the majority of the outstanding thinkers, scholars, scientists, and artists of the age were intellectuals who had dropped out or withdrawn from the middle-class Establishment, but never joined a political or social movement.

The final essay enters virgin territory, by trying to outline basic categories in the social perception of the lower classes, based on some letters written during the First World War. This unexplored medium offers new insights into the radical shifts toward an increasingly revolutionary mood among people in Hungary (and all Central Europe), and into the causes behind this. The letters present graphically the "sub-historical" masses, with their nonintellectual, noncognitive awareness of past and present. Their rationality about daily tasks blends with their common beliefs; the pursuit of magic rituals, intrinsic in people living close to nature, transgresses their down-to-earth realism.

Another term I used to designate the genre of this book was "comparative." Again, rather than contemplating a general definition of this as used in historical methodology, I would like to deal with its local significance, in the comparison between Vienna and Budapest already touched upon in connection with the divergent metaphors of "garden" and "workshop." The essay on the urbanization of the two cities refers at one point to a specific and tangible difference. While the Ring in Vienna is surrounded by greenery, all the way from Döbling to the City Park, central Pest has scarcely any parks, gardens, or green squares at all. From its earliest years, Pest has been surrounded by factories. The dichotomy of the garden and the workshop, a metaphor in the volume's title essay, runs through the whole book as well.

What, then, explains the differences in character between the two capitals? One springs to mind all too readily. History has been kind to Vienna, but not to Budapest. Buda was still under the baneful crescent moon when Vienna already boasted strong bastions around its ancient core and a girdle of outer defenses, circled by flourishing townships. At that time, the area that was to become the great boulevard of Budapest was still sprinkled with manors, open fields, and sheep pastures.

Such an answer is simplistic, however. Vienna in modern times was the seat of rulers and capital of an empire, housing powerful government offices. It was the home of aristocrats and magnates from Austria, Bohemia, and Hungary, and of affluent Greek and Jewish merchants, who furnished their palaces with the insignia of power and wealth. Meanwhile Pest and Buda were small provincial towns. It was a good century after the end of Turkish rule before Buda regained its status as the country's capital. Vienna had a Baroque period, crucial to city development, whereas Pest did not. *That is the key difference.* The Baroque style defined Vienna's development, as the Burg, the string of mansions on Herrengasse, Am Hof and Wipplingerstrasse, and the Karlskirche, Belvedere Palace, and Schönbrunn—masterpieces of Fischer von Erlach and Hildebrand—all testify. But the Baroque was more than just an influence on the cityscape or a style of art. It was an expression of a way of life. The Baroque coincided with the Counterreformation, full of piety, religious sensitivity and zeal, and of bigotry—when heresy and paganism were intolerable, but the human failings of the faithful might be forgiven. Religious intolerance was perfectly complemented by tolerance of splendor, religious ritual, and adoration of secular beauty and sensuality. The closed circles of the Viennese court, and the courts of the aristocrats in its wake, imitated the civilization of Versailles and Paris. Display, representation of rank, was their canon. The court was the stage of public life on which everyone played an assigned or self-assigned role. From this derives the love of illusionism, the fusion of appearance and reality in Baroque art and mentality, the fascination with theater, with the illusion of reality on stage, and the attraction to nature in the garden. The gardens of aristocrats in the Baroque period were settings for recreation, beauty, and the magic of nature. Rather than sweeping all this away, the Enlightenment and Classicism simply tamed it to suit bourgeois tastes, rendering it acceptable to a rising new social stratum of Vienna: the educated middle class (*Bildungsbürgertum*).

Pest reached maturity in a spirit of Classicism and liberalism that could readily coexist with a romantic zeal for patriotism. Initially, Pest was marked by a classically puritan simplicity and bourgeois intimacy. Later came the neo-Renaissance line of Eclecticism. The city's nobility was declining into the middle class, while the middle class mimicked the nobility. Art to this public was not an expression of piety and sensuality, nor the stage an evocation of the illusion of reality. They were media for awakening national consciousness—effective tools for educating the nation. Pest was driven by a desire to rise to be a capital of European rank. It sought to turn its meadows into crammed apartment houses, not gardens or parks. Whole streets were lined with buildings and factories. It sought to be industrious, and to industrialize.

There was a vast difference between the one city—growing up in the age of Baroque and the Counterreformation, marked by illusionism and an adoration of beauty and ornamentation—and the other—maturing under Classi-

1. Statue of Eugen, Prince of Savoy, Square of Heroes, Vienna

2. Statue of Eugen, Prince of Savoy, Budapest Castle

cism, in an atmosphere of tolerant enlightenment and love of the renaissance of liberal humanism. The garden represents display, the workshop industry and profit. The social structure and whole historical situation of the Monarchy and its two capitals were changed radically in the nineteenth century, especially by the events of 1848 and 1867. Vienna's new elite—its upper middle class and artists and intellectuals—adopted and guarded much of their city's Baroque culture as they climbed the social ladder and assimilated. They retained their love of the theater, of the play between illusion and reality, music and art, secret and suppressed eroticism, and of course of the splendid villas, with their secluded gardens, havens for withdrawal and contemplation, on which the soul could draw in times of crisis. With the fin-de-siècle, the soul actually became the garden for those who wanted to flee this world and, at the same time, the source of their neuroticism.

The younger and more restless city of Pest had no Baroque tradition. In fact it lacked any tradition, since it had been divested of its continuity. In the late nineteenth century, at a time when the romantic spirit of noble tradition was waning, intellectuals and artists in Pest looked to the questions of the hour, to the future, society, and reform. They did not withdraw (and would have had nowhere to withdraw to), because in spite of their gut feelings of impending catastrophe, they harbored a positive vision of the future. They wanted to set about building a new Hungary, through art, literature, and culture.

So much for the origin and historical validity of the metaphor in the title of this book. History has the peculiar ability to absorb the future of the events that it relates, and the distance that this creates lodges in the consciousness of historians. Time, in a historical perspective, is able to undergo magic transformations. Looking back after almost a century, a historian feels that the Viennese garden was also a workshop in a way. No matter how much the great minds retreated into the solitude of their mansions or their souls, they met together, nonetheless, at the Café Griensteidel or the Central. No matter how often their works were consigned to the flames, they created, nonetheless, something enduring. They created a culture whose products are admired today, in exhibitions in cities ranging from Budapest to Paris and New York. When I as a historian look back on the Hungarian capital almost a century later, it seems to me that the workshop of Pest was also a garden in a way, sprouting flowers and fruits that were frequently uprooted but never eradicated by the storms of history.[3]

Budapest, August 1997

The Garden and the Workshop

Chapter One

URBANIZATION AND CIVILIZATION:
VIENNA AND BUDAPEST
IN THE NINETEENTH CENTURY

URBANIZATION AND THE SHAPING OF CITY CENTERS

The existence of a link between modern urbanization and the processes of embourgeoisement, the rise of the middle class, can be taken as self-evident. It hardly needs proving that the expansion of the production of goods and development of capitalist production were the underlying requirement and main stimulus for modern urbanization, and that the resulting urban development differed in kind from medieval development. Modern urbanization, with its complete openness, dynamic expansion, and fast acceleration, differed indeed from the slow growth or frequent stagnation of medieval and early modern times, when towns were still surrounded by walls, privileges, and other constraints. So one requirement before urbanization could begin, in the mid- to late eighteenth century, was for the walls, privileges, and restrictions to come down and for the common lands of the town to be parceled out as building land. Another was for citizens to acquire civil rights. A third was for the functions of a capitalist economy and bourgeois administration and culture to begin a steady process of development. A nineteenth-century metropolis was no longer just an artisan settlement and a marketplace. It was an administrative, legislative, and cultural center, tending increasingly to fashion a way of life and cast of mind that served as the pattern for society as a whole.[1]

With the process of embourgeoisement, modern cities gained a new functional structure and economic and social topography. Corresponding with the pace and depth of embourgeoisement, there was a steady division of job from home, public from private life. The business center and office area became separate from the shopping, trade, and industrial areas. These in turn became increasingly divorced from the residential areas,[2] which for their part took on a variety of social complexions, and provided socially and visually an accurate topographical guide to the character, consistency, and culture of the city or quarter. This separation of the manufacturing, commercial, administrative, and cultural zones from the residential areas presupposes a developed infrastructure and a high degree of mobility.

There were no walls or dikes, however, to make a sharp dividing line between a preindustrial town and a modern city. There was normally a continuity, in fortunate cases an integral one, between the two types and periods—

which again is a self-evident, easily verified statement. Vienna, the rich, privileged burgher town of the Middle Ages, developed continuously in the seventeenth and eighteenth centuries from a protector of the Hungarian border cas-
tles and bastion of the power of the Habsburgs into a resplendent Baroque
capital.[3] The development of Buda and Pest became stunted at the turn of the
fifteenth and sixteenth centuries and paralyzed by the subsequent Ottoman
occupation. They rose again out of the dust and ruins to form a commercial
burgher town, and to a lesser extent an administrative center, through a great
process of reconstruction in the eighteenth century. The growth was remarkable even in the preparatory stages: an estimated population of 20,000 became
50,000 by the time of the Josephine census in 1787, and 60,000 by the turn of
the next century. The physical expansion and planned "embellishment" of the
city began.[4] All this was provincial and meager, however, by comparison with
the imperial capital. Vienna's preurbanization period began as soon as the
Turkish siege was broken in 1683, so that its population reached 100,000 in
1700. With 233,000 inhabitants in 1800, it ranked as Europe's third largest city
after London (one million) and Paris (over half a million), with which it could
vie in terms of its power, refinement, urban character, and cultural creative
force.[5] Pest-Buda's 60,000 or so inhabitants, on the other hand, lived in almost
as many buildings as Vienna's 233,000 citizens: 5,600 as opposed to 6,600.[6] Its
public buildings, educational institutions, and university were provincial in
character, freshly founded or still only dreams in the minds of ardent patriots.
The central importance of Vienna was beyond dispute. There were strong
walls around the old city with real fortified bastions and a moat, a 500-yard
military parade area or glacis without buildings in front of it, and even a wide
masonry wall thirteen feet high to protect the suburbs—the Linienwall, along
the line of today's outer ring road, the Gürtel. Curiously, this had been built
not against the Turks, but in 1704 against the forays and incursions of the Hungarian insurrectionist "kuruc" forces.[7]

    If some worthy counselor of Maria Theresa had extrapolated the trend of
development from the initial signs of urbanization in his time, he would have
logically predicted that Vienna would enjoy a place in the front rank of Europe, while Pest, on the edge of the Hungarian plains, would have secondary
status, as the economic and cultural center of an agricultural province. The
course of history often belies such logic, even with a process such as urbanization, strongly determined by material factors. In the event, the relative rates
and intensities of development in Vienna and Pest-Buda were reversed in the
first period of urbanization, which extended from the French wars to the revolution of 1848.

    Pest and Buda began to pick up only in the second half of the eighteenth cen-
tury, during Maria Theresa's reign. Even then they were small provincial
towns by comparison with the Baroque splendor of the imperial capital, and
even when compared with Pressburg, proud venue of the Hungarian Diets, or

Debrecen, with its traditions of national identity. Although the royal court had moved to Pest in 1723, and the university established by Cardinal-Archbishop Péter Pázmány moved to Buda in 1777 and a few years later to Pest, Joseph II chose the quieter, more secluded Buda as his administrative seat, leaving Pest as a bustling commercial market town. As yet no thought was given to merging them. Pest especially spread quickly in the second half of the eighteenth century. But Józsefváros and Terézváros, new districts named after members of the royal family, which grew up among the meadows, manors, and gardens to the east of Pest, were still semi-agricultural in character, home to small craftsmen, artisans, workmen, journeymen, and peasant farmers squeezed out of the walled Belváros (downtown), rather than being hotbeds of urbanization.[8]

Pest-Buda started to become a real capital city at the end of the eighteenth century, when the rate of urbanization speeded up, reaching fruition in the Age of Reform in the first half of the nineteenth century. Let us look at the figures. The population of Pest-Buda, including Óbuda (Old Buda), tripled between the 1787 census and 1848, from 50,000 to 150,000. Within this increase, Buda's population grew by 63 percent while Pest's almost quintupled. Development was sluggish, almost stagnant in the districts of Buda, except Krisztinaváros (250 percent), to the west of the historical center on Castle Hill. Development in Pest was fast, but uneven. The population of the original center, Belváros, merely doubled over the half century. That of Józsefváros in the southeast increased two and a half times, and that of Terézváros in the northeast three and a half times; the population of Lipótváros to the north more than quintupled.[9] There is further evidence in the qualitative indices of a shift in the center of gravity. In terms of the proportion and weight of the middle classes, both Belváros and Józsefváros fell back during the half century under consideration, while the middle-class share of the population in Terézváros and Lipótváros increased significantly. The difference between the last two lay in the fact that mainly artisans and petty traders and newly arriving Jewish petty and middle bourgeois settled in Terézváros. Lipótváros attracted more prosperous merchants, public officials, and the intelligentsia. Indeed, it is apparent from the list of first owners of houses and sites and surveys of later house owners that the characteristic strata in Lipótváros society were made up of rich Greek and German merchants, high-ranking public officials, and members of the learned professions—joined later, in Nádor utca (street), by some of the aristocracy and the most mobile sections of the Jewish haute bourgeoisie.[10]

So in terms of origins and character, Lipótváros differed substantially from the old Belváros and the other new parts of the city. With its foundation, the town walls began to be pulled down—Vác Gate was demolished in 1789, Kecskemét Gate in 1794, and Hatvan Gate in 1808. It then took on new functions that Belváros proved no longer capable of fulfilling: a new fairground, wharf, and marketplace were established there, and new stores, hotels, and inns were built, along with a theater and dance hall (*Redoute*) in the square known today as Vörösmarty tér. Naturally the new district was chosen for the Trade Hall—the later stock exchange—so that this became Pest's "City," the center of the credit institutions and commerce. Certainly in keeping with these new functions and sometimes closely related to them were the attempts to use advance plans and regulations to ensure that there would be broad, orderly streets and squares, and that attention would be paid to outward appearances.

In a matter of decades, rows of three- and four-storied mansions of an urban character went up in and around Színház (now Vörösmarty) tér (square), Nádor tér, Fürdő (now József Attila) utca and the area of present-day Roosevelt tér. Some of the credit for this planned, aesthetically pleasing development is due to the Embellishment Committee set up by Palatine Joseph in 1808, more still to the plans for the townscape drawn up by János Hild in the same year, and not least to Mihály Pollack, Ferenc Kasselik, and several other excellent architects who designed the new city center.[11]

Apartment Buildings

Another sign of modern urbanization, apart from the arrival of town planning and "embellishment," was the appearance of blocks of apartment houses. These went up in large numbers in Lipótváros, and to a lesser extent in the upper part of Belváros and on the western edge of Terézváros. Apartment buildings are a type of housing characteristic of the capitalist system, built not to satisfy the living and working requirements of one family—the owner and his household—but for gain, as a business venture.[12]

The imposing appearance produced by the first phase of urbanization in Pest is due largely to the simple, noble, uniform Neoclassical style of architecture employed. The style, which became ubiquitous all over Europe at the end of the eighteenth and turn of the nineteenth centuries, marked a departure from the ostentation, ornamentation, and complexity of the princely, aristocratic Baroque. It brought a return to the geometrical archetypes of the Greek and Roman building tradition, emphasizing its calm dignity and architectural evenness and simplicity.[13] This ambition was rooted in the middle-class values held proudly, and not without a measure of dissembling in some cases, by the rising bourgeoisie, which was already dominant in the West. In Central Europe in particular, the style eminently suited the tastes of a nobility that was taking on bourgeois characteristics, and the aspirations of princely courts that were keen to display bourgeois virtues. Classicism can really be seen as the first of the great nineteenth-century revival styles. In this capacity it became a favorite with the Hungarian nobility, so that a somewhat clumsier, more parochial variant of it developed in provincial towns and on country estates.[14]

The popularity of Classicism can also be ascribed to the fact that it was better suited to the multiplied demands of urbanization and the erection of civil offices and apartment houses than the Baroque mansions, which were more closed, expensive, and structurally complex, or Baroque dwelling houses, which were difficult to enlarge. Neoclassical architecture rejected the notion of finely balanced units superimposed on one another, in favor of an ensemble of parts equal in rank and repeatable at will. A Classical façade could be symmetrical in every direction simply by continuing the axes of the windows; it could be extended and expanded in any direction.[15] Thus Classicism came to provide the dominant architectural type for the massive apartment blocks and public buildings of Central Europe.

But in outward appearance and antecedents, blocks of apartment houses and public buildings were derived from two different lines of development. Different types were constituted by the upper-class mansion blocks and by the apartment buildings for the masses. The former displayed inside and out the ornate signs of their origin as an expansion of the medieval burgher's house or the Baroque mansion translated into Neoclassical terms. Meanwhile the "courts" of mass housing, such as Wurm-udvar, Marokko-udvar, Orczy-udvar, and so on, harked back to monastic architecture, especially monastic farm buildings. From the latter there developed in Austria during the rise of urbanization what was known as the Grosswohnhof (great residential court). This became a prototype for army barracks and for working-class tenements during the post-1867 period of the Dual Monarchy, and produced a rather poignant affinity between them.[16]

Apartment blocks differed from burghers' houses in the size of the dwellings and their arrangement. The flats, in line with their new functions, were small in scale, with an average of three to six rooms of much reduced size. But they were more intimate and less disturbed by noise from work or outside life than the dwellings of earlier periods. If there were a more elegant reception room at all, it would not be a sumptuous one. Visitors were normally received in the afternoon. Full-scale soirées were ruled out by the size of the rooms and the difficulties of illuminating them with candles or rush lights.

There is not a large body of materials or research to draw upon for information on living habits during the first phase of urbanization in Budapest. A general type can be reconstructed clearly enough, however, from contemporary descriptions and from some exemplary works of Viennese art history. A rented apartment, sheltering behind a Classical façade and furnished in Biedermeier style, would be eminently convenient and comfortable.[17] There steadily developed a division of functions among the rooms, beginning with the bedroom, which was filled with a double bed and symmetrical furnishings. Illustrations from early in the nineteenth century still commonly show a four-poster or a divan in the parlor, but from the 1840s onward, more depictions of separate bedrooms are found. The separate drawing room known as the "ladies' room" also appeared, but in general the dining room and drawing room were not separate in the middle-class homes of the period. Affluent families had a separate nursery as well, although this tended to be a miniature of an adult's room, with a little bed and a great many mixed pieces of furniture.

The most cogent and lasting legacy of the Biedermeier life style is its furniture and fittings. In fact the furniture style also sprang from Classicism. As Georg Himmelheber says, "Its anthology of forms was ultimately created by Antiquity." Surfaces are flat, and decorative elements are developed out of geometrical shapes; it is more comfortable in every way than the rigid forms of the Empire style, having elegant curves and upholstered seats, couches, and armchairs. It also differed from the previous and subsequent styles, respectively, by being no longer artist-designed and not yet mass-produced. Craftsmen made these pieces of furniture by hand, for bourgeois families of the same social standing as themselves.[18] The favored suite in this style consists of a couch and armchairs, or chairs arranged about a round or oval table, suggesting the intimacy of a family or group of friends. A typical piece of comfortable furniture in the period was a rocking chair with a footstool; a glass cabinet or shelved stand would be used for display.

Classicism and Central European Biedermeier, however, should not be represented as a trend by which the way of life in the period can be judged. After all, the appearance of the home was still influenced by inherited Baroque furniture, Baroque stoves, and Romantic pictures. Apart from that, it is inappropriate to make a judgment in terms of art history or cultural history. The early period of urbanization was imbued with a spirit of modernization and em-bourgeoisement, from town planning down to furnishings. This was the common denominator between the values of traditional Belváros guildsmen, capitalists from Lipótváros, and petty bourgeois artisans or traders from Terézváros, even magnates moving up to the capital, or professionals or officials of noble family already resident there. To this can be added the circumstance that the urbanization did not occur under the benign protection of an absolute ruler. To a degree such rule was the target of this conscious course of urban development, which formed part of the process of acquiring nationhood. It was led by the liberal opposition nobility and supported by the upper middle class, one might say with the deliberate intention of founding a capital city.

CHANGES IN VIENNA'S URBANIZATION IN THE MID-NINETEENTH CENTURY

Urbanization in Vienna differed radically from the process in Budapest and in most big European cities. Something of this is apparent from the fact that the population, in an era of dynamic change, did not more than double, and even this increase occurred in the city's unincorporated suburbs. The population of the old city stagnated at a time when provision of the new economic, administrative, and educational functions was expressly being concentrated or rather crammed in there. The aristocracy and high-ranking bureaucrats drawn to the imperial city had squeezed out the traditional petty bourgeoisie, so that the artisan district became the Adelsviertel (noble quarter). But as the Adelsviertel then turned into the Regierungsviertel (government quarter) in the nineteenth century, space and patronage were also claimed among the Baroque palaces of the imperial high authorities by members of the financial aristocracy and the elite of the capitalist and professional upper middle classes—the Besitzbürgertum and the Bildungsbürgertum.[19] So the old city had to perform the new urban functions for another sixty to seventy years, largely because the surviving town walls and the glacis before them, coupled with criteria of rank and repute, drew a sharp dividing line between the city and the burghers of the suburbs, who were "beyond the pale."

Questions of power had much to do with this strange stagnation. Unlike other big cities in Europe, Vienna kept its inner walls and outer walls (*Linienwall*) until 1857. This was not due to any threat from the Turks, which had quite receded, nor since the time of Maria Theresa to any fear of a Hungarian uprising. The walls symbolized power and dignity, and were seen increasingly under Metternich as a means of keeping the turbulent working people of the suburbs at bay.

The salient feature of this phase in Vienna's urbanization, then, is that its expansion ran up against barriers. There was no development of a modern business center. The urbanizing transport connections and integral social links between the city and the suburbs that now belonged to it failed to emerge. What little industry arrived in Vienna went to the outskirts, and the infrastructure failed to develop. Crowning all this was the way the ruling imperial elite more or less deliberately distanced itself from modernization and modern urbanization.

What corresponded in the middle-class suburbs to the rank and pomp of the princely and aristocratic inner city was a Biedermeier life style and frame of mind that imbued private tastes and public life. The effect was a lasting one only in private life, where the Biedermeier domestic style spread throughout the empire.

The Ringstrasse

The year 1848 brought resounding evidence that no Metternich, no walls and towers, and no imperial will could be proof against the people of Vienna, now that it had grown into a big city. It was neither expedient nor feasible to curb modern urbanization. A new era in Vienna's history opened with the patent of 1857, which ordered the demolition of the walls and introduced planned urban development. After the walls had come down, development took off rapidly, as if the city were determined to make up for lost time. The suburbs were merged into the old city, and in 1890, the outer suburbs (*Vororte*) were incorporated as well. During this founding period (*Gründerzeit*) of sudden development, Vienna's population grew from 470,000 to 800,000 in the three decades to 1890, or 1,342,000, including the outer suburbs. A lasting achievement was the construction of a range of communal utilities. The city was supplied with mains of good water from the hills, main drains, and gas lighting. Later came electricity and a modern system of roads and transport.[20] The city's new appearance and the concurrent shift in its center of gravity came with the building of a boulevard, the Ringstrasse, and its surroundings, on the wide belt left by the demolished walls and bastions and the glacis.

In 1860 an ornate map was published of the urban development plan, endorsed by His Majesty. This presented a draft for developing a broad heptagonal zone round the old city, along the line of the new Ring and the Danube Canal. One side of the decorative border of the map has a female figure of Vienna in diaphanous clothing being dressed in a new robe by a serving maid, over the legend "Geschmückt durch Kunst" (Bedecked by Art). The other side has two female allegorical figures with the motto "Stark durch Gesetz und Frieden" (Strong through Law and Peace).[21] The grandiose plan advances the idea of a constitutional state blessed by science, scholarship, and the arts, to replace one of absolute rule based on force of arms. So what parts of it were realized? The Vienna Ring as a whole, an avenue two hundred feet wide and two and a half miles long, with vast squares and resplendent public buildings and residential mansions, stands as a monument to nineteenth-century Historicism. It is a work of art worthily representative of its period and empire, and is still imposing to this day. Citizens and visitors can sense in the Renaissance Revival museums opposite the Baroque Hofburg, Parliament, the Neo-Gothic City Hall, and the University the ethos deriving from the self-confident burghers of the Gründerzeit, the commitment to "Recht gegen Macht" (right over might). But only at first sight, on a level of appearances, does the picture seem so uniform. Observant onlookers may notice how a statue of Maria Theresa stands on the Emperor's Forum between the two Renaissance Revival museums, with equestrian statues of her indeed forgotten generals at her feet, and the block of the former Life Guard headquarters and military stables behind her. It may also be remarked how the Reichsrat or Parliament, representative of right and law yet of little weight at the time, was housed in a building that would make a good temple of Pallas Athena. Meanwhile the Rathaus or City Hall, reminiscent of German Gothic, is quite dysfunctional as an office. The University, radiating Renaissance beauty and scholarship, stands opposite the Neo-Gothic Votive Church, built in thanksgiving for a lucky escape by the emperor. The Stock Exchange, with its atmosphere of an ancient temple, is faced by the barracks known as the Franz-Josef-Kaserne, built in the shape of a fortress. So the Vienna Ring is an eclectic composition in ideological and political terms, as well as architectural, expressive of the Austrian compromise between right and might.

So what happened in this paramount stage of Vienna's urban development? The surge of building that followed the demolition of the walls moved the limits of the city center to the edges of the Ring zone and even the squares next to it. This caused a partial shift in the city's center of gravity, as the business, ad-

3. The changing of the Imperial Body Guard, behind the Parliament
and the City Hall, Vienna. About 1900

ministrative, and educational center became divided between the old Burg-
viertel (Castle District), the Graben district and the Ring. Into the new zone
moved the aristocracy by birth and ex officio, the wealthy upper middle
classes, and some of the rich intelligentsia. Naturally enough, a third of the
new householders came from the nobility, half from the capitalists, and the re-
mainder from the professional middle classes. The social composition of the
Ring zone can be conveyed accurately by saying that in 1869, in the midst of the
building, 20 percent of its inhabitants belonged to the nobility and upper middle classes and 56 percent to the middle classes, whereas in 1914, 14 percent belonged to the top ten thousand, 19 percent were rentiers and 66 percent were
from the middle classes. (The statistics found only 1 percent from lower down
the social scale.)[22] These figures also show how the Ring belonged, functionally and socially, to the Baroque imperial capital, as its modernized shell. Instead of linking the old city with the mass bases of embourgeoisement in the
former outer districts, it shielded it from them.

  The Ring was indeed a border area, and not a single radial avenue led off it
into the old city. Traffic is halted at the Ring, and the outer districts have their
own business centers, linked not by the Ring, but by the Gürtel, the outer ring.
Thus the Ring, in terms of settlement structure and social structure, plays the

part of the old town walls. It shields the residence of the court, the imperial nobility and bureaucracy, and the imperial haute bourgeoisie from the quarters of the lower-middle, middle, and working classes. This feature of urban development was to have serious social and political consequences. However great the artistic and educational merits of the institutions gathered along it, the Ring from the outset was a scene of display, serving less to perform modern urban functions than to express a sense of historical authenticity, greatness, and dignity. It was a rendition of power in urban architectural terms. What its imposing squares, monumental public buildings, and palatial blocks of apartments lack are the attributes of a town: a human scale, a communal binding force, and a sense of home.[23]

BUDAPEST IN THE FOUNDING YEARS

The urbanization of Budapest did not lag behind Vienna's in any way, during the decades of the founding period, as the figures make clear.

The population of the capital rose from 270,000 to 880,000 between 1869 and 1910, or to 1.1 million, including the suburbs. Meanwhile the number of buildings rose from 9,300 to 17,000, and the number of dwellings from 50,000 to 170,000. Around the time of the 1867 Ausgleich or Compromise with Austria, a good three-quarters of the buildings were single-storied; only 6 percent had three stories and 2 percent four or more. In 1914, on the other hand, only half were still single-storied, 35 percent had two or three stories, and 15 percent had four, five, or more stories.[24] This is a significant outward and upward growth, even though Budapest houses were still on average one to one and a half stories lower than those of Vienna. The essential change was that the urbanization, having been concentrated on Lipótváros, shifted east toward Terézváros and Erzsébetváros. Its boundaries at the end of the second phase in the 1890s reached the Nagykörút (Grand Boulevard), while its axis was formed by the great avenue of the Sugárút (Radial Road), now Andrássy út.

The main consideration behind the design and execution of the Sugárút was that it should be imposing, a broad, spacious promenade expressive of Budapest's status as a great city.[25] Even its elegant shops and the department store and cafés added later were determinants of class and character, for the architecture of the city—the prevalence in Hungary of Renaissance Revivalism—and for its history as well. The Nagykörút, started in 1871, took a good quarter of a century to build due to the enormous economic difficulties met. It performed functions of commerce and transportation from the outset. (Indeed the city architect, Ferenc Ritter, had plans in 1862 for a navigable waterway rather than a boulevard.)[26] By 1896, celebrated as the millennium of the Hungarians' arrival in the Carpathian Basin, the two and three-quarter-mile Nagykörút was open for its full length from Boráros tér to Margaret Bridge, binding the inner and outer districts of the city together.[27] Although it bore

4. The Opera House, Vienna, designed by Eduard van der Nüll
and August von Siccardsburg, 1861–1869

5. The Opera House, Budapest, designed by Miklós Ybl, 1875–1884

some resemblance in its outward appearance and transportation functions to Vienna's "divisive" Ring, Pest's grand boulevard had a combining and leveling nature, binding together the inner area and the rapidly integrating outer areas. It differed from the Ring inasmuch as the radial streets all crossed the Nagykörút and continued outward to Zugló, Kőbánya, Kispest, and other neighboring places. The Pest Nagykörút can hardly be called imposing. Apart from the National Theater and the later Vígszínház (Gaiety Theater), it was hardly adorned with any fine public buildings. Instead it was crammed with a railway terminus and numerous road junctions and intersections. Its buildings, three to five stories high (most had the average number of four), were by no means resplendent like the palaces along the Ring. They were plain apartment houses densely occupied by shops, workshops, and crowded dwellings.

These two main arteries of the capital were strongly influenced by the fact that the government and the Council for Public Works had promoted their construction and had imposed their own notions of urban development on their appearance. That was also why Neo-Renaissance came to predominate among the revival styles characteristic of the Gründerzeit.

Revivalist Historicism is a ubiquitous stylistic trend, lending to the city an exacting, spectacular, varied appearance that emanates a traditional respect for the past and a desire to impress. It has often been called the architecture of an upstart haute bourgeoisie unable to create a style of its own, aspiring to display mastery over the past as well as the present, and hiding its inward paucity and pretense behind outward pomp and pageant.[28] But an explanation of this kind, laced with social psychology, is too simplistic and superficial. It can hardly apply to Hungary or its eastern neighbors, where the forces promoting the revival styles remained for a long time the same aristocracy and liberal nobility that had stood behind Classicism. As for the upper middle classes of the West in this period, they were far from being so parvenu and uncultivated as to need to borrow stylistic ideas from the waning nobility.

In reconsidering this question, there are a number of theoretical, aesthetic, technical, and social factors to allow for. First and foremost, the whole nineteenth century is marked by an overall historical revivalism, ranging from Herder's Romanticism and Sir Walter Scott's tales to positivist science, biology, and Darwinism. Even historians were not immune. The great architects of the period, erudite professionally and in their knowledge of history, shared Ranke's view that all periods are equidistant from God. They abandoned the simplicity of Classicism in favor of adopting what was best in every tradition.[29] Their ideal was not slavish reconstitution or imitation, but a combinative revival, a re-creation. Let us add that the new, up-to-date building materials and technologies were not yet ready for use in the middle of the last century. Although people were becoming conversant with and using iron and glass, they stuck for several reasons to tradition—columns, arches, and thick dividing walls. The obstacles to choosing the functionally most suitable structure and materials, and to lighting upon a new union of function, structure, and form were initially the availability of materials and then the prevalent outlook.[30] What had to take place was a technical revolution in engineering and architecture and a rebellion by the artistic intelligentsia against the prevailing outlook and values.

Middle-class society during the Gründerzeit underwent a marked rise in its standing. There was a trend toward a kind of egalitarianism, expressed well in real life in the blend of historical styles known as Eclectic. This is found in grand apartment buildings, and appears also in the blocks of uniform tenements, where the motifs of an impoverished Historicism were applied externally. Significantly, such tenements provided homes for both the wealthy middle and the skilled working classes, but hardly at all for the petty bourgeoisie.[31]

Revival architecture was ultimately close to the mainstream of modern urbanization and the needs of its main social strata. It can be rated as a trend that wrought a radical change on the townscape. Only with the decay of the middle-class family in the more advanced period of technical and social transformation did the obsolete, dysfunctional character of its forms and substance become apparent.

The Buildings

There are no accurate records of who owned the houses on the Sugárút and the Nagykörút at the turn of the century, or who their tenants were. It has been more or less possible, however, to reconstruct the ownership of the first houses in the Sugárút at the time of their completion, in 1883–1884: No. 1 Leó Baumgartner, and then Carl Leopold von Stein; No. 2 the Foncière Pest Insurance Institute; No. 3 the Saxlehner family; No. 4 Baron Frigyes Harkányi; No. 5 Lipót Keppich; No. 6 Baron Frigyes Harkányi; No. 7 Náthán Latzkó; Nos. 8, 9, and 10 Ármin Brüll and Auguszta Kohner; No. 11 Sándor Ullmann; Nos. 12 and 13 Baron Frigyes Kochmeister; No. 14 —; Nos. 15 and 17 Sarolta Politzer and Ármin Politzer; Nos. 16 and 18 —; No. 19 Zsigmond Brüll; No. 20 Lajos Krausz; No. 21 —; Nos. 22 and 24 the Opera; No. 23 Zsigmond Brüll; No. 25 the Drechsler Palace; No. 27 Ede Loisch and Ottília Melczer; No. 28 Rezső Fölsinger and Hermina Traub (see Figure 6).[32]

This yields quite a clear social picture. The great apartment blocks in the innermost section of the Sugárút were mainly built or acquired from the Capital City Council of Public Works for investment or speculative purposes by members of the commercial and entrepreneurial haute bourgeoisie. The owners themselves did not live in the tenements. They had family residences in Belváros or Lipótváros, and a good many of them moved out at the turn of the century to the new villa district along the Sugárút beyond the Körönd and in neighboring side streets.

Less is known about the social status of the tenants. The annual residential registers show only the name and occupation of each tenant, and not even that in all cases. To arrive at the social composition, it may be taken as sufficient to

6. The beginning of the Andrássy út. Budapest, 1896

use the residents of the first twenty-seven houses as a sample. Of the 140 tenants, only 15 families can be placed in the haute bourgeoisie (including just one aristocrat), 35 in the strata of officialdom and the intelligentsia, 78 in the trader and artisan middle class, and 12 expressly in the more impoverished middle class. With the additional fact that almost half the tenants ascribed to the middle class were on the borders between the middle and lower strata (21 master craftsmen and 13 factors or agents), it becomes clear that the first section of the Sugárút presented a mixed social picture. The registers of residents and sizes of the flats show that the haute bourgeois tenants of the statelier first- and second-floor apartments with numerous rooms made up only a fifth of the total. The bulk of the tenants were members of the middle and petty bourgeoisie or modestly endowed members of the official and professional classes.[33] The prestige of the Sugárút rose at the turn of the century, when aristocrats and plutocrats also moved in. In general the standing of the Sugárút (Andrássy út), Erzsébet körút, and Lipót (Szent István) körút has tended to rise in the twentieth century.

The surviving register of residents from 1921 for one of the well-to-do blocks (Lipót körút 17) will serve as an example. Six of the tenants of the twenty-five flats were haute bourgeois, four of them were landowners (one was an aristocrat), five belonged to the stratum of high-ranking officialdom and the learned professions, and ten to the lower end of the middle bourgeoisie.[34]

The planners and "founders" of the Sugárút, the actual house-owners, and finally the tenants differed widely in social status. The most they might have had in common was a loose adherence to middle-class, liberal values. As for the buildings, it was mainly the façade that was imposing and ornamental, rather than the contents. The design and taste reflected the liberal nobility, while the execution was more in line with the interests and requirements of the new bourgeoisie. This duality of grandeur and functionalism was not a peculiarity of Budapest. It was a Central European characteristic, more conspicuously present than usual in the contrast between a revival façade and a humbler courtyard behind it.

The houses themselves divided functionally into three parts. The ground floor would be taken up with shops, or more rarely offices and cafés, and with stock rooms on the courtyard side or in the basement. The second part can be called the "service" sector. It contained the premises that could not be incorporated functionally into the flats: coal cellars in the basement and drying area and lumber rooms in the attic, with a laundry and ironing room, usually on the ground floor. With each flat went a proportionate coal cellar and attic area, and use of the communal laundry. The assignment and upkeep of these premises were among the manifold duties of the concierge, for whom there would be a one-room-and-kitchen flat on the courtyard side of the ground floor. In larger blocks of mansion flats, where the concierge could assume the rank of a senior porter, his assistant, the "vice," would also be provided with a meager room. Also part of the service sector of the building were the usually ornate front staircase (paved in marble or reconstituted stone in many houses on the Sugárút), the plainer back or servants' staircase with one or a pair of servants' toilets on each floor, and the square paved courtyard.

The third functional part of the building, the residential section, was differentiated in social terms. The largest in area and highest in status was the grand apartment on the second floor, sometimes occupied by the landlord and sometimes by a wealthier bourgeois, noble, or even aristocratic family. The third floor was largely the same as the second, the distinction in status being marked mainly in symbolic differences—simpler windows, no balcony, smaller reception rooms—so that this was still a floor on which the more well-to-do middle class lived. The fourth floor differed substantially, usually being divided into smaller flats, including some that looked out on the courtyard and lacked a servant's room and bathroom. In larger houses there were small room-and-kitchen or two-room flats on the ground floor, and in the Nagykörút flats of a similar kind were found on the top floor as well, specifically for the petty bourgeoisie and lower middle and working classes.

Pest apartment buildings possessed a social hierarchy. There was a continuum from the second to the fourth or fifth floors—from the haute bourgeoisie to the lower middle class—and another from the front to the back of the house—from the upper middle class to the petty bourgeois craftsmen and right down to the "vice," a member of the servant class. Let us look at a few examples.

The ground floor of the palatial tenement building at No. 5 in Sugárút had eight shops on the ground floor with five adjacent stock rooms, a one-room-and-kitchen flat for the concierge (250 sq. ft.), a small two-room courtyard flat (231 sq. ft.) and a communal laundry. The house had two courtyards separated by the stair well, with areas of 1,400 and 585 sq. ft., respectively. The grand apartment on the second floor had seven rooms with two vestibules and the usual offices (2,340 sq. ft.), while the equivalent on the third floor had seven rooms with only one vestibule and a smaller dining room. Next to the grand apartment on each floor was another smart, four-room apartment (1,440 sq. ft.). On the fourth floor, however, the 3,800 sq. ft. of living space were divided into three flats instead of two: two more genteel flats with four full-size and one half-size room, and one with two full-size and three half-size rooms (900 sq. ft.). So there were altogether eight flats in the building. Two were let to haute bourgeois families, four to well-to-do middle-class families, one to a more modestly endowed middle-class family, and one, opening onto the courtyard, next to the servants' toilets, to a working-class family.[35]

The house is imposing and dignified outside. The façade is reminiscent of Renaissance style in its spatial proportions, but has the windows on all three upper floors arched in a Baroque fashion. It resembles its Viennese counterpart in outward appearance and proportions and above all in the mentality embodied, although it lags behind in size and grandeur.[36] The differences in social level become even clearer in the blocks in the Nagykörút. According to a contemporary account of the original arrangement of No. 35 in Erzsébet körút, the grand apartments on the second and third floors had only six and seven rooms, respectively. The second floor had two other flats—one with three rooms and a servant's room, and the other with two rooms—and so did the third floor—one flat with two rooms and a servant's room, and another simpler two-room flat facing the courtyard. The fourth floor became poorer. For more modest middle-class occupancy, there were four-room and three-room flats, but the two-room flat on the courtyard side was laid out with petty-bourgeois requirements in mind. The ground floor was occupied by four shops, each with a separate room for the shop assistant, a room-and-kitchen flat for the concierge, and finally a laundry.[37]

So only five of the seventeen flats in this genteel house with a respectable façade, right in the middle of the Pest Nagykörút, can be described as of middle-class standard, of which only two had six to seven rooms, while the remaining ten flats must have been occupied by petty bourgeois, shopkeepers, artisans, public servants, and in some cases workers.

At the opposite pole, let us look at a large haute bourgeois villa in the outermost section of the Sugárút, belonging to Manfréd Weiss, the great industrialist.[38] The two-storied villa was built in the 1890s, with an arching loggia in front and a veranda behind. The villa, of course, had no "commercial" section, but its "service" section was extensive, including a separate wine cellar and tap-room in the basement, a kitchen, a servant's room, and small laundry, ironing, and mangling rooms. There was a separate little house for the upper servants: the concierge, the gardener, and later on the chauffeur. The street side of the ground floor was taken up by three smart rooms: a salon, a music room, and a reception room, covering a total of 1,170 sq. ft. Adjacent to these was a 540-sq.-ft. dining room, from which opened a conservatory or winter garden, while at the back there were a drawing room, bedroom, nursery, schoolroom, bath-room, and two toilets. The street side of the second floor contained further re-ception rooms, bedrooms, and living rooms, while the separate back part con-tained the rooms and conveniences for the indoor servants. So the owner had twelve living and reception rooms with varied and ornate conveniences, whereas the servants had three rooms in the house and three small flats.

When we measure the urbanization of Budapest by European standards, the most conspicuous feature is its feverish speed, expressive of an almost patho-logical determination to catch up. There was, however, much that was superfi-cial about it, which appears in some of the skimping, meager solutions used for the problems of urbanization. One sign of this is the high density of building. Construction in the inner areas was not in a grid of blocks divided by side streets, but in rows of contiguous houses interrupted relatively infrequently by cross streets, which would have raised the cost of construction. The city has no emphatic center, few spacious squares, and relatively little green open space, at least in the seven inner districts of Pest, where the proportion of open space is a tiny 1.3 percent of the built-up area.[39] Apart from the Városliget (City Park) and Népliget (People's Park), which were on the edge of the city at the time, the bleak stones of Pest were unrelieved by more than a few pockets of green or small squares, except for the trees lining the Nagykörút and Üllöi út. In terms of parks and gardens, Pest was far behind the major European capitals. Their place was taken not only by crowded housing, but by workshops, warehouses, and factories, which were moved further out time and again over the decades, but were still encompassed anew by the rapidly growing city. Pest was a city of factories, not gardens: the *workshop* of Hungary's bourgeois development.

While the pearl of the Hungarian capital, Margaret Island, remained closed to the general public until recent times, the Prater and Augarten in Vienna had already been opened by Joseph II, who also planted out the glacis before the town walls with limes and false acacias as a promenade area for recreation.[40]

The foundations of Vienna's great garden cult were laid by the vast Baroque gardens of the Schönbrunn, Belvedere, Esterházy, Schönborn, Schwarzenberg, and Arenberg palaces. Parks and gardens were maintained by the magnates, and during the period of urban development by the city fathers. New ones were added when the Ring was built: the Volksgarten (People's Garden) be-tween Ballhausplatz and the Burgtheater, the Burggarten before the Hofburg,

7. Everyday life on the Károly Körút and Deák Square, 1900

the promenade park fronting the Votive Church and City Hall, and the Stadt-
park (City Park) stretching from Schwarzenbergplatz to the Landstrasse. It
was the city's social policy at the turn of the century to aim explicitly at expanding the "social green belt," and later, after the First World War, to parcel
out hitherto private parks and provide allotment gardens (for example, at
Schmelz).[41] So Vienna has larger and more numerous squares than Pest, and
they fulfill the real functions of a square. The total area of open space is several
times that in Pest. The traditions of Baroque gardening were continued uninterrupted by the bourgeoisie, both in the public open spaces and around their
private villas. By the standards of Eastern and Central Europe, Vienna is truly
a *garden city*.

Another characteristic of urban architecture in Pest is an ornate façade coupled with a rather shabby interior. The fronts onto the main streets are conspicuously decorated in revival styles, but the imitation marble and painted
plaster work cease as one goes through the doorway. The contrast appears
most clearly in the courtyard, which normally has open corridors running
round three or four sides, from which the kitchens and the courtyard flats are
approached (see Figure 8). Traces of this kind of architecture with all-round
galleries can be found in early nineteenth-century Vienna in buildings of the
"Pawlatschen-Hof" type. This arrangement became widespread mainly in the
outer districts, but had been superseded completely by the end of the century.

8. Typical courtyard in Budapest with open corridor
and back staircase for servants, 1900

It was clearly derived from the conversion of the originally monastic Grosswohnhof, where the covered corridors were opened out, so that they adhered
to the outside of the several-story building.[42]

There are two factors to explain the expansion of Budapest. Originally
there had been large manorial estates owned by townsfolk or nobles on the
outskirts of the city. These were usually parceled out and developed as units.
So the blocks of housing along the boulevards and radial roads were large,
with fewer intersections than in Vienna, Munich, or Prague. Moreover, there
was a higher average number of inhabitants per building, to reduce unit building costs and help to keep the flats cheaper in spite of the spiraling land prices
fueled by the speed of the city's development.[43] This criterion also led to rejection of the typical Viennese layout of a deep entrance and several staircases.
One result was to produce open corridors leading to the corner flats at the

front and the back courtyard flats, which had to open onto the corridor because they were inaccessible from the stair well.

This open-corridor pattern of building had far-reaching social consequences. The bourgeois principles of strict privacy and as full a segregation from the "lower orders" as possible applied less fully in Budapest than in other big cities of Western or Central Europe. As mentioned before, there were petty bourgeois families in the courtyard flats and working-class families at the back of the building, living in the same block as the well-to-do and able to observe their private life. A central role in such open-corridor buildings was played by the all-seeing, all-hearing concierge. On the positive side, Pest tenement buildings contained a more socially interactive community than was usual in their equivalents in Western European capitals.

The Arrangement of a Home

Before entering, so to speak, a bourgeois home in Budapest, it is worth considering one or two figures.

The largest flats in the Sugárút and Nagykörút houses examined had eleven or twelve rooms and an area of 2,200 or even 2,700 sq. ft. The average middle-class home, however, had three or four rooms and an area of 900 to 1,340 sq. ft. The height of the second- and third-floor rooms in the Sugárút reached almost fifteen feet, which was reduced to twelve feet on the fourth floor. The figures were similar for buildings in the Nagykörút. The heights of buildings and of stories were laid down in the building regulations and in certificates of planning permission.

The houses in the inner parts of the city appear to be very varied. Eclecticism gave rise to much stylistic variation in façades, but on the stairs and still more in the flats themselves there was a high degree of uniformity in terms of layout and appointments. The arrangement of a middle-class home was determined by the routine of daily life. Sleeping, eating, daytime activity, and personal hygiene were functionally and spatially separated in middle-class homes. The simplest and most modest arrangement was a flat with three main rooms: a bedroom, a parlor, and a dining room, with the usual adjuncts of a hall, a kitchen (see Figure 9), a pantry, and possibly a bathroom and toilet. These auxiliary rooms open off the hall, off the middle of the three main rooms (from which the other two are reached), or from any of the three rooms.

The three-room flat was a standard attribute of middle-class life in Central European cities.[44] Geographical differences tended to be apparent in the proportion of them to flats with four or more rooms. By this yardstick, each status group in Budapest had an average of one room fewer than its equivalent in Vienna and Munich. In a three-room flat, a child would sleep on a divan in the parents' bedroom while small, and later on in the parlor. The modest receiving and rare entertaining in the home would take place in the dining room or parlor, tidied for the occasion.

9. The kitchen of a modest petty-bourgeois home. Budapest,
end of the nineteenth century

This simple type of dwelling could be developed in two directions. If the
family grew and prospered, there would be a further division of functions and
segregation of private life in the flat, with the addition of a nursery, a room for
the wife, and a study for the husband. This reflected the middle-class needs of
autonomous individuals for privacy and a separate "living space." One innovation in the period that deserves attention was the introduction of a nursery
for the children, adapted to the requirements of their age group and their qualitative differences from adults, and equipped with white or colored furniture,
pictures, toys, and space for play. The nursery was a reflection of new middle-
class principles of child raising. In more well-to-do middle-class families, the
sexes would be segregated at puberty into separate rooms for girls and boys.
The other line of development was a tendency for the grander rooms used for
receiving visitors to proliferate. The dining room was joined by a drawing
room, and among the haute bourgeoisie by a morning room, a reception hall,
a music room, and a library. After the turn of the nineteenth and twentieth centuries, the majority of the middle class had a bathroom with hot running water
and a toilet.

Class distinctions were reflected not only in the number and size of rooms,
but also in the auxiliary rooms and the number of servants kept. Any decent

middle-class family kept at least one servant, a maid of all work, who in the basic type of flat with three rooms and a kitchen would sleep in the kitchen on a folding iron bed. Most genteel flats had a small servant's room leading off the kitchen, sometimes unheated and unlit. More well-to-do families kept two servants, a parlor maid and a cook, with the former conveying status when guests were received and the latter assisting in the running of the household. Also part of the middle-class household was a washerwoman casually employed for the heavy washing, a hairdresser (*friseur*) who would come every two or three days and, among the upper strata, a governess (*Fräulein or gouvernante*), who would live with the children and eat with the family.

As with the city and the building, there was a threefold division on functional lines in the arrangement of the flat. Bourgeois homes observed a strict division between the private, reception, and "service" spheres in spatial and personal terms.[45] This segregation was accomplished architecturally by a long vestibule without windows, shaped like an L or a T, from which opened all the rooms, or at least all the groups representing the spheres. There was a clear line between the living rooms and the group consisting of kitchen, pantry, and servant's room, and in two-story dwellings, between the ground-floor reception sphere and the private sphere upstairs. But there were usually only the virtual boundaries of unwritten house rules between the private sphere of daily life, primarily the bedroom, and the more elevated and protected salon or drawing room, opened on more formal occasions. Middle-class citizens tried to give themselves a private life cut off from the outside world. This desire for privacy and cult of the individual led to the development of single-function rooms, even though it seldom applied in a pure form, and then mainly among the upper classes.

The degree to which respect for private life also affected the reception sphere can be seen in the formal, almost museumlike quality of the salon and the rarity of the occasions on which it was used. The residents of middle-class dwellings resorted to outside help in performing public functions: cafés, clubs, and commercial catering and entertainment places. A middle-class home was too cramped and secluded to be a scene of daily social contact, let alone of afternoon social occasions. This role was adopted increasingly by the cafés, where there were fresh cakes and newspapers and tables for billiards and cards. Gentlemen frequented clubs, known as casinos, which appropriately combined the pleasures of socializing with the need to keep up political relations.[46] The times had passed when people made music, held dances, and played in aristocratic and bourgeois mansions. Such functions were steadily assumed by theaters, dance halls, and concert halls.

How Homes Were Furnished

There are several kinds of source material from which to reconstruct how flats were appointed: sensitive but not wholly accurate reminiscences and literary

descriptions, furniture dealers' and department stores' price lists and cata-
logues, and inventories for probate, which are authentic and accurate but reflect the multiplicity of real life, which makes them harder to categorize.[47]
Luckily a good many inventories of the estates left by tenants of the houses and
flats surveyed have survived.

The first tenant of the four-room flat on the first floor of No. 5, Sugárút was
a physician, Dr. Ármin Hercog. The inventory of his estate mentions that the
bedroom contained, for example, two beds, two bedside lockers, a three-door
wardrobe, a two-door wash stand with a marble top, a writing desk, and a
looking glass with a gold frame. The main pieces of furniture in the dining
room included a sideboard with three doors, one smaller square dining table,
and a larger expensive one with extending leaves, six cane chairs, an upholstered divan with six matching chairs, a wall mirror with a console, a sewing
table, a pendulum clock, a porcelain service for twelve, and a coffee and tea
service for six. The salon had one glass cabinet with three doors and one with
two, two round side tables, a sofa, four silk-covered armchairs with four similar upright chairs, a gilt-framed console mirror, a large glass-bead chandelier,
pictures, and vases. The simpler nursery had two wardrobes, a wash stand, a
bedside locker, a small table, and an expensive piano. (The inventory curiously
fails to mention a bed.) Each room was lit by a petroleum lamp. A moderate
estimate of 1,246 forints was put on the furniture (equivalent to about US $500
of 1890, although price structures were not directly comparable).[48]

The contents of one of the seven-room grand apartments in No. 27, Sugárút, are known from the inventory of Imre Róbert Goldberger's estate, taken
in 1892. From the description it is possible to reconstruct clearly the appointments of the bedroom, dining room, salon, and nursery. The other three rooms
probably had several functions. Let us mention here just the elegant dining
room, which contained an American walnut dining table with twelve chairs
upholstered in leather, a six-door oak sideboard with a marble top, two oak
console cabinets, a gilt porcelain dining service for twenty-four and three different services for twelve each, a coffee service for twelve, and a similar tea service. (Here the teaspoons, which would be silver, are not mentioned.) The
value of the entire contents was put at 5,000 forints (perhaps US $2,000).[49]

The owner of No. 35, Erzsébet körút, and the occupant of the grand apartment on the first floor, was the member of Parliament Gusztáv Fröhlich.[50] It is
not easy to reconstruct the actual furnishings from the inventory. It is known
from an authentic description made at the time that the flat had seven rooms,
but the inventory only lists the contents of four of them. (Fröhlich was a wid-
ower and may not have used all the rooms. He may have joined his bedroom
with his study and his dining room with his parlor, or kept some of them
locked up.) The bedroom contains, besides the bed, a bedside locker, a wash
stand, a strong box, and the writing desk and card table that would have belonged in his study, and a suite of furniture consisting of a divan, four armchairs, and three upright chairs. The salon was very mediocre in standard,

while the "young lady's" room appears to have contained a mixture of what you would expect to find in the bedroom and the sitting room of a young lady of modest means. The piano and harmonium are listed as being in the dining room, although the drawing room would have been more usual. The furniture was valued at a mere 754 forints (about US $300 of 1890).[51]

These inventories of estates point to the flats being congested. With fifteen to twenty items recorded per room and sixty to a hundred per apartment, counting the suites as one item and the carpets and cushions in each room often likewise, these middle-class homes were plainly stuffed with furniture.

So what can the furnishings of a bourgeois home at the turn of the century have been like? An attempt has been made, with the help of inventories of estates, literary descriptions, and price lists to compile a list of what can be considered typical, although it must be realized that a real home would alter according to changes in the number, ages, financial position, and rank of family members, and with widowhood, divorce, and marriage; furniture would be replaced, and the function of certain rooms could change, too, over a period of time. Bearing all this in mind, let us confine the attempts to define a type for three relatively stable rooms: the bedroom, the dining room, and the salon.

THE BEDROOM

This was the part of a middle-class home that changed least, and probably the only one where the tradition embodied in the bourgeois ethic extended over the full social range from the haute to the petty bourgeoisie. The function and structure of the bedroom did not essentially alter during the century. As the place where the married couple lay and slept together, it was off limits to other members of the family and still more to outsiders, and entered only by the couple themselves and a servant to clean it.

The structure of the bedroom was determined by the twin beds standing side by side, at right angles to an uninterrupted main wall. Close to each bed would be a bedside locker, so that the candle or lamp (and perhaps a glass and medicines) were within reach, along with the chamber pot and slippers inside. Other items integral to the room were a wardrobe for hanging clothes, another cupboard with shelves or a chest of drawers for underwear, and a wash stand opposite the beds, usually with two bowls and jugs, and a mirror behind. In smaller flats there was often a divan at the foot of the beds, where a child would sleep until the age of puberty. Other pieces commonly found were two to four chairs or armchairs and possibly a separate dressing table.

As bathrooms became common, the size and importance of the wash stand decreased. But even in the early twentieth century, there was hardly a bedroom in a middle-class home without one, even though there was a bathroom as well.

So the furnishings conveyed a feeling of intimacy, and the symmetry of the appointments symbolized the equality between husband and wife prevalent in the bedroom. This symmetry was broken by the dressing mirror (and perhaps it was to compensate for this that there was a symmetry in the three glasses arranged as a triptych), and in the opposite corner by the tile stove in warm-colored tones. The intimacy and privacy of the bedroom lent it a kind of festive mystery that gained an almost ritual character from the ornamental elements in the structure. Above the beds hung pictures of saints, devotional objects, and family portraits and photographs, as expressions of intimate piety. In families that were not religious, and wished to demonstrate the fact, the place of the devotional pictures was taken by stereotypes of intimate eroticism—oil-painted or cheaply printed reproductions of nudes, odalisques, and piquant scenes from mythology. The bedroom also contained the family valuables that were not for display: the jewelry, gold, and money. Many inventories list among the bedroom items a jewelry casket or a larger strong box or safe.

The appointments and structure of the bedroom were so pronounced that they influenced the common people and survived two world wars. Only with the chronic housing shortage after the Second World War and radical changes in the way of life did the traditional pattern break down.

THE DINING ROOM

The other more or less unifunctional and structurally stable element in the home was the dining room, which normally opened off the hall, so that access from the kitchen could be as direct as possible. The furniture consisted of solid hardwood pieces stained dark, with the table in the center. The use of a long rectangular dining table was inherited from the great households of earlier centuries. The size decreased in this period as the family itself shrank to four to six members. Many households had extending tables, and there was a trend toward oval or round tables, which made for a better use of space. The dining chairs were more solid than comfortable, with cushions rather than upholstery.

Also part of the dining suite would be two sideboards, one large and one smaller (referred to by various names in different periods, regions, and styles). The larger sideboard, known generally as a "Kredenz" in the south German, Austrian, and Hungarian regions, consisted of two parts: a lower part with double doors and two drawers, and an upper part with the middle open. It was made of fine wood, and in the period of revival styles it would be carved and have pillars. The top of the lower part tended to be French-polished or covered with a marble slab. The upper part contained the porcelain and stoneware (including cups, jugs, and drinking glasses) and the lower part the plates, table-cloths, and silver cutlery. Vases and a fruit bowl would be arranged on the marble. The smaller sideboard, known as the buffet or "Anrichte," could also be in two parts, with a serving counter below and a glass case for glassware above, but it could also be in one, in which case it was normally referred to and used as a server. Apart from a stove not placed centrally and a none-too-bright

10. Middle-class salon of the Pscherer-Verebély family in 1900

lamp, the dining room would also have a mirror and a long-case or wall clock. In a sense foreign to the room, but occasionally to be found there, was a divan, a sofa, or possibly a small table or an armchair.

The furniture of the dining room was suggestive of order, restraint, discipline, and ritual, matching well the rules of the house and the ceremoniousness of eating. It was typical of the middle-class way of life to eat together three times a day. Poorer families would not heat the dining room in winter, eating in the hall or the drawing room instead. For the upper strata, the dining room was also the place where guests were entertained in a more lavish fashion on a larger scale, when the doors would be thrown open to the salon and the master's sitting room, to give the scale of a banqueting hall of old.

THE SALON

The heart of the salon was provided by a suite of drawing-room furniture, which was usually arranged asymmetrically and diagonally, with a table lamp or standard lamp. Here too there would be a sideboard, a console table, and a console mirror. A salon differed from a simpler parlor mainly in possessing a few important items for display (see Figure 10).

A characteristic item was the glass case (*vitrine*), a graceful, four-legged cabinet with glass sides and shelves, where the family would place a display designed to represent itself: decorations and medals, family heirlooms, objets d'art, and curios (see Figure 11). Also ubiquitous was a chandelier to give light

11. The glass case in the same salon

and sparkle to the whole room. It would usually be of the Venetian type favored in Central Europe. If the family was not musical, the piano would also be placed in the salon as a decorative piece. (It would normally stand in the music room, or among the less well-to-do, in the parlor.)

Also associated closely with the salon were the appropriate clothes. For an evening occasion, the parlor maid would wear a simple black dress with a white apron and cap, the male members of the family would don dark evening wear, and the ladies' dress would be transformed as well. Daytime female attire in the nineteenth century was notable for completely covering the body with long skirts, long sleeves, and tops buttoned up to the neck. Ladies would be covered from head to foot in a looser, more comfortable fashion in the daytime or while working, and be laced in more tightly for the street or afternoon calls. But when the evening parties came, the ladies suddenly sported bare arms, shoulders, and backs.

How can these conflicting habits of dress be explained? On festive occasions, the ladies of the family themselves became exhibits: the family was putting its valuables on show. The attractive décolletage of the wife was an enhancement of the husband's prestige, while the seductive shoulders and bosom of an available daughter increased her value on the marriage market. Display as a public act reflected the free-thinking, profane appreciation of beauty to be found in the bourgeois ethic, just as in business it betokened a practical, profit-oriented outlook.

These descriptions are of ideal types, which only reflect in imperfect outline the chaotic abundance of practice in real life. This could hardly be demonstrated better than by the apartment of the wealthy, middle-class lawyer from Pécs, who in social position belonged to the political elite, where the salon was used also as a common parlor, even though he often received distinguished guests there,[52] or by the descriptions and inventories, which make it plain that the dining room was also used as a parlor, or the parlor as a nursery. Least commonly was the ritual nature of the bedroom infringed.

More recent researches have shown that in the middle class and above, the head of the family often reserved a room for himself, known as the study, the gentleman's room, or most commonly the master's room.[53] Items commonly found in such rooms included a writing desk, a gaming table, a bookcase, a divan, a sofa, a leather suite of armchairs, and sometimes a strong box, while on the walls there would be weapons and game trophies. In the case of provincial manor houses, the villas of gentlefolk, or the flats of professional people in the city, there was justification for a separate room in view of the head of the family's occupation—he might be a lawyer, a magistrate, or a structural engineer. But it seems that separate master's rooms were socially more widespread than that. Further investigations will decide whether the frequency of such rooms was a Hungarian specialty or a phenomenon general in Europe, or perhaps Central and Eastern Europe. Certainly the presence of a separate salon, a formal dining room, and a master's room signifies that the bourgeois way of life was tending toward greater display at the end of the century.

The Somberness of a Middle-Class Home

Having tried to type the arrangement and appointments of a middle-class flat, it is worth considering what life must have been like in such a home, not in terms of mode and quality but of what it felt like to live there at the turn of the century. Certainly the buildings and flats of a modern big city brought many innovations, conveniences, and civilizing elements for the middle classes, who built up for themselves a secure island of private domestic life that provided intimacy and protection, and fully accorded with the illusions built up of security in public life, internationally and within the Monarchy. So did people actually feel at home in their flats, particularly the younger generation? The vast majority of reminiscences point to feelings of unease. Most of the young professionals at the turn of the century felt uncomfortable in their parents' homes, despite the comfort they lived in. Many of them turned against middle-class values and morals, and moved out as soon as they could.

The form and structure of these late nineteenth-century houses and flats in revival styles were at odds with their functions. Both literally and figuratively, flats in the Ring and the Sugárút were cold, with large, high-ceilinged rooms that were unwelcoming and costly to heat. Narrowish windows and an abundance of curtains and drapes left the rooms quite dark, and even after electricity was installed, they could not be lit well with the technology of the day. As for the furniture, it took up too much space and was hardly designed for practicality. The abundant decoration, carving, and curves were often at the expense of the utility of the space inside, while the columns, volutes, and reliefs were hard to dust and clean. So form and structure were dominated by display at the expense of functionalism. The grander and fancier a middle-class home, the more dysfunctional and cheerless it became.[54]

Take, for example, the plan of a house in Renaissance Revival style. There was harmony between structure, form, and function of a Renaissance palazzo of old. There was good reason, in terms of life style, for the living quarters to be on the second and third floors and good reason for the ceilings to be high. The house had several dozen inhabitants; the sala was the center of public life, and the smoke from the lighting needed to rise into the upper regions. The same could hardly apply in a nineteenth-century flat inhabited by four to six people, lit by gas or electricity and heated with a tile stove. It was an age, moreover, when ironwork, masonry, and concrete were making new kinds of structure possible. Only the salon, the main reception room, still largely served its purpose. The other rooms were cheerless and their atmosphere was cold and hollow because their functionalism was lost. It was no use a rich tenant trying to fill the void with showy art works and knickknacks, no use trying to combat the coldness with velvet drapes and curtains, for that only made the home less commodious and cheerful than ever.

Ultimately, the hollowness and pretense could not be disguised by the life style or outward forms. The inconsistencies of the bourgeois ethic came into sharp conflict in the final third of the last century. Out of the bourgeoisie arose a new, detached aristocracy, a stratum of barons and other nobles that had spent much time and money on promoting their prestige and dignity. These were admired and imitated in their values and principles in life by most of the middle class, in whom the bourgeois expansionism of old gave way to respect for tradition, and respect for liberal principles to ever more hesitant lip service to them. There was still a great respect in word and principle for humanism and cultivation, when humanist culture and the bourgeois way of life as a whole had reached a state of crisis.[55]

It was against this display-oriented culture and morality that younger intellectuals at the turn of the century rebelled, rejecting profit-oriented liberal values in favor of aestheticism, artistic revival, and a total reform of life style.

Sezession Architecture and Youthful Rebellion

Several explanations have been suggested for the change of architectural epoch and the pathfinding that began with the Sezession, the Viennese school of Art Nouveau. Both the bourgeoisie's weariness and decadence and the freshness, vigor, and brash joie de vivre of the new style have been put forward. It has been ascribed to a new attitude to life on the part of the alienated intelligentsia, and to the creativity of an intelligentsia freed from the bonds of "style architecture." Such epoch-making changes, however, are always generated by several more specifically definable motivating factors. Without venturing to establish a causal relationship of any kind, let me mention the social and technical requirements of modern urbanization as certainly being among the underlying factors.

The technical innovation began among architects familiar with the potential architectural applications of steel structures, reinforced concrete, and glass, who wanted to release the opportunities presented by the new materials from the prison in which the revival styles had immured them.[56] The new trend, as demonstrated by its well-known symbol, the Eiffel Tower in Paris, emphasized structure and function. It found a formal idiom in American skyscraper construction and the ongoing development apparent in the building of family houses in Britain. More and more, traditional architects also began to feel weighed down by revival architecture, although they managed to incorporate the new materials into the old forms. Their protest was partly artistic and aesthetic in motive: they really did feel that the stylistic ideas of great periods in history were empty and obsolete, and made conscious efforts to alter tastes and the system of aesthetic values.

A contribution to the change in tastes was also made by the aesthetic demand for harmonious assimilation into the environment and the ideological demand for use to be made of local and national tradition. It started in England in the final third of the nineteenth century, primarily in the form of housing and family houses that remained formally within the bounds of Historicism, but created a model for a provincial, simple, intimate house, drawing mainly on the creative imagination of Philip Webb and Norman Shaw. Influenced by Morris and Ruskin, however, English architects rejected iron, concrete, and everything machinelike.[57] The new building techniques gained ground in bold, advancing America, where a new aesthetic outlook combined with the commercial spirit to engender the experiments that led to the development of new types of iron and steel structures, above all the skyscrapers.

So the impetus behind this second architectural departure was economic, social, and ideological. It elicited a favorable response in society and among architects in Central Europe, where those with the breadth of vision to think in terms of townscape increasingly turned away from the empty stereotypes and insincere, superficial solutions of Historicism. The motives and proposals of these pioneers were very diverse, as the Ringstrasse Debate at the turn of the century went to show. Camillo Sitte considered the Ring to be bleak and inhuman, and a breach of urban tradition. His target was not Historicism as such, but the employment of it in contemporary architecture in a utilitarian, rational way that was divorced from the community. A city, he declared, was not a housing estate, but a work of art: "A city must be built so that its citizens feel safe and happy. Urban architecture is not a technical question, but an aesthetic one in the loftiest sense."[58] Opposing him was Ludwig Baumann, who supported the principle of plasticity of spatial effect and spectacular monumentality.

The most influential critic of the architecture of the Ring was Otto Wagner, whose point of departure was likewise social. His basis for comparison, however, was no longer a conservative, backward-looking cultural critique, but that of a forward-looking person engaged with the new demands of the turn of the century. To suit modern mankind, everything newly created in architecture, he wrote, "must match the new forms and new demands. . . . Display us as a better, democratic, self-aware, ideal being, and embody both the colossal technical and scientific advances obtained and the practical streak running through modern mankind—that is self-evident!" This makes two assumptions that double as attributes: "Maximum comfort and maximum purity."[59] Wagner ends by summing up the underlying principle of modern architecture in the following sentence: "An architect should develop the form out of the construction," which is closely akin to the thesis of Louis Sullivan, who raised American engineering architecture to the status of an art: "Form follows function, and that is a law."[60]

Wagner laid down his basic principles as a theorist and applied them as an architect. He would choose his material to suit the purpose of the building, and the structure was tied to both of these. From these premises the form was derived, not automatically but in an artistic configuration. Notably progressive was the way Wagner combined social commitment with artistic exaction. For he certainly traced the changes of style back to the great social transformations,[61] although he was well aware that it was the master builder, not "society" as such, who designed the dwelling place and environment: "In every case of urban development, there is one primary question: the floor must be given to art and the artist, thereby displacing the engineer's antipathy to aesthetics and the 'vampire-like power of speculation.' "[62]

The critique made of the Historicism of the Gründerzeit and the ideal put forward by the new architecture found enthusiastic adherents and disciples among the second and third generation of the successful haute bourgeoisie— young people no longer brought up in trade, but in the best universities, academies, and artistic workshops. The sons of this well-to-do middle class of the

12. Part of the Majolika House (left) and the adjacent
apartment building, Linker Wienzeile 40,
both designed by Otto Wagner in 1899–1900

fin-de-siècle were educated, susceptible to new ideas, and sensitive to social
and moral issues. They turned in disillusionment and revulsion against the hypocrisy of bourgeois morality. The crisis and desire for change arose out of a
strong reciprocal reaction between the established order and the younger generation. The revolt of the young was naturally born of and fed by the structural
crisis of capitalism and the ideological and value-related crisis of liberalism,
although the latter was exacerbated in turn by the strongly anticapitalist cultural criticism and not infrequently the socialist criticism aimed at the milieu
of their parents by young people disenchanted with the bourgeois family and
morality.

The revolt of the younger generation extended to all aspects of work and
way of life and thinking. Except in the case of the revolutionary socialists, it
found expression in great reform movements aiming to change life as a whole.

This wholesale reform of life embraced labor safety and environmental protection, garden-city planning and family planning, health and education. It covered the emancipation of women and the end of male domination, rejection of religious and moral tradition, rejection of stays, adoption of healthy dress and nutrition, care and freedom of the body—from bathing and sunbathing to love making—through more tolerant sexual morals, universal franchise, and the secret ballot, and reform of psychology and penal law.[63]

Fitting into this aim for a complete modernization of life were the new architecture and style of living. The revolt of the younger generation met with a searching, innovating ferment among artists and architects. *Der Zeit ihre Kunst—der Kunst ihre Freiheit* (To the age its art, to art its freedom) was the motto of the Vienna Sezession, expressing this encounter of desires for innovation and release.

Artem Impendere Vitae

The change of epoch—during the quarter of a century leading from Historicism to modern architecture—took place through stylistic trends and degrees that penetrated and permeated each other. Within every style there was a multiplicity of variants and local types. (It may be this cavalcade of variety that makes it so attractive to people today, when economic and political rationality tend to impose uniformity and drabness on the environment.) Certainly the structural and stylistic solutions of the "late Eclectic" resemble those of the adolescent Sezession in many respects. Similarly, it would take a smart art historian to draw a clear line between the ways the mature Sezession and premodern architecture used space and form. So to a certain extent it is wiser to avoid a categorization in art-history terms in favor of concentrating on what was new and common in the change of epoch at the turn of the century.

In the early period of the Central European Sezession (and Art Nouveau and Jugendstil in general), the elements of outward form are conspicuous. It broke down the harmony, symmetry, and dignified motionlessness of the traditional historical styles, bringing façades to life with curves and waves on cornices and balconies, and various protrusions and projections. Keen use was concurrently made of sinuous, tendriled, floral, or geometric decorative elements, the ornamentation suited to the decorative art of the period or to the newly discovered folk tradition. Perhaps more important than the ornamentation was the fact that the Sezession increasingly took advantage of structural changes appropriate to function, and to functional solutions to interior use of space. So it displayed the structurally oriented nature of the building in its outward form as well. Structural clarity was seen as a sign of honesty and was steadily applied. Having conveyed the view of Otto Wagner, we can also quote Hendrik Berlage: "Falsehood has become the rule these days in art as well. . . . We architects must now rediscover the truth, which means reinterpreting the essence of architecture, [namely,] construction."[64] Henry van de Velde, one of the first

13. The Sezession Building, designed by Joseph Maria Olrich,
with Naschmarkt in the foreground. Vienna, 1897–1898

great innovators, can be cited as well: "Comprehend the form and construction of every object in relation to its most strictly elemental logic and justification for existing."[65]

So the highest principle of the mature Sezession was to judge objects by the
way they satisfy human needs—functionalism, in other words. This did not
imply a rational, utilitarian approach, only that functional objects were to be
fashioned in an artistic manner. The principle was applied in the execution of
the outward surface and of the space inside, in the varied external and internal
decoration, and in the careful crafting of every element of the building and
item of furniture and fittings, by hand where possible. Façades, cornices, roofs,
windows, furniture, wallpaper, lamps, door handles, and railings were all
works of art, and the resulting house or flat an aggregate work of art, a Gesamtkunstwerk. Behind all this, however, was a glaring inconsistency. The
apostles of the "new art" who departed from tradition were imbued with good
intentions of fostering social improvement. They wanted to influence life
through art, everyone's life, but only the rich could afford their handmade

14. Atelier of the Malonyai Villa, designed by Béla Lajta. Budapest, 1905

pieces of artistry and craftsmanship, or their Gesamtkunstwerke to beautify their environment. Only from the wealthy, art-loving haute bourgeoisie and the prosperous artistic intelligentsia was there a demand or appreciation for it.

The Sezession brought relief to the interiors of the revival period with their hefty, oversized carved furniture, curtains, and hangings. Sezession furniture was simpler and more graceful and functional. But a more radical change in interior design and furnishings came only toward the end of the 1900s, along with the transition to modern architecture, affecting both Vienna and Budapest, primarily in the construction of villas. Both in the practice of architecture and the life's work of certain practitioners (such as Otto Wagner, Josef Hoffmann, Adolf Loos, or Béla Lajta) there ensued a cleansing, continuous transition from the mature Sezession into the pre-modern, in which the simplified, proportioned surfaces and forms really were adapted to function and structure, while ornamentation became simple or was replaced altogether by cool rationalism in the architectural treatment of space. This shift lasted for a short while in some cases, but was permanent in the case of forerunners of the Bauhaus movement. The main purpose really became the performance of function, in the context of the great principles of an overall reform of life style: spacious, comfortable, clean, and sunny flats, not just for the top ten thousand but for the lower-middle and working classes as well.

This produces a duality in the architecture of the early years of the century. On the one hand, there are luxury Sezession and "pre-modern" villas for the haute bourgeoisie and the scientific and artistic intelligentsia. On the other, there are comfortable, homelike tenement blocks and flats and later family houses and housing estates for the common man. From England to the eastern rim of the continent there resounded among artists and artisans, Utopians and realistic social policy makers, a call for the building of smaller flats, for design inspired by popular craftsmanship and intended for popular use, for cheap, tasteful furniture,[66] and for an affordable life style. Ebenezer Howard's book *Garden Cities of Tomorrow* had appeared in 1898. The building of Letchworth began five years later, and the movement soon spread to German soil. Darmstadt's Mathildenhöhen, built in the early years of the century, was still a villa district of artists' homes and luxury houses for the haute bourgeoisie, but in 1908, the Deutsche Werkstätte announced plans for a garden city for the middle and working classes in Hellerau, near Dresden.[67] Hellerau set out to realize the noblest aims of the movement for life-style reform: to circumvent the crowded, unhealthy life in big cities and speculation in building land and housing, by putting up small, cozy, comfortable, tastefully appointed homes. For Hellerau was at once functional and painstakingly and tastefully designed and executed, a kind of socialized Gesamtkunstwerk, one might say.

Tessenow worked there, and so did Le Corbusier for a while. There, in the garden city's modern theater in 1913, Paul Claudel's verse play *The Annunciation (L'Annonce faite à Marie)* was first performed, together with Kafka, Rilke, Werfel, and Buber—quiet renovators and rebellious innovators alike.

A Transformation of Housing in Hungary

Finally, let us take a brief look at the transformation of architecture and housing arrangements in Hungary. The aim is not to provide either a historical overview or an artistic assessment, since both have been done comprehensively and with great erudition in the compendium *Magyar mûvészet 1890–1919* edited by Lajos Németh.[68] The question instead is how the new architecture fitted in with the global change of epoch and the development of education and cultivation in Hungary.

It is worth emphasizing first of all that the development in Hungary almost caught up with the change of era in Europe, following it in its multiplicity and its architectural and social principles and solutions by only a few years. A special feature in eastern Central Europe is the conscious cultivation of local and national tradition. The period's emphatic search for a style, according to *Magyar művészet,* "appeared most plainly in architecture, where it became interwoven with the problem area of national character."[69] "National art held a central place in public thinking" about art in the period, "as a goal chosen . . . by the widest variety of schools of thought and form."[70] It was stated categorically that "the architectural theory of the time can only be studied in conjunction with the interpretations of national art."

These aspirations should not be seen solely as the effects of the period's enhanced nationalism, even though this certainly helped to inspire the investigation (and frequent exaggeration) of the national character. For the roots of the matter run deeper. A whole century before, in the age of Romanticism, the smaller nations of the eastern Central European region had already been prompted by instincts of self-preservation to research keenly into their national attributes, as the foundation on which to justify their existence and identify themselves. It can be considered fortunate that the Sezession, having exhausted the veins of Historicism, turned to indigenous art, in the work of the pioneer Ödön Lechner, although Lechner did not gather the material for his folk characteristics from his own experience or collect them himself, and in fact used folk motifs as ornamentation that was still not subordinate to function (see Figure 15). Instead he adopted the stock of forms and the solutions of the European Sezession in his treatment of exteriors and internal space (such as his Post-Office Savings Bank and the Sipeki Villa).[71] Perhaps this is not even a shortcoming. Perhaps the art critic Lajos Fülep was right to say, "In seeking the national, he arrived at the international . . . in seeking the specific, at the universal, and in seeking the ancestral, at the modern and immediate."[72]

The great masters of the main architectural schools that derived from Lechner or independently of him at the beginning of the new era discerned the national quality they sought in the realm of the popular or folk. (For a folk character predominates even in the applied art of the Gödöllő school, which revived medieval tradition.) Apart from borrowing motifs of folk decoration, the mature Sezession in Hungary tried integrating functional elements and techniques of rustic architecture its plans, structures, and technologies.[73] This drive toward innovation was not specific to architecture. It had a more general significance in Hungarian culture. The liberal, rational scale of values—empty and exhausted by the turn of the century and to be equated in Hungary's case with the tradition of the nobility, that is, Romanticism, National Realism, and Historicism—could not be ousted simply by the formal idiom of the global artistic upheaval. Nor did the folklore already explored, with its commonplace, pastoral popular character, offer a fertile soil for renewal, as its

15. The Sipeki Villa, designed by Ödön Lechner, Marcell Komor,
and Dezsô Jakab. Budapest, 1905–1907

accessories, chansons, and Gypsy bands had already been absorbed into traditional taste. So deeper, more archaic layers of Hungarian popular tradition
had to be explored, as the poet Ady did with the language of the Hungarian Bi-
ble, Protestant preachers, and songs of the eighteenth-century kuruc (peasant)
rebellions, and as Bartók and Kodály did with their research into the ancient
sources of folk song. The turn-of-the-century architects with a folk-art orientation (above all Béla Lajta, Károly Kós, and Ede Thoroczkai-Wigand) belong,
in my view, to this educational process of renewing Hungary's national self-
image and artistic tastes.

Of course it was and remains questionable whether such structural loans
from folk architecture to the townscape and types of building produced by
modern urbanization could yield a viable solution capable of functional and
aesthetic development. In practice certain elements of folk art—techniques of
building and furniture making—proved usable in environments and on scales

16. The Babochay Villa, designed by Aladár Árkay. Budapest, 1905–1906

similar to the originals, that is, in family houses and residential areas. Examples of this are the center of the Wekerle Estate in Kispest, designed by Kós, the master's own house at Sztána, Árkay's estate of villas on Kis-Sváb Hill, and some other Buda villas (see Figure 16),[74] to which can be added Kós's Zebegény Church. But in metropolitan surroundings, on massive public buildings and apartment houses, the transfer did not succeed even where the scale and structure were modified, because the radically different proportions and function caused the original structure to break down, leaving trappings like gateways, balconies, or verandas reduced to ornamentation.

In the case of modern public buildings, residential buildings with several stories, and the villas of the well-to-do, it proved feasible to combine folk ornamentation with functional principles of structure. The happiest combinations were accomplished by architects who started out from Lechner's Sezession style and were conversant with folk art and respectful of it, but subordinated it to the general ordering principle of functionalism, as in Marcell Komor and Dezső Jakab's Town Hall for Marosvásárhely (Tîrgu Mureš); Béla Lajta's Malonyai Villa, Vas utca Commercial School, and classic Rózsavölgyi Emporium; the Vágó brothers' National Salon and City Theater; and József Vágó's Schiffer Villa. On Lajta's Rózsavölgyi building on Servita tér (square) in central Budapest, the tasteful, original folk ornamentation that serves to decorate and divide up the front marks a direct continuation of the Lechner tradition, and the way the functional structure—half commercial, half residential—is resolved reflects the architectural influence of the best British, German, and

17. The Schiffer Villa, designed by József Vágó. Budapest, 1912

Austrian premodern buildings of the time. Yet the synthesis remains essentially original.[75]

Especially pertinent to the subject under discussion is the Schiffer Villa, a two-story house built in 1910–1912, on the watershed between two eras, worlds, and architectural styles (see Figure 17). The external surfaces are clean, severe, and devoid of ornamentation, so that the structure emerges in the form. As a recent study put it, "The arrangement of the internal areas of the building is reflected in the consistent asymmetry of the façades."[76] The lower floor coincides with the reception area. Almost a third of the 4,300 sq. ft. of floor area is taken up by an imposing hall, which extends up into the story above. This is flanked by an L shape consisting of a spacious dining room, a large salon (650 sq. ft.), a smaller salon, and an art gallery and library known as the study (600 sq. ft.). The stained-glass window covering a complete wall of the hall and the panel covering the space over the entrance are the work of Károly Kernstok, and Vilmos Fémes Beck did the marble pool and flower trough. Decoration for the other rooms was done by Rippl-Rónai, Iványi-Grünwald, István Csók, and Kisfaludi Strobl. All the furniture, wallpapers, and other items of furnishing are carefully designed works of art. The arrangement and appointments of the upper story are functional. One wing contains the master's and mistress's bedrooms, with a breakfast room and sitting room next to them, and next to these the nursery. Whereas the 4,300 sq. ft. of the ground floor are divided into five large reception areas, the upper story of 3,000 sq. ft. contains eight main rooms with auxiliary premises. So each room had an area of about 300 sq. ft., making them homelike and human in scale, and this feeling was supported by spacious windows and furniture in keeping with each room's purpose.[77]

The Schiffer Villa's combination of the livable, the usable, and the decorative, along with its marriage of engineering skills and artistic creativity, gave rise to a model for a dwelling in which functionalism and display could once again complement each other harmoniously.

The Schiffer Villa, the Rózsavölgyi Emporium, a good many of the pavilions at Budapest Zoo, and the center of the Wekerle Estate were all works of art that would stand their ground in any great European city. But the other side of the coin is that such buildings as the Schiffer Villa, or Sezession villas and stores, banks, and homes designed by Lajta in general, were so few and rare. Was it because of the country's poverty? Were there too few enterprising and rich bourgeois? Were the state and the city too mean with their money? Could the backwardness of the country have left too little time for the new architecture to reach fruition, so that it flowered, only to be engulfed immediately by the war, followed by penury, crisis, and jerry-building?

In fact it was not a shortage of enterprise or capital that caused Hungary and its capital to fall behind the more prosperous countries in the field of urbanization, and the lag was not even very striking before the Great War. The backwardness was apparent less, I think, on the creative side than in the reception—the public, the level of taste in society. Hungary at the beginning of the century was at a stage where the revolt of the younger generation (and concomitant movement for reforming the life style) was just breaking out, and then only among the educated bourgeoisie, the intelligentsia, and the conscious working class. Elsewhere it was incubating and stimulating artistic renewals. Although the great movements for renewal during the change of era influenced Hungary as well, the social basis was too weak, and somewhat too isolated, for the country to join the mainstream of them.

Hungarian urban architecture and residential design enjoyed, without being able to utilize them fully, two fruitful decades in which architects, freed from the rigid dogmas of Historicism, were still not entangled by the economic constraints of mass construction or the abstract rationalism decreed by modern architecture.

Chapter Two

THE IMAGE OF THE GERMANS
AND THE JEWS IN THE
HUNGARIAN MIRROR OF
THE NINETEENTH CENTURY

THE AUSTRIAN Museum of Ethnography preserves a table of the Peoples of Europe (*Völkertafel*) from the early eighteenth century.[1] The table gives us an amusing description of the main features of ten European peoples—ranging from Spaniards to Turks—evidently according to the imagination of some Austro-German writers of that age. The representatives are depicted in characteristic national costumes: the Westerners in elegant civil dresses with knee-stockings and shoes (the Englishman in riding boots), the Eastern men in parade dress with boots. Except for the Frenchman and the Italian, they all wear a sword, showing that they are gentlemen. Let me concentrate on only two of the ten nationalities here represented, the protagonists of this chapter, the Germans and the Hungarians.

The representative of the former appears in this table as open-hearted and charitable, sharp-minded and invincible, and thus both lavish and given to drink, a man whose main entertainment is drinking but whose character is that of a lion. The Hungarian, on the contrary, is unfaithful and treacherous, cruel and bloodthirsty, with little mental capacity; he is lazy, his sole military virtue is that of mutiny, and he resembles the wolf. In the illustration, the German wears festive dress whereas the Hungarian appears in Hussar uniform.

From the same period, the time of the anti-Habsburg uprisings, we are well informed of the image of Germans as depicted by the Hungarians.[2] Contemporary kuruc poems and manifestos call on Hungarians not to believe Germans because they are treacherous and perfidious, merciless jailers, and vicious even when cultivated: they are "learned worms." These images of the enemy are mainly negative imprints of one another. The common feature of these images is that they are not based on unbiased experience but on prejudices, inherited sympathies, or dislikes. These stereotypes, unfolded in the depths of the past, have been the natural consequences of the disharmonious coexistence of dozens of nations, ethnic groups, and vernaculars in the Danube region.

For a very long time, and particularly since the emergence of nineteenth-century romantic nationalism, the region contained a motley garden of national character perceptions and self-images, a garden that supported a dense vegetation of prejudices directed against other ethnic communities and minorities.

How can this variety of national images be investigated? The sources we have at the moment are overabundant, pamphlets or scholarly works imbued by national spirit, supporting or condemning former or existing minority policies of the ruling nations and their governments. The bulk of such papers are only recent sources of mutual prejudices, flattering self-images, and hostile images of "others." But we cannot approach a realistic view of our neighbors without a scholarly self-discipline; we have to measure our own virtues and faults using the same norms and terms as we do those of "others."

One of the earliest Hungarian ethnographical studies coupled statistical geographical information with a description of national character, and with a self-image and an image of the other that were not free of prejudice. Elek Fényes, an excellent statistician, wrote of his own nation in these terms: "Hungarians are haughty and overbearing, and this haughtiness is combined with a measure of gravity; they are honest, generous, straightforward and cordial, intense in love and hate, quick of temper but soon calm again, friendly, and hospitable; and they are soon drawn to all that is great and fine, but if their ardor is not constantly fueled it soon expires; their valor, courage, and fortitude are respected even by their foes." This splendor is dulled by a few shortcomings: complacency, a fondness of luxury, the love and pursuit of rank and office, extravagance, and a lack of steadfastness.

The image given of others is far less flattering and tactful. The Slovaks are "mild, humble, often meek to the point of cowardice, hardworking and fit for trades, but for the most part mean, sly, and two-faced." The Serbs "are marked by cordiality, hospitality, a heroic spirit, religious fervor, and good humor, but otherwise are quite lazy . . . intemperate, treacherous, superstitious, and vengeful." The Romanians love frippery; the women paint themselves heavily and wear many trinkets. The Romanians are "warmhearted and quick-witted, and make good soldiers . . . but at the same time are idle, treacherous, and very superstitious and bigoted."[3]

Early statistical and ethnographical studies were rich in descriptions of national character, but most mixed observations and numerical data with conjectures, and were replete with prejudiced opinions and stereotypes. For us they serve primarily as source material, alongside nineteenth-century pictorial illustrations and pamphlets. Indeed, during the course of research into the subject of this study, it emerged that one could mainly rely on caricatures, parodies, and sketches of speech and mentality, and in general on the comic features in the daily press, on the feuilletons, on literary periodicals, and on literature itself.

For our topic, the press has three advantages as a source. First, the simultaneous confrontation of the press representing a variety of schools of opinions provides material for examining opinions and prejudices in social depth, and politically differentiated; a comparison of several periods discloses change, the spirit of history. The second advantage of press material is that it largely employs distilled, simplified, commonplace stereotypes and clichés, evolved over a long period, from which ordinary readers could easily identify the figure concerned and by which ordinary readers might easily be influenced. The third advantage, particularly of the comic press, is the visual element: a drawing or a pictorial story is usually easier to perceive and more transparent in its essentials than a verbal abstraction. Consequently this source material to some extent allows one to progress methodically from the surface to the essence, from the outward to the inward. I shall therefore begin describing the images that were born in nineteenth-century Hungarian society, then undergoing a bourgeois transformation, by giving a description of the outward characteristics, the figure and clothing. I shall continue by introducing the variants in ways of speaking and thinking, and then conclude with a delineation of character.

This present study confines itself to examining two minorities, the Germans and the Jews, largely but not exclusively for reasons of space. The restriction is also suggested by certain considerations of content: as can be seen above, the images created for the Slovaks, Romanians, and Serbs are very laconic and general. They largely repeat attributes and describe characteristics (not upright, sly, treacherous, primitive, stupid, barbarous, lazy, cowardly, wild, brutal) which the opinion-setting nobility also applied to serfs, even to those of their own nationality. (In any case epithets such as these stem from the prejudices encountered in every community where different groups live together in discord.) By contrast, the image created for the Germans and the Jews, who were at a much higher level of bourgeois development, is far more differentiated, colorful, and varied, since these two minorities occupied an outstanding place and played an important role in Hungary's bourgeois transformation. Although both were initially alien or immigrant ethnic groups, the majority became assimilated to a greater or lesser extent in the nineteenth century. By the end of that century they were not considered as strange or alien nations, but as "different groups" within the nation, toward whom the leading strata's rational interest, motivation, and emotional capacity for acceptance was ambivalent. So through the example of these two minorities the socio-political differentiation and the chronological changes in the form taken by prejudices can be well observed.

DEPICTION

The models for the Hungarian comic papers that were launched in the 1840s must probably be sought in Britain's *Punch* and France's *Charivari*. The greatest and most direct influence, however, came from the almost contemporary illustrated comic papers in Berlin, the *Fliegende Blätter* and the *Kladdera-datsch*, which were close to the Budapest comic papers in social character and spirit.[4] (The influence of Kaspar Braun and Wilhelm Busch can clearly be discerned.)[5]

The German archetype (Maxi the German) was a "pan-German" figure that embraced several variants, including the "Austrian brother-in-law," the "Swabian" settler-peasant imported from Germany, and the old home-grown *purger* (burgher). He assumes his full historical and social shape only when juxtaposed with his Hungarian counterpart, Magyar Miska (Mike the Hungarian), who is a handsome, well-set stout lad in pelisse with frogging and loops, in boots and feathered calmuc (headdress). The German, by contrast, is an insignificant weakling. His face is smooth, with no pointed moustache, and his arms and legs are thin. He wears the German knee breeches with braces and a waistcoat (in hot weather just a shirt). He has a typical German *Zipfel-mütze* (skull cap) with a tassel on his head, and mules on his feet.[6]

The more elevated, slender, intellectualized variant of this basic type is the bureaucrat, one of the upper-class élite. He is usually depicted as skinny, with a meager, oval face reminiscent of the Habsburg family. In some cases, as a sign of enervated intellectualism, he is clean shaven. He has long spindly arms and legs, and although dressed in keeping with his official position, he is not really elegant: a frock coat; light, striped, or plain trousers; a stiff shirt front; a bow tie or a wide tie with a pin; and walking shoes, patent leathers, or soft boots. The typical bureaucrat is bald or thinning, wears pince-nez or spectacles, and smokes cigars or cigarettes. Even at first glance he looks sober, gloomy, severe, hostile, and repugnant.[7]

Német Maxi (Maxi the German) also spawned the figure of the city *purger*. He wears a shirt, a waistcoat, a jacket, and a cravat, but on his head is the traditional skull cap. In his mouth there is a cigar or a long-stemmed pipe, which is the visible sign of assimilation, but on his feet he still wears the mules that to Hungarian eyes were specifically German. It is not his conspicuous wealth and exploitive nature that make the Hungarian German burgher a comic figure in the drawing, but his commonplace, bourgeois narrow-mindedness.

A distant relation of Maxi was the figure of a Swabian peasant which turned up in the papers later. Initially he was thin, and worked in simple peasant clothes and wooden clogs. Only later did he put on weight and become a rich and fat farmer (*Landwirt*).

There is a very informative caricature showing the assimilation and rise in social rank of the eighteenth-century German settlers, and the transfigurations that accompanied the process. The first part of the caricature, which pokes fun at the career of Sándor Wekerle (prime minister in 1892–1894), is called the "Mecklenburg forefathers": it shows an earlier Wekerle in typical German peasant clothing, with a skull cap on his head, knee breeches, and wooden clogs, sowing seed and killing rats. The second part ("Scythian grand-

children") depicts the assimilated descendant, in Hungarian gala dress complete with headgear with an egret's feather and a sword by his side, seated in a
ministerial armchair, while ugly little Jewish rats jump about in his lap, on his
shoulders, and around the chair in their delight at the introduction of civil
marriage and the acceptance of the Jewish religion. The essence of the caricature is its anti-Semitic political implication, but the picture also illustrates the
point that an assimilated German, even though he has become Hungarian in
appearance, clothing, and behavior, dons the *summun symbolum Hungari-
cum* of Hungarian gala dress in vain, for in "spirit" and mentality he has not
become Hungarian at all.[8]

Still more differentiated and richer in forms and ideas is the manner of depicting the types and transformation of Jewry. Initially, in the liberal press the
Jew was seen more as a ridiculous figure, despicable rather than repulsive: a
pedlar in patched clothes and scuffed slippers with a pack on his back. He was
a *handlé* (peddler), a rag collector, or in a more upstage version a Jew who
deals in wool, leather, or feathers, who retains his old features even after settling and becoming a rich shopkeeper. During the constitutional period that
followed the Ausgleich of 1867 there appeared a self-portrait by Magyarized
Jewish writers, showing assimilated figures who alternately criticize and reflect the society that has received them.
    The character to survive longest was created by the Hungarian Jewish sati-
rist Adolf Agai: that of Solomon Seiffensteiner, the yarn-spinning commentator. He is immediately recognizable as typically Jewish in appearance: thick,
fleshy nose, shifty eyes, thick hair, thick lips, and broad gestures, appearing to
"talk" and gesticulate with his hands all the time. On weekdays he performs
his "reflections" in a cap and waistcoat with a smiling face, and on festive occasions in a top hat, jacket, and overcoat. He was the clever, shrewd, still
"charming" Jew.[9] But a different version of the "ugly" figure comes from the
increasingly strong anti-Semitic camp at the end of the nineteenth century. In
the papers of this group the Jew was repellent and mercenary, and the Jew who
had grown rich was a repulsive, shylock figure even in his mildest form. He had
a thick crooked nose, thick lips, big ears, wooly hair, two shabby locks in front
of the ears, a short fat body, short, bandy legs, rough hands, and most characteristic of all, a devilish grin conveying greed and desire for possessions.[10] Surrounding him are the pitiful figures of his victims.
    These distorted depictions imported from German comic papers, in all the
variants, convey the same essential message. Irrespective of what he wore,
whether it was a Jewish cap, long hair and sidelocks, a skull cap on the head,
and face covered with thick, curly hair, or a top hat on a bald head and a clean-
shaven face, the Jew represented something anomalous or demonic in which
the spirit of witchcraft and destruction dwelt. This was conveyed in the distorted ears, nose, and lips, and the obligingly servile, cynically shallow, or

hair-raisingly rapacious grin that all anti-Semitic caricatures wore. Undoubtedly the Jew, from the peddler to Baron Rothschild, was becoming increasingly civilized, but these depictions suggested simply through the outward features that the essential character was unchanged.[11] The Jew, however rich, is ugly, pot-bellied, club-footed, and badly dressed, even when wearing an expensive frock coat. No upstart can ever be elegant.

The merciless Jew who wheeled and dealed everywhere and with everything became the stereotype of the bald, fat, cigar-smoking, pot-bellied capitalist in the anti-Semitic press of Central Europe. That figure, with his thick wallet and purse stuffed with gold, marched on from those German, Austrian, and Hungarian papers to the pages of the Nazi *Stürmer* and other fascist papers—and from there straight to the death camps of the Second World War.

The change over a few decades in the image of the Jew, and at the same time the deeper causes of anti-Semitism, can easily be comprehended through the comic paper of the Hungarian clericals, *Herkó Páter*. The mid-nineteenth-century Jew with a pack on his back was a modest, humble beggar to whom the noble owner of a country mansion talked down in an offhand manner. By the end of the century the situation had changed. The Jew had become a landowner, the new master of the mansion that had been auctioned off. He now wore a tunic and trousers with frogs and loops, smoked a pipe, and treated the old gentry in an offhand way.[12]

SPEECH AND MENTALITY

In the bourgeois period, when differences of outward appearance are slowly standardized, the outsider, whether he is a foreigner or a fellow citizen belonging to a different national group, can be identified less by figure and dress than by speech. The pronunciation, vocabulary, structure, rhythm, and intonation of speech as a whole make it easy to identify an outsider, an assimilated member of another ethnic group, or even one who belongs to a subculture within the same ethnic group. To any community, a foreign language sounds strange, and in most cases is considered ugly and ridiculous. (Even the medieval Hungarian chroniclers likened the sound of German to the growling of bears and Italian to the twittering of swallows, while the latter likened Hungarian to chattering or bawling.) To the majority, the minority that learns the majority language slowly and uses it imperfectly is a constant inspiration of ridicule and feelings of superiority. Hungarian literary works and the Hungarian press both took great pleasure in aping and mocking the broken Hungarian of assimilated Germans, Jews, and other minorities; this broken speech became a major part of the image that was formed of them and a useful method for depicting their character.

Hungarian is unrelated to any of the Indo-European languages. It contains many front vowels, and among them open, long vowels (like é, ô, and û) which cause pronunciation trouble to Slav speakers. It also contains many digraphs, softened consonants (like gy, ny, and ty) that are difficult for German and French speakers. Other features that cause difficulties for nonnative speakers of Hungarian are the accusative -t suffix, the distinction between the objective verb conjugation that accords with a defined object and the subjective conjugation that accords with an undefined object, and strict rules of usage for the definite and indefinite articles. Speakers of Indo-European languages wrestle with the problems of using suffixes instead of prepositions, of positioning verbal modifiers, and with the innumerable variants of word order.

It would be a hopeless task to illustrate in English translation the conventions by which Hungarian writers imitated and characterized the bilingual, partially assimilated minorities. It would involve translating the rules and irregularities not of one but of two languages into a third language, while paying particular attention to the specific mixture of the first two. The result would be an incomprehensible travesty. The best one can do is to attempt to describe a few of the regular transgressions made in this specific linguistic assimilation.

For the Germans in the process of Magyarization, the problems were clustered around Hungarian vowels and the digraph soft consonants. In most cases they improperly used the accusative case and the objective conjugation, and under the influence of their first language, they made constant use of personal and possessive pronouns (which in Hungarian are required only in cases of emphasis). They hardly ever managed to compose sentences with a correct word order. Another general practice was for the learner to supply words in his own language with the suffixes of the new language, or the other way about: to use certain words of the new language according to the rules of his mother tongue. Examples of such mixtures are the Hungarian participle form *unterminirozva* being substituted for the German *unterminiert* or *triumphál* instead of *triumphiert*.

The Hungarian spoken by the assimilated Jews was even more mixed and represented a more characteristic way of speech. The majority of the immigrant generation spoke German, or rather a dialect of German with an admixture of Hebrew: Yiddish. They later mixed their Yiddish with literary German, and then with Hungarian words. In pronunciation their main problems were a partiality for back vowels, modification of labial and dental consonants into Hebrew gutturals (a lot of k, kh, and ch), disregard for word order, expression of statements in question form, the throwing back of questions, a singsong manner of speech, and frequent admixture of German and Hebrew words.

The manner and style of speech of the minority in the process of assimilation into the majority is more than a linguistic or socio-linguistic question. It can also serve as important source material for examining mentality. When one reads the "Preschpurger purger," Kraxelhuber's poem of greeting on the occasion of Prince Alfred Windischgrätz's appointment as Austrian prime minister in 1894: "Polldok [boldog] szem, te mit is látsz? Mekind tyitt [megint jött] ó Windischgrätz!" (Happy eyes, what do you see? Windischgrätz is back again), it is not only the linguistic oddities but the rather typical mentality that make one smile.[13]

The anecdotes of Solomon Seiffensteiner, who has been mentioned above, are likewise interesting from the point of view of the history of mentality. The wise Rabbi Hillel goes for a walk with his students on a Saturday (Sabbath). They notice a Jew smoking a pipe beneath a bastion. "The bastion will fall on him," the students shouted angrily. "It won't fall on him," says Rabbi Hillel mildly, and "Gattes Wünder! It did not fall on him either."[14] Again, it is not only the linguistic oddities and the joking at the expense of political forecasters that is interesting, but the rational prophesying of the Jew educated in the Talmud.

ETHNIC GROUP AND CHARACTER

Since the imitation of speech can be considered to convey an opinion or illustration of the other group's mentality, one can arrive, by following the same kind of opinion-forming mechanism at a deeper layer of the image, the character, which is a favorite theme in prejudiced thinking.

The national self-image and the image of the other derive from social and psychological processes that influence each other closely. Social psychologists in our time have proved by many and various methods that the awareness of identity in both small groups and macrocommunities is created and shaped during constant communication and friction with the other group, the neighbors.[15] Many groups owe their very existence to having defended their members against external threats and dangers and to the need for a "common refuge," as Henri Tajfel puts it.[16] Yet the individual in many societies is faced with a network of complex group formations into which he must integrate. Whereas his self-identification depends on his relations with various groups, his behavior toward his own group and other groups depends on his self-identification. Just as the individual's sense of identity and awareness can take shape only in relation to a specific group, so the identity of a group can only gain sense and content through the constant process of confrontation with other groups far and near. According to Allport, a child conceives his parents, his neighborhood, his dwelling place, his nation as parts of a given environment. As his existence is part of these constraints and these constraints are parts of his existence, they are in any case good.[17] By the age of four or five a child can conceive of himself as a member of various groups, and so can identify himself in the ethnic sense. Of course his connections with his own group and the opinions he forms of "the others" are precognitive in nature, since they antedate his acquisition of geographical, ethnographical, and historical knowledge and personal experience. He learns what kind of people the neighbors are before he learns exactly who they are. This primary image certainly derives from a prejudiced formation of opinion. In most cases its basis is ardent, passionate identification with his own community and similarly ardent antipathy toward the other group and outside communities.

Although the subtle detail in the process of cohesion has yet not been analyzed sufficiently, modern national awareness is recognized to be at once a
combination and development of older awareness of ethnic, territorial, cultural, or religious communities. Thus the awareness of national identity that
arose in the nations of Central and Eastern Europe in the first half of the nineteenth century derived from ethnic, regional religious, and other traditions,
from the myths of origin that became canonized at about that time, from the
awareness of vocation, and from the study of national character that was compressed into stereotypes.[18] It was the writers, poets, scientists, and politicians
(in the passionate decades of Romanticism often one and the same person)
who made the sensational discoveries that all the small nations of Central and
Eastern Europe could be traced back to Biblical ancestors, at least to Noah and
his sons, and more immediately, back to the Scythians, Sarmations, Romans,
and Huns, thereby coming up with the evidence to secure them the rights of indigenous peoples.[19] For they were all indigenous to this region, this Babel of
small nations, even though some may have been more indigenous than others.
They were also alike in that each group regarded itself to be a people who
loved freedom, a creator and repository of culture, a defensive bastion of
Christendom, and a pioneer of modern civilization, while the neighboring
group, of course, was either a barbarian intruder and savage conqueror, or a
timid, conquered—in other words a primitive—people.

Despite the numerous similarities, national awareness, and character, identi-
ties in Central and Eastern Europe show some typical differences that stem
mainly from the social nature and conditions of the leading strata in the nation
in question. In Hungary's case, the national awareness and character identity
were determined by the nobility. At the top of the nobility's traditional scale of
values was ownership of land, "farming," rule over an army of serfs, servants,
and livestock. This was accompanied by cults of horse breeding, horse racing,
dog breeding, and hunting. Another occupation that ranked high was political
activity at the county or national level, through holding suitable official positions: the *officia nobilia*. A career as an army officer, in the diplomatic corps, or
in the church belonged to the same category.[20] But the list of prestigious positions for the nobility did not, of course, include manufacturing, trade, speculation in money or goods, banking, or official "business pursuits" in general. "Is
perfidious trade suitable for a Hungarian?" asked an outstanding poet of the nobility in the final quarter of the eighteenth century, and the answer was obviously no, since it was the source of all "moral distortion." In any case, why
should a nobleman trouble himself with trade if there were wheat in the granary
and good wine in the celler?[21] Trade and business in general were passed on by
the Hungarians to the Greeks, Serbs, Germans, and Jews, who were then looked
down upon, or if they happened to grow rich through trade, angrily despised.

The backward-looking Hungarian nobility had long considered Pest-Buda,
with its German, Serbian, and Greek population, as alien and repellent. According to the early nineteenth-century nobleman and writer Miklós Révai,

"the flames" of all that was "Jewish, Armenian, Serbian, and German money-grubbing, blood-sucking usury and meanness in the Hungarian world are to be found here in Pest." He considered that any Hungarian must feel lost among the Germans and Jews in this alien city.[22] Even as late as the mid-nineteenth century, János Arany, a poet from the provinces, complained that all he found in Pest was dust, dirt, and German speech. Yet to a large extent the capital's well-to-do citizens tried to adjust themselves to the noble estate and the nobility's scale of values. They preferred to invest their accumulated capital in land, houses, and vineyards rather than trade, and were more inclined to deal in viticulture and viniculture than urban culture. In 1808 the guild trades-men of Pest complained that the "peddlers scurry from house to house, under-mine morals by encouraging a desire for luxury among the mob, and often manage to cheat even a cleverer man. . . . The bulk of the Jews spend the whole day loitering in the coffee houses, in the streets, and in the offices . . . dis-covering what articles are in demand and what are on offer." These Jewish dealers did business on their own account "so as to deprive Christian and middle-class tradesmen of their livelihood," in other words, of the advantage of guild privileges.[23]

One can also read of a hierarchy among the minorities. The Hungarian no-bleman had little liking for the urban German burgher, but both alike despised the Slovak, Romanian, and Serbian tradesmen, artisans, and peasants, all of whom joined them in a common hatred for the Jews. (Of course, this phenom-enon was not confined to Central Europe. Allport writes that although the British in South Africa did not like the Boers, both groups were against the Jews, all three against the Hindus, and all four despised the native Negro population.)[24]

There was an outstanding period in Hungarian history, the twenty-five years known as the Vormärz before the revolution of March 1848, when the great reformers, the generation of István Széchenyi, Ferenc Deák, Lajos Kos-suth, and József Eötvös, attempted to modernize the outlook of the nobility. Features of bourgeois morality like tolerance, liberalism, and equality gained a place in Hungarian public thinking. This was the period when the leading strata accepted the *Hungarus* German as a good Hungarian patriot, and a congenial picture arose of the Jew in process of assimilation as diligent, practi-cal, and useful. Thus the majority of the Hungarian landed nobility accepted bourgeois transformation as the inescapable requirement for survival, and re-spected bourgeois morality, but at the same time retained their own scale of values and rejected the bourgeois ethic of making money by diligent, regular work and relentless accumulation.[25]

Let us mention just one highly characteristic anecdote. In 1900 one of the Károlyi counts, a real grand seigneur, invited the German consul-general in Budapest to his home. At the end of the visit the guest asked the count how it was that no one in the family or household played music. Why should they? en-quired the count, that was what the Gypsies were for. "As we keep the Gypsies to play music for us, since we are too lazy to do it ourselves, so we keep the Jews to do the work for us."[26]

By the end of the nineteenth century a self-image had crystalized of the true Hungarian as being marked by a love of the land, sobriety, and honesty, but most of all by a contempt for business and speculation. Even prominent writers and scientists declared that Hungarians lacked the spirit of business, enterprise, and speculation, not only in the stock-exchange sense but in the philosophical one too.[27] The Hungarian lacked an ability for abstraction, he was not mystical, and he was not interested either in philosophy or in purely instrumental music. The Hungarian was open, upright, honest, and distanced himself from anything revolutionary, conspiratorial, or furtive. As the nineteenth century drew to a close, a code of norms for Hungarian behavior, a real aesthetic of the Hungarian character, was born.[28] And the image of the others living in Hungary, and particularly of the assimilated middle class, was created with reference to this national character of noble origin, adopted by Hungarian public opinion.

REDUCTION IN THE VALUE OF TRAITS LACKING IN THE HUNGARIANS: THE IMAGE FORMED OF THE GERMANS

The image Hungarian public opinion formed of the German character was very varied. A separate type that was often described and mocked in literature and the press was the Austrian, the *kaiserlich-königlich* official. The Hungarian public vented its rage on him for his "insolence of office," mocked the duplicity with which he was humble to those above and overbearing to those beneath him, his shortsighted concern with regulations and files, and his meticulous orderliness, in which he betrayed that he saw his official position not as a noble office but as a tiny part of the apparatus of state, perhaps even as a mere source of earnings. The general antipathy to him was dissipated only after the Ausgleich of 1867.

Another type was the urban German citizen (the Saxons of Transylvania and the Zipsers of northern Hungary—bourgeoisie of the Hungarian towns). They had lived in the country for centuries. In the eyes of the Hungarian nobility they were the embodiment of profit making, and were moreover profiteers who had acquired their wealth in dishonest ways (that is, not through royal grants, inheritance, or robbery). The models of this type of bourgeoisie had for centuries been the English and Dutch merchant. "The Dutchman has no regard at all for honesty, only for profit; in any matter his first question is: Will there be any profit in it?" wrote a Hungarian nobleman back in the late seventeenth century. The true "Hungarian, on the other hand, puts honesty before the profit of the trading cobblers."[29] The German bourgeois likewise considered profit the main thing of value and spared no time or effort in pursuit of it.

On the other hand, he was a hard, stout, untiring worker, unfamiliar with the pleasures of a comfortable life and merrymaking.[30]

In the house of a German citizen there was thought to be order and cleanliness and no hands were idle, and they drove themselves and their servants alike without mercy. Germans were marked by "the sombre fanaticism of the asceticism of work." According to one anecdote, a bourgeois German housewife went out at six in the morning on a visit before her son made a proposal of marriage, and since she found her would-be daughter-in-law still in bed, she canceled the marriage, saying, "Such a genteel lady will never do" in her simple bourgeois home.[31]

The image of a third German type, the Swabian peasant, has several features in common with that of the bourgeois. The Swabians are hardy, obstinate, unsociable, and cool; they are difficult to make friends with and they will do nothing to oblige. Their houses are always carefully locked up, and rarely opened to strangers and guests. In Swabian areas, life is always frenetic. Horse and carts are always driven at a trot, "people always goad one another along, and one constantly hears the panting of workers laboring under a burden, the rumble of barrels and the clatter of hammers. With their dreadful haste and brutal noise, the Germans have startled and embittered the whole of the Banat, which used to enjoy sunshine so sweetly among its flowery marshes."[32] Finally, the German's main mistake was that he was a German. "Do not believe, Magyar, the German"—warned the old *kurutz* verse.

Through the prism of the Hungarian nobility's traditional scale of values, the bourgeois virtues become distorted. The industry of the Germans appears to be a scramble for money, and their economy becomes avarice. Their disciplined, regular activity and reliability are seen as servility and Philistinism, and their German professional knowledge as pedantry. A spirit of enterprise, particularly if successful, arouses an immediate suspicion of profiteering.

But this suspicion overshadows the image of the German less than it does the image of the Jew.

The Shift of Responsibility for Hungarian Shortcomings and Mistakes: The Image Formed of the Jews

The image of the Jews (and this is clearly a universal phenomenon) is a typical product of prejudiced thinking. The emotional content is strong, and is scarcely influenced at all by fact, evidence, or even experience. Both chronologically and in content the image is somewhat contradictory.

The leading strata of Hungarian society saw the Jews as a primitive, uneducated, and dirty people, but as the most intelligent and most highly educated of the ethnic groups in the country, as well. The Jew is a withdrawn, very conservative and even "invariable" type of man, but from another viewpoint he is

a very accommodating, pliant, variable element in society, receptive to everything new.[33] On the one hand the Jews are a merciless, wild people who despise
the Christians and are aware of their own superiority, while on the other they
are a humble, opportunist, even cowardly people replete with inferiority complexes and neuroses. Opinions differ even as to whether the orthodox Jew is
the one who is initially wild and haughty; or whether an original modesty and
timidity give way to impertinence only when the Jew has become assimilated;
or whether is it the other way about: assimilation makes the Jew progressively
more uncertain, cowardly, and opportunist? In spite of assimilation in a linguistic sense, the Jew never became a full-blown patriot in the opinion of the
majority Hungarian community receiving him, yet it was quite commonly believed that the neophyte Jew became a representative of extreme chauvinism,
"a great and valuable factor of cultural nationalism."[34] Some were also of the
opinion that the Jews in particular were advocates of a better, wealthier, and
more humane Hungarian community.[35]

These contradictions can be resolved, of course, on the basis of the historical development and social stratification of Jewry and the social and intellectual differentiation among the Hungarian majority. It is probable that the
views of the Jews as a primitive, withdrawn, thoroughly traditional people imbued with a belief that they are the chosen race apply more readily to the first,
immigrant generation, and to the orthodox, Yiddish-speaking communities
fresh from Galicia, whereas the views that stress their intelligence, intellectual
superiority, flexibility, and Hungarian nationalism refer to the assimilated
Jews. "He does not study, he does not become cultivated, and he does not
wash. He does business and breeds children. . . . He prays out loud and cheats
in silence." He is as resourceful and cheeky as a sparrow.[36] According to one
anti-Semitic self-styled "expert" between the two world wars, the Jews at the
beginning of the nineteenth century formed a secluded social stratum "dirty in
outward appearance and dreadfully behind in cultivation."[37] At that time the
Jew was still a timid, humble, caftan-wearing peddler with a pack on his
back—that is how he was pictured and how he was depicted in nineteenth-
century popular plays and cartoons. Due mainly to repeated waves of immi-
gration from Galicia, this type still appeared at the beginning of the twentieth
century, obstinately continuing to live in orthodox communities that maintained the forms and rules of a secluded ghetto life despite emancipation. To
the ghetto Jew, irrespective of whether he lived in a Hungarian, German, Polish, Slovak, or Romanian environment, there accrued superstitious images and
an aura of secrecy. He was the living symbol of foreignness and the classic target of xenophobia. His clothing was strange and unusual, and so were his language, religion, and customs. He was clever and energetic, traveled a great
deal, and spoke even more. It was easy to identify him with the mystical figure
of the "wandering Jew" who had denied and crucified the son of God, never
stayed still, never rested, was always barefoot, understood all languages, and
had no purse, although there was money even under his skin.[38]

Adding to this foreignness and increasing xenophobia was the fact that he lived and worked in a different way from those around him. He neither farmed nor did manual work—rather a hypocritical criticism from the part of the "genteel middle class"—and instead spent most of his time trading and doing business, that is, cheating people, for in the conservative eyes of the nobility, falsehood was the probable basis of any business.[39] The prejudice was not dispelled even when the Jew had virtually left the ghetto and become citizen and Hungarian. The process of becoming civilized and rich was treated as evidence that wealth had been gained by fraud. According to the anti-Semitic sketch of his character, the assimilated Jew had changed only his clothing and language, not his spirit and features, which remained unchanged, so that he remained an alien element incapable of change or assimilation.[40]

And just in this comportment lies a characteristic ambivalence. The majority of the leading political and intellectual strata of Hungary, which had been raised on liberal nationalism, encouraged the assimilation of the Jews; they saw many advantages of this policy, particularly a growth in strength at the expense of neighboring minorities. Many had personal ties and a regard for certain members of the Jewish elite. But even for the liberal elite the broad-scale assimilation of the Jews was not entirely free of problems, for they saw in it a triple threat. Assimilation rendered the Jewish characteristics, "alien to the Hungarian character," more clandestine, and so liable to destroy the genuine "Hungarian character" through the press, mass culture, and increasingly intensive social interactions. Another reason for anxiety was the continued loyalty of the Jews to their old community, despite their assimilation. It was as if Jewish solidarity were stronger than devotion to the Hungarian community, people said. This anxiety was considered as having a solid basis by one expert on the minority problem, who said Jewry "forms a mass distinguishable from the others, in that it does not always identify its interests with those of the Hungarians, even though it speaks Hungarian and claims to be Hungarian."[41] A church dignitary at the time did not hesitate to label the assimilated Jews as "agents of the Jewish community" who were dangerous precisely because they did not form a separate minority and were seemingly good Hungarians.[42]

The liberal elite of Hungarian society was receptive and tolerant up to the end of the nineteenth century. They favored assimilation without any kind of discrimination. But at the turn of the century a growing part of Hungarian society considered the assimilated Jews a separate element, as did all other societies in Central Europe. They recognized in the Jew their own mistakes and bad qualities more easily than they did in the other assimilated minorities. The Hungarian gentry, and even the parvenu bourgeoisie of German origin, identified easily and criticized with a supercilious irony the snobbery, selfishness, extrovert way of life, and the noisy, overbearing behavior of the assimilated Jews, while failing to recognize these in themselves.[43]

In the course of bourgeois transformation a few, probably universal, stereotypes took root in the minds of the Hungarians, and these they used to charac-

terize the "timeless," "immutable" Jew irrespective of the stages of assimilation or the local variations.[44] The Jew was seen as selfish, mercenary, and
profit-seeking, as a cunning speculator and as a materialist in terms of his
greed and mentality—in other words, as a king of "incarnation in Hungary of
the capitalist world concept."[45] The Jew's orientation toward success was so
strong that nothing could deter him, and that was why he could triumph over
the "thoroughbred merchant nations," the Greeks and the Armenians. He was
so worldly that many considered the Jews to be a *populus carnalis*, a pattern
of man living for carnal pleasures alone.[46]

This stereotype led to another: the Jew had no ethic, or rather he had a double ethic. The dislike that was initially felt for the Jew's business morality soon
extended to a sense that he had utter disregard for the rule of law, and later grew
into a general moral disapprobation.[47] The Jews, particularly the metropolitan
Jews belonging to the wealthy bourgeoisie and intelligentsia, did not honor the
institution of the family and destroyed ancient customs, prestige, and family
life.[48] The degree to which the qualities ascribed to the Jews were qualities of
basically bourgeois, urban society received little attention in the thinking of the
conservatives, although they talked with similar feelings about the Dutch and
English business spirit, and they condemned with a similar disgust French decadence and the immorality of Paris.[49] The double commitment and dual culture
that was accepted as natural in the case of the minorities that were assimilating,
particularly in the case of the European emigrant group to America, was explained in the case of the Jews as some kind of "racial solidarity."[50]

THE MOTIVATION BEHIND THE IMAGE OF THE JEWS

There were significant variations in the way the origin and causes of Jewish
characteristics were explained. These explanations and arguments can be divided into three main groups, and one might say that these groups of arguments largely correspond to social trends that developed in the quality of rela-
tionships to the Jews and the intensity of prejudices.

The first and most numerous group insisted upon a racial determinant. To
many of them "racial" meant the traditional notion of race and ethnic group,
and traced back to the character of the chosen (later accursed) people of the Bi-
ble. But the number of new-fangled racists grew rapidly. They discovered with
a pseudo-scientific, biological affectation of seriousness the ethnogenesis of
the Jewry of the ancient times to have been a mixture of the "oriental Semitic
and Armenoid races" with some negroid blood as well, a mixture that had not
changed over the intervening millennia.[51]

On a higher plane was the historical explanation that linked the Jewish
character with the fate of the Jews and their socioeconomic position in relation to other peoples.[52] Ghetto life, involving a lack of all rights, a prohibition
on the acquisition of property and the holding of office, had forced the Jews in
the Middle Ages and the early modern period into trading and finance. This

centuries-old situational determinant provided an explanation for the many acquired and transmitted abilities and skills that made the majority of European Jewry more capable of pursuing capitalist business than were the rigid agricultural societies. The faculties that rose from this situational determinant (an ability to live in state of constant preparedness, a high degree of mobility, and acceptance of the existing order, values, and truths) gave Jewry the ability to espouse rational scepticism and to view life in a relative fashion. Reflective and speculative thinking, utilitarianism, distrust of their environment, and scant appreciation for law and social prestige seemed to be results of the ghetto life.

The truly educated, thinking members of the Hungarian intelligentsia, mainly scholars and writers, found the situational determinant too one-sided to serve as the dominant principle of explanation. They particularly questioned the identification of Jewry with capitalism and the close correlation of the negative image of Jewry with capitalist economic activity. "It is wrong to bring up economic reasons," wrote Marcell Benedek, a scholar and writer, as there were many more gentiles then Jews among the exploiters, and there was a fast-growing number of Jewish workers and employees among the exploited.[53] The negative image of Jews was thus considered to be driven chiefly by factors of social psychology.

Left-wing intellectuals consider the real situation to be that in Central Europe the ghetto was eliminated only legally and not socially. The majority of liberal Christians were still "anti-Semites between you and me" (entre nous). In Marcell Benedek's experience, Hungary contains "no Christian capable of a perfectly unbiased and purely humanitarian standpoint toward Jewry."[54] This often-concealed rejection and disdain hurts the sensibilities of the assimilated Jew and increases his feeling of uncertainty, which can often and easily turn into discourtesy and aggression. All these features originate in nervousness and are symptoms of a kind of social neurosis. To be a Jew, it was put rather pointedly by Anna Lesznai—a member of the circle in which Endre Ady, Oszkár Jászi, and then later György Lukács moved—is a special, "abnormally excited, nervous state."[55] The assimilated, "cultivated Jew" inherited from his ghetto ancestors a worn-out nervous system that is constantly disturbed by "the lack of stability toward which he is impelled by his uncertain social situation." He has deserted orthodoxy and ghetto Jewry both in their outward features and in spirit, but his social environment still denies him full acceptance.[56] In fact he belongs nowhere, he is a renegade everywhere, which makes a painful dent in his self-respect. "A man whose self-respect has been disturbed will arrive in a false relationship with the notion of authority." Although he respects authority and fears power, he finds it desirable to obtain authority and power, and position and security as well, but at the same time he disdains authority and subjects it to ironic criticism. This "belonging nowhere" becomes the basis for understanding everything, since the Jew is less bound by intellectual tradition and so is well able to see the reverse side of any matter. Thus the ability to view things in a relative way and to arrive at abstractions and the special ability to "turn ideas into realistic life-shaping factors" can all be deduced as well from this socio-psychological isolation and from the Jew's "state of nerves."

"Such influences and conditions," concludes Anna Lesznai, "make the Jew a lonesome, intimidated, and affronted neurotic, who thinks a lot of himself, and yet sincerely denies himself, and who is deprived of earthly and eternal joy in all its forms."[57]

The character deduced from the historical and social situation and from factors of social psychology undoubtedly provides a more realistic and considered explanation of the visible and apparent, as well as the hidden and prejudiciously imputed features of the Jewish character. One can argue about whether it is the distorted external and internal features deduced from the "racial" qualities or the "Jewish conditions" qualified as social neurosis that reflect more tragically the fate of the Jews.

Self-Image and the Image of the Other

Finally, let me emphasize that self-image and the image formed of the other are complementary elements in the community's awareness of a social or ethnic group. One can add that these are complementary elements that do not, even when juxtaposed, show a realistic overall picture, because the elements of reality they contain are fragmentary and overlaid with the mud of prejudice. Certainly national culture, rather than character, does have objective historical, cultural, and psychological bases. But it is extremely important not to confuse the actual national culture with the image by which particular peoples describe each other's national character.[58] In the latter, facts and fragments of facts are mixed inextricably with the prejudices and values of several generations. This social psychological statement is supported by concrete ethnographical observations. Ethnographers have discribed very expressively the differences in the farming, building, house-furnishing, and eating customs of the Romanian and the Hungarian peasants in Transylvania.[59] The results of convincing research point to the difference in mentality between the Swabian and the Hungarian rural communities in Transdanubia. Whereas the Swabians are economical and rationally thrifty, and lead a modest life, the Hungarians are extravagant and prestige-oriented.[60] Again there are objective data to show that the Jewish population has a higher than average level of schooling and cultivation. But these actual differences are transmitted into the image formed of the other through the prism of petrified prejudices.

The main part in the formation of the image of other social groups and of ethnic minorities, and in the turning of them into stereotypes, is played by the following factors.

First, the primary factor is the distancing of our own group from all other groups, which is the basic condition for group identity and at the same time provides the first outline for the opinions formed of the other group. Regular contacts and steady interactions between different ethnic groups, and the formation of a positive identity for one's own group usually lead to a negative image of the other group.[61] If "we" are friendly, honest, unselfish, and orderly, the "neighbor" must certainly be treacherous, mercenary, malicious, dirty, disorderly, and so on. Lasting interactions can lead, however, to positive images, too, particularly in cases when economic and cultural exchange has brought fruitful contacts, or in cases when ethnic groups are sympathetic with each other due to common enemies.

Second, the primary, impressionistic image is modulated right from its birth by the social situation and function of the group that forms it. In Hungary, for instance, the image of the other, of the Slovak and Romanian serfs, the German bourgeoisie, and the Jewish peddlers and renters was formed by the landed nobility and later by the "middle-class gentry." In the eyes of a Hungarian nobleman, any serf would obviously bear the features of a "servant," and consequently was stupid, dirty, lazy, rough, and rude; in the thinking of the minority peasantry, the "Hungarian" became identified with the bloodsucking landlord, who was as a matter of course haughty, merciless, barbarous, mean, selfish, extravagant, and so on. Great and small in the cumbersome, inert agricultural society saw in the merchant, whether Greek, Armenian, German, or Jew, the usurer, false huckster, wandering member of a swarming mob that sold and upset everything; to the mobile Jewish businessman the agrarian population embodied a thick-headed, lazy, extravagant, and unpractical Asian race.

Social condition, position, and function as a set of factors that establish the local color and differentiate the images, lead to a third quality: the image of the other always contains, in a magnified, sometimes caricatured form, the qualities that are lacking from our own group, those the group envies and would like to, but cannot, copy. The missing qualities that blossom in the rival community gain in most cases a negative aspect. If the German shows an inclination toward abstract thinking and philosophy, the Hungarian dislikes abstraction and will only accept what is realistically conceivable and tangible; if the German is hard-working and economical with money, the Hungarian must be generous and comfort-loving; if the Jew is practical and has a developed business sense, the Hungarian despises commerce and business and remains an honest farmer.

The achieved level of civilization was an important element in the national images formed in the nineteenth century. Early in the social transformation the backwardness of eastern Central Europe, and toward the end of the process a decline caused by the process of "bourgeoisification" gave the qualities that were lacking in Hungarian agricultural society a blacker and blacker hue when seen in others. Trading and shrewdness, which "had never suited a Hungarian" and were in any case despised, turned into detestable characteristics of the detrimental "Jewish spirit" that was ruining Christian society. At the

beginning of the twentieth century, the elements of opposition to modernization in the Hungarian self-image were upgraded and given the attribute
"Christian," which was synonymous with what was honest, noble, and identified as ingenuous.[62] On the other hand, the efforts at reform and the spirit of
enterprise, ranging from industrialization to the avant garde in the arts, and
from universal suffrage to tolerance of sexual mores, were labeled as "non-
Hungarian," "decadent," and "Jewish."[63]

Another factor that operated in a similar way was the projection of qualities
that one's own group had but disliked and felt ashamed of onto the image of
hostile groups. It is a general phenomenon, well proven by psychologists, that
a group either canonizes its own bad qualities and mistakes as virtues, or
hangs them around the neck of an adversarial group. Nevertheless, this projecting mechanism in the image formation of nineteenth-century Central and
Eastern European nationalities operated mainly in the case of stereotypes of
Jewish character. Every bourgeois or would-be bourgeois was seen as a selfish,
profit-oriented individual.

The belief that such nasty qualities as trade were unsuited to "the Magyar"
was part of the self-image of the nobleman. These qualities were shifted onto
the Jew or ascribed to the overwhelming influence of the Jews.[64] In just the
same way, monks of long ago, unable to resist temptation, shifted the odium of
their fall onto the magical demonry of "witches."

In conclusion, it should be emphasized that the displayed image-stereotypes
are not particular to Hungarians; they can be found all over the world. In Central and Eastern Europe, perhaps, they will prove to be more deeply rooted,
more petrified, and more harmful than in the West. This chapter has tried to
show that the image of the enemy derives from the mutual effects of complex
social and psychological processes. Paralleling the appearance of increasingly
distorted elements of the image formed of the enemy—whether neighbor, inner minority, or assimilated "alien" group—the deficiences and mistakes of
one's own nation were transmuted into "national virtues." The self-image of
all Central and East European nations became idealized, not only during and
immediately after the first and second world wars, but particularly after the
most recent change of 1989–1990. The restitution of a dark image of the enemy, and at the same time the justification of our own bravery and innocence
are more virulent than they ever have been.

Chapter 3

THE GARDEN AND THE WORKSHOP:
REFLECTIONS ON FIN-DE-SIÈCLE CULTURE IN VIENNA AND BUDAPEST

THE ENIGMA OF A BELATED GOLDEN AGE

Vienna as the hotbed of European culture, the maturing metropolis of Budapest catching up to it, cultural florescence thriving throughout the Austro-Hungarian Monarchy—these were some of the subjects of concern to cultural historians over the past quarter century. Historians have repeatedly posed the question, "How could such a flower garden bloom on the depleted soil of a worn-out and eroding empire?" Impressionism, Sezession, Jugendstil, psychoanalysis, the New School of Music—were they merely the fleurs du mal, the "flowers of decomposition," of the Monarchy? Was this culture inspired by the "slight rapture of death," or was the whole structure void of a foundation and its glitter nothing more than a mirage?[1] Such reflections by modern historians are postscripts, of course. Contemporaries, if they saw or experienced the deficiencies or sensed the decline at all, had no foreknowledge of the inexorable collapse.[2] Stefan Zweig, the Austrian novelist, wrote in his memoir that the period before the First World War was the "golden age of security." Everything in the thousand-year-old Monarchy was made for eternity, "and the state itself was the foremost guarantor for this durability."[3] Security in one's life and one's life's course, the durability of objects and institutions, were taken as self-evident by the people of this time.

Of course a writer need not be a prophet, especially in Austria a good quarter century after the decline of the era of peace. The retrospections of Zweig and many other contemporaries will not invalidate the premonitions among impregnable writers and intellectuals, premonitions that we present-day historians are so eager to expose. What the Monarchy's, and specifically Vienna's, intuitive, perhaps even neurotic, intellectual prophets sensed was a malaise on a societal scale and a growing feeling of foreboding. The outside world became ever more frightening, the liberal-rational outlook grew ever fainter, and centuries-old European values became shallow. Vienna's vibrant culture experienced what Carl Schorske fittingly called the "crisis and dissolution of the liberal Ego." In looking at fin-de-siècle Vienna and present-day interpretations of it, one readily accepts the notion that this wonderful culture fed on the

chronic failures of the Austrian bourgeoisie; the middle class was impelled to
retreat into the private sphere, into the seclusion of Gardens.[4]

The notion is certainly valid for Vienna; but what about Budapest, Prague,
or Cracow, "the provinces"? Here also the decline of liberalism and the signs
of upheaval were evident. Impressionable artists could sense the anxiety, and
decadence infiltrated the public mind. In Budapest the spark of liberalism
flared up once more, most prominently in the 1890s. With the new century political radicalism caught fire—as it did, for example, in France. The phenomenon might be called a late reaction, a feverish "catching-up complex" of a
backward agrarian country, an argument with ready evidence to support it.
When Hugo von Hofmannsthal and his literary group Junges Wien appeared
in Vienna, Budapest had only one politically loyal and diffident literary journal, A Hét (The Week); when in Vienna Klimt and his friends were provocative
and bold enough to launch their Ver Sacrum and erect the brilliant Sezession
building, in Hungary a group of young painters withdrew to Nagybánya in the
far corner of the country to grasp open air and the fleeting image in provincial
reclusion.

Between Vienna and Budapest there was a delay of a decade or two; yet to
use this circumstance to explain the essence of the differences between the two
would be a gross oversimplification. There were similar signs of what has been
called "the decadence of the Monarchy" in the two neighboring strongholds of
Munich and Berlin as well, and even beyond the German borders it is evident
that Sezession, symbolism, the search for novel forms to express the intelligentsia's new sentiment, the crisis of tradition, and cultural upheaval were
phenomena not confined to the Monarchy or to Central Europe. They affected
Europe overall, a fact that underlines the argument that the turn-of-the-
century cultural boom was by no means an outgrowth of the decaying Monarchy. The boom was not the result of failure, retreat, or confused identity on the
part of the Austrian bourgeoisie. In fact, no single factor or tendency can account for the complex historic phenomena of a whole era. There must always
be several factors that happen to coincide at a given time, and they defy hierar-
chical classification.

THE INTELLECTUAL CAPITAL AND THE UPSTART METROPOLIS

In the case of Austria, one wonders why liberalism was so weak here. Why was
it defeated in such a short time? How was the Austrian liberal elite's social and
political character different from, say, the Hungarian? The impotence of Austrian liberalism was due not to an economically inconsequential or culturally
insignificant bourgeoisie and its intellectuals (or to use the more precise German terminology for this group, Besitz- and Bildungsbürgertum). Rather, its
impotence stemmed from its being rooted in a traditional, dynastic state patriotism and not, as it were, true nationalism, which was the dominant ideology

of the time. Consequently, Austrian liberalism could never persistently rebuff absolutism and the Habsburg *Hausmacht;* it submitted to the dynasty's almost unlimited sovereignty as a concession for retaining favorable economic and administrative positions.[5] There was also another, more fundamental reason than common interest and opportunism. The stratum that gave the Austrian bourgeoisie its character, namely its intellectuals, with businessmen and bankers, bureaucrats, scientists, and artists at its core, consisted largely of assimilated immigrants, Slavs, Jews, and to a lesser extent Hungarians and Italians. Despite the fact that they absorbed German culture, they did not identify with German nationalism.[6] Neither did the native Austrian patriots within the bourgeoisie. These groups saw their quest for identity best fulfilled by a cosmopolitan liberalism and dynastic state patriotism.

It was undoubtedly this distinctive power structure and social make-up that led Austrian liberals to brush aside Western-style parliamentarism—which banned monarchs from affairs of government—and collective rights; rather they stressed the need for the full guarantee of the right to liberty for the autonomous individual.[7]

Liberalism tailored to individuals and a supranational humanism of a Weltbürger (citizen of the world) may have been genuine ideas at the time of the famous Austrian playwright Franz Grillparzer, and the naiveté of the Austrian Vormärz of the 1830s and 1840s with its proclamation of universality. How self-confident and proud ring the words: "Man and his spirit I esteem above all else, and they know no national tendencies."[8] "The best thing man can be is simply to be man, whether he wears an *atilla* [gala coat] and speaks Hungarian or walks about in an English tail coat and French hat, his German tongue notwithstanding."[9] However, such "pure humanity" bowed to the emperor's and tsar's reactions as early as 1848–1849. And despite all its splendid rhetoric, it proved useless some decades later, when Bismarck forged his empire (also sparking nationalism in Austria among those who felt drawn to the empire and demanded the Monarchy's resubmission to German hegemony). The Austrian-German middle strata had a double cause, nationalist and social, for turning away from the upper bourgeoisie with its state patriotism and liberalism. Thus the leading stratum, and the liberalism that came with it, was defeated not by political events in 1879 or later in the Reichsrat, but by losing social influence and the power to affect the general consciousness of the middle strata among its own people. For the most part, in the 1880s, they turned to anti-Semitism and nationalism.

The dually motivated confrontation of the middle strata is still not enough, however, to explain liberalism's quick denouement and specifically the Austrian bourgeoisie's traumatic defeat, with its sense of crisis and its retreat. The ruling power was still there and did not cease to patronize the parvenu bourgeoisie as it always had, although no bourgeois was allowed to enter its magic circle. Protectionism also existed in the outgoing nineteenth century, though in time the state had undergone a strange metamorphosis. What had been patriarchal rule hinging on the person of the emperor or the dynasty became the paternalistic absolutism of the bureaucracy. It absorbed the monarch himself, and gradually became statist, with ever-growing control. The metamorphosis is an historic one, the Habsburg Monarchy its classic example; from a human approachable imperial bureaucracy it transformed slowly, almost imperceptibly, into an intangible and anonymous Castle.[10] The deceptive element of reality that made the process possible was the fact that for the most part the insiders of traditional cabinet politics came from the aristocracy. Not even the wealthy members of the bourgeoisie were fully able to identify with the elite statist bureaucracy, and the intellectuals, the Bildungsbürgertum, felt just as uneasy about the growing power of bureaucracy as about the revolt of the nationalist and socialist masses.

There were several reasons for this ambiguity. In Germany and Austria, the backbone of the traditional Bildungsbürgertum was made up of the "free intelligentsia," university graduates with academic careers. The stratum played a highly significant role in the modernization, and in the intellectual and political life of these territories, from the period of Romanticism, which brought the awakening of a national consciousness to the Frankfurt Parliament of 1848, and all the way to unification, after which it quickly lost in prestige and influence.[11] The clublike *honoracior* (the educated—often academic—intellectual elite) to some extent was replaced by the bureaucratically organized party of the masses, and the humanist intellectuals, professors, and lawyers, by the technical graduates and bureaucrats of the administrative apparatus. The part of the bourgeoisie that was uniquely Austrian—the creative intellectuals of Vienna—had nothing left to identify with, neither viscous nationalism with its Christian Social demagogic agitation, nor the Socialist movement, nor even the baneful technical civilization and statist bureaucratic rule.[12] The substance of their liberal creed was the liberty and security of the autonomous individual, and when powerful, obscure, and uncontrollable forces loomed on all sides there was really no escape but retreat—Sezession in its broad sense—to their villas' real, or their spirits' virtual, Gardens. Here they were surrounded by an aura of secureness in the classical cultural flora, the harmony of beauty sheltered from the chaos of the outside world, and the illusion of salvaged autonomy.

The general political and cultural trends of the outgoing nineteenth century also affected Budapest. In Hungary, too, there were signs of foreboding that arose from social and national minority conflicts, which may have been even stronger than in the Austrian territories. Again most of the bourgeoisie and bourgeois intellectuals were assimilated Germans, Jews, and other non-Magyar nationalities. There were outbreaks of wild nationalism and anti-Semitism; liberalism was growing weak and ossified into an ideology of the status quo. Eruptions of nationalist and socialist mass movements provided ample grounds for the sensitive intelligentsia to feel terrified and to take refuge in their Gardens, be they ancient family property or a paternal acquisition, or be they dreams. There were those impregnable souls whose desires found expression in art. In Hungary, however, the intellectual trends of the period were never precipitated in a yearning for reclusion.

Regarding the social structure and intellectual make-up of Austria and Hungary, at least three differences can be discerned. First, in the shadow of the fervently nationalistic German empire, the Austrians were losing their patriotic attachment and with this the very essence of their sense of identity. By contrast, the Hungarians' sense of identity became manifest as part of their self-concept, a patriotic creed, and concurrently a precondition for social integration.

Second, in Hungarian society the ossified remnants of feudalism were still very potent, visible, and tangible. The Hungarian Castle was not as mythically symbolic, impersonal, and remote as Kafka's. It stood just outside the villages, all over the country. It may have been inaccessible to intruders, but was present as a fact of everyday life. In other words, it was the petrified past and its symbol in the feudal Castle that the impressionable intellectuals of the rising Hungarian bourgeoisie were up against. To them the weakening of liberalism signified that the liberalism of the nobility was in crisis, especially since the Hungarian bourgeoisie never really partook of political power but accepted the aristocracy's and the gentry's traditionally leading role. There was never a Bürgerministerium here, nor a constitutional party, nor did this stratum carry any weight in public life, as its Austrian counterpart did. The Hungarian bourgeoisie had nothing to withdraw from.

The third difference was that while the Austrian Bildungsbürgertum took refuge in their Gardens to evade a persistent foreboding and lost sense of identity, the Hungarian bourgeois intellectuals found their legal emancipation politically acknowledged and gained a sense of identity on entering public life.[13] To them science and art became public matters, and thus such works dealt with public concerns. A ready-for-action culture such as this would never choose the esoteric Garden for a setting; its breeding ground was the Workshop, the seat of collective work: perhaps the offices of a newspaper, a club, or a café. Viennese intellectuals experienced the crisis of the outgoing century from the inside, as something uniquely Austrian and human. Budapest intellectuals, in contrast, saw in it the anticipated demise of a world that was foreign, hostile, and an obstacle to advancement.

The Garden: An Illusion-and-Reality Play

Structural differences between the two societies provide the background for comparing their cultural history, but it was in art that this period found its most typical vehicles of expression. As it happens, in 1890 a group of young writers, spurred by author and critic Hermann Bahr and playwright and poet Hugo von Hofmannsthal, gathered in Vienna to form Das Junge Wien. The same year in Budapest the journal *A Hét* (The Week, but initially planned to be named "Young Hungary"!), was launched as the herald of a new literary age.[14] What these young people in both capitals wanted was a modern literature. Their definition of "modern," however, was not quite the same.

In Vienna modern meant submersion into an inner reality, the psyche, and reality was the world created in a work of art. "Man either researches the anatomy of his own psyche or he dreams. Reflection or fantasy, mirror or dream image," wrote the young Hugo von Hofmannsthal.[15] To be modern was to listen to the grass grow and the tremors of the soul, an instinctive, somnambulant surrender to any expression of beauty. Hysteria, neurosis, and dreams were favored subjects, not to say symptoms, of the erudite elite well before Freud. Das Junge Wien started out as an outright antinaturalist literary movement, which was a strange or, as Karl Kraus put it, downright humorous paradox, because in Viennese culture, with hardly a trace of naturalism, there was nothing there to defeat.[16] The movement, or call it "the gathering of a generation," was motivated by social and political influences rather than literary ones, even though their ideals and criteria were purely aesthetic.

To jump ahead for a moment to Budapest and what the young writers there considered "modern," it was, more than anything else, to do away with the outdated popular-national art of epigones and replace it with trends prevalent in the west of Europe. In other words, modernity was realism and naturalism—though at the end of the century Symbolism and the Sezession also seeped into Budapest. For a more concrete sense of the differences between the two cultures one must look at their experiences, the subjects and styles they dealt with most often.

The intimate home and figurative setting of the Viennese youth was the Garden. Behind its symbolic interpretation there was just a trace of the golden age of prehistoric innocence and a faint reference to paradise lost.[17] The Garden meant either what it is by primary definition, a closed-off piece of preserved nature or, metaphorically, a place of solitude and retreat; or as with Rilke, the antithesis to the bleak concrete landscape of the chaotic metropolis.[18] So the Garden was not just a refuge for body and soul but was the vehicle for aesthetics, the unity of man as a product of nature and the work of art as a product of man. The final conclusion coming from this interpretation was expressed by Leopold Andrian-Werburg, in a psychological novel in which the Garden stands as the setting for uncovering the self, as the obscure depth of the soul.[19] The Garden and solitude, solitude and the narcissistic self—these are ready metaphors. More involved is the relationship between the Garden and the theater, which was the other decisive experience of the young Viennese in their cultural renewal.

To them the Garden was often a stage, a theatrical setting. What comes to mind most prominently is Hugo von Hofmannsthal's prologue to Arthur Schnitzler's cyclic drama *Anatol*.

> Eine Laube statt der Bühne,
>   Sommersonne statt der Lampen,
>   Also spielen wir Theater,
>   Spielen unsere eignen Stücke . . .

> A bower, not the stage,
>   The summer sun, not lights,
>   Thus we play theater,
>   Act our own plays . . .

Even so refined a critic as Hermann Broch saw in this Garden-theater, this arbor play, a Rococo motif, a nostalgia for the eighteenth century.[20] Of course Baroque theater did have a strong tradition in Vienna, but the fin-de-siècle Welttheater was Baroque only in its respect for tradition; its content had nothing to do with morality plays or pastorals. It was, rather, a moment snatched out of the cycle of life and death. To continue with the prologue,

> Also spielen wir Theater,
>   Spielen unsere eignen Stücke,
>   Frühgereift und zart und traurig,
>   Die Komödie unsrer Seele,
>   Unsres Fühlens Heut und Gestern,
>   Böser Dinge, hübsche Formel,
>   Glatte Worte, bunte Bilder,
>   Halbes, heimliches Empfinden,
>   Agonien, Episoden

> Thus we play theater,
>   Act our own plays,
>   Matured early, tender and sad,
>   The comedy of our soul,
>   Our emotions' past and present,
>   Of evil things, pretty idiom,
>   Smooth words, bright images,
>   Half- and secret sensations,
>   Agonies, episodes

The same thought appears again in another prologue by Hofmannsthal (entitled "Zu einem Buch ähnlicher Art").

> Wir haben aus dem Leben, das wir leben,
>   Ein Spiel gemacht, und unsere Wahrheit gleitet
>   Mit unserer Komödie durcheinander
>   Wie eines Taschenspielers hohle Becher.[21]

Of the life that we live we have
Made a play, and our truth interglides
With this comedy of ours
Like the hollow cups of a sleight-of-hand artist.

Fin-de-siècle theater in Vienna was not a gallant Rococo play but a tragic life experience. In life we take on roles, we feign, "put on an act," and only on the stage do we act out the tragicomedy of our lives, only there do we show our true selves. An interpretation such as this of the relationship between stage and reality may have been inspired by Kierkegaard or Nietzsche: we must live life as a piece of art because art is true reality. If that is so, then illusion and reality are not opposites but mutual substitutes, two states of one and the same reality; the concept runs through many of Schnitzler's dramas, most eloquently in his *Der grüne Kakadu* (The Green Cockatoo). The scene is an inn in the outskirts of Paris, where on the eve of the Revolution they are staging a play. The protagonist Henri acts out the murder of Prince Cadignan, and because of their genial performance and the situation at hand everyone believes it to be true. But when Henri later really kills the prince, the audience at first takes it as part of the play. "Is this play or reality?" someone in the audience asks. To which the narrator Rollin replies, "To be . . . to play . . . Do you know the difference so well, Sire? . . . I do not. . . . And what I find so peculiar here is just that all apparent differences have been dissolved. Reality turns into play, and play into reality."[22] Moreover, real actions have no value in themselves; they are valid only in a given context, because the masses that storm the Bastille celebrate as their hero Henri as the murderer of a prince. Illusion and reality can be substituted for one another because both are qualified and relative to the given situation that history, ever changing and always in motion, presents.

Closely related to the subjects of Garden and theater is a third notion, that there is a continuity of, and relation between, life and death, a continuity that is symbolized by dreams, or Psyche, and love, Eros. What are the objects of the world around us, what are the palaces and poems?—"the dreamlike images of reality." "We are such stuff as dreams are made on," says Hofmannsthal in one *Terzine*, using the words of Shakespeare.[23] As we know, dreams play a central role in Viennese art. They inspired Freud, just as he in turn inspired art when he uncovered the depth of the psyche. Aesthetics and medical therapy reciprocally affected one another and went hand in hand in staking out the way to *Der Zauberberg* (The Magic Mountain). Freud believed dreams to be both the fulfilment (though simultaneously also the suppression and distortion) of secret, hidden everyday desires,[24] and a transitional state between waking consciousness and the unknown unconscious, between being and not-being. The same ambiguous, transitional interpretation of dreams appeared in Gustav Klimt's great works of the Sezession, most likely inspired by psychoanalysis. One of his symbolic murals commissioned by the University of Vienna (*Medizine,*

18. Arthur Schnitzler, playwright and novelist.
Vienna, 1900s

1901) shows Hygeia in the foreground holding up the symbols of healing, the snake and the chalice with the water of the Lethe; behind her are floating figures, half awake and half in slumber, nascent or dying.[25] Even more expressive, even in its title, is Death and Life, where Death stands apart, robed in a splendid cape with a pattern of crosses, and directs the circulation of sleeping beings, nascent, resting, and dying.

Yet Klimt, and other Viennese artists of the Sezession, also saw dreams in another way. Dreaming, or closed eyelids conveying surrender and transfiguration, expressed the timelessness of sexual ecstasy. The mutual influence of dreams and reality is already discernible in Klimt's earliest picture on the subject (*Love*, 1895), and became a more and more frequently recurring motif in his erotic pictures (*Danae, Judith-Salome,* the kiss motif in his *Beethoven* frieze, and so on). We might explain this accent on sensuality with the Sezession's idolization of beauty, or the erotic atmosphere of the Viennese art world, or even take it as a kind of war of liberation against prudish academicism, which tried to take the erotic even out of mythological nudity. But there is more behind such eroticism: something mystic, metaphysical, and philosophic.

Recent research points out the effect of Schopenhauer's pessimistic philosophy, and especially his concept of the tragedy of existence, on Klimt (in the mural *Philosophy,* in *Nuda veritas,* or the *Beethoven* frieze). Schopenhauer had a direct influence on his contemporaries' philosophy of intuitivism and its transubstantiation in painting.[26] The endless cycle of natural existence, the individual being a mere speck in this cosmic cycle of life and death, was a philosophy in which sexual ecstasy, the timeless moment, became the sanctified act within the mystery of this cycle. New life was conceived, and the lovers, their task fulfilled, met symbolically in death. The Sezession's interpretation of death differed from the heroic death of the Romantics, as it did from the redeeming, transfigurational death of the Baroque, with which it had a lot in common. In the Sezession death was nothing horrifying, neither hostile nor glorifying, not a superhuman principle. It was life's partner and escort, admonishing when all went well, and embracing at the time of tribulation and suffering. A wonderful example of this view is one of Egon Schiele's masterpieces, *Death and the Maiden,* where Death is an old Franciscan friar softly embracing the Girl, whose life is as worn as her dress.

Perceiving death as an organic part of existence and treating it as something aesthetic were central ideas in the Austrian empire. The most competent to make a statement about the concept was the young Rilke. He was the ever-inquisitive poet, ubiquitous at the turn of the century with the question he addressed in his *Das Stundenbuch* (The Book of Hours).

> Lass mich nicht sterben, eh ich weiss
> Wie sich der Tod zu dir verhält!
> Ist er der Widerspruch der Welt? Ist er ihr Heil?
> Ist er ein Teil von dir, des Lebens Teil?[27]

> Do not let me die before I know
> How Death behaves with you!
> Is he the contradiction of the world? Is he its good,
> Is he a part of you, a part of life?

And he himself responds by saying,

> O Herr, gib jedem seinen eignen Tod.
> Das Sterben, das aus jenem Leben geht,
> darin er Liebe hatte, Sinn und Not.[28]

> Denn wir sind nur die Schale und das Blatt.
> Der grosse Tod, den jeder in sich hat,
> das ist die Frucht, um die sich alles dreht.[29]

> O Lord, give everyone his own death,
> The dying that issues from that life,
> Wherein he had love, reason, and dearth.

> For we are merely shell and leaf.
> Great death, inherent in us all,
> That is the fruit, that's what it's all about.

But Rilke's fine intuition did not fail to also sense when the perception of death changed.

Denn dieses macht das Sterben fremd und schwer,
   Dass es nicht unser Tod ist; einer der
   Uns endlich nimmt, nur weil wir keinen reifen.
   Drum geht ein Sturm, uns alle abzustreifen.[30]

For what makes dying strange and hard,
   Is that the death's not ours; one who
   Finally takes us, only because we do not mature.
   A storm is coming for that, to scrape off one and all.

In his *Aufzeichnungen des Malte Laurids Brigge* (Diary of Malte Laurids Brigge) he elucidates, "Man dies by chance, with a death that comes with illness" and that is not his. "Before, everyone knew (or perhaps surmised) that we bear death within ourselves like the seed of a fruit. . . . It was inside us, and this filled everyone with a sublime dignity and quiet pride."[31] Very similar is the perception of the young Hofmannsthal. In his first drama *Der Tor und der Tod* (The Fool and Death) the protagonist Claudio, his life squandered, is led by the hand by a gentle fiddler who personifies his death. Enlightened, Claudio submits, "you shall be Life, Death!"[32] In the same vein is also a gentle *Terzine* of Hofmannsthal:

Die Stunden! wo wir auf das helle Blauen
Des Meeres starren und den Tod verstehn,
So leicht und feierlich und ohne Grauen,

Wie kleine Mädchen, die sehr blass aussehn,
Mit grossen Augen, und die immer frieren,
An einem Abend stumm vor sich hinsehn

Und wissen, dass das Leben jetzt aus ihren
Schlaftrunken Gliedern still hinüberfliesst
In Baum und Gras, und sich matt lächelnd zieren

Wie eine Heilige, die ihr Blut vergiesst.[33]

The hours! When we stare upon the bright blue
Of the sea, and comprehend death,
So lightly, festively, and without dread,

Like little girls, who look so pale,
With wide eyes, and who are always chill,
Staring ahead one evening in silence

And know life is passing from their
Languid limbs over into
Tree and grass and, smiling wearily, play coy

Like a saint shedding her blood.

The beauty of dying, such a refined, perhaps decadent, pleasure, is also what hinders Anatol in Schnitzler's *Agonie* (Agony) from breaking off with his lover. As he says, living with the past is an illness that leads to beautiful death.[34] In the Viennese Sezession, the aesthetic treatment of death directly gave rise to regarding death as something erotic.

That death was not just aesthetic but also erotic and associated with love, or to put it differently, that Eros and Thanatos were alternates, has long been discovered and written about in literature. The Salome theme had a revival at the turn of the century, in Beardsley's stirringly erotic drawings or Wilde's forceful play, which in turn inspired Richard Strauss's musical drama (conceived in Vienna but premiered in Dresden because of its provocative, erotic treatment of death),[35] and *Tristan and Isolde* was extremely popular. Less known are Schnitzler's variations on the love-and-death theme in short stories and dramas, his danse macabre of love in his *Reigen* (Roundelay), or the ecstatic agony that was *Professor Bernhardi*'s source of conflict.[36] Little known today is the pertinence of this idea to Hofmannsthal's dramas set in antiquity, or his blithe verse on Grandmother's death, where the grandson visits his grandmother on her deathbed and she tells him in her final hour how she looks forward to death with the same feeling as she once, as a young girl in love, flung herself into Grandfather's arms.[37]

Solitude, Garden, illusion and reality, the play of life and death, are all evident in the works of the rebellious young writers and painters of the fin de siècle. However, the Viennese Sezession forked out into another direction as well. It was the Wiener Werkstätte, the renowned studio of applied arts of the Viennese Sezession, which while abnegating eclectic art did not retreat from public life, and while working a garden also erected a real and famous workshop. The Wiener Werkstätte opened a new era in applied arts. Does this offshoot signify an ambivalence, or was there more to it than that?

No doubt there was a sort of ambivalence to this sort of abnegation without retreat. A foremost representative of the Garden culture, Hofmannsthal was quite deliberate when he claimed that its refined aesthetics and ornamentation brought to light a well-defined social stratification in Vienna that had been present since the baroque. To break entirely with tradition was to be rejected, to sustain it rigidly was impossible.[38] Beauty in art, knowledge, must be shared with the people, yet it is questionable and uncertain whether the people wish it. Several of Hofmannsthal's short stories and dramas testify to his social conscience and also to his fear. His retreat was motivated not so much by what Horace called *odi profanum vulgus* but rather an intellectual attitude saying *timeo vulgus* (that is, "I hate the uninitiated crowd" turned into a fear of the crowd). What prevented the fin de siècle from running smoothly, and what stirred up the emotions of the masses, was what the conscious registered as the norm of existence: that no sensible relationship can be established between art and the world, or between one person and another. "Look," Hofmannsthal wrote in 1900, "if I pronounce: I and you, chaos breaks out. So leave me be, let me read my dictionary."[39] Two years later he formulated his famous *Chandos* letter, a document on the impossibility of human communication.[40]

Branching out of Junges Wien and the fin-de-siècle artists of the Sezession was another, socially more open and active, group, hallmarked by Hermann Bahr and the art of Josef Hoffmann. In the introductory words of their organ, *Ver Sacrum*, in 1898, they declared war against "Byzantinism and all bad taste." This young generation was out to take on art that addressed its own age and people. "We know no difference between 'high art' and 'mass art,' or art for the rich and art for the poor." And should the simple folk fail to understand the culture that was to become public property then it must be instructed on how to gain a firm knowledge, to understand and get involved, "so that you shall rule over the spirits! That shall be our mission."[41] Hermann Bahr called on his fellow artists to create something entirely new. "You must accomplish something that has never before existed, you must create Austrian art. . . . I long to live among such objects that are a part of Viennese art. . . . Envelop our people in Austrian beauty!"[42]

The initial slogan of the Viennese Sezession had been a militant "Der Zeit ihre Kunst, der Kunst ihre Freiheit!" (Art to the Age, Liberty to Art!). It was passionately social and extroverted, with a determination to make life better. It knew that the artist "has to stand with both feet in the thick of life."[43]

It may appear as a mistake, a self-contradiction on my part, to label as an esoteric "Garden culture" a trend that is so consciously aware of its mission. But paradoxical as it may seem, the label fits. Rarely were intention and execution so disparate as with the rebellious generation of the Sezession. Their ornamentation was charming, impressing even the man in the street, yet their choice of form, their philosophy and subconscious symbolism remained alien to him. The contradiction lies much deeper than could be gauged by the man in the street, however. The Sezession was detached and therefore in a bad mood, full of existential anxieties. This was not something that could be expressed by decorative, stylized beauty, any more than a cripple can find a cure in beauty or art.

Nor did the household objects the Wiener Werkstätte created really reach the man in the street. The tenet that everything the group put out must be fully handcrafted drove up the prices beyond his means. The Sezession's aim was to deliver man through beauty. They offered clearly laid-out, hygienically polished houses, handcrafted wallpaper and furniture, door knobs and dishes, in short, industrial art. But in the end only the wealthy and only the ones with refined tastes and a sense for art were able to move into such houses, because only a select few could afford these paintings, jewels, silks, and tapestries. The Viennese Sezession failed in lifting the barrier between high and mass culture, in making art a public treasure, and even its most typical workshop, the Wiener Werkstätte, failed to break out of the Garden. Instead it remained confined to the greenhouse, remained a peculiar Garden-culture workshop. That became its downfall.

Typecasting always holds the risk that from the overwhelming mass of data one selects the ones that best fit one's intellectual disposition and preconceptions. Typecasting is arbitrary; it shows things to be either simpler or more important than they really are. What I treated as typical in the intellectual cast of fin-de-siècle Vienna was its aesthetic focus, even though there were also (aside from the light, operatic genres) the popular, socially committed dramas of this period in Germany, and pamphlets and fiction dealing with the Austrian's confused sense of identity.

Nor have I mentioned as typical Karl Kraus, as the relentless and acrimonious critic of the Monarchy's political system, and the society and literature of his time. I omitted him not only because he was a self-declared outsider (who said that Vienna's population of 2,030,834 consisted of 2,030,833 inhabitants and Karl Kraus)[44] nor because in spite of all his sympathies he refused to join the Social Democratic party (who took offense and called him an ivory-tower aesthete). The reason I did not mention him lies in his own explanation for his self-isolation. "If my choice is only the lesser of two evils," he replied to a critic, "I prefer to choose neither."[45] Kraus also lashed out at the young artists of the Sezession, at their flight into the Garden world of illusion, and he predicted the catastrophe that was to befall the Monarchy and subsequently mankind. His "therapeutic nihilism" brings him closer to the avant garde of the following age, even if he was born the same year as Hofmannsthal, in 1874.[46]

Out of all the parallel and contradicting tendencies I took Junges Wien as typical because it best represented the unity of tradition and the break with it, that ability to strike a balance that is an attribute of the Austrian intellect.

But is there such a thing as the Austrian intellect? And if there is, how can it be defined? To Thomas Mann it was a "life-blessed mediator" that balances lack and excess of form; to Rudolf Kassner it was the gauge that, wedged between life and death, holds both together.[47] Hermann Bahr characterized the Austrian intellect by its inability to choose between antipodes, so that by avoiding saying no to anything it strikes a balance between extremes. Everything is true and at the same time interchangeable. At the point of utmost happiness come tears; in greatest suffering is a trace of happiness; in life and art happiness and pain, illusion and reality blend.[48]

It must have been exactly this modern reinterpretation of the relationship between illusion and reality that was the specific and lasting achievement of fin-de-siècle Vienna. It set forth not only the illusiveness of the real world and the realness of the illusory world but also the relative relationship between illusion and reality. How far reality is an illusion, or to what extent illusion—call it play—is relevant to reality, is determined by the given social-historical situation and individual psychology. The thought must have come from Ernst Mach;[49] it was he the young rebels took it from, as did also the sober physicist Einstein.[50] But with them all, Mach included, the thought sprang from, and was nurtured by, the Monarchy itself. Here was the hopelessness of a declining empire that according to Kraus was "an experimental station of the end of the world," and to Broch "the symbol of vacuum."[51]

The Workshop: The Attraction between Life and Public Life

As seen from Vienna, the Monarchy was inspirational and nurturing. In Budapest the old world's expiration was perceived and depicted differently. Here the young generation, a newly maturing age group, grew up, lived, and worked not in gardens and villas but for the most part in editorial offices and cafés. The question arises whether the cultures of the two capitals may be compared at all. Can we put Garden and Workshop in the same balance? What can we hope to gain from searching for exotic flowers in a bustling editorial office or by trying to discover the Viennese's experiences in the background of the people in Budapest? Or if we take the Budapest Workshop, with its own works and its belief in a utopia, how could we possibly compare it with the aesthetics of the Viennese, who renounced utopia altogether? The answer is that we can gain something from the comparison, namely, an understanding of the differences in social commitment and orientation between the two cultures.

Cultural renewal in Budapest was launched by the young staff of A Hét. All were in their twenties, with only the editor József Kiss in his late forties.[52] A Hét reveals hardly a trace of fin-de-siècle ennui and melancholy; the paper was fresh, full of ideas, and open to everything. Its aim was to refine middle-class tastes and to instill the value of freedom; its subjects were social problems and inequities. It latched on to anything having to do with public life at home and abroad. How could it have been otherwise? As the philosopher Bernát Alexander put it, "For decades literature to us was something much greater than a source of aesthetic pleasure. . . . Our writers served aesthetics with one hand only, with the other they took on . . . the defense of the national spirit. Our literature was to us not our entertainment but served as our temple."[53] There is no question that such a commitment was made to the detriment of aesthetic values. Still, A Hét was founded on the values of fiction, but at the same time it was grounded in reality. Literature must be artistic in such a way as to keep in touch with the realities of life and the affairs of the public. Life and public life merged in this philosophy on art, where life was relevant to the artist only insofar as it was an integral part of public life.

The central theme of the new Hungarian culture was the country's backwardness, which this generation may have thought more severe than it really was. They decried the country as medieval, beset with social injustice. Their sensitivity found expression not only in journalism but also in fiction and writings on art theory. In the solitary, mystic painter, László Mednyánszky, they saw someone who "revealed to us the world of suffering, exposed the wounds of life, proclaimed for us the doctrine of relief."[54]

Of course, poverty upset young writers everywhere, even in Vienna. As the young poet Sándor Bródy wrote about Budapest, "And amidst the almost listless prosperity of the happy city came to mind again and again the poverty of the metropolis." It was not uncommon for young writers like Bródy to be in love and willing to face death for the sake of their ladies, or perhaps to write an aesthetic "Thanatology." But it is surely a Budapest specialty that the kiss of the muse inspired a volume on poverty. "How could I have chosen not to write it if she, too, wished it?" Bródy was to argue later.[55]

The young people of Budapest were enthusiastic about the Sezession, though perhaps less for its style than for the revolutionary spirit that came out of it. "My Sezession is the struggle of progress against narrow-mindedness," wrote Ady, and in the trendy philosophy of intuitivism he saw not the irrational élan vital, but a love for life and the belief in human progress.[56] "The Sezession is not a style but a liberty, the artist's revolt against art which is not created by him but which governs him," wrote an admirer about Ödön Lechner, the pioneer of the Sezession in Hungary. He saw Lechner's greatness in his being a truly "heroic freedom fighter who helps tear down barriers and overthrow tyrants."[57]

In this sense the young painters who followed their master, Simon Hollósy, to Nagybánya were freedom fighters also. Far from the bustle of the capital and public life they nevertheless propagated a bourgeois culture in painting that opposed the traditional trend with its aristocratic/national/historical themes and its rigid academism.[58] In this sense the Vígszínház Theater that opened in the late nineteenth century was also innovative. It was established as an alternative to the inveterate National Theater, and looked out to Europe; it popularized Ibsen, Chekhov, the German social dramas, and the fashionable French plays, and at the same time established a veritable workshop for modern acting.[59] A decade later the avant-garde company Thália was established for the express purpose of propagating progressive ideas. It came to symbolise the coming together of radical intelligentsia and socialist workers.[60]

The solitary heroes, life's drop-outs, were given a place in Hungarian literature and on the stage, provided they were the bearers of the real historical and social drama. Of this type of solitary writer, László Arany, and his disillusioned hero Tamás Kóbor, wrote, "That is the almost customary tragedy of the really outstanding figures in the history of our day," to rise above the masses wishing with all their souls to make their country a great one, but faltering for the indifference they encounter. "Our Fate is that of the albatross thrown on the dry shore, helplessly stumbling in the sand, to the great amusement of the shore-dwellers."[61] But on the Hungarian stage mysticism was hardly a factor, and there were no mystery dramas. Also missing were episodes or agonies of private concern. Only the nation was entitled to a "wonderful death"; common individuals were not given the right to put their trite death before the public, the country. "Death is ordinary, it stinks, a thing without any poesy at all," wrote Ignotus, one of the notables of the young generation.[62]

The Hungarian cultural elite set only its ideals and not its life before the public, and showed tangible reality in an easy-to-understand, naturalistic form. Death from Love was frequently written about in the newspapers, pamphlets, and sometimes in fiction, but this was not the kind of death the Sezession spoke of. It was the usual romantic version, like a Biedermeier oil canvas. One young A Hét writer, Dezsõ Szomory, neither a romantic patriot nor at home in the Biedermeier, presented a touching drama about romantic love. A sick husband gets out of bed on his wedding anniversary to buy a gift for his beloved wife, thus causing his death, which in turn drives his equally loving wife mad.[63] A feuilleton with the promising title of "Halálos szerelem" (Fatal Love) will leave anyone looking for traces of the Sezession even more disappointed; the love-death of the mating roebuck is caused by a hunter's bullet.[64]

In the workshop of A Hét lyrics, daydreaming and dreams were the tools at hand. The basic experience in Zoltán Ambrus's moving short story is an agonizing dream; a boy comes under the spell of a beautiful but wicked fairy, and though he wishes to flee in terror he cannot. Later in his life the fairy of his dream pops up repeatedly, in the guise of a friend or a lover. We are almost swayed to believe that this is the death symbol of the Sezession, but in the end of the piece we find just the opposite. Death brings the writer out of his sweet dreams about dying and awakens him to bleak reality: when he was young death had wanted to bind him, in his old age and with death approaching it is love that leaves him by the wayside.[65]

In comparing the cultures of fin-de-siècle Vienna and Budapest, negative parallels present themselves more readily than positive ones. In Budapest the culture was very public, as we have seen. Men of intellect did not appear on their private arbor-stages but in the forum, and did not reveal a private reality but lived the trials and tribulations of public life, which they turned into their personal problems. The trend became even more pronounced and more gripping in the first decade of the twentieth century. That is especially true in one significant sense, namely, that in the literary consciousness of the young generation backwardness was now perceived as a self-evident fact. It was even bestowed a metaphoric name, taken from the poet Endre Ady's symbol of the Hungarian "wasteland" with its smell of death, a grave of souls. The symbol is there also in Mihály Babits's "Fekete ország" (Black Country), where everything to the marrow of the bones is black; or more directly in his "Szimbólumok" (Symbols), where the speck of the country that is home lies abandoned and lightless:

fortune's great current dropped you halfway
and you stand motionless, like an idle lake[66]

The same picture shows up in Dezsõ Kosztolányi's poems about the Hungarian Great Plain, where in the motionless, ancient land everything sleeps, "dreams still hover here, sluggish dreams," and "even the earth dreams of Asia."[67]

"Socially we live in prehistoric times," Ady wrote in an article. This society had not come of age; it was uneducated, superstitious, and sick. "In this country only aristocrats, priests, and asses can exist. And those who want to accommodate them."[68] "Oppressed, backward, and beggarly, that's what we are. . . . Our people perishes because fate wants to destroy it."[69] But fate has its names: class society, class state, gendarmes. Oszkár Jászi, the leading figure among the young radicals, saw the problem similarly, in the system of the great estates, in the power of the landlords over the villages, in the towns and industrialization that had not come of age.

The sense of backwardness and of perishing had a double source: the structure of society with all its remnants of feudalism weighing it down; and the strong sense of national identity felt by the Hungarian intellectual elite. So their slogan was not, as in Vienna, "Liberty to Art!" Instead it was "Liberty to the people!" meaning that they did not want to redeem man through pure art but to mobilize the people with art for the war for the liberation of society. In Vienna modern political science was replaced by a subjective and relativistic philosophy. In Budapest it was founded on a positivistic sociology.

Literature and the newly evolving drama ran along the same lines as science and journalism. In the powerful play by Sándor Bródy entitled *Tanítónõ* (The Schoolteacher), the heroine takes on a mission in hope of gaining social reform. Flóra, pretty and educated, leaves the capital to teach in a godforsaken village. When questioned about her views she flings them at the petty village lords, "I am a socialist . . . on emotional grounds. I've created my own prayer, the same as I've created my own political creed, individually. Decent rich people must not be harmed. To poets . . . we must erect palaces. And the concept of fatherland is beautiful, don't anyone dare touch it. . . . My dream: I'd like a big, an enormously big school that all peasant children would attend. I love peasant children. Did you ever see an ugly one? One is prettier than the next."[70]

"What is Magyar lies in the reforms," wrote Ady around this time.[71] If anything, it was a belief in reforms that still drove this unfortunate "ferry-country" on, a country navigating between two worlds, two cultures, between Asia and Europe—and back. A few thousand Hungarians, the "Sacred Heralds," run ahead but the millions fail to follow behind.[72] Tradition, order, and impotence hold the people captive. What is the source of the inadequacy? Why can't Hungary ride at anchor in Europe? What is it that makes its leaders turn the ferry back toward Asia? Because the aristocrats, the gentry, the upper class are afraid of Europe, of progress, of the city, of industry, of schools, and the maturity of the people. To continue Ady's quote, "Oppressed, backward, and beggarly, that's what we are. But this is not the worst of our woes. . . . The people of Góg and Magóg were shut away behind iron gates, but . . . at least they could pound on the iron gates. Our people cannot do that. Their arms have been chopped off and they cannot pound even the gates of hell, only tumble into its grave as cripples, with bodies putrefied."[73] Out of such a tragic national condition and individual reclusion must come disillusionment, a longing to escape, the loss of a sense of identity. It did. In the early twentieth century almost every great artist felt compelled to retreat, and faced a crisis of this sort. It was a time "when autumn, winter, spring, and summer all came together."

THE WORKSHOP'S DOUBLE IDENTITY: LIFE ON THE RUN AND A SHARED FATE

In the one and a half decades after the turn of the century, the generation that made the journals *Huszadik század* (Twentieth Century) and *Nyugat* (West) (and perhaps all major Hungarian progressives) worked wonders. Here, where Asia was the product of the soil and of dreams, the time had come when they were catching up with Europe. Europe was there in the subject matter, the way they perceived things, in their depth of thinking—in short, in the society's way of responding to the challenges and problems of becoming bourgeois. And much more than that, it was in their power of expression, their aesthetic treatment, their modern approach to the language of music, painting, and writing. Without self-glorification, the generation was able to "elicit letter, line, color and belief" in the adherents they recruited (though this with varying success). They did it first of all by rebelling against the cliché that artistic expression had become, against imagination turned bland, against puffed-up platitudes and the deterioration of the language. In a single decade they caught up with, brought home, and instituted what there was to European culture. Intellectual rebirth was by no means directly and unambiguously in line with positivist rationality.

While one branch of the intellectual turbulence in Hungary came out of the Enlightenment, the other had its roots in Romanticism, was familiar with Schopenhauer and Nietzsche, later took from the philosophy of Intuitivism and Bergson, from Baudelaire, Wilde, and Rilke, was at home in Impressionism and its moods, in the Sezession's outlook of life, and in the depths of Symbolism. This was a process of fermentation and by no means did it proceed without drawing disbelief, or as unambiguously as these belated followers of the Enlightenment imagined the progress to human perfection to go, and as their successors conceived the "second reformist generation" to be.

In approaching the ideas, the intellectual content, of these years it becomes evident that the subjects of concern to Symbolism and the Sezession in Europe years earlier were dealt with in Hungary only in the decade preceding the war. Clearly the main theme here also was loneliness, chilling solitude, the severing of the communal transmission lines between communication and understanding—and along with that and from the same roots, the desire to escape, either into the self, the soul, the tower, or the Garden if you will, the harmony of the Garden before the Fall, and the adoration of beauty. Solitude, a lack of understanding, anxiety, the wish to escape—these might be seen as a legacy of Romanticism or a bohemian eccentricity, if only in the meantime there had not evolved a stratum from the urban intellectuals that, having lost its footing and become marginal, sustained this type of thinking. Creative solitude was making its way into the depths of the soul: Mihály Babits, Endre Ady, Dezsõ Kosztolányi, Frigyes Karinthy—all arrived at psychoanalysis, the recognition and acceptance of ambivalence as the modern form of existence. Resolve was sought in art, there was reverence for beauty. Out of this grew the *Nyugat* generation's euphoria about language, their belief in the magic of the word; and this gave rise to the thesis of György Lukács and his circle that artwork is the primary reflection of reality. Now it became a constituent of literary taste to express amorous desires outright, whether that meant confessing to masochistic and autoerotic narcissism or the portrayal of sensuality in the nude.

With the decades-long delay of these subjects, their counterpoint came almost automatically. Ugliness, sin perishing, and death were expressed and made aesthetic. To Ady, Babits, and especially Kosztolányi, Gyula Juhász, and Árpád Tóth the prime mover of existence was a fear of death coupled with a desire for it.

Literature and art suddenly became colorful and polyphonic. In Babits's words,

> the old idea shall wear a thousand coats,
>   and the old form shall reappear
>   as the suit of the new idea.[74]

Such was the renaissance of the capital and in part of the country at the beginning of the twentieth century.

Where there is such a polyphony of thought and form, there must be people with quite different views and from different subcultures, as was the case with this young generation. Temperament, tradition, and taste drew a chasm between, for example, Endre Ady and the young Mihály Babits and Dezsõ Kosztolányi, as they did between Zsigmond Móricz and Frigyes Karinthy and Milán Füst. Or taking the broader circle, it seems strange in retrospect how Oszkár Jászi and György Lukács could have been of one mind if only for a fleeting moment in history, or both of them with Dezsõ Szabó. How was the *Nyugat* able to embrace a man like Endre Ady, a scion of the arrogant gentry yet an heir of rebellious plebeians, echoing such poets as Mihály Csokonai Vitéz, Sándor Petõfi, and János Vajda, to whom poetry was but a fancy lackey;

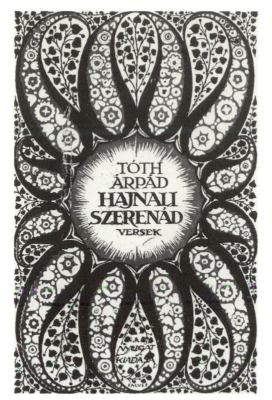

19. The title page of Árpád Tóth's book of poems, *Hajnali szerenád* (Morning Serenade). Budapest, 1912

and a man like Babits, who deferred to János Arany and continued that poet's deliberate art, "objective poetry" with an aristocratic spirit, an erudite mastery of the humanities; and Kosztolányi, the clever artist of language, the generation's most characteristically European and most subjective, narcissistically egocentric poet? And what was it that attracted to the capital's intellectual elite the loners from Debrecen, Szeged, distant Fogaras, or faraway Székelyudvarhely? What was it that attracted, and what repelled them? Perhaps the promise of Europe and modernity; and then the spiritual emptiness of their environment that became animated only when it came to uttering curses.

I think we may accept a "yes," the answer that has been consecrated by posterity. We can accept it unconditionally, and can at most underscore the arguments for it. If there was ever a time when Hungary was left-wing and progressive, it was in the early twentieth century. Everything, even the tiniest clearing, was still overshadowed by the Castle, by the County Hall, and by the Church.

The achievements of modernization, the new inventions civilization offered, were received with aversion by the traditional middle class, even if they profited from it. And even a minor change in taste or ideas was viewed with suspicion and even hostility. Here even the Muse of Parnassus was distrusted if her tune was not the popular-national one, and true folk music was suspect if it was not in rhythm with the folksy *verbunkos* recruiting songs. Abominable were all things modern; the public, in line with the gentry, promptly attached to them the label of "immoral," "decadent," and was especially quick to denounce them as "not Magyar."[75]

It is a well-known fact that Ady's relentless political anger was incited by those "Pumpkinseed Johnnies" who questioned his Magyarness and sought his downfall. They also kindled his poetic fire.

> How I should wish to hate myself.
> But God! they hate me too:
> I must not, cannot cease.[76]

Babits chose much the same tone in his *Darutörpeharc* (Crane-Midget Fight) and his subsequent memoirs speak of the same theme. "I was openly rebelling even then. . . . I didn't drink, didn't hunt, and didn't talk politics, which in itself was considered revolutionary in Hungary at that time, where even poetry was tolerated and permitted only for politics' sake. They began to regard me as unpatriotic, which I was proud of, considering its horrendously wild, base mouthpieces."[77] Not the desire for, nor the idea of, social truth but a compulsion for it was what drove these tower-recluses back from Paris and Rome and into the forum. And something else: the fatherland, the Magyar nation, that lay hidden in and under the ground, somewhere below the present.

How often, and perhaps most pressingly in the critical year of 1905, did Ady write about having to become free of "this hideous, murderous filth," and about his suffocating here. "My whole being is an almost pathological burning feverish longing for Paris and to get away from the filth at home. . . . I am leaving and that is that."[78] And he stayed on. It was not so easy escaping from here. He was held back, bound by the common fate. It was impossible to flee for someone who had relinquished the traditional framework and had preserved his popular and national identity even at the cost of losing his political home.[79] Just when he was most impatient to leave, Ady asked in his programmatic poem whether one may cry at the foot of Carpathians. Babits, even under the blue skies of Italy, was tortured by the memories of his "woeful land." No matter how much he wished to rest idly, he was compelled to run and search. When he saw how obscure delusions were lulling his country to sleep he turned to Ady. Without denying all the differences between them,

> But we had one mother: Hungary.
> Still we're of one blood, we two,
> Though opposites, together one;
> My struggle is the continuance of yours.[80]

20. Endre Ady (right) and Mihály Babits in the 1910s

In search of the truth and in concern for the Magyar nation, otherwise reclu-
sive poets like Árpád Tóth and Gyula Juhász were driven to the Workshop, the
public forum, and even Kosztolányi, a man of European horizons, was also
forced to raise his voice. To the latter, however, it was of no consequence where
he was; at seeing the unstirring Hungarian Great Plain in full bloom he was
driven to cry out,

> You send me to revolt now, to brawl,
>   A drunken Magyar in the tavern of the world![81]

Instead of withdrawing from the national community, the generation that
made *Huszadik század* and *Nyugat* solved its identity problems by modeling
a new national idea. Without exception they demanded that it be antifeudal,
self-examining, critical, and resting on the people.

At this point I must clarify a question of semantics. The terms "national,"
"popular," and "the people" covered different things for the radicals and socialists of the early twentieth century than for their Russian *narodniki* contemporaries or the popular writers of the thirties in Hungary, and had nothing to
do with the German *Volk* and *völkisch* between the two world wars. To them
"the people" simply meant workers who made their living by the sweat of their
brow, the poor peasants, servants, and day-wage men, or the "fourth estate" if

you will, who spoke out in concert but without identifying with the bourgeoisie against domination by the aristocrats and bishops. Perhaps I am not exaggerating in mentioning that as great a deed as it was in 1789 for the nation to identify with the third estate, redefining the relationship between the nation and the people, the national idea and social reform in the early twentieth century had the potential to be an equally great deed.

The rethinking of the national idea and self-concept also affected the perception of history and society, the landscape, and redefined public ethics.[82] Labels like sad, sick, tired, downcast, rebelling in vain, brooding are expressions of a general feeling that pervade Hungarian literature and art. This feeling, this attitude was as ambivalent as the Workshop itself. It could signify a sense of disillusionment and renunciation, but also the will to revolt and mobilize. The tragedy that lay in the former significance unfolded not in this generation but the history of the ensuing half century.

The Budapest Avant Garde: A Synthesis of Hungary and Humanity

In following a logical train of thought I have broken the chronology and stepped over an important demarcation line. Both in politics and in culture the quarter century before the war was cut in two by the crisis of 1905–1906. In the middle of the first decade of this century there were new signs and events indicating that time was swerving off its track. There were the first Russian revolution and in its wake the great upsurge of social movements, the birth of the entente block and the speeding up of the immediate preparation for war. At the same time, in only a few years new trends were making themselves known in art, with Picasso, Braque, Leger and Cubism, the German circle Die Brücke, Kandinsky's group Der blaue Reiter, Marinetti's manifesto and Futurism, and later Russian Constructivism; and in literature Apollinaire, Proust, Gide, and others all pointed to the coming of a new age.

In Hungary the date is marked by the printing of Endre Ady's volume of poetry entitled *Új versek* (New Poems) in 1906, the launching of the literary journal *Nyugat,* and the breaking away of the group of eight painters who formed Nyolcak in 1908. The time-span here was not as narrow, but the change went consistently and embraced different branches of art, languages, and forms of expression, and entirely different artistic personalities even within one group. I have spoken of the social and national links and the new ideals that tied them together. There were a few more connecting threads within the fabric of art, however, which, though related to the ones I already mentioned, were less obvious.

One such link was language, the renewal of the literary language of the nineteenth century, meaning both its modernization and its archaization. Again *Nyugat* was the germinator. Ady's linguistic innovations at the end of the 1910s came as a revelation when he discovered kuruc (peasant) poetry, which lent itself to renewed passions for the fate of the kuruc rebels. Taking up arms for "fatherland and liberty," repeatedly betrayed and forced into hiding, the kuruc served as the popular antithesis to the hollow patriotism of aristocrats and gentry leaders, those "gentlemen kurucs."[83] This was more than mere political or historical opposition. In his verse form, language, and rhythm, and even his poetic imagery, Ady reached back to sixteenth- and seventeenth-century Hungary, buried by the language reform movement at the turn of the eighteenth to the nineteenth, and the journalistic language of the late nineteenth century. He used the language of Hungarian and Transylvanian Calvinist preachers in a number of his poems with themes about the kuruc war of liberation.

These poems were followed by leaner and more bitter ones during the war, but the language and form were there. There was a peculiar, chilling mixture of an archaic, biblical tone and the modernized, reformed language. Mihály Babits also reached back to seventeenth-century language, though he was more deliberate and crafty, while his fellow poets Dezsö Kosztolányi, Milán Füst, Árpád Tóth, and Gyula Juhász refined the reformed language with the temperament of the deliberate, twentieth-century man of intellect in mind.

The same motivation that spurred the launching of Nyugat gave rise to a search for identity in music. Béla Bartók and Zoltán Kodály turned away from well-liked gypsy music and the composed "folk songs," in demand on the stage and in the cafés, in search of the early source of the music. To offset the gentry taste for a tearfully jolly "Magyar" sing-along they found something that was even older than the verbunkos recruiting songs, embraced by the romantics, in the villages of Hungarians, Slovaks, and Romanians. True folk music was pentatonic music that the tribes had brought with them from the East, with its own rhythm, melodic line, and store of songs.[84] The folk-music arrangements by Bartók, Kodály, and Leó Weiner, Bartók's études for the piano, but also Dezsö Malonyai's folk-art collection[85] and the use of motifs from folk art in the architecture of Ödön Lechner and his followers as well as Béla Lajta,[86] and the integration of the structural and decorative elements of Székely peasant houses into modern architecture, all became the ingredients and propagators of the new national idea.[87]

Integrating archaic and living folk culture and finding the "pure source" were only one part of the cultural synthesis, which by itself might have resulted in the mere romantic idealization of popular tradition. Another part, of cultural historical significance, supplemented and balanced the former. The folk music these composers set before the public was the modern musical expression that dissolved the tonality of the Sezession of the twentieth century, of Symbolism, of the avant garde that dug below the surface of artistic form. Take the Nyolcak, for example, who claimed to believe in nature, but without copying the approach of old schools they were carefully selective in adapting nature to their constructivist pictures inspired by the European avant garde.[88] Or the best-known examples, Bartók's *Allegro barbaro* or *Blue Beard's Castle,* with their folk motifs and rhythms, but which, in addition, changed the whole of late-Romantic musical harmony and tonality.[89]

The writers who rallied around *Nyugat* were alike in more than just their desire to renew linguistic form or their search for a synthesis. Take the favorite subjects of the turn-of-the-century modernists:

Solitude. This is a motif that runs through the generation's poems and prose works. It is a universal feeling, but with an East and Central European flavor, or perhaps particular reference to a small people. First of all, complete solitude or withdrawal was not possible to Hungarian writers for the simple and pro-fane reason that they had no villas and gardens, estates or fortunes; they could not even withdraw from the editors' offices. Second, if they did get away now and then they were never able to be entirely alone, their loneliness could never be totally existential, because they were always grounded in the land and the people, pulled back by their urge to accept the common fate. And finally, even if one or the other writer did get away for brief moments it never became a qualitatively new state of being, but lead to destruction, voluntary death, or the madhouse.

Sin. Since Baudealaire elevated a motif of modernism into a literary subject, sin has become something aesthetic and accepted. The motif was not alien to Hungarian poets, either. But in its unconventional sense what did it mean to Endre Ady? More than anything, idleness, backwardness glorified, the sick century. The sins of great backwardness and great thieveries fall on the high lords, the country's leaders who allowed the fatherland to go to waste. Cow-ardliness and servitude, however, are the sins of the people.

> It never dared to live its life . . .
> And is now punished by its past.

But from a historical perspective, even common individual sins are elevated to become national sins.

> If my sins sometimes pull me down,
>   If I fall into the wallow of my blood,
>   Is it not the torpor of the ancient wine
>   Of revenge that kills me, unexplained,
>   Of an old, great sin and grievance?[90]

Accepting that the primeval cause for the national sin, that centuries-old sick-ness, was backwardness, it is logical that anything new was considered a sin, unpatriotic, and immoral. But for the *Nyugat* group it was just this "tearful daring," this "destructive creating" that was the redeeming sin which could be dealt with aesthetically. Babits wrote an ode to Sin.[91]

Sin was not lasciviousness or love, nothing of the conventional vices; it was not the sluggish and inert who were labeled sinful but the vigorous innovator who ventured to take an axe to clear hitherto untrodden paths.

> Yet bravely I enlist in your service,
> The best remuneration of your servants, great Sin,
> Hand me your bright axe! Anoint me with
> Wrestler's oil!

Babits set inaction, "unsinfulness" without virtue, against the sin of creating, innovation, discovering. This is not Baudelaire's sin in his aesthetics of decay, nor Dostoevsky's ethics where goodness redeems sin, but again very much a public sense. The same goes for a related term, decadence. As György Rába put it, in Babits's vocabulary decadence was synonymous with "the unaccustomed, the original, what's more, the complexity of the soul."[92]

Death.   This third motif lends itself especially readily for comparison. Western Symbolism and fin-de-siècle Vienna's affinity for death were not foreign to the Budapest Workshop. Next to a public death of national rank, a private death now gained justification in art. Dezső Kosztolányi was especially close to the modern concept of death, to Freud's Thanatos thesis or Rilke's death experience. Most of Kosztolányi's early poems revolve around death. Death and suicide, if only as a chilling game, are hauntingly present in the small child's complaints, and even more so in his later, schizophrenic dialogues.

> Often it is as if a coffin clutched me,
> I am covered by a cool shroud
> And know that this is the head
> On which hence a grave cap must be.[93]

For Kosztolányi death is a tangible presence that follows him, modulates his life and attracts it like a magnet.

> I want you like life wants death,
> For my heart anticipates signs from beyond,
> The impossible and death are its desires.[94]

The fear of death and the longing for it are feelings that run through Endre Ady's volumes, as well. The spell of perishing, the affinity for death, the readiness for self-destruction, and the erotics of death are all preferred subjects for him. Granted, the death motif was a fashion of the time, a fin-de-siècle mood, and initially perhaps a morbid game and pose. Ady himself later said so,

> I have amused myself quite enough
> With Death.

But as private death gained the same acceptance as national death, and as that was no longer a display but an internalized experience, death became a companion, a supplement to life, a constituent of the great cycle.[95]

> On the snow-covered path of Life
>   (The errant path of my life)
> This slight servant was my escort,
> This nothing: Death.
>
> Perhaps Life would not be
> If Death were not,
> Albeit he is there behind us,
> Our Mysterious Lord,
> Something ancient and wild, awful,
> The orderless order,
> A very big Persecutor.

The great persecutor, the "Unknown," as Kosztolányi's "great unknown Lord," is mysterious, not to be comprehended by the rational mind.

It is perhaps not contrived to associate with this train of thought Babits's *Esti kérdés* (Evening Question), with the well-known lines,

> Why does the grass grow, only to wither?
> Why does it wither, only to grow again?[96]

the poet questions the sense of being, as the poet Ágnes Nemes Nagy interprets it: "he puts between two fires the nonsensicality of existence."[97] This is the most specifically existential question of the early 1900s; we come across it with Rilke, Hofmannsthal, and dressed in a unique pictorial symbolism with Klimt. It comes up again with Kokoschka, Kafka, and Brecht, the avant garde's agonizers.

It is very likely, and I venture to say it is certain, that Babits's *Esti kérdés* (Evening Question), and Ady's and Kosztolányi's Great Unknown expressed an ambivalence about the sense of existence. Only a thorough analysis of their entire oeuvres can judge the validity of my thesis, because only a comprehensive philological analysis can reveal whether the cycle of life and death conveys the absolute absurdity of existence or a hidden, nonrational sense. There is plenty of evidence, with Ady fading away while turning to God, with Babits solitary and sick, with Kosztolányi bearing within him the proximity of passing, with Árpád Tóth, and up to István Örkény, to support another possible interpretation: that life wants to be lived "for reasons that are sacred," and it is precisely in the cycle of death and renewal wherein lies its axiomatic "sense." It is also very likely that this question about the sense of existence was the subject on which in Hungary the public connection was made with the existential doubts of the early 1900s. Again, to accept the absurdity of being as a state of existence led to voluntary death or the mental institution.

It seems that neither the mood of the times nor the affinity for death, neither modernity nor aesthetics loosened the ties; solitude and the desire to escape did not break the bonds that bound the reform generation's great artists to their country and their people.

VISION AND ECSTASY: THE DECEPTIONS OF THE MIND

Not all creative intellectuals may be assigned to the workshops, however. For the sake of integrity the itinerants as well as those who stayed at home must not be omitted. In the cultural ferment of this time there were also in Budapest those who dropped out of community and public life. Their outlook on life was like the Sezession's, to escape from a reality they perceived as dismal and threatening, coupled with the bitterness of not belonging. Their mouthpieces were not from the assimilated wealthy bourgeoisie and intelligentsia but the sensitive, impoverished gentry and petty nobility who were going through an identity crisis much like the "freely fluttering" bourgeois intelligentsia to the west. Their withdrawal from the shoddy gentry present was as voluntary and deliberate as the retreat of the Viennese from their well-to-do bourgeois existence. In spite of having lost much of their property and being forced to take up office work, these families surely would have had enough left to get their most hopeful young into the county hall or secure them a protected status. But the young chose to walk into editors' offices, from there into cafés and theaters, and from there into art, a dream world of their own creation.

Of the artists of the Sezession I wish to present two notable personalities, two true artists, the writer Gyula Krúdy and the painter Lajos Gulácsy. Both came from impoverished gentry families and inherited neither wealth nor rank, only tradition, passion, and outward gestures. There was nothing extraordinary about Krúdy's early career; from a provincial newspaper he went to work for a paper in Budapest, in short, the Workshop.[98] In the bohemian setting it was an accepted way of life to stay up and make merry till the early hours; and no one found anything remarkable in his pieces of fiction reminiscent of Kálmán Mikszáth. But soon it became evident that it was only gestures that linked him to his origins, and only card debts and amusements that tied him to his new friends. In reality he joined neither the radical reformers nor the keepers of tradition, because he was not a part of the present. Deep down inside Krúdy was an outsider, just as his dreamy and erotic characters were. He lived in a dream world transposed to the past, or rather a world of dreams created by the waking imagination, of visions.

He brought Sindbad the Sailor of *The Arabian Nights* to Hungary where, left without oceans, he roamed the small country and "the dead seas of the past," the small towns suspended in the night; he came upon women longing with love, friendly pubs and inns, and the sweet scents of memories.[99] The present was to him merely a backdrop, a surface from which gradually rose the ever more luring and realistic layers of a sunken past, as rapture comes to an opium smoker. The dream existence needs no interpretation because it is the natural world, compared to which waking demands relief from endless neuroses. This is not the exact Hungarian copy of the Viennese play of illusion and reality. With Krúdy, vision and ecstasy stood opposed to everyday sights, the external to impressions, the internalized self-love for loneliness in the outside world, which were connected only by a thin thread of self-irony.

Such characters straying on the beyond of society could be created, as Ady remarked, only by a man whose own place in society was unclear, who "incessantly oscillates between being day-wage man and God."[100] In this marginality come true, not just the present was suspended but also the vision of the future. And as there was no longer a clear image of the future, life was perceived not as backward but as ephemeral. Consequently Krúdy's struggle was not with the Hungarian Wasteland but with a death without dreams.[101] That the two were connected somewhere in the deep, imperceptible to common sobriety, was to be sensed when it came to affronts and duels or in the aftermath of what Ady called "the hours of great euphoria," and only in the greatest clash, the revolution in the fall of 1918, was the connection unmistakably apparent.

Krúdy's closest spiritual counterpart in the early 1900s was Lajos Gulácsy. Without any antecedent in Hungary, Gulácsy began to paint in the style of Dante Gabriel Rossetti (who died in 1882, the same year Gulácsy was born) and the Pre-Raphaelites. He brought home the trademark style and subjects of the Western European Sezession, the Garden, solitude, escape, the aesthetic treatment of eroticism, fine lines, and mysteriousness. Sharp-eyed art experts did not fail to note the new phenomenon, his lyricism, his "sacred languor," his "wilted colors of autumn," yet they associated him with Symbolism.[102] Very few understood him, and fellow painters rejected him.

Like Krúdy, Gulácsy did not belong anywhere, not to any workshop, and for his part he did not go to pubs or participate in the nightlife. He was no small-town Sindbad but a living wanderer in, and lover of, far-away Italian and French landscapes and times still extant after their decline. This painter, in search of his identity, was really closest to the Sezession of his own time. He longed to go away, to escape from the strange present, from irrational anxieties and interrogation, into love that never was, into Dante's Italy and Florence of the quattrocento, the gardens of sorcerers where sad, languid, and sensuous lovers meet, and are there for him to meet. The adoration of beauty, sensuality, art saturating life—these were clearly feelings and ideals of the Sezession.[103] Use of decorative elements in his paintings was modest, his symbols were simple and unambiguous. There was no devastating love or erotic death; dreams were not the transition between being and not being, consciousness and unconsciousness, but a quietly pensive, sometimes visionary state where imagination was free to create, dissolve, and reconstitute time. The world of illusions conjured up by the imagination is free from bias—Gulácsy saw that well.

The "beautiful, sacred lies are great noble dreams that constitute the significance of reality and life."[104]

But if "sacred lies" are the most noble of dreams and they have the value of reality, then it follows that they are of a different quality from the unconscious dreams that switch off the waking state. They are the mind's special ability of letting the waking imagination wander freely, of being able to grasp that which never did and never will exist, which is intangible and invisible, the substances of the imagination, and the ability to reproduce and find symbolic expression for them. It is not this commentator, seduced by Gulácsy's painting and the imaginary beings and landscapes he brought to canvas, who came up arbitrarily with an interpretation such as this. It was Gulácsy who created a utopia in his *Naconxypan,* suggesting how much he himself considered vision to bear the significance of reality. Deeply enthralled by female sexuality, he wrote that sensation surpasses life. "It is no impression. You have never seen it—because it did not exist. You have never dreamt it—because it is no imagination. You cannot shape it into marble—because it is forged of bodiless bodily desires. And still you seem to hear every throb of its heart. Its lips burn you."[105]

Perhaps Gulácsy's was more a presentiment than the recognition of the characteristic tendency of the times, which gave rise to two artistic and scientific perceptions: a psychoanalytic new anthropology, and abstraction that probed into the structure of matter. The first took figments of the imagination as realities of the soul, the second searched under the vacillating and incidental surface for the construction, and provided the basis for Cubism, Constructivism, and today's physical concept of the world. Gulácsy was one who created a world of the imagination, which may explain why he accepted and always kept features of the Sezession, but also readily identified with the Baroque and the Rococo, while his late paintings may be assigned to the Surrealism just then emerging. It may also explain why he sided with the activists during the war, perhaps out of the similarity in perception, perhaps for his identification with the progressives in Hungary.

I do not think that a single principle could, or should, be applied in judging an artist's complete oeuvre. May it suffice to say that Gulácsy's painting depicted a visionary reality, if a little poetically and grotesquely, but to a greater extent and more enduringly than any other artist's.[106] His figures are for the most part imaginary, yet part of our reality. Clowns and fools, or fools dressed like clowns, old women in Rococo fashion, on the peripheries of the times and of life, hunchbacks and the disfigured, the mad and eccentric, but pensive without exception—just like Hofmannsthal's young girls, intoxicated by dreams, who so readily understand death.

To single out one picture to illustrate what I have said, it is Gulácsy's *Az Ópiumszívó álma* (The Opium Smoker's Dream), a panel painting he did during the First World War. On top, blowing bubbles, are the heads of a clown, a Negro woman, and others. In the center an attractive young lady, a Rococo figure, reclines in an armchair; her feet are fins entwined in seaweed, and one arm reaches into a lake out of which grow aquatic flowers. Every detail—the heads, the flowers, the jewels—all are real, but overall the picture is illusory, possibly truly an opium vision. What holds it together is its mood, and it is very suggestive, intuitable, perhaps comprehensible.

With Gulácsy, art and life were in tune, since he was himself an eccentric, a fantasist, who succumbed to mental illness at a young age. As a painter he was to the end deliberate in being one of the modern and progressive, radical reformers.

Krúdy and Gulácsy bring to mind another visionary painter, Tivadar Csontváry,[107] and a writer little known in his time and since, Géza Csáth. The latter's short stories, diaries, and some of his plays reveal the same aesthetic and erotic treatment of death as that of the Viennese. Csáth still remembered the Garden, knew the magician's garden with all its strange and unreal flowers, its secrets and tales. He also knew the death of the magician, who smoked opium so much that even the most unselfish and erotic love could not help him. Csáth was a heavy morphine addict who knew well the euphoria and suffering of poison and loneliness.[108] Csontváry and Gulácsy died in mental institutions; Csáth, after killing his wife, committed suicide.

The Austrian Avant Garde: Absurdity Attained

The Viennese Garden was not able to provide security for long for the seekers of solitude. To use Carl Schorske's description, the Garden "exploded."[109] The apt metaphor comes from Oscar Kokoschka's childhood prank; after being shown the gate of an exclusive garden, he actually set off an explosion there. The artistic explosion came more than ten years later at the 1908 Kunstschau, when Kokoschka broke out of the Garden of Sezession, just as did Arnold Schönberg in music, Adolf Loos in architecture, and Robert Musil in literature.

The Austrian avant garde that came into being in the first decade of the twentieth century definitely rejected the narcissistic adoration of beauty. Most of this generation was born in the 1880s, when one crisis topped another. To the avant garde it was already obvious what Hofmannsthal and his friends had been forced to learn through bitter experience, that "everything disintegrated into parts, and the parts again disintegrated, and nothing wanted to fit into its concept," and that the possibility for intelligent communication was lost.[110] It is true that the great artists of the Sezession did not hibernate in the Garden, as demonstrated in the above quote from what is known as *Ein Brief des Lord Chandos* (A Letter from Lord Chandos). When their own insecurity and bad disposition became a concern to society at large and coincided with doubts about the endurance of the Monarchy, Junge Wien, now on the threshold of adulthood, also became aware of the symptoms of decay. The change is perhaps implied in Hofmannsthal's drama of 1905, *Das gerettete Venedig* (Venice Saved), and Arthur Schnitzler's novel of 1907, *Der Weg ins Freie* (The Way into the Open), when it became clear that it was not art that infiltrated life, but that life was making its way into art.

The avant garde was more sensitive than the preceding movement to the disintegration of the whole, of concepts, institutions, the system of values, and to the relative value of illusion and reality, of what was possible and what was not—in short, to the absurdity of the world. There were also other differences between the avant garde and the fin-de-siècle Garden culture. To the former, anxiety and threat came no longer from nationalistic or socialistic mass revolts, which were gradually turning into institutionalized movements and becoming part of the "establishment." Their feeling of helplessness came rather from the establishment itself, the inscrutable power.

A second, crucial difference was that for the avant garde illusion and reality were not set on any stage but in villages, towns, and above all in the dominant, imaginary Castle, the fictitious Court of Law that pronounced judgment on the autonomous individual; and the Prison, whether that meant the school, the barracks, or the middle-class home. "I seem to be going home," Kafka once said to his young friend Janouch, "but I am crawling into the prison established for me." It was all the more difficult to endure because it resembled the traditional middle-class home, which made it impossible to break out of. "Everything sails under false banners, not one word covers the truth."[111] The decisive experience in avant-garde literature and art was not voluntary solitude but incarceration and claustrophobia. Breaking out, escaping, flying were their frequent themes.

Closely related to this is a third difference between the two groups, and that is their concept of what is aesthetic. The Austrian avant garde rejected the Sezession's idea of beauty, and what their expressionist aesthetics termed as art was the representation of psychological reality, desires, fears, and suffering. The aesthetic treatment of death was now eclipsed by representing the relationship between death and erotics in the dark tones of brutality and aggression. Decorative beauty and aesthetic suffering that had been the Garden now gave way to distortion, mythic perversion, and the absurdity of attainment.[112]

In an absurd world the identity crisis became complete; there was a loss of the self and a homelessness coming forth from the pictures of Egon Schiele and Oscar Kokoschka, and from the music of Arnold Schönberg and his followers. The young Törless, Robert Musil's "Hamlet," had the distressing experience that as he watched objects, people, and himself he felt ultimate incomprehension coupled with a vague sense of affinity for them. And when for a moment something seemed comprehensible after all, he could not entirely put it into

words or shape it into thoughts because between his own feelings and his innermost self there "ran an inobliterable demarcation line."[113] The incompre-
hensibility of the outside world grew inside him into a sense of terror on learning of the theft by one of his schoolmates, the feminine Basini, and he almost
involuntarily became an accomplice to the sadist tortures carried out in the
"dark chamber." If all this, all these underground games, are admissible,
"then anything is possible"—even that "from the bright world he once
thought to be the only one there was a gate leading to another, musty, gushing,
passionate, naked, exterminating world." But what is more terrifying than
stepping over the threshold from the regulated and transparent, bright world
into a world of darkness, blood and filth, and debauchery, is that the two
spheres are very close, and "their secretly touching border we might cross at
any moment."[114] Karl Kraus came to the same conclusion, that in the empire
of Franz Joseph the demons of mediocrity had gained the upper hand and had
established a regular border traffic between the ordinary, rational, constitutional state and the world of bloody and aggressive passions run amok. The
doomsday of the Monarchy, and symbolically of mankind, had to come.[115]

The war, whose coming the majority of intellectuals in Budapest thought
absurd right up to that ominous night in late July, proved to those who were
able to see clearly how in our age absurdity can easily turn into reality. Again it
was Endre Ady who was the first and most perceptive in recognising this. He
knew from the beginning that this was "a war of the Prussian Junkers, the
Habsburgs and the Magyar upper-class bandits."[116] "I am very much afraid,"
he wrote to Oszkár Jászi not much after the outbreak of the war, "that I won't
be able to bear for long what must come. . . . The horrors are inexhaustibly in-
ventive, man is more disgusting and more hopelessly pitiful than anyone ever
imagined."[117] Ady felt doubtful whether the future would still need him and
the Magyar people.

> It's all the same, my friend, to me
> If wolves eat me, or the Devil,
> But surely we will be eaten.
> If a bear eats us, it's all the same,
> The sad, age-old thing is:
> It's a matter of chance who eats me and you.[118]

And then a postscript, similar to Karl Kraus's words but perhaps more painfully subdued, on the destruction of the Magyar nation and mankind, a bitter
consolation in the argument "now all is very well because it can get no worse,"
and a resigned, "now the Devil shall lead us."

What remained of the one-time revolutionary belief was only a wish to protect what there was. It was less a creed than a defensive reflex to remain a seed
under the snow, so that mankind and the Magyar nation, rejected by an absurd

world, would have the potential to continue on. Again at the nadir of absurdity there was attained the deferent acceptance of the sacred reason behind subsistence.

In Conclusion

In their self-concepts, attachments, the subjects they treated, and their forms of expression, Vienna and Budapest at the fin de siècle were very different. As they were nearing collapse their intellectual peaks came so close as almost to converge. They had a quarter century of magnificent efflorescence behind them. The aim of this chapter was to show a few of the characteristics and presumably enduring features, innovations, and makers of this efflorescence. Describing and interpreting nevertheless fall short of explaining it. I have not arrived at a full and coherent answer to the question I posed in the introduction, what were the reasons behind this extraordinary cultural boom in Central Europe? In my conclusion the answer is still not there—because I wish to avoid quick and easy explanations.

Chapter Four

THE ALIENATION OF DEATH
IN BUDAPEST AND VIENNA AT
THE TURN OF THE CENTURY

DEATH, as the disjunction of the mortal body and the immortal soul, was once a self-evident part, an accepted event in the cycle of nature. Death was present in everyday life; the members of the community lived with the dead, for they saw them dying and then lying draped on the bier. The dead slept their everlasting sleep among them, in a graveyard in the middle of the town or village, in the church or the churchyard—until the Second Coming. The whole community shared in the mourning and funeral rites. The church performed these rites according to a ritual perfected over centuries in which the magic of old had become spiritualized, and each word, song, and action was a well comprehended and experienced element in a global, symbolic interaction. Though Death reaped without favor or forebearance, cutting down king, bishop, and peasant alike, however, there were vast differences in the way people were buried. The differences corresponded to the rank and wealth of the deceased. The lord patron and the bishop were laid to rest in the crypt, the well-to-do burgher in the front rows of the churchyard, and the beggar and suicide in the cemetery ditch. Apart from the ritual, there was something else about death that was communal in the Middle Ages; it belonged within the local community and congregation and expressed their integral way of life.[1]

Then came the absolutist state and its rational, official form of organization, which could not tolerate the integral entanglement of life and death. The fact of death, the placing of the dead in the ground and the whole matter of burial, became subject to official procedures and regulations. During the Monarchy, Maria Theresa was the first to divorce the graveyard from the church, in 1775. Joseph II added to the empress's decree: from 1783 on all new cemeteries were to be placed outside the Linienwall (the Gürtel of today).[2] The new decrees forbade burials around the church, amid the houses. The measures were designed to be useful from the points of view of public health and urban development, but the establishment of public cemeteries outside the towns was an extremely protracted process. Many churchyards continued to be used for burials, and the expanding towns frequently swallowed up the newly opened cemeteries. Only in the middle of the nineteenth century, when urbanization gathered momentum and enlightened citizens also wanted to be rid of the daily presence of death, did the public cemeteries of the great cities open—the Währinger and the St. Mark cemeteries in Vienna, the Farkasrét in Buda, and the Kerepesi úti and later Rákoskeresztúr cemeteries in Pest.[3] By the end of the century they occupied their present sites and functioned in accordance with their present systems. Public utilization of the cemeteries, at least as far as Christian denominations were concerned, was regulated in Hungary by Act LIII/1868.

Although the law permitted churches and private individuals to run cemeteries, the authority to license and oversee them and to maintain and tend public cemeteries was given to town and village councils, and in the case of the capital to the Budapest City Council. In 1882 and again in 1902, the capital issued by-laws that reflected the mentality of the local government bureaucracy.[4] These laws laid down precisely how the cemetery was to be parceled out (usually in a geometrical fashion), the dimensions of vaults and tombs and the distance between them, the height of grave markers, and their utilization and decoration as well as the date on which the lease for the grave sites expired. Apart from memorials granted in perpetuity to the great men of the country and its capital, all other burial places could only be leased—vaults for a hundred years and tombs for thirty.[5] The by-laws laid down in detail the rent to be paid for vaults, monumental tombs, double graves, and, at the bottom of the list, common graves, as well as the charges for turfing, watering, tidying, and mending memorials, and other maintenance tasks. The laws established procedures for keeping the register of the dead and the grave ledgers. Cemetery bureaucracy extended to the living, as well. It laid down visiting hours, what visitors should wear, how they should behave, and what objects they might bring in and take out. Administratively a cemetery was treated like some kind of closed institution, a reverently run hospital or prison whose inmates needed ordering and disciplining before as well as after their deaths.

Administrative logic dictated that burial could only take place when the subject thereof had deceased according to the official procedure. But who might be officially considered dead? Joseph II made an attempt at institutionalized certification of death, but it was thwarted by lack of qualified personnel. Even half a century later the certification of death was only issued by a doctor in the larger towns. Elsewhere, in accordance with ancient custom, it was the parish priest who filled out the solemn certification of death. Almost a century later, the Hungarian public health act of 1876 (Act XIV, para. 110), which applied to the entire nation, declared that "All dead persons shall be examined by the person designated thereto by authority as to whether death has actually occurred and whether the party has not died by violence or from some contagious disease."[6] If the certifier of death—the coroner—found no suspicious circumstance of any kind, he set the time of burial and issued a death certificate on the basis of which the local authority gave the burial permit and entered the death in the register. If infectious disease or violence were suspected, the coroner notified the state and police authorities. This procedure, quite rational and useful in itself, became steadily more complicated. Regulations were issued on the qualifications required of coroners; those without medical qualifications were placed under the authority of the district medical officer. The procedures to be followed in cases of infection and violence were more precisely laid down and expanded to cover more thorough examination of the stillborn and the corpses of persons unknown. A perfect example of public health bureaucracy occurs in the handbook of 1910, a voluminous book which extended to all imaginable cases and stipulated a scale of fees for the examination of the dead.[7]

Death cost money, a lot of money, and it became increasingly expensive as every stage from the final heartbeat to the grave and beyond became commercialized. The house of the dead man, which had once been decorated by the family and the narrower community, such as the religious congregation or guild of the deceased, was now clothed in mourning by the staff of the undertaking establishment. Transportation, which in the towns steadily replaced the funeral procession on foot, had to be paid for, as well. By the beginning of the nineteenth century the bodies of great lords were transported in hearses drawn by six horses; the well-to-do had four horses; and ordinary people two horses. The bodies of paupers and beggars were hauled in a barrow. The pomp began with the bier and the transport, complained a Pest chronicler of the time, and even the poor sold what few valuables they had so that their dead could be taken to the cemetery by at least two horses.[8] But this was a mere side expense compared with the costs of the burial place and the funeral.

As we have seen, the capital city controlled most of the burial places, with a smaller number in the hands of individual denominations. Funeral services were conducted by the churches and the burials as a whole by capitalist companies. Depending on the standing of the cemetery and the elaborateness of the memorial, a hundred-year lease on a vault cost between 1,000 and 8,000 crowns in 1900. (A crown at the time was worth about 20 US cents.) Another 600 crowns had to be paid for every new burial in the vault, and 30 crowns every time it was opened or walled up. The cost of a burial place, from a double monumental grave down to the simplest, undecorated grave in the furthest rows of a suburban cemetery, was from 1,200 crowns to 2 crowns, and the scale reflected several hundred distinctions of rank and status.[9] The dead with no possessions or surviving relatives, known as "gratis corpses," were buried at public expense in common, unmarked graves.[10] It follows from all of the above that a funeral indicated the position (or pretensions to a particular position) of the deceased in the social hierarchy and the social reference group of the family.

Since burial places were so expensive, the Budapest City Council tried to drive down the price of laying the body out, transportation, and funerals. In

1886 it signed a contract with the First Hungarian Haulage Company, which undertook to transport "paying" corpses individually with a moderate degree of ornamentation and "gratis corpses" in common collecting wagons (but with not more than six corpses to a wagon), for the relatively modest price of 2 to 10 crowns. As in Vienna, the laying out of bodies was offered in four categories costing from 10 to 80 crowns, the last including the rental of a large hall with torches, candles, silk, and velvet.[11] It is very telling to look at a receipt for the burial expenses of an average middle-class man. The second-class burial of the physician Dr. Philipp Wenzel cost precisely 486 crowns in 1911.[12] This sum included an expensive coffin of oak, the place of eternal rest, the bier, and the expenses of the funeral ceremony. Later, the gravestone and some additional expenses ammounted to approximately 200 crowns. Taken together, the total expenses of an average middle-class burial came to about 700 to 1,000 crowns.

However expensive a funeral might be, most members of the lower classes avoided burial at muncipal expense, feeling that it was beneath their dignity. Even the workers preferred to scrape together the fee for a modest fourth- or fifth-class burial rather than incur the shame of a pauper's funeral. Only the poorest of the poor took advantage of a municipal burial.[13]

In this respect Vienna went further than Budapest. In 1907 it bought up the Entreprise de pompes funèbres and Concordia, the two largest undertaking companies, and despite reducing prices, managed to make a substantial profit. Nevertheless, the city never really overcame the competition of smaller undertakers or gained the sympathy of the general public.[14] On the one hand, the private companies were cleverer and more energetic, and had influential shareholders, and on the other hand, the religious denominations, with their stake in the funeral ceremony, likewise competed against both municipal and private funeral companies.[15] In the end, funerals in the Monarchy's two capitals, and presumably in every large town, were by and large conducted by private companies that held permits from the authorities and received assistance from the churches.

The body was hardly cold before sales representatives were calling on the bereaved family, and exploiting their sorrow by offering a wide variety of funeral arrangements. The first step was to decorate the house and erect the bier. Under the Dual Monarchy it was not compulsory to lay out the body at the cemetery, and most people set up the bier at home. The undertaker charged for the entire decoration of the home: the coffin, the mattress, the hire of the candlesticks and the candles used, the lamps, the shroud, the pillow, the hand-held crucifix, the wreaths, the veils, the cross on the grave, the bier, and the cloth that went with it. A simple suburban laying out in Budapest cost at least 50 crowns. Then came the transportation: a simple black carriage drawn by two horses with two attendants, followed by an omnibus for the close relatives, meant another 30 crowns. Of course, great lords were still taken in a six-horse hearse with such dignity that even the masked, crested horses covered in black saddle cloths and the pages who accompanied the hearse appeared sorrowful. The price of such dignity was several hundred crowns and, like the quality of the coffin, tangibly reflected the rank and status of the dead man. In turn-of-the-century Budapest and Vienna a Greek-style bronze sarcophagus cost 4,800 crowns, and a Renaissance-style one 4,000 crowns. On top of that came the appropriate six-horse ornamental hearse with six pages. A simple bronze or oak coffin and a four-horse, first-class hearse cost 1,000, an oak coffin with a third-class hearse 400; and a pine coffin with a two-horse hearse 80 crowns. The poorest had to be content with a cheaper coffin still of unpolished spruce, no bier, and no hearse (the coffin was carried on the shoulders). In Vienna that cost 55 crowns.[16]

The clergy had to be paid according to a scale of fees that varied with the area, time of day, and quality of the ceremony. Afternoon funerals were more expensive than morning ones, particularly if the family wanted the last rites celebrated in style with the priest in a cope or surplice, servers, a choir, a mass with organ accompaniment, and tolling of the great bell. A funeral of that kind cost 300–400 crowns, whereas a simpler, more modest service with one priest, a low mass without music, and tolling of only the small bell could be had for 15 to 20 crowns.[17]

At a rough estimate, the cost of the finest of funerals in either of the capitals, with burial in a family vault, a bronze coffin, and full ceremonial, must have come to 15,000 crowns, but even a simple, poor man's funeral cost more than 100. The figures exclude the cost of the tombstone, usually raised a year later. Memorials in marble, granite, or sandstone were often made by well-known artists and excellent stonemasons on whose work one could not put a standard price.

Death and burial during the nineteenth century became not only bureaucratized in every detail but commercialized as far as the professional parts were concerned. Elsewhere bureaucratic regulation and the formation of a free-market price tended to work at cross purposes, but in the death industry they complemented each other perfectly. Official regulation dovetailed with social differentiation, and so elicited prestige prices according to the rank-reflecting quality of services. The popular press often fulminated against "the outrages of the undertaker-hyenas" and "the depredations of the usurers of death," calling for elimination of capitalist businesses that squeezed profit out of grief and reverence for the dead, but to little avail.[18] State bureaucratization and free-market capitalism were the prevailing tendencies in the nineteenth century.

Encouragement for bureaucracy and commerce came from a third concomitant of the modernization process: urbanization. In the big cities the traditional community of the village and market towns had broken down. Daily life had become private, and city dwellers isolated. The dead no longer belonged to the whole community, only to the family and friends. Not even they could always accompany their dead on the last journey: the new public cemeteries were several miles out of town, and foot processions with banners and candles could not be held in the busy streets. In most cases the priest conducting the funeral had not known the departed personally, so that the final farewell became impersonal. Mourning became emotionally as empty as the mortuary chapel after the carefully timed half-hour or hour of the funeral had elapsed.

For a time a personal element remained in the old custom of erecting the bier in the house, but this too steadily changed. In 1879 the lawmakers of Budapest decreed that the laying out had to take place at the mortuary if living conditions did not permit the dead to be accommodated separately from the living, if death had occurred at an inn or during travel, if the dead had been fished out of the Danube or found, or if death had resulted from an infectious disease.[19] The first provision in particular affected vast numbers of families, for 54 percent of Budapest flats in 1911 had one room and 25 percent two rooms, while over half looked out onto airless courtyards.[20] As a result, the practice of laying out the body at the mortuary in the public cemetery steadily spread until it became generally compulsory in 1919.

A significant contribution to the process of the estrangement of death was made by the swift advances in medicine and public health. It was not just that the number of doctors and pharmacists doubled in Hungary under the Dual Monarchy, or that the number of hospital beds increased tenfold, or that a quarter of the country's doctors and hospital beds were found in Budapest. What medical progress did was to spread faith in the healing power of science and the efficacy of a succession of new drugs and therapies among the capital's middle classes. Although it was still the custom among the "better families" at the turn of the century to have their loved ones breathe their last amidst the family circle, the educated middle class no longer took fright at the idea of dying in the hospital, which divorced the family and the narrow community from the fact of death and the body of the dead. Modern urban civilization wrenched death out of the integral entity of daily life, and shriveled and formalized the ritual of mourning into a few hours and a few ceremonial acts. Death did not belong any more to the man but to the illness, and illness became a simple medical case—an *exitus lethalis*. Man became deprived of his own personal death. Rationalizing death meant alienating it from life and the living community.

Creeping bureaucracy and the rule of commercialism, coupled with urbanization and scientific rationalism, led to a change in the relationship of city dwellers to death. Whereas death was increasingly excluded from their lives, they became familiar with the natural history of pathogens, the causes of constitutional disease, the risk factors, and the likely effects of drugs and treatments. Many things changed with the advent of alienation and rationalization, but one thing that remained and perceptibly increased was the fear of death.

What consolation, what equipoise remained for the inhabitants of the cities, and particularly the educated middle class, at the turn of the century? The folk customs surrounding death, still current in country districts, were largely extinct in the cities. All that remained was the consolation of religion and the catharsis produced by the mourning rituals of the church. In the Christian and Jewish religions death is denied not only through removal of the dead and burial of the body but through the basic principles of belief, which sanctify and transform death into everlasting life. Outwardly, a Catholic funeral at that time was the most moving. Religious devotion and reverence that spread forth from the ceremonious blessing at the bier and the graveside, the offering with incense, the priest in his black cassock and white surplice, adorned with stole and mitre, the choral singing in which the congregation joined in, and the familiar melodies of the *Circumdederunt, Kyrie, Libera,* and *Requiem* stirred the soul. Even the Latin language of the liturgy, the Catholic theologians said, helped to deepen the experience, because the esoteric twilight it spread had a strong influence on the emotions.[21]

As the bier was decorated with flowers, so the funeral oration was adorned with its flowery expressions proclaiming everlasting life, the soul's salvation, and the resurrection. The stereotyped phrase in the sermons was St. Paul's statement that the body "is sown in corruption; it is raised in incorruption." The priest and his followers prayed that the deceased might slumber in peace, find salvation, and be resurrected. Whereas a Protestant funeral "wears out and depresses one with its simplicity," as one Catholic apologist put it, the pomp of a Catholic funeral "restores one's spirits, and its majesty forces one to come to oneself to a marked extent."[22]

A Protestant funeral certainly was simple and somber. It lacked the repeated blessings and the promise of salvation. In the liturgy of the Reformed Church the emphasis is on this life, not the afterlife, and the prayers are said not for the dead but for the living and their consolation.[23] Of the promise of everlasting life after death only the resurrection remained. The dead were buried "In the Hope of Blissful Resurrection" (*A boldog feltámadás reménye alatt*), and the letters BFRA were cut into the wooden headpost.

The Jewish religion did not differ in its perception of death. The soul in death returns to its Maker: "And the Lord God formed man of the dust of the ground, and breathed into his nostrils the breath of life; a man became a living soul" (Gen. 2:7). The body is perishable and expires, but the soul lives forever. Jewish funeral orators quoted the prophet Daniel (12:2): "And many of them that sleep in the dust of the earth shall awake, some to everlasting life, and some to shame and everlasting contempt." This religion, too, consoled people with the soul's immortality and resurrection, and spiritualized its believers into the transcendental.[24]

Jewish mourning manifested itself in penitence rather than outward splendor or cathartic apotheosis. Although the body was dressed in the white robes of a bridegroom or bride, it was buried in a plain coffin. Members of the community helped in washing and dressing, and this counted as a particularly good deed (*Mitzvah*) since it could not be reciprocated. After the simple, somber burial the closest kin stayed at home for a week, seated on the floor and not shaving or working. Every morning and evening a prayer (*Kaddish*) was said for the dead person. For a month they did not appear in public places, go out to the cemetery or celebrate in any way. A lesser degree of mourning and prayers for the dead were compulsory for a year, and after that on every anniversary of the death.[25]

This Judaic-Christian spiritualization of what had once been magic to placate and exorcize spirits may well have provided solace and refuge for devout people, but it was less able to do so for the enlightened elements in a rational age, for Jansenists and Josephinists and the great mass of liberal Catholics and Protestants and reform or indifferent Jews. In these enlightened circles, not only the funeral became formalized but the funeral banquet, still fashionable in the provinces, was tamed into a quiet family tea.

Nineteenth-century evolutionists summoned science to assist in combatting the fear of death. A growing part was played in the modern concept of death by the rationalization of magic, or from the opposite point of view, the mystification of scientific rationality. The reputation of medicine and science, declining since Moliere's day, suddenly grew, and a veritable cult arose around doctors, medicines, and healing. The doctor was a charismatic figure again, assuming the role of the priest, and his instruments and drugs were the modern symbols of that charisma. After the discovery of bacteria, hygiene and sterility became cultic elements, involving, for instance, the white gowns of and constant handwashing by doctors and nurses. Drugs, to ordinary people and the intelligentsia alike, came to possess the same power as prayer or incantation, with both of them often used at once. A cure at Carlsbad or treatment at the Lukacs spa in Budapest gained an equivalent ritual and psychological effect as a pilgrimage to Lourdes. The classic piece of literature on the ritual of therapy and how magic becomes rationalized, gaining a scientifically tinged symbolism, is Thomas Mann's novel *The Magic Mountain*.

From the angle of the history of mental attitudes one can also include among the symptoms of the mystification of rationality the counterculture: the great movements for a return to nature and a natural system of healing (*Naturheilkunde*). One cannot deny either the kernel of rationality or the magical religiousness and cultic nature of such reform movements as cold-water cures, vegetarianism, or nudism, which all spread in central Europe and the countries of the Monarchy at the turn of the century. In this regard, one thinks of Vincenz Priessnitz, the clever Austrian peasant's son, who first developed the water cure; then of his follower, Sebastian Kneipp, a German priest, amateur physician, and health propagandist in one person; and of Heinrich Lehmann, who introduced the water cure into medical practice.[26]

A quite different way to tame death was through the aesthetic. Decoration of the cemetery and the grave spread widely and became established in popular culture, as well. Memorials, previously the preserve of the well-to-do nobility, appeared on the graves of rich bourgeoisie, the intelligentsia, and then ordinary people, and were sometimes adorned with a statue, relief, or verse. These became so common on tombs and gravestones that cemetery art has become a separate branch of study among art historians, and a small specialized literature has been written on cemetery poetry.

A specific high-cultural, local variety of the aesthetics of death grew up in Vienna. The upper middle classes there lacked a national allegiance and were not bound to anything but a decaying state and a supranational tradition. The creative spirits of Vienna were unable to identify with the existing reality, with any kind of retrograde reform, or with any progressive Utopia. They did not embrace nationalism or adhere to socialism. They found a home in the realm of relativized possibilities, particularly in the garden of art.[27] The idealist endeavor to reclaim personal death was not, originally, an enterprise of existentialist philosophers but of poets like Rainer Maria Rilke and André Malraux—according to Jean-Paul Sartre.[28]

To show the part that death, and particularly the aesthetics of death, played in the culture of fin-de-siècle Vienna, it is enough to cite the poetry of Hofmannsthal and Rilke. As is well known, Rilke's main concern was the "good death" that "belongs to us," to our life.

> Death is immense.
> We are all his
> with laughing mouths.
> When we are in
> the midst of life
> he dares to weep
> right in our midst.[29]

Or as he writes elsewhere:

> O Lord, give everyone his own death,
> The dying that issues from that life,
> Wherein he had love, reason, and dearth.
>
> For we are merely shell and leaf.
> Great death, inherent in us all,
> That is the fruit, that's what it's all about.[30]

In *The Diary of Malte Laurids Brigge* he writes that a person in a sanatorium dies the death organized for him by the institution, which is what is expected of him. But thinking back to his parents' house, it occurs to Rilke that things used to be different: "Formerly we knew . . . that we carried our death within us, as a fruit bears its kernel. . . . Death [was] within them, . . . that gave one a singular dignity, a quiet pride." [31]

Death as a partner of life is the protagonist in Hofmannsthal's verse plays such as *Titian's Death* (1882), *Death and the Fool* (1893), and *The Little World Theater* (1897). Death is present also in Arthur Schnitzler's dramas. One need only recall *Professor Bernhardi* (1912). The conflict in the play develops around a young girl who attempted an abortion, got a general sepsis, and is brought to the hospital in agony and near death. In order to alleviate the girl's pain, the professor gives her a morphine injection that makes her feel happy and sinless; in a dream she sees herself united with her lover. At this point, however, the church intervenes: the hospital's priest demands that he be allowed to administer confession to the girl and give her extreme unction. The professor resists, maintaining that it would only disturb the happiness of her death. She cannot be happy, replies the priest, dying as a sinner doomed to eternal damnation. While the professor and the priest wrangle over the issue, the girl dies.[32] Two opposing concepts of death clash in the drama. In the end the church's concept is vindicated and the doctor's reputation is ruined, but the idea of personal and peaceful death—euthanasia—subsequently makes great advances.

Death as an immanent principle of life and aestheticized death were recurrent topics in the fine arts and music of Vienna at the beginning of our century. These were the years when Mahler composed his *Kindertotenlieder* (1901–1904), and Richard Strauss created in terms of music the lethal-erotic figure of *Salome* (1905). One can also mention the discovery by Freud of the death wish and the interchangeability of Thanatos and Eros. Moreover, Freud's central theme of dreams is closely linked to the new perception of death, since dreaming is a transitional and ambivalent state between consciousness and the unconscious, between being and nonbeing. This same ambiguous transitional nature of dreams appears in Klimt's *Sezession* works: in *Medicine* (1901), the great symbolic mural he did for Vienna University, or in the picture *Death and Life* (1916), where Death stands to one side dressed in a robe adorned with crosses and directs the circulation of sleeping—nascent, relaxing, and dying—figures.[33] Although European—particularly Viennese—art nouveau is rooted in congenial Baroque and heroic Romanticism, it substantially differs from both. For Viennese art nouveau, death is nothing fearful, nothing hostile or glorious. It does not constitute a principle beyond or above man. Instead it is the partner and companion of life. One only has to think of Schiele's wonderful painting, *Death and the Maiden* (1915) in which Death, appearing as a wise old Franciscan friar, gently embraces as a true friend the girl whose life, like her clothes, has been rent.

An aestheticized perception of death like the Viennese one cannot be found
in the culture of Budapest at the time, except in a few extravagant, totally marginal figures of the final decade of peace. The central theme of the Hungarian
culture was the country's backwardness, its medieval character, and its outra-
geous social injustices. No mysticism, no mystery plays or episodes of individual death and agonies could be found on the Hungarian stage or in belles
lettres. The tradition for that kind of thing was missing, for personal death
did not emerge either in the literature of the Reformation and Counter-
Reformation, or in Hungarian Baroque. The Hungarian aristocracy and the
gentry had a "genealogical" mentality, a clan-awareness that esteemed and
cultivated a heroic death for the nation. Miklos Zrinyi's seventeenth-century
epic *The Peril of Sziget*, which commemorates the defense of Szigetvar from the
Turks, is representative of this idea. According to this prevailing tradition,
"glorious death" was due only to the Nation. The man in the street could not
aspire to take his ordinary death before an audience. "Death is vulgar, smelly,
and altogether devoid of poetry," wrote Ignotus (Hugo Veigelsberg), an
eminent writer and critic among the younger generation of fin-de-siècle
Budapest.[34] The young Hungarian writers also understood love death differently from the Viennese. They regarded the yearning, melancholic, and self-
sacrificing Viennese as a soupçon, concocted of Biedermeier with good help-
ings of romanticism and sentimentality.

   The mixture of fear and love of death did appear in Hungary among poets
like Endre Ady and Mihály Babits, or in deviant figures like the painter Lajos
Gulácsy, the crazy genius of Hungarian art nouveau; or the morphine addict,
doctor, and writer Géza Csáth, or the dream knight of the transitory, Gyula
Krúdy, Hungary's Sindbad.[35] But these were creative spirits of a marginalized
intellectual elite, mostly homeless dropouts of the decaying nobility, and not
sons of an anguished bourgeoisie who had lost their identity.

   The relationship to death and the perception of it differed markedly between the high cultues of Vienna and Budapest. In Vienna death was a protagonist. In either Freudian psychoanalysis or the neo-Kantian philosophy of
life, one encounters an aestheticized picture of individual death that has
grown cosmic, that is, the new sensation of life for the isolated individual.
The culture of Budapest, on the other hand, was strongly committed to social
and political ideas and imbued with the problems of public life. Its writers,
artists, and radical scientists still thought within the community of their
nation and class. To them death was principally a social and political problem, or at least something that only took on artistic or scientific relevance in
that capacity. Humanized and aestheticized death was a rare visitor in Budapest, and its appearance and exponents were considered as oddities by public
opinion.

   Yet there was one point of contact between the aesthetically oriented creative intelligentsia of Vienna and their socially committed counterparts in Bu-

dapest. If by different routes, they both arrived at the idea of euthanasia. Ultimately, Schnitzler's controversial play, *Professor Bernhardi,* says the same thing as the periodical of the Budapest radicals, *Huszadik század* (Twentieth Century): one can and must rob alienated, awesome death of its myths, and one can and must reconcile man to his own death, to natural death.

Chapter Five

THE START OF ENDRE ADY'S
LITERARY CAREER
(1903–1905)

THE OVERTURE

Endre Ady burst onto the Hungarian literary scene—and started a new epoch in Hungarian literature—with an unusual, gripping verse:

> The son of Góg and Magóg, I
> vainly pound on door and wall
> Yet I asked you after all:
> May one cry with the Carpathians nigh?

Although these lines have been much quoted by both his followers and posterity, no satisfactory explanation has ever been given of the biblical reference to Góg and Magóg, of the vain pounding of a people locked behind bronze doors, or of the past tense of the sad questioning.

It is clear enough that he'd been banging on the rusty doors of medieval Hungary since the beginning of his career, as indeed he is right now; but when did he in fact ask liberty to weep? At first glance, one might be inclined to think of an article of his that had appeared a few weeks before the poem was written, a disturbing piece entitled "Notes on an Unknown Corvin Codex," with the subtitle "Weeping and Complaining." This article, however, appeared so close to the time of the poem's writing that had he had it in mind, the use of the present continuous tense would have been the more natural. The past tense of "I asked" really is, I feel, a reference to the past, to past battles waged in vain.[1] An interpretation of the rhetorical question thus involves interpreting Ady's life or, put another way, the process of his maturation as a poet.

Ady came from an historically noble family whose fortunes had declined. His father lived in circumstances no better than that of the peasantry; self-consciousness, not wealth, distinguished him from his peasant neighbors. For his son, who showed talent even as a child, he had bigger plans: he wanted him to be a county clerk, a politician, a member of parliament. Ady, however, was likely to fulfill his father's dreams only with respect to his interest in politics, for very early he had chosen journalism as a vocation. He was motivated both by respect for tradition and by the wish to break with it; literature and politics held an irresistible fascination for him, and he was also a modern intellectual who rebelled against the canonized order of things, against the hold the feudal past had on the present, and against the capitalist present that left room for no illusions concerning the future. Ady waged a war on two fronts: he fought against religious superstition, against the institutionalized forces of darkness, against despotism and feudal prerogatives; but he also cried out against the worship of the golden calf, against a civilization become mechanical, and destructive of all that was individual.[2] Like so many critics of modern civilization he, too, questioned the validity of the European value system: of efficiency, competition, speed, and the greatest virtue of all, work; and advocated natural simplicity, beauty, and the dreaming of dreams as alternate values.[3] Many of his articles and poems were variations on this theme: "Life is the only truth, life is the only end."[4] "Life has the holy purpose of living."[5] But just as frequently he declared himself an incorrigible positivist, and the supporter of progress and common sense.[6]

The radical antifeudal social critic in him was inextricably intertwined with the anticapitalist Kulturkritik of his times, for he had been shaped as much by the rational evolutionism of Comte, Spencer, and Darwin as by Zola's naturalistic anatomy of society, Nietzsche's prophetic Zarathustra, the fin-de-siècle contempt for the rational, Ibsen's and Dostoevsky's psychological insights, and Tolstoi's quest for salvation. "Do you want to know what became of the monkey's biped descendent, who is commonly called man? Three men at the end of the nineteenth century have told us: Ibsen, Spencer, and Tolstoi."[7]

It would be easy enough to explain this duality as the immature eclecticism of one growing up not only on Europe's but also on the country's periphery. This would, however, be to no purpose, just as it would be to no purpose to indulge in the philological pedantry of ordering the different ideological trends according to the periods of Ady's activity. Ady was no illiterate in philosophy, nor was he an eclectic committed to reconciling opposites. His "being of two minds" was not some disharmonious coexistence of the two halves of a split personality, but "both liberation and thralldom in one fork." Nor was this a particularly idiosyncratic ambivalence, but rather one specific to a particular period and to a particular social stratum: the intelligentsia, the men most sensitive to the alienation and existential solitude of the age, the ones who had no place in a disintegrating society, those who, as the young Ady had put it, "stood outside the world."[8]

Ady's diversified and apparently contradictory Weltanschauung then, was eclectic only in respect of its origins; it was, however, no haphazard collage. Though he saw the Art Nouveau as the first clash in the battle for a new world, he by no means saw it—as did its devotees in Munich and Vienna—as the road to salvation. "Let no one consider me a devotee of the fashionable Art Nouveau," he said. "My Art Nouveau is progress struggling against academic pedantry."[9] As a philosophy of life, too, he grounded the popular current of his

day in rationality and humanism: a real man and a real thinker had to arrive at
"a love of humanity and of life, at faith in mankind's progress. . . . It is indeed
work that will bring us salvation, that will bring us a world of beauty, of wisdom, and of tranquillity."[10]

THE QUESTER JOURNALIST

Ady, as we have seen, broke with the nobility's traditions, but capitalist
money-grubbing was no less alien to him. An evolutionist social criticism was
dominant in his thinking at the beginning of the century, a politically committed faith in progress that was to find full journalistic expression during his
years at Nagyvárad. Any attempt to give a brief sketch of Ady's journalism
brings us up against what is perhaps the greatest challenge of the historical art:
the methodological problem of selection and summarization. Ady wrote more
than nine hundred articles at Nagyvárad, and these in every field and in every
kind of column. What can we take as essential and typical from the plentiful
selection of improvisations, passing fancies, credos, and essays of profound
conviction? How can we typify and choose in order to escape the all too insidi-
ous methodological trap of finding quotes to illustrate a preconceived notion
of how it all was?

I think it a fair and historically precise method to regroup all the functional
categories of journalism—editorials, commentaries, special columns, and reviews—according to historical content and relevance. Our criteria might be
how far each exposes the Hungarian scene on the one hand, and how well each
shows Ady's development as a writer, as a poet, and as a human being, on the
other. On these grounds, we can regard as secondary—or even negligible—
the articles, polemics, reports, and theater reviews of fleeting or but a day's relevance, and disregard all these standard products of a journalist's daily routine. It is especially important to leave out all articles of transitory actuality,
those dealing with some passing political issue, not only because these have
lost their historical relevance but also because the stand they express is frequently that not so much of the author as of a given political group, the editorial board. Chiefly of tactical value, these statements must be seen within the
context of the changes in the group's tactics.[11]

What concerns us, rather, is the group of articles touching on matters of
principle, those with lasting sociopolitical relevance.

Written apropos some current event or inspired by some passing mood, the
account these articles of Ady's give of the domestic situation or of the international scene has a more general validity, and expresses his own personal views.
Obviously, this method of selection by no means eliminates the methodological difficulties; in fact, it gives rise to new ones, dependent as it is on the selec-
tor's subjective judgments, on his valuations, and on the type of evidence required by the issue being discussed. Its shortcomings, however, can be kept to

a minimum if we carefully analyze the articles themselves, and if we keep in mind what we are aiming to shed light on: the Hungarian scene of Ady's days, and his own artistic and personal development. At any rate, the method seems to be less misleading than that of randomly collecting quotations from the range of all the articles that appeared.

In the five years between 1901 and 1905, Ady wrote about twelve hundred articles, an average of two to three hundred a year. At least three-quarters of these were on some event of the day, a commentary or a theater review. No more than a fifth or a quarter of all his articles can be considered writings of lasting value. Nor are these distributed evenly throughout the five years. The ratio rises from 1901 on, reaching 40 to 45 percent of all his writings by 1903, and dropping back to about a fifth in 1904 and 1905. In 1900 and 1901, it was the theater reviews and cultural commentaries that predominated; from 1902 on, it was current events that most preoccupied Ady, but by the end of the year 1902, and even more in the first half of 1903, even these articles were full of more general observations on domestic politics, on the great trends of the times, and on the worldwide clash of the forces of progress and of reaction. At first glance, all this suggests that Ady's political activity curve reached its peak sometime in the spring of 1903, and then fell until the fall of 1905, to rise again in the years that followed.

We draw the same conclusion from a content analysis of the "ideological" articles. Most of these express Ady's political thinking, principles, judgments; a smaller percentage—especially those dealing with the arts, with the cult of beauty, and with the destiny of man—are verbalized moods voiced in terms that are an amalgam of Nietzsche's philosophy of life and of a kind of irrational mysticism. These latter types occur rather frequently in the articles written in Debrecen (1898–1899), and during Ady's first years at Nagyvárad (1900–1903); in 1902 and early 1903, however, we find very few of them, to find all the more from the summer of 1903 on.

An examination of both the outlook and the genre of Ady's writings thus indicates 1903 to have been some kind of turning point in his political development and career as a journalist. What about the content analysis, then?

We can hardly undertake here to give a systematic treatment of the ideological articles Ady wrote at the beginning of the century; there are, at any rate, already a number of fine works on the subject.[12] We shall, rather, sketch the development of the chief categories of his political program, of his political thinking. From the very moment of his becoming a self-conscious journalist, he was dedicated to the service of the "ideal," having "pledged his life in the service of progress."[13]

In Debrecen, during the last years of the century, however, Ady's "ideal" was still the conventional one of the Independence party; and his notions on the direction progress was to take were rather faint. It was only in Nagyvárad that he began to see his goals, his ideals, and his task more clearly. Looking

back then, he could write: "During my chauvinist 'kuruc' years, I gorged myself with the most naive enthusiasm on the Magyar air of Debrecen, until I was
very shortly and very definitely sick of it. Even now I've hardly managed to recover. In Debrecen, . . . one falls out of love with the Magyars."[14]

This disillusionment was facilitated by two external factors: Nagyvárad
and the Széll government, but the two were probably quite closely related. In
Debrecen Ady had already noted the growing reaction behind the hypocritical
liberalism of Prime Minister Kálmán Széll.[15] But in that city of oriental indolence and conservatism, where there was no interest in or receptivity to whatever was new, he was unable to see it for what it really was, nor pass judgment
on it in the name of a radical progressivism. It was only in Nagyvárad, in this
intellectually alive, modern city, working in the neoliberal "workshop" of the
Nagyváradi Napló, that he came to recognize the threat posed by the alliance
of political Catholicism and agrarianism—these old and new forms of conservatism—to progress of every kind, and especially to the development of democratic patriotism.

It was when he saw the growing ultraconservatism of the Széll government
that he finally came to understand "the spirit of Debrecen": "the roaring for
the nation, gold lace, shepherds' cloak, braiding, round hats, grease, wine, and
Philistine morals," the indolence and the pot bellies; and behind all these external signs, their essence: a conservative nationalism.[16]

"The Magyar nationalists," he wrote in May of 1902, "are a great deal more
stupid than the French, and a great deal more dangerous. Magyar nationalism
is a copy of the French, except that it's augmented with the ultramontanism
[*sic*] of the Prussian junkers, with the camarilla and the anti-Semitic clericals
of Vienna, and has kept Rome as the conductor directing them all."[17]

The Ady speaking here is no longer the anticlerical radical, much less the
chic cosmopolitan. His new ideal for Hungary was shaped by Nagyvárad, that
modern, bourgeois town: "I love, admire, and esteem this town because it's
Magyar, bold, industrious, and modern. Its soul well expresses my own
credo."[18]

THE KNIGHT OF THE HOLY SPIRIT

There is no room here to trace the stages through which this credo grew into a
political program. In numerous articles—"A Short Walk," "Let's Go Back to
Asia," "The Hungarian Two-Headed Eagle," "Which Gives You Care and
Shelter," and many more—Ady brought the entire reactionary camp under attack, revealing its overt brutality and its underhanded instigations. He opened
fire on the clergy, on the big estates, on agrarian reaction, on the "barking" patriots, on the corrupt counties, and on the forces of literary reaction preaching
religious morality. He wrote of the poverty of the peasants, of starving seam-

stresses, of illiteracy, of bad taste, of the feudal "justice" being done, of the persecution of thought. The topics appear to be diverse enough, and there is a free association of images and ideas, but the overall picture gives a map of Hungary's social ills: "Socially speaking, we're still in prehistoric times. The money we'd have to spend on culture is swallowed by Austria and the army. Above and beyond all this, the fate of the nation is decided in the casino. Hungarian politics . . . is totally at the service of the privileged class."[19]

By 1902, the various points Ady had been making—behind all of which stood his commitment to a radical democracy—began to take the shape of a program: "We consider the social relations of today to be untenable. We believe and proclaim that Hungarian society—if we can speak of one at all—is immature, uneducated, superstitious, and sick. . . . We believe and proclaim that militarism, clericalism, and feudalism must be razed if we are to live."[20]

We find frequent outbursts of bitterness at the fact that the country could not be kept from total demoralization, for the Magyars were "a historical people," and tradition required that "the country belong to a few lords."[21] At Christmas of 1902, he wrote,

> In this country, only magnates, priests, and donkeys can live. And those who seek to please them. . . . They've decapitated Jacobins here, played Ides of March, made a revolution and a compromise. . . . And still there are only a few people who can really live here, and we, many millions of us, live . . . for the benefit of these few. Anyone who still wonders at this can play Jeremiah. As yet, he may still sing his laments. . . . For all that, we keep chewing on the innocuous cud of the legend of salvation. And yet! . . . perhaps one could still make something of this little country. . . . Perhaps one could do a little justice.[22]

It is a bitter and skeptical article, *Societas leonina,* in which Ady reviews two years of ceaseless struggle to shake this empire of backwardness; still he concludes on a note of "perhaps," and "and yet," refusing to give up all hope. It is not a despondent, but a defiant "and yet" that we have here; there is something in it of the spirit of Christmas, of the hope of salvation. A few days later, Ady greeted the New Year with a radical program of bourgeois reforms: industry, trade, urbanization, universities, the satisfaction of the peasantry's land hunger, an end to the miserable living conditions of teachers and public officials, the equality of all religions, and the secularization of ecclesiastical property. Here, he is not far from the Socialists' program; and in fact he concludes the article with noting that every working Hungarian is already a Socialist at heart.[23] The motif is not altogether a new one. Meditating in August of 1902 on how the *Marseillaise* had become hackneyed, he noted: "For the battle of the future, we shall need a greater, a more courageous song than the Marseillaise."[24]

Half a year later, the idea had grown to be the most radical element of his antifeudal program. In his famous "Nostra res agitur," he notes that Hungary had had no French revolution, had not yet seen the third estate come to power, "and yet it was already something anachronistic, while feudalism was hardly different from what it had been in Dózsa's days."[25]

It was at this point that he wrote the sentence that was to become so famous; the third estate, too, must be done away with: "rank, privilege, the cruelty of centuries, the aristocracy and the clergy, and exploiting capital must all be done away with at once."

It is a passage that has been much quoted and often exaggerated, with some people seeing it as the germ of the theory of "permanent revolution," when in fact the context shows it to have been the words of a radical who sympathized with the Socialists. The closing lines of the article, which shed more light on just what *nostra res* was, have been less widely quoted: "If we want to live, let's start living. Let's find a *Magyar* solution to our problems. For it's hardly an attractive prospect, is it, to picture the successors of Prussian Bebels or of Slav Bakunins doing it for us—when the German or the Slavic ocean sweeps over our helplessness!"

The cause of progress was not only the people's cause, or the cause of the radical intelligentsia, but also the cause of Hungary. Ady was making war not only on the proud feudal counties, on the bishops and the magnates, but also on Vienna. He was struggling to rescue Hungary from her dependency, but considered the destruction of the country's own two-headed eagle, clericalism and nationalism, and the renewal of Hungary's sick and corrupt society the precondition of success. Ady's idea of a Hungary reborn was part and parcel of the radical antifeudal program he worked out during his years at Nagyvárad.

What is significant in the political profile of Ady the journalist, however, is not so much the details of this program—which came very close to the one the Social Democrats presented in 1903, which he heartily supported[26] —as the sense of commitment that it testifies to. "We are," he wrote in February of 1903, "the disciples and soldiers of radical democratic progress. That's why we fought against the old county, against the contemporary county, against the superstitious, proud, familiar, feudal, anti-Semitic, repressive, and brutal County of Bihar. More precisely, against the county's petty monarchs. And our creed is the true one. Our prophecy is marvelous. The end is near."[27]

On the first of March, Ady published his journalist's credo written in the form of a letter to his father:

What, then, are we? . . . Tired Olympian gods and ostracized, despised pariahs. . . . Often we are comedians. More willing to make a deal than a horse trader, and more flexible than a reed. . . . As long as the murderous steel-nibbed devil does not beckon us. . . . Then, all the world is full of faith, all of life is worth living.

[At this point, we work ourselves into a frenzy of love] . . . for a better life, for a more decent world, for progress, for light, and for that most ephemeral, wildest, and most beautiful of all phantoms: for truth. We are the knights of the Holy Spirit.[28]

There are few more beautifully lyrical confessions of rational faith in progress than this letter. Ady had just won his first literary award; he was full of faith and confidence. His convictions, as much as all the passions of his inestimable love of life, impelled him to play an active political role. "I have never hated and loved more than now. . . . Father, you need no longer weep for your son, for he has more faith in himself and in life than ever!"[29]

His self-confidence was at its zenith in the winter and spring of 1903. Yet, strange as it might seem—and the pattern was to be a recurring one—there was also a note—at first faint, almost an overtone—of disillusionment. The first signs of it we see in his comment on the latest parliamentary maneuvers: after four years of peace, the parliamentary opposition resorted to obstructionism the winter of 1903. "The political comedy played in Hungary is worse than an amateur production, and is less honest than a racket, where at least you get no worse than you expected," he wrote in February of 1903.[30] "Who takes politics seriously? . . . One party is more loyal than the other!" he exclaims bitterly at the lack of principle displayed by the Independence politicians. Ady, however, does take politics seriously. And he is confident that the political Ash Wednesday cannot be far off.[31]

In mid-March, he goes to Venice, and is taken by the urge to travel, to see the world; he is taken by the sea. Still, a few days later, he is impatient to get home. "I long to hear the petty noises, to be part of every drop of it, to fight, to grow worn. . . . It's the only kind of life I can tolerate. . . . Addio mare, addio Venezia. I think I'll never write poetry again."[32]

He was mistaken, and not for the last time in his life. Soon he is again writing poems, and finds the spectacularly active political scene dull, and then disgusting. At the end of July, he writes: "A poor unfortunate little pauper of a country is in its death throes. . . . I accuse no one. I'm sick of politics."[33]

At the end of November, in front of his alma mater at home in Zilah, he makes a symbolic renunciation of his profession: "I've run the first great course. I was a knight of the Holy Spirit: a decent journalist."[34] The knight unbuckled his sword, and fled to the life throbbing in Paris.

THE REVOLT AGAINST POLITICS

But why this sense of hopelessness, why the defection to Paris at the moment of his greatest triumphs as a journalist? Before we try to explain it, let us do a chronological review of the developments. The first clues, as we have seen, take us to the parliamentary maneuvering around the "army question"—that is, the demand that Hungarian be introduced as the language of command in the Imperial and Royal Army. Ady is irritated by this comedy, but is not put off by it.

For quite some time, he uses the steel-nibbed devil to level some masterly blows at the ongoing nationalist demagogy. For all that, the spring was a bad time for him. Perhaps it was the broad support the obstructionists seemed to be getting, the flood of patriotic jargon that put him off; perhaps it was the after-effects of the trip to Venice. For it was there that he first noted that "the modern man of nerves" can find satisfaction only in feverish activity; and he longed to be in Paris even while he knew that "a little Swiss retreat was a more real, a more human place than Paris."[35]

His passion for life, for so long concentrated exclusively on politics, now found a new object in the expanding world around him, and in the symbol of all that he desired in it: Paris. In this frame of mind, the pettiness of domestic politics was bound to seem ever more boring. "Everyone is sick of everything," he wrote at the end of April. Public attention was on the ever more frequently occurring strikes. "The Marseillaise is no longer enough for this seething, sick world," he noted, returning to the need to go beyond liberalism to radicalism. "What we need is some new call to arms, a resistless clarion to give vent to the despair of the oppressed millions, to the sin, to the filth, and the sickness that has come to rule the earth."[36]

The image we have here might have come from Bakunin; we should note it, for we will see it again in one of Ady's poems.

By May, the daily sensations of the *ex lex* leave him practically cold. Why should this people care if there is lawlessness or not; absolutism is absolutism, implicit or explicit.[37] It is for freedom of thought that he fights his greatest battle to date, defending the Nagyvárad professor Bódog Somló from the attacks made on him by the narrow-minded forces of reaction. Throughout the country, his defense met with support, and Somló was acquitted; but Ady's sense of foreboding only grew. For though Somló was safe, reaction had made headway everywhere, even in the Freemason lodges.[38] "There's no progress here, no hope. This is Dante's sad world."[39] In early June of 1903, Ady went to jail; he was sentenced to three days' confinement for his article "A Short Walk." It was not so much the days in jail as the indifference of the liberals and the judges' willing compromise—the forces of medieval darkness—that discouraged him. "They let me have no jury; they let me call no witnesses and no experts; everything was already fixed."[40] Then the bitter jail philosophy: "I was kept awake during one of my prison nights wondering whether the only way to save mankind from its eternal suffering might not be to reorganize all of society along the lines of a prison. I'll not deny it: I still find it an attractive idea, and I don't think it . . . too foolish."[41]

Ady's doubts and disgust soon led to somber visions of the nation's destruction. His article "Bilek"—written in the biblical tone of some of his later great poetry—blames militarism for the death of the soldiers who fell victim to the rigors of the military exercises held in July. Soldiers, gendarmes, class, and state were slowly killing the people.

> Oppressed, backward, and beggarly, that's what we are. But this is not the worst of our woes. The greatest is that some horrible work is afoot here. The people of Góg and Magóg were shut away behind iron gates, but . . . at least they could pound on the iron gates. Our people cannot do that. Their arms have been chopped off and they cannot pound even the gates of hell, only tumble into the grave as cripples with bodies putrefied.

It is a frightening prospect, to see the nation degenerate and perish along with the people. In this country, it is only the dregs of the people that survive— those who get used to the diet of bread and water, who don't revolt, don't get themselves shot by the gendarmes, don't escape to America, those who resign themselves to it all. "They've gradually wiped every progressive trait off the souls of our people. Our people is doomed, for fate wants to see it doomed." But it was a fate whose name could be told with scientific precision: class society, state, gendarmerie.[42]

This article marked the zenith of Ady's journalism in the rebellious, prophetic, nation-lamenting vein. For the moment, there was no way to go on from here, just as there was no way to break out of the growing power of nationalist reaction with the sheer force of a steel-nibbed pen. There had to be a revolution, an all-destroying, apocalyptic flood; or flight to lethal love, an secession to art. It was a few days after the conclusion of the Somló affair and his own imprisonment, around June 10 of 1903, that Ady wrote his poem "Vision in the Fens." All of Ady's biographers and critics have analyzed and interpreted it. The general consensus is that it was in this poem that Ady first found poetic expression for his emotions, found his symbolism, and even his task as a poet.[43] There is good reason to doubt, however, that he also found some kind of harmony with the outside world, "a symbolic mode of expression that does not conceal, but rather depicts reality with a visionary force."[44] The circumstances in which the poem was written and its extreme flights of fancy make another interpretation much more likely. "It was the soul's consuming fever that was given linguistic form, the disenchantment with everything around him, his impatience with the future."[45]

One pole of the poem is the reality Ady saw around him: the world of the fens, grey, poor, squalid. It is a sorrowful world of evening mist and frightening visions. (It is here that we first find Ady's favorite adjectives and key symbols.) The other pole is the volcanic mountain with the sun about it—light, flame, wonder, and victory. The mist-enveloped marsh dweller longs for the brightness of the volcanic mountain. And at this point there comes the vision of the two alternative modes of escape: the salvation of all men through revolution, and individual salvation through love.

The question, of course, is whether it really is breaking out that is at issue, and whether the two modes really are alternatives.

> Perhaps it's volcanic peaks I'll climb
> My blood-red standard proudly high
> And go howling over barricades
> My bombshell words a call to ruin,
> I'll let loose a sea of sin . . .
> That it might thoroughly cleanse the earth.

In respect of both form and content, these lines are reminiscent of the specter Ady had conjured up in his articles of the previous weeks—the specter of an absolving, purifying revolution. And as much as we might be tempted to make our portrait of the young Ady a thoroughly revolutionary one, a close contextual analysis of the text warns us to forbear. For though Ady was fond of conjuring up the specter of an all-consuming revolution, he did not plan one, he did not want one.

It was in the already quoted article "Bilek" that he made clear how far he was from the popular revolutionary demagogy: "We love the sovereign people from a safe distance of three paces off."[46] Two years later, in the most dramatic moments of the Russian revolution, he noted: "One must come to terms with the people—before the conflagration."[47] Ady's real commitment was to radical democratic reform. It was his realization that this was a hopeless dream that drove him to the vision of a cataclysmic revolution, which he saw, however, not as an alternative but as total negation. It is this interpretation that is suggested by the conclusion of the poem, too: at a smile from the daughter of the devil, with her golden red hair and skin of alabaster, her red-hot breath and murderous eyes, he would cast away his banner, and

> Race, plunge to meet her,
> Burning to scorch, and aflame.

It hardly needs saying that this life-and-death plunge into passionate love was no alternative, no way out, but rather the repudiation of the social and political environment, an antipolitical escapism. Ady's view of love here was basic to both the irrational philosophy of his day and to the cult of beauty of the Art Nouveau, for love was seen as life at its most vital and intensive, and love consummated as an embrace with death. In this context, revolution and love do not appear as alternatives: the former is not the collective, the social, and the latter not the instinctive, the personal way out.[48] In reality, revolution and love were, perhaps, mutually exclusive; but in the philosophy of the fin de siècle, a purging devastation and the consummation of a mortal love were one at root. In this midsummer night's dream, revolution victorious and love consummated were of the same substance, just as abortive good intention was as sterile as a barren night of love. "Vision in the Fens," far from being the symbolic depiction of reality, much less the formulation of a realistic alternative that transcended Ady's earlier attempts to break out, was thus in fact the negation of the system, the negation of all he had attempted in the past—it was, in short, an escape from reality, an escape into an ecstatic, miraculous redemption.

In these summer days of disillusionment and desire, when Ady had lost all hope of a democratic turn, the female phantom of the fens was made flesh: Léda appeared because she had to appear, and in the eleventh hour.

> I worked for a newspaper, and wrote editorials, and would most likely have perished or started on a very wise way of life if someone had not come for me. She was a woman. . . . she took me by the hand and we never stopped until we'd got to Paris.[49]
>
> I was beginning to see the Hungarian clouds in ever sadder hues. . . . It was a woman who wanted me to speak. For I was consumed by heart-breaking thirstings and infinite desires. I felt life here to be miserable, and had long ceased to be at home here.[50]

The role that Ady's "Léda"—the beautiful and cultivated Adél Brüll—played in his life is clear enough today: it was around her that his scattered, amorphous, whirling desires took shape, and because of her that he learned to hope again though all political hope was lost. Ady stepped out of the fog enveloping the fens, and found himself in an expanded world.

"A dazzling star rises in the August sky. Venus pales beside her, and the moon takes flight," wrote Ady a few days after he first met his love.

> The whole world is consumed by fever. . . . The Cosmos is restless is in labor. Secret, mysterious streams of chaotic forces swirl. . . . Shall I be unhappy because the king is angry? Or take the fate of the national concessions to heart? Shall I trouble over foolish problems? . . . whether it's light that's coming, or reaction? . . . When the world is in a burning fever, as it is now . . . mankind is led to see the sole truth: life *is* what you take it to be; its goal is you yourself; its happiness is when, content with yourself, you make your peace with everything.[51]

Clearly enough, it was not the world but Ady who was in a fever; the truth he preached was the irrational one of one's being his own salvation. True enough, until he returned to his native village in mid-October to take stock of himself before the great step, for a few weeks he conducted a valiant rearguard action on the side of progress. But his letters revealed a restless will to be gone. "I must get out of this squalid, murderous filth; I feel I'm veritably suffocating in it," he wrote to Léda in September.[52] He was torn by doubt and self-recrimination: "It is as if I would have constantly to suffer for the last wasted, useless years. . . . Here at home, this nothing, this stupid silence is killing me."[53] "My whole being is an almost sick, burning, feverish longing for Paris, and to be gone from the filth at home. . . . I'm going and that's all there is to it."[54]

IDENTITY CRISIS

Here we might attempt an interpretation: whence this acute nausea, this feverish need to escape? Ady's friends and biographers alike see the political scene—ringing with the noise of obstructionism, and infested with corruption—as its main source. Ady, who expected that with Kálmán Száll's defeat in 1903 the powerful forces of agrarian reaction and clericalism would be pushed into the background, was ever more disappointed to see that all the excess of obstructionism not only failed to resuscitate democracy, but failed even to keep alive Tisza's brand of liberalism. The "barking patriots" terrorized public opinion; no talk of social reform, no argument was tolerated, but the agrarian and clerical nationalists, and the anti-Semites were seen as allies. After the Socialists, Ady was the first to notice that the patriotic "struggle" for military concessions and Hungarian military commands was nothing other than the expression of Magyar imperialism, and the patriotic tricolor covered nothing but the oppression of the people. Sick as he was of it all, and about to retire, Ady could not help but cry out against this pseudo patriotism: "The patriotic swineherds come, and woe to him who will not agree that Hungary has no other problem" than the issue of Hungarian as the language of command. "The herd of magnates comes, and then the camarilla, and it is summarily proclaimed that absolutism may come next."[55] With amazing clear-sightedness, Ady shows that verbose obstructionism and absolutism with its references to the Army Order of Chlopy are, in fact, the two heads of one and the same imperial eagle.

Ady's disillusionment with all this might—perhaps should—have led him to seek comrades in arms among the Socialists. Though he fights on the same side, however, Ady does not fight hand in hand with them, and does not seek his salvation in identification with them, or anyone else. This aloofness has rightly been explained in terms of the individualism characteristic of a poet, of a genius, in terms of the rigid isolation that he both complained of and so jealously guarded.

But although Ady was never one to become a part of the "holy, maltreated multitude," what kept him from total identification was not his isolation so much as the vulgar rationalism and linear evolutionism of the social democratic leaders. Nor was he the only one to be so put off. The eschatology and prognoses offered by the Second International could not offer a new intellectual identity even to those sympathetic to its aims—to, for instance, Karl Kraus, Max Weber, Kafka, and Kokoschka, to say nothing of Lukács and his circle.

The social democrats, with their vulgar materialism, understood the capitalism of Marx's days better than their own. They were unable to give a really valid account of the structural changes of capitalism or of the absurdity of the nascent imperialism, nor were they able to solve the crises of consciousness and of adjustment that these had given rise to. Their propaganda was aimed at the ideal, abstract rational man of the nineteenth century; anyone who deviated from this model was considered a servant, or dupe of reaction. They considered the ever more frequent outbursts of irrationality, mass nationalist and religious fanaticism the work of the devil; they held neuroses to be a bourgeois fashion; and they saw the anxieties permeating the alienated world of imperialism as an intellectual disease. It was not faith, but a sceptical faith, not a structured, rational utopia, but—as the contemporary Russian revolutionaries put it—a plan for "god-building," a concern for spiritual order that they lacked.

How could Ady ever have identified with this Weltanschauung?—he, a quintessentially twentieth-century man, who from early youth had premonitions of the absurdity of the century to come, who knew and understood Symbolism, the Art Nouveau, Nietzsche, Ibsen, and Bergson, who looked beyond the primal superstition of the priests and the primal crudeness of the magnates for the real causes of the crises of the religious and social order, for causes that could no longer be fathomed by an obsolete Rationality. Truly the poet of the new age, he wanted to see beyond the incomprehensible. At the same time as Rilke, Freud, and Musil, but first among Hungarians, he put the question of what would become of "spirit" denuded to a bare word,[56] and captured in poetry the demons of a spirit shivering in solitude.[57] In the spring and summer of 1903, in those days of a growing sense of political homelessness and an increasingly acute identity crisis, he realized that during the past "wasted" years the poet "had been eaten by the newspaperman, the editor, the journalist. . . . Suddenly, however, the poems wanted again to live."[58]

ART NOUVEAU AND POETRY

No direct road led Ady from the politics he had outgrown and grown weary of to a new, revolutionary politics. The first stage was the repudiation of politics as such.

Three ways of secession—emigration, love, and the psyche—opened to Ady the fall of 1903, all at once, and all together. Paris, Léda, and poetry were all parts of one great renewal, a renewal inspired, unified, and organized by Léda. Léda, the incarnation of the vision on the fens, who was at once Salome, or murderous desire, and Lou Andreas-Salome, the understanding literary mistress; at once Alma Mahler—whom she resembled even in her appearance—and first and foremost, Psyche awakened, the white woman of the castle of the spirit, who smiled at him from windows now flung wide.[59]

Ady, escaping to poetry, did so following the road typical for European writers and artists from Paris to Petersburg: *l'art nouveau*. Here I use the term not simply to refer to an artistic trend, but in the broader sense of an entire approach to life, of a withdrawal from public affairs: that is, "secession" in a broader sense. Different as the various irrational philosophies, Freudian psychoanalysis, Impressionism, Art Nouveau, Surrealism, and atonal music were, all were based on the conviction that classical philosophy and liberal-rational ideals and values were outdated and empty. The shell of academic culture, too, was left behind, as writers, artists, and scientists—alienated and traumatized by the dehumanizing effects of imperialism—withdrew from public life. Politics were left to monopolist vested interests, statist bureaucrats, and bureaucratically organized mass parties, against which the intellectuals, disappointed in their faith in Reason and the autonomy of the individual, had no adequate defense. Sezession in this sense can be seen as the antipolitical revolt of an intelligentsia divorced from its environment and from the ruling bourgeoisie, as alienation became a way of life, or as the "abreaction" of malaise and of existential anxiety. The forms it took were various: there was nihilism, the disintegration of reason; and there was also the revival of humanism, where the goal of the cultural revolt was the salvation of man.

Sezession, in this sense, was particularly vital and fruitful in Austria, in Vienna, where an all-too-soon devalued liberalism and a soon pointless Austrian national identity made for a particularly acute crisis among the intellectuals. It was in Vienna—and in a great measure, in Prague—where nationalism had been an elemental force, where National Socialism had come into being, and where the integration of modern bureaucracy with traditional absolutism appeared in its most naked and purest form, that the escape into the emotional, into sexuality, into the psyche appeared at its most suggestive and most urgent. The Viennese cultural ferment was expressive of a historical situation in which the central problems of the age were formulated not in political but in cultural terms. This being so, the repercussions they did have in public life were weak and of moot validity.

In Paris, Ady found himself exposed to a similar set of influences: a functionally disturbed political life, rationality shaken at its roots, Baudelaire's images and moods, Symbolist poetry, and love that consumes itself in the moment of consummation. Nothing shows their effect better than the four cycles of his *New Poems* (1906). The first he called "Léda's Psalms"; the second deals with home affairs from the perspective that distance gave: "On the Hungarian Wasteland." In both, we see a passionate attachment that is indissoluble, and, at the same time, a passionate arousal that is abortive. In the Léda psalms, love is not only the consummation of life, but also its completion for love was akin not only to life but also to death. Eros embraces not only Psyche but also—as in Freud—Thanatos, the god of death, for all three principles can be both linked and interchanged one with the other. In the "Hungarian Wasteland" it is the same attitude that finds expression: the knight of Nagyvárad, who would gladly blow everything sky high, ends on a note of renunciation and negation. The guffaws of the "patriotic swineherds" and of the "magnate herds" are here met with suppressed curses and the whistling of feigned indifference. Seen from Paris, the impoverished but rebellious country is a "graveyard of souls," "a plain with the stench of death." The polar opposite, the city of sunshine, singing Paris, becomes a refuge not only for the knight banished from his homeland but also for the poet fleeing from the reality of his home. The Tisza-Danube opposition gives way to the Danube-Seine parallelism. It is on the banks of the Seine that that other life comes into bloom, Life itself. It is this self-deceptive illusion of the city of sunshine that is the fulfillment of the fen dweller's vision of yore.

The "Wanderer on Virgin Peaks" cycle seems, at first glance, to be heterogeneous indeed; without a real leitmotiv, the collection seems an assemblage of "leftovers." (Let us leave open for the moment the question of how far this is a fair impression, and return to the matter after our analysis of Ady's articles of 1905.)

I do not want to analyze the *New Poems*. Plenty of literary critics have already done so. All I want to say is that the *New Poems,* and Ady's next volume, the *Blood and Gold,* are not the documents of an unambiguous, revolutionary poetic development. From the point of view of poetic technique, they certainly show maturity and artistic rejuvenation; but as political, public acts, and from the point of view of Ady's becoming a revolutionary they are undoubtedly a break, a regression—are signs of the Sezession.

THE PUBLICIST IN 1905

Ady returned in early January of 1905 to a country mad with election fever, to "Grand Guignol country." "I cried, I wept when I got on the train," he wrote to Léda's sister, Berta Brüll; "I was overcome with nausea, anger, and bitterness when I got into this rotten, hopeless city."[60] Weeks passed and he was still unable to get used to it; he kept wanting to flee in panic. Quite out of keeping with this largely politics-inspired nausea and anger was the intensity of Ady's political activity at the time. For as soon as he got home, Ady started electioneering: he wrote his daily articles, he poked fun, he fought as in the old days. This activity and his self-confessed mood are in such stark contrast that many researchers are inclined to regard Ady's chronic complaints as simply a neurotic's attempts to gain sympathy, and tend to emphasize his energetic entry into the political fray. They justify their approach by pointing to the number of his brilliant articles, and also to the fact—variously interpreted as a mistake on his part, and as a laudable stand for progress—of his having accepted a post at the prime minister's office, and of his willingness to support the nonparliamentary Fejérváry government at the end of 1905.[61] Convincing as all this might sound, for my own part I cannot accept it. On the contrary, I see 1905 as the continuation of the period of his secession from public life; it was a unique year of antipolitical revolt.

But let us reexamine the evidence. I shall not adduce as an argument a consideration that, in reality, we cannot think to have been totally irrelevant, namely, that Ady made his living writing for newspapers. He had neither a rich family nor shares in the stock market to support him; he had to write, and if at election time, then about the elections. Still, I will not dwell on this, for material considerations never influenced his thinking or his willingness to take a stand. It seems much more important to consider that of the truly great number of articles written in 1905—287 in all—a third dealt with foreign affairs, another third with theater reviews and cultural affairs. In the first month, until mid-February, we find 9 articles on foreign affairs, 9 on domestic political affairs (5 of them on the elections), and 6 cultural notes. In March, however, he wrote 8 articles on foreign, 4 on domestic political, and 10 on cultural affairs.

From then on, up to October, we find a surprising dearth of actual political articles. Of his regular columns, the "Friday Evening Letter" contained mostly theater reviews, while "This Week" and "Very Strange Stories" gave mostly anecdotes, "minute" articles that referred only indirectly to public affairs.

It is very telling that Ady did not deal with István Tisza's defeat, with the agony of the Liberal party that had been in power for thirty whole years; nor with Fejérváry's appointment, or the new government's program. His articles during these days dealt with gossip from abroad, with scientific congresses, with the colorful trivia of apolitical daily events. On carefully studying Ady's articles of 1905, we are most likely to conclude that he had become apolitical—which, of course, was not tantamount to neutrality on questions of principle, still less to ideological indifference. It is for this reason that I should like to concentrate on the motivation of those articles that did touch on questions of principle and ideology.

Of the first group of these, the better articles dealing with foreign affairs, we can easily say that their message and their function were to contrast the progress, the culture, the democracy found abroad with the reactionism and backwardness prevailing at home. The burden of these articles we can take to be summed up by the following: throughout the world, throughout Europe, "the forces of volcanic ideas have reached every society. We, too, live in Europe. To prepare for the imminent, great, and inevitable earthquake, we had better equip ourselves with some European ideals, and with some sympathy for the Hungarian people!"[62] His brilliant articles on the Russian revolution, too, show that he saw in it the new, rejuvenating earthquake that would reshape the world, a conflagration "that the whole world must pay attention to, that the whole world must attend. The time is ripe."[63]

Ady saw all too well that world progress—political as well as ideological—was accelerating, and that Hungary was getting left totally behind. What there was in this country was a "gentleman's hullabaloo," the infuriating continuation of the parliamentary comedy.

The second main point of his political articles, thus, was the revelation of the lies with which the coalition of opposition parties—the genteel ruling stratum—duped and exploited the people. Ady put words in the month of the cheated peasant, and conjured up the kuruc (peasant rebel) traditions that had been betrayed: "What's this playing kuruc all good for? . . . Do they want to discredit the days that we hold to be the best, the bravest? . . . In politics, in literature, in the arts . . . they mouth, they melodramatize away our most precious historical treasures."[64]

Much as Ady made fun of the Coalition, he saw very well what power it wielded: its power over minds and souls was nothing but taking advantage of the people's patriotism, it was the clever and dangerous demagogy of nationalism.

It was at this time that Ady developed in depth his third main topic as a journalist: the relationship between nationalism and progress, between nationalism and patriotism. In the spring of 1905 we already find the "Am I not a Hungarian?" motif which was to return again in hurt and defiant poems. "I'm no homeless villain," he wrote at the beginning of April; "But I'm beginning to feel homeless, for I can find no corner free of fatuous patriotism in all this homeland. Is this the way to build the great land of culture, where thirty million Hungarians will think there's no other merit than knowledge, ingenuity, and hard work?"[65]

That patriotism was the ideal of "honest laboring men in a common culture working for common social aims," while nationalism was nothing other than obfuscation, repression, and genocide, he explained in his excellent "The Twilight of Nationalism." Nationalism in its purest form, he tells us, that found among the Czarist ruling élite, openly cries anathema on liberty and culture. Nationalism in Western Europe is more refined, but both have a common root and a common goal: to delude the intoxicated masses. Where progress is no mere phrase, an enlightened people will tear up this poisonous plant by the roots.[66]

At a distance of seventy years, we can admire Ady's clear-sightedness in matters of principle, but we cannot help but note his naiveté in prognosticating the twilight of nationalism. Perhaps Ady watched for the signs of this twilight only to wait for it all the more impatiently. At any rate, in the months that followed, he thought to discover some hopeful signs from Tibet to Paris, and even in Hungary: "The revision of patriotism," he wrote at the beginning of July, "is coming here too. How little we will talk of our homeland then. . . . How unbiased, how cultivated, how cosmopolitan, how industrious, and how Hungarian we will be then. . . . I would be sad indeed, if we did not believe that this must come."[67]

It is here that we see that Ady's talk of the end of the bigoted, provincial, loud-mouthed, and lazy nationalism of his days—his talk of the revision of patriotism—was not so much a prognosis, the statement of a probability, as the expression of a need, of a self-sustaining faith without which the nation would be lost.

POLITICS VERSUS CULTURE

There can be no doubt that such writings of Ady, when measured against the nationalist propaganda, had some value as counter-propaganda. The *Budapesti Napló* (Budapest Journal), where he worked, was very critical of the nationalist type of opposition. In this sense, then, Ady did belong to a definite political trend, and played an indirect part in the political struggles. But that he nevertheless condemned as destructive politics as such we find from his very articles on patriotism. For he regarded creative work and cultural creativity as the essence of patriotism; their development, however—and this is the leitmotiv of his articles of 1905—was frustrated, disturbed, or forestalled by politics.

Ady had very well-defined views on the relationship of politics and culture. In 1848 and in 1867, something had gotten under way: the nation had started on the road to a European Hungary. "Besides all the patriotic phrases a bit of science, a bit of literature started to crop up. We began to look and to live a little like a cultured society. Of course, one needs politics, we especially need it, but politics is, after all, a rather low sort of thing, and everywhere throughout the world it does more harm to culture than good." But when a bit of civilization had finally gotten going, here too "there came the flood, and inundated everything. Today again, there's no one in this country interested in anything except politics."[68] In externals, we have come a long way, "But our soul! . . . That's still backward. . . . And now here comes politics. They've already got the clubs out to smite at the writer's hand. Barren heartlessness, culture-cide: all in the name of the nation."[69]

When Ady's own poetry was attacked, at the beginning of July, he exclaimed, "This air of Coalition. This new world. The world of the inquisition. Of Asia let loose. When even innocuous poems make uneasy uncultivated nervous systems not used to restlessness. . . . Intellectual life, too, is sat on—by swineherds."[70]

Commenting on the suicide of Sándor Bródy, the distinguished writer, he saw him as the victim of a tragic mistake: he believed that Hungary had become a cultured Western country. However, "self-deception can never succeed. As the example shows, not even in politics."[71]

The cause of backwardness in the sciences Ady saw in the predilection for merrymaking and disputing, and in "politics, which puts a pot belly on all."[72] We get variations on this same theme when he wrote about the great men of the past: the poet, Csokonai; Wesselényi, the reformer; the great novelist, Jókai; or a contemporary, the socialist member of parliament, Vilmos Mezőfi.

Is there any internal correlation, any consistency among the chief topics and motifs of the articles written in 1905? For my part, I find the examples of the progress to be seen abroad, the judgments passed on the Coalition for its destructive backwardness, the revision of the conservatism of the current patriotism, and the idea of an antipolitical culture to be coherent parts of a comprehensive thought. The idea Ady had in mind might be formulated as follows: since politics—nationalist politics—had become an enemy of progress and of culture, culture—the true, patriotic culture—had to be antipolitical and progressive, and had to take the lead in the nation's progress and renewal. This was the mission of the educated Hungarian intellectuals, of those who had become European in culture and in spirit—and this was also their tragedy, as the examples of Csokonai, Wesselényi, János Vajda, and Sándor Bródy indicated. Ady gave fullest and finest expression to this conception in the key essay of this stormy year, "To the Margin of an Unknown Corvin Codex."[73]

The first part of the article, "Complaint and Faith," which appeared in the spring, puts the anxious question: what will become of the Hungarians? Will they move forward, will they create something; or will they get bogged down, remain crude raw material to be shaped by the chemical processes shaping the world? The danger of decomposition and destruction was great indeed; but the ideal of a European Hungary, of the continuation of the great traditions of Transylvania, might perhaps prove the saving inspiration.[74] The Ady we have here is not the doctrinaire deprecator of the issue of military commands in the vernacular; what is at stake is Hungary's progress. For in that critical year of 1905, in Hungary, too, there came about an historical situation analogous to the one we have mentioned in connection with Vienna: the questions of the nation's fate were formulated not by high politics but by literature.

Even the title of the article's October continuation, "Weeping and Complaining" shows that all hope is now lost. The intervening six months have shown Asia to be stronger than Europe. "Strong you are, Pusztaszer, stronger than Jerusalem . . . stronger than Rome, stronger than Paris. Fear not to flaunt your glory: you'll prove stronger than Vienna. . . . Stand still, stand firm. . . . Live in the marvelously foolish faith of a Hungarian globe."[75]

But what of the European Hungarians? Those few thousands who had run ahead, "who have become European in nerves, in blood, in thought, in pain, in thirst"? Now, "when the Tartars roam free round the Carpathians," the fate of these holy couriers, of these new Gerhardts—these Hungarian Messiahs, as Ady was soon to call them—could only be crucifixion:[76] "Morituri te salutant . . . those who'd run ahead, those who'd been despoiled, the . . . Hungarians marked for martyrdom" . . . those "on whose brow Thought carelessly shows," those who can be proved to sacrifice to the god, Ideal: "the lost."[77] It is Ady's sense of doom and readiness for death which helps us make sense of his support for the government.

It is a touchy question, this issue of his progovernment stance. For the most part, we do not speak of it, or excuse it with clever and tactful reasoning. Yet it is something which, unless we think of it as an expression of political faith, needs no excusing. It is no more and no less than the flight to Paris, or the withdrawal from public affairs in the spring and summer of 1905. Ady's support for such a government was a logical step for one committed, as he was, to secession from public affairs.

For just as Paris, Léda, and his poetry of that time had been the antipolitical repudiation of the reign of terror of the nationalists' phrases, so his progovernment stand, far from being some kind of identification with the other head of the imperial eagle, was in reality a similarly antipolitical repudiation of its separatist, domestic head—was, in fact, the form of escape best suited to the scene of 1905.

A closer look at his well-known "The Danger of the Word"—the article generally adduced as evidence for his having become a government supporter—will show that its message is essentially the same as that of his "To the Margin of an Unknown Corvin Codex." Instead of phrases, the people need bread, he wrote in October of 1905, at the time the government announced its plans for social reform. It wanted to introduce a bit of Europe onto the Hungarian plains—"a terrible crime indeed." But Ady wanted to aid and abet this crime: "Reform is the only way to Hungary, to life, to truth, to culture, to liberty, to progress."[78]

RETURN TO A POLITICAL CULTURE

It might be well at this critical point to go beyond Ady's journalism, and to take into account also his moods, his state of health. "I'm very sick. Close to a total nervous breakdown."[79] "Except for the contacts I can't do without for my daily bread, I see no one," he wrote in October.[80] "It's a sick and comfortless life I live. Politics paralyzes everything here. . . . If there's an election, I'll run. . . . If I live that long. For even yesterday I was so strongly determined, there in your garden, to meet the midnight express train with my neck. . . . If there are no elections here by February 17, I'll leave Hungary."[81]

"In politics, everything is yet more topsy-turvy and hopeless than ever it was,"[82] he complained to Léda in December. Again he was thinking of flight, to Paris, to St. Petersburg, anywhere. "How I'm suffocating in Budapest, you know. . . . I don't even want to die here."[83]

Flight, however, was not so easy. His sense of responsibility for his people kept him back, more powerfully than sheer politics could have done. What hurt him most was not the flood of vilification let loose on him for his articles but the anathematization of his poetry. The conservative leading circles immediately branded his love lyrics immoral and sick, and cried out against his hard and sobering "Hungarian" poems. Anywhere else in the world these poems would have been debated in cultural reviews and literary circles. But in Hungary the new rhythms, the new imagery, even symbolism itself were counted as revolutionary—not to mention the apotheosis of modern sexuality and his

21. The title page of Endre Ady's book of poems,
Szeretném ha szeretnének (I Would Love if I Were Loved).
Budapest, 1910

declaration that Hungarian conservatism was a burial ground. There could be no flight for Ady; for though he had lost his place in the declining gentry world both socially and politically, he felt his national identity all the more deeply, and suffered for it more keenly in these critical days than ever he had as a young journalist. He had no choice but to stand his ground, though tragedy hovered over him.

As soon as Ady read the venomous reviews of his earliest poetry, he knew that he had hit upon a field of action where the Hungarian progressives had the better of the nationalist reactionaries. And, sitting behind closed doors in the editorial office of the *Budapesti Napló*, looking over the proofs of his first book of poetry just before Christmas, he suddenly realized that revolutionary revival had to start—or had, perhaps, already started—not in the political but in the cultural sphere. And then, in the midst of his consuming sickness, politi-

cal disenchantment, the scars of lost battles, and persistent yearning to be
gone, there came back to him the bewildering experience of that restless summer of 1903: the sons of Góg and Magóg pounding vainly on iron gates, the fu-
tile struggles of the journalist trying to find an answer in politics. And then,
looking for a motto for his poems, there came to him the defiant "and yet."[84] It
was this recollection that made him use the past tense in "and yet I asked you";
that inspired the new song that he was determined to sing after all, inspired the
faith that was "victorious, new, and Magyar after all," with "victorious" being a call to battle, "new" standing for the "renewer," and "Magyar" for the
people as opposed to the decadent nobility.

It is in this context that we can try now to answer the question of why the
"Wanderer on Virgin Peaks" cycle, especially the mood and atmosphere of the
closing poem, "I Walk on New Waters," differs so greatly from the pessimism
of "Notes on an Unknown Corvin Codex," an article with a similar motif.
Ady, the journalist, saw no hope of convincing the masses intoxicated with the
heady wine of nationalism; he saw no hope of overcoming Pusztaszer. Ady, the
poet, however, knew that Pusztaszer could deride him and anathemize him as
it would, the future would claim him for its own. This might well be the reason
that although the tone of the other cycles of the *New Poems* are sadder, more
pessimistic than the tone of the articles written at the same time, this last cycle
ends on a hopeful, victorious note.

There are two conclusions that we can draw from the decline of Ady's radical journalism, and his withdrawal from public life in 1903, and then his return
to the public stage in 1905 as a poet. The first is that the sociopolitical complexion of the country was not one that would tolerate artistic secession, the
escape into pure aesthetics; nor would it permit a retirement from politics. The
second conclusion is that the progressives were not yet prepared for a political
offensive; to rally their forces, they had to start in the cultural sphere. The revolt of the intellectuals in Hungary, then, had to be political, although its advocates were exorcised from public life a hundred times over; and it had to have
faith in progress, although its champions had long ceased to regard a rationally instituted liberalism as the road to salvation.

The "And Yet" Morality

This—the point at which the Hungarian "genteel estate" took the offensive,
and Ady returned from his secession a revolutionary poet—brings us to the
end of the period to be discussed.

In the years that followed, during the Coalition government of the former
opposition, the scattered forces of Hungarian democracy gained in strength
and organization. Ady appeared to be firmly committed to radical, active politics, although he was often moody and sceptical about it all. Had this remained a constant state of his, we could take 1906 to mark the end of a definite

phase of his life, of the start of his career. The two motives that determined his conduct during these years, however—secession and return: antipolitical, artistic revolt against the political order, and a politically committed radical offensive—stayed with him throughout his life. From Hungary, from this "graveyard of the soul," where there was "the stench of death," Psyche would always want to flee; here, she would always be tempted to accept alienation as a form of existence. But here, where Death had been sown but the "seeds of anger" were coming to fruition, here, along the Danube, the rebelling intellect must choose not alienation but the veto and protest decreed by fate, setting community ethics up against the cult of the aesthetic, and the "and yet" morality against the sense of hopelessness.[85] After 1906, too, the revolutionary poems and calls to arms are followed by the tired gestures of resignation; in fact, the two moods seem, at times, to coexist. It is at this time that Ady—perhaps the first in modern Hungarian literature to do so—formulated the creed of a faith without illusions.

> Every one of our ideals
> Is everywhere else tired junk,
> We go to battle
> Already knowing we fight in vain. . . .
> There's no Easter for Hungary
> Yet to write, to do
> We're still driven by great commands

—he wrote this in early March of 1910.[86] A few weeks later, after the commemoration of the 1848 revolution, he noted, almost as a challenge, that the March sun had not ignited a revolution in Hungary in a thousand years: "We've always sat in icy languor."[87] Not long after, he gave a prose formulation of the tragedy of "men of two minds":

> We demand the most complete democracy, and shout for universal and equal suffrage and the secret ballot with the integrity of martyrs, although the results these have brought to societies hundreds of years ahead of us have secretly cured us of any real desire for these things. . . . Our philosophy . . . would fain embrace a bit of metaphysics. We smell God everywhere . . . and being decent men we feel obliged . . . and indeed are duty bound . . . to organize liberal societies . . . without God. . . . These people are really tragic heroes, for they are right to hold discourse with themselves, and they are right to look around this colonial, factious, mixed, impoverished, priest- and magnate-ridden country. . . . I am proud to declare myself a man of two minds in this unfortunate country.[88]

The thought of revolution seemed least hopeless in 1912, that dynamic year in Hungary's history. Seeing the huge crowds of demonstrators, and hearing of the planned general strike, Ady felt that the earthquake had come, that events were rushing toward the revolution.

Instead of the general strike, however, it was István Tisza who came, and with him the rule of more overt force; and instead of the revolution, there came the world war. Ady saw the turn that events had taken as early as 1913.

As yet the guns could be heard only in the Balkans when bloody specters rose up before him.

> It's all the same to us; it can be no worse here.
> The earth is shaking, my young friends
> . . . And we'll put something better for all that there is,
> Or all is lost here, amen, for ever.[89]

Then, when all hell really did break loose, Ady—sicker and sicker—withdrew completely. His place as leader was "at the head of the dead." Practically from the first moment he knew, and then declared with growing certainty, that what had started was a ghostly horror story. It was a game in which mankind would be the loser, and Hungary many times over. It was during the war years that an existential anxiety came completely to rule him. He had a presentiment of the apocalyptic times to come; and as for Hungary, he could only resign her to her fate with an "it's all the same."

In the spring of 1915, he wrote:

> It's all the same, my friend, to me
> If wolves eat me, or the Devil,
> But surely we will be eaten.
>
> If a bear eats us, it's all the same.
> The sad, age-old thing is:
> It's a matter of chance who eats me and you.[90]

But even in these deadly years, the "and yet" morality confronted and contested this "it's all the same." What it enjoined now, however, was not participation, but preservation; not revival, but survival. In these years, not much remained for a committed intellectual but to safeguard the seed under the blanket of snow, to preserve man in the flood of inhumanity, to fan the flames of faith in beauty when all around was a mindless and bloody horror.

Chapter Six

THE CULTURAL ROLE OF THE
VIENNA-BUDAPEST OPERETTA

OPERETTA is one of the most rewarding topics of cultural history. Imagine a performance in an average musical theater. Its libretto is primitive and silly (if not idiotic), unbelievable, and ridiculous. Its music is a mélange of cheap opera arias and fashionable dance music full of sentimental commonplaces and a few melodious hits for everybody to whistle at home. In most cases, operettas cannot be measured by high aesthetic or dramatic values. Yet, despite all its deficiencies, operetta always was and is very popular, particularly in Central Europe, the old Habsburg Monarchy and its successors—not only with ordinary people and the lower middle classes but also with the educated upper classes, creative intellectuals, musicians, and writers. Operetta effortlessly cuts across regions, countries, and nations, and across social strata; it is interregional, international, and transpersonal. Its success is really an intriguing question for cultural historians.[1]

Answering the question requires a short historical overview of operetta's genesis. The mixed ancestry of the operetta ranges from such elegant forms as opera buffa, through the specifically German Singspiel, down to the knockabout farce of the fairground. Included among its precursors are a few glittering names (Pergolesi, Mozart, Donizetti) and many more that are dimly remembered or simply lost in the passage of time (Schenk, Dittersdorf, John Gay, and Papusch).[2] Operetta that is merely elevated Singspiel, or debased opera, however, belongs to the infancy of the genre. Operetta proper arose in the Paris of the 1850s and represented the most conspicuous cultural product of the emerging middle classes. Its creator, who brought it to a high state of perfection, was Jacques Offenbach.[3]

The overwhelming success of the Parisian operetta (and shortly afterward the English and Viennese offerings in the same genre) may be attributed to three principal factors: first, the freshness and wit of the music, which drew inspiration from the most melodious elements of opera but which avoided opera's sentientiousness and melodrama. (Indeed, these aspects of opera were frequently mocked in operetta.) Its music was also sufficiently uncomplicated to make it suitable for home rendition and to supply amateur musicians with a ready-made repertoire of dance music and stylized "folk music."

Second, plots of operettas dexterously combined escapism with gentle political and/or social satire. Thus, they pandered to the sentimentality while exposing the hypocrisy of the audience and that of the ruling classes.

Third, operetta provided its audience with spectacle on a grand scale—glittering costumes, elaborate scenery, slick choreography—theatrical elements that are nowadays known as lavish production values. In operetta, the formerly exclusive hybrid art of opera broadened its appeal and was transformed into a medium of metropolitan mass entertainment. Clearly, the one indispensable prerequisite of the birth and development of the operetta was the metropolis. Each form and genre of public entertainment had its social setting and spatial environment, from the antique polis and the Renaissance princely court to the modern city. The nineteenth-century metropolis developed a massive need for typically urban forms of entertainment and professional groups of critics, writers, composers, and actors. In the second half of the nineteenth century, traditional opera became increasingly a minority interest whose elite audience of connoisseurs was able to follow it into the abstract and intellectual realm of Wagner and of post-Wagnerian music. Belles lettres, theater, and music of the urban high culture segregated rather than integrated the society of the metropolis. But operetta constituted popular culture, appealing equally to the upper and middle classes and even more to those down the social scale.

In Vienna, specifically advantageous circumstances came together for the new genre. Vienna was the European city whose multiethnic society had always inclined to cosmopolitanism; its loyal subjects admired but at the same time ridiculed the aristocracy and the absolutist bureaucracy. The Baroque and Biedermeier traditions of the city complemented each other: piety and sensuality, loyalty and ironic skepticism—all brought music and humor together at the same time in the operetta.

The genre had deep roots in the country. The old Viennese folk comedy, with its hundreds of well-known roles, goes back to the eighteenth century.[4] So does the dance music of the empire in the first half of the nineteenth century (the Austrian and German waltz, Länder, the Czech and Polish polka and mazurka, and the Hungarian csárdás). The type of play known as Singspiel, however, influenced by the Parisian operetta, received a new name and new sense in the second half of the century. This was shown by the stormy success of Offenbach and the French operetta and its quick adoption by Suppé, Millöcker, and above all, in Johann Strauss's works.[5] Viennese operetta conspicuously differed from its Parisian model from the very beginning, however it was not so relentlessly ironical. In its music it did not adopt an acrid, playful humor, but rather a daydreaming melody, a sweetness, a sentimentality, as its leitmotiv. This is what audiences liked so much in Suppé's *Die Schöne Galathée* and *Bocaccio,* and especially in Strauss's great operettas.

I shall not analyze Strauss's oeuvre here.[6] But I do want to introduce *The Gypsy Baron*, which I regard as the most representative of his works, from the cultural historian's point of view.

Strauss was close to sixty when he started work on *The Gypsy Baron*. He himself, just like the genre, seemed to be tiring out. Oh, those 1880s! That was the exceptional decade when peace and quiet reigned in the Habsburg empire. The Compromise of 1867 between Austria and Hungary had created a climate of political stability in which a Central European version of constitutional liberalism could exist, underpinned by a period of economic prosperity and international security. In this climate Strauss, as well as the public, desired something entirely new. His Hungarian friends—who constituted a specific bilingual channel between Vienna and Budapest—had been suggesting for some time that he pick a Hungarian subject and that he turn to the famous writer Mór Jókai. The summit between the King of the Waltz and the Hungarian Prince of Writers took place at the beginning of September 1883.[7]

Jókai offered a ready-made formula for a romantic play by turning to a topic of the past in the Hungary recovered from the Turks. There you will find wasteland, swamp, and burnt-out villages wherever you look. He populated this romantic landscape with romantic people, in this case with Gypsies: "This nice, vagrant people will automatically bring success on the stage of the opera house."[8] The formula also called for some treasure to be found in the play. An operetta in which the hero scraped together his fortune by hacking and grubbing the soil for thirty years would hardly have any impact; the public would say, we can also gather together a little fortune penny by penny. More effectively, money should fall from heaven, or it should emerge suddenly from the belly of the earth. And in this romantic landscape, lovers should find each other while looking for buried treasure; they should not be married by a priest, at least until the end of the play. The music to accompany the wedding of Jókai's lovers should be supplied by birds and crickets.

Strauss immediately liked the subject, especially when Joseph Schnitzer presented him with a libretto translated into German and improved by witty lyrics. He took his time, however; he worked on the operetta (which, incidentally, found its way to the opera house, too, at the end of the century) for almost two years.[9] In *The Gypsy Baron*, which opened in October 1885, all the ingredients of a romantic musical play are brought together. There is Barinkay, the Hungarian nobleman in exile, who will be pardoned by the kind empress (Maria Theresa), and who will also recover his lands; the upstart pig dealer, who will allow only a baron to marry his daughter; honest, kind-hearted Gypsies; and Saffi, the beautiful Gypsy girl, who turns out to be a princess, the daughter of the last pasha in Temesvár. There is also some hidden treasure in the play, which the lovers will find. The Austrian bureaucracy is duly mocked, yet the Hungarians' patriotism will protect the Monarchy and its young empress from the Spanish. The final product is an ingenious composition extracted from the musical treasury of almost all the peoples in the Monarchy. We can hear polkas, recruiting music (the *verbunk*), and Gypsy songs, with the waltz binding them all together.[10] At the end of the second act, a recruiting song is heard that had been composed by a genuine Gypsy musician in 1848.[11] At the seventy-fifth performance in 1886, even the Rákóczi March, which had been strictly banned since the Revolution of 1848, rang out for the first time on stage in Vienna. Again, the ingeniously constructed finale is bound together by Viennese music.[12]

The piquancy of the story is that the operetta was constructed of elements rooted in real life. The original model of Barinkay was an actual man (Botsinkay), an artiste in a circus touring abroad before he was given back his land.[13] The romantic story pieced together from romantic fragments and Strauss's well-spiced, Hungarianized, sweetly plaintive Viennese music brought him a worldwide success that reverberates even today.

It was a sweeping success. Up to the end of the last century there had been more than three hundred performances in Vienna, and over a hundred in Budapest; it was translated into seventeen languages and performed in several dozen cities ranging from New York to St. Petersburg. Theater critics received it with praise, even with adulation at times, although there were some critical remarks as well.[14] Critics in the Budapest press disapproved of the fact that Barinkay was played (in the absence of a tenor) by a pretty prima donna, Ilka Pálmay, with a boyish grace. But gone was the projection of Hungarian manly strength.[15] The press objected most of all to the fact that Schnitzer, who adapted the story written by Jókai, had changed the essence to suit Viennese taste. Jókai's compliance with the change was deemed a mistake. "If somebody is a big enough star to illuminate all of Hungary, why does he want to be a tallow candle on the music-stand of a Viennese musician?" wrote one of the comic papers.[16] Some praised him, saying that "the alliance between the Viennese waltz and the Hungarian csárdás is piquante and new," while others protested against the "waltzification" of the patriotic Hungarian world of music.[17] There were also critics who considered this romantic idyll to be outdated: "waltzes do nothing but thump emptily," wrote a critic in the Viennese *Extrablatt*.[18] This type of cultural criticism was expressed most sharply by Hermann Broch.

Broch compared three types of operettas: one by Offenbach, one by Sullivan, and one by Strauss. Even the best of the satirical tendencies is lost in Strauss's operetta. The ironic notes in Raimund and Nestroy "have disappeared, too, without any trace, and nothing has remained but a copy of the comic opera simplified to idiocy. . . . This is how the operetta form founded by Strauss has become a specific vacuum product: it is only as a vacuum decoration that it has proved to be maintainable."[19]

There is some truth in the contemporary criticism and in Broch's views. In Strauss's operettas, social criticism was mild, the irony sugary; and there were more sentimentalism and drive for reconciliation than in operettas staged in Paris or London. Nevertheless, we would be unfair not to appreciate the softer ironies of the Jókai-Schnitzer-Strauss trio. On the stages of Vienna and Budapest, it was not outdated at the time to mock the extremely formal and old-fashioned bureaucracy and the hypocritical "Commission of Morals" (*Sittenkommission*), and it was very much in vogue to praise the freedom of love and even the legality of marriage without the clergy's blessing—especially in the years of frustrated clerical reforms. In *kaiserlich-königlich* Vienna, even at the end of the century, it took considerable courage to play a Hungarian military song of the 1848 Revolution, especially the Rákóczi March. The fact that this piece of music was oppositionist and critical is made manifest by the disapproval of the authorities and its success with the people.

It would be unfair on our part, however, to measure the Viennese-Budapest operetta on the scale of London or Paris. In those two cities, characterized by a relatively homogenous national atmosphere and a strong middle class, the critical function of the operetta was to provide social and political satire. In the Dual Monarchy, however, other priorities prevailed. It had been only one and a half decades earlier that the Compromise was signed; the grudge was still vividly alive both in Budapest and in Vienna. It was very much up to date to pacify the grudges and hurt feelings created by the absolutist retaliation of 1869. Franz Jauner, director of the Theater an der Wien, who was among the really well informed, said after the premiere,

> The performance of the Gypsy Baron has been the greatest theatrical experience in my life. . . . The Gypsy Baron is a victory: a demonstration for the Hungarians, for democracy. A wonderful manifestation of fellow-feeling which has been glowing in the air for more than half a century but only exploded now . . . this operetta has been due to come on the scene since July 3rd, 1866, when Benedek lost the battle of Königgrätz. After the catastrophe, the thought occurred to many responsible: the Hungarians must be conciliated. . . . Consequently they were happy that someone at last stepped out in front of the Hungarian audience, made Barinkay a hero, and laughed loudly at the caricature of Metternich censorship.[20]

By the way, the Hungarian verse to the song mocking the Commission of Morals was written by Jókai himself. Hence it is not an exaggeration to say that *The Gypsy Baron* itself was also a part of the compromise process, the reconciliation of hearts, a political agreement narrated in words and music. Its integrating effect was not confined to the Austrian and Hungarian public. In the

Monarchy, fading state patriotism, history, and belles lettres proved incapable of creating a common civic ethos, which could be accomplished only through music and the arts. In the Empire, it was only within the army that German prevailed as the language of service. In public and private life, a dozen languages, idioms, national feelings competed with each other. Only Mozart, Haydn, Schubert, Brahms, Liszt, Smetana, Dvorák, Goldmark, Strauss, Lehár, and Kálmán were able to create a language commonly understood by all peoples, lands, and cities, a kind of community of cultural identity. Accordingly, we agree less with Hermann Broch than with Franz Werfel: "In this banal form of art the old Austria is reflected with all her rhythm, all her wit." Moreover, "the whole old opera form could keep itself cleaner here and this way survive in the people's minds."[21]

In the Monarchy, the integrating function played by operetta did not confine itself to the creation of a city culture or the integration of multicolored group cultures: it had a wider scope—a role that was much more important from a cultural-historical point of view. The Viennese and the Budapest operetta gathered something from the music and dances, the characteristic figures, and mentalities of all the peoples living in the Monarchy; it had an overall "Monarchic" character. In this way it related to every nation. The vacuum that Hermann Broch had shrunk back from in horror perhaps did exist in the aesthetic and philosophical sense. But in everyday life, although very faintly—only as a second theme—a realistic value existed. This was the coexistence and peaceful cultural interaction of the nations and peoples in Central Europe. The Viennese-Budapest operetta definitely contributed to the formation of a common mass culture in the Monarchy, thereby contributing to cultural integration.

Operetta was able to enjoy a new lease on life at the beginning of the twentieth century, when a fundamental shift took place in historical and cultural attitudes. National and social tensions accumulated within the Empire along with diplomatic conflicts abroad. Romanticism lost its attraction, and styles of historicism and naturalism also became outdated. The primary source of the operetta form, the Viennese Singspiel and the Budapest play about the idealized peasant, dried up, and the operetta of "the golden age" fell into a crisis. It is enough to say that the home of the musical theater, the Theater an der Wien, was closed down at the beginning of the century, and all other theaters also had to struggle.[22] In the turbulent and decadent fin-de-siècle atmosphere, the question was raised as to whether the Viennese-Budapest operetta could be rejuvenated and adjusted to the sentiments and expressions of the new age.

Just at this time of crisis, signs of a real rejuvenation appeared on the stage. In Vienna it was mostly Leo Fall's modernized operettas that became popular; in Budapest it was the work of Jenö Huszka, whose *Prince Bob* (called *The Vagabond Prince* in the United States) was the first hit of the new century, in both city and countryside. Referring to the amazing success of *Prince Bob,* a young journalist of *Nagyvárad* pointed out how misguided it would be to de-spise operetta as a naive and foolish genre. As a matter of fact, "the operetta is a most serious theatrical genre. It is the one with which we can freely strike out kings without danger. . . . It can destroy more of this rotten world and better prepare the future than five protests in Parliament."[23] The young journalist was Endre Ady, Hungary's greatest poet of this century.

Yet another Hungarian poet, Gyula Juhász, wrote with good reason several years later that "the center of the European operetta had shifted into the Austro-Hungarian Monarchy, and it is slowly but surely coming to Hungary." Juhász attempted to explain the reason for this successful shifting of the genre toward the East. The drama had not yet found its new form, he argued; it does not correspond to the requirements of the age of the newspaper and the movie. The operetta, however, "is a quickly moving story with much easy lyricism and music, much decoration and little earnestness." These are just what the audience is longing for, particularly in eastern Central Europe, which is not mature enough for Ibsen and Hauptmann.[24]

The most representative figure of the rejuvenation, "the silver age" of the operetta, is Franz Lehár, and his most representative play is *The Merry Widow*. Lehár was a characteristic figure of the old Empire: a man of a "Habsburg na-tionality."[25] His family came from Moravia; they were probably the descen-dants of Germanized Slavic peasants and craftsmen. (According to family leg-end, however, a French officer by the name of Le Harde stayed in Austria during the Napoleonic wars; his descendant would be the military musician Lehár.) What we know for certain is that the composer's father was the con-ductor of a military band and that he traveled throughout the Empire with his family, from his birthplace Komárom to Kolozsvár (Cluj), from Prague to Sa-rajevo. The young man had a promising musical talent and attended the con-servatory in Prague. He was a great admirer of Antonin Dvořák. He was study-ing to become a violinist, but decided to follow his father's path; he became the leader of a military band for twelve years and toured the Empire from Losonc to Vienna. The long time he spent in the military band had two advantages. This institution, which was so popular in the Monarchy, also had an inte-grative role (see Figure 22). Its conductor was expected to know all musical genres, the novelties of Vienna, the local folklore, and the changes in taste of the mass culture. It was in this atmosphere that Lehár's musical talent un-folded, together with his sensitivity toward the public. The new director of the Theater an der Wien, Vilmos Karczag, a Hungarian theater entrepreneur, made the right choice when he offered the young Lehár a position as a com-poser by the side of two talented librettists.

The two librettists, Victor Leon and Leo Stein, discovered a work gathering dust among secondhand librettos, written by the witty playwright Henri Meil-hac, entitled *L'attaché*. They made some cosmetic changes and placed the lo-cale of the story in a small state in the Balkans, which they called Pontevedro.

22. Military band in the Prater. Vienna, 1896

The embassy of this small state was commissioned to save Hanna Glavari, the immensely rich widow from Pontevedro, for her homeland—together with her millions, of course. To achieve this, the handsome attaché of the embassy had to win Hanna to his side. However, Hanna was afraid of dowry hunters, while Danilo was afraid of being taken for one. A passionate breakup was followed by an equally passionate reconciliation and a most passionate embrace. Boy wins girl and the fatherland is saved.

What is so new, so fascinating about this story? In the story line, nothing, but there are significant innovations in the lyrics. Gone is the Biedermeier sentimentality: frivolous city humor and criticism of capitalism, bourgeois morals, marriage, and diplomacy take its place. "We widows are in demand. . . . But when we poor widows are rich, why then, our value is doubled," signs Hanna in her entrance. Marriage, Danilo retorts, is like a Dual Alliance in the beginning, "but soon the league's increased to three [Triple Alliance]. . . . Madame too readily adopts the policy of open doors!" For these new cavaliers even the fatherland is not sacred any more. What do we hear in Danilo's famous Maxim song? "And then the champagne flows, and often can-can goes. And there's fondling, kissing, with all these charmers . . . they make me forget, then, the dear father-land!"[26]

The real novelty and attraction, however, lay not in the lyrics but in Lehár's music. When he finished the first song, he called his librettist well after midnight and played "Dummer, dummer Reitersmann" (Foolish, Foolish Knight) to him, and though Mr. Stein was sleepy and irritated, he had to admit that "the waltz had a strict but flexible rhythm, it was seductive, and explicitly erotic."[27] In describing Lehár's music, Bernard Grun holds that the absolute novelty of the piece lies in the ingenuous boldness by which the plot musically interprets the ever-vibrating sensuality. The melodies speak about nothing but desire, passion, instinct, embrace, lovemaking. "Libido has dominated there where pure love, . . . psychology where simpleness once prevailed." But the interpretation is new, breaking all conventions; it freely alters major keys with minor keys and uses different musical elements. Hanna's entry begins with a mazurka and ends with a Parisian slow waltz, her Vilia song. A soft and sentimental romance is finished off with a fast and sarcastic polka rhythm played by the orchestra. No doubt Lehár uses musical colors and harmonies that he must have heard in the works of Debussy, Richard Strauss, and Mahler.[28]

The operetta takes place in Paris, with Parisian scenery. This local color is, however, merely a façade behind which the story resembles scenes from Vienna and east Central Europe. Both the mocking spirit (making fun of the aristocracy, the nouveaux riches, and ardent patriotism) and the heroine, Hanna, who could be from Budapest, Prague, or Zagreb, are first and foremost Viennese.

In *The Merry Widow, The Count of Luxemburg,* and some other works, Lehár performed a real feat of daring. With his remarkable compositions of rejuvenated operetta he managed to reintegrate a very differentiated city culture in which the more and more esoteric and alienated high culture was sharply segregated from the mass productions of the entertainment industry. Lehár's operettas spoke about the city to the people of all strata and kinds living in the city; even the people of the nightclubs in working-class neighborhoods danced to the new and refreshing sounds of the dance music seeping out of the upper middle-class saloons.

The Merry Widow opened in Vienna on December 30, 1905. During the first ten years it was performed four hundred times there and one hundred fifty times in Budapest. The fact that Budapest accepted and became enamored of the lovely, sensual widow with the wonderful voice shows that the capital had truly become a metropolis. On the other hand, the other half of Budapest's heart was still drawn toward modernized national romanticism represented by *János Vitéz* (John the Hero), composed by Pongrác Kacsóh. The enormous success of this musical play surpassed even that of Lehár and Strauss, testifying that the new metropolis was strongly attached to the glorious past, a national nostalgia that inundated the eastern Central European mentality.[29]

Together with Lehár, the independent Budapest operetta blossomed in the first decade of our century. What were the main features of its spectacular rise in popularity?

As we saw in Lehár's *The Merry Widow,* some Budapest operettas also became more "democratic"; they were imbued by a strong antifeudal and anticapitalist spirit. This meant at first a more explicit ironical criticism of the "feudal-capitalistic" society, and a growing importance of popular figures. Not only attractive actresses and music hall girls advanced into the ranks of higher society, but also common people, waiters, and stable boys played protagonist roles, as in Albert Szirmai's play, the *Mágnás Miska.*

Together with "democratization," structural changes also took place in the librettos. Beside the usual couple who embodied great romantic love, a second couple appeared in the new librettos: the soubrette and the comic dancer. They counterbalanced and made fun of the first, often boring couple: they brought humor and nonconformity onto the stage.[30]

Finally, the rising Budapest operetta rejuvenated the world of music, too. Beyond traditional waltz and csárdás, it adopted more popular elements and later incorporated modern ragtime rhythms. Outstanding composers like Jacobi, Juszka, Kacsóh, and Szirmai were not ingenuous amateurs but musicians who had graduated from music academies, who had learned composition and orchestration.

Claim to the most vigorous talent could be made by Imre Kálmán, who was born on the shores of Lake Balaton, in Siófok, in 1882.[31] The family consisted of rich bourgeois entrepreneurs who went bankrupt when Kálmán was only a child. Like Lehár, who had wanted to become a violinist, Kálmán longed to be a pianist, but his chronic myositis was a deterrent. What was left was composition—and operetta. His operettas represent an overall Monarchic identity: they are set in the Empire, the protagonists are the aristocracy, the army, soldiers, Gypsies, and citizens. The music of the *Tatárjárás* (The Autumn Maneuver) and the *Gypsy primás* (the leading violinist in a Gypsy band) embodies Viennese waltzes, military marches, couplets, and Gypsy music like that of his greatest hit, *The Csárdás Princess.*[32]

The subject of the libretto of *The Csárdás Princess* is banal hackwork—the romantic love story of a Budapest music hall prima donna, Sylvia Vereczki, and Prince Edwin Lippert-Weilersheim. Their love is so strong and pure that it overcomes all obstacles—the resistance of aristocratic parents and all the machinations of high society. The libretto, a buffoonery of the Golden Age, was born in the cloudless spring of 1914. When war broke out, Kálmán lapsed into silence. It took him a year of solitude in a villa in Bad Ischl to compose the operetta, perhaps as a protest against the worldwide massacre.[33] *The Csárdás Princess* opened in Vienna on November 17, 1915, during the fourth Isonzo offensive in northern Italy. That prolonged attack resulted in 440,000 deaths and more than double that number of casualties.

In spite of daily tragedies, the new operetta had startling success. By April 1917, there were five hundred performances in Vienna, two hundred in both Berlin and Budapest, and in Stockholm, Gothenburg, Hamburg, Cologne, Munich, Hanover, Leipzig, and Frankfurt over a hundred performances.[34]

The people, heavily weighed down by the calamities of war, misery, and death, wanted to forget: they delighted in this operetta that evoked the world of the music hall, in which love and song, not lords and death, prevailed. And in *The Csárdás Princess,* Kálmán crystallized all the inventions, tricks, and accomplishments of the Budapest operetta. He created a stylistic mélange out of the piquant wit of the Parisian operetta, the sweetness of Viennese music, and stylized Hungarian gypsy music, blending them with the typical figures, jokes, and musical expressions of the opera buffa and the Budapest-Berlin cabaret. In his fairy tale, dreams of the glittering marriage of a poor girl symbolizing the triumph of love were intertwined with a satire on the idiotic conventions of the nobility. This ambivalence can be seen in the main characters of *The Csárdás Princess*—Prince Edwin and the prima donna Sylvia. He is a handsome, pleasing man infatuated with Sylvia, and his love seems sincere and serious. But he possesses neither a strong moral character nor even a mediocre intelligence. Sylvia provokes admiration. She comes from a small, distant village on the banks of the river Tisza, and achieves a miraculous career evolving from a village elf to a music hall angel and finally to a real court princess, without losing her innocence. Because of the absurdity of such a character in twentieth-century Central Europe, the libretto relativizes here genuine chastity. In the opening song she declares: "If you only want to have fun, keep away from me, darling!" And for the sake of unequivocal understanding, her partner adds the warning: "You cannot get Sylvia for 'something' [for a conventional love affair]." She does not permit stupidity. Here one must make an offer of marriage or go away."[35]

Characteristic of the operetta is the unmasking of Prince Edwin's mother, who firmly resisted the planned misalliance. At the end of the play, however, it is revealed that the mother once had been a music hall performer too, and had preserved her reputation only by marrying each lover in turn. Having thus been unveiled, she succumbs and gives her blessing.

Finally, we have to mention an important ingredient of the operetta's success—lyrics that greatly contributed to keeping an ironical distance from the fairy tale. The lyrics and the Hungarian translation were written by a talented humorist—an expert of the theater and the music hall—Andor Gábor. His sparkling lyrics are witty couplets mixing folklore and metropolitan elements, creating an unmistakably Pest slang of aristocratic, Jewish, German, and other idioms. Gábor's text is parody at its best.

The deepest secret of *The Csárdás Princess,* however, lies in its fascinating music. "Melodies that go on lying in our hearts entwine our souls like the odor of wonderful flowers," wrote a viewer in the magazine *Szinházi élet* (Theater Life). "Imre Kálmán is a magician. . . . His music drives all sorrow away and tells about a wonderful love. . . . We believe him as the little child believes his mother when she relates to him a fairy tale."[36] The operetta is "bubbling over with blood-boiling Hungarian rhythm, Hungarian songs, brilliant orchestration," said a Budapest daily, the *Budapesti hirlap.*[37] "His greatest merit is that he refreshes the operetta with the enchanting aura and pulsating vitality of the

Hungarian folk song, whose ability to get the blood circulating had already been slackening . . . because of sugary Viennese sentimentalism." The reviewer of the *Pesti hirlap* was not enchanted, however. Kálmán has sacrificed his art for "cheap effects . . . regarding popularity that brings happiness as the only major objective." There are many lovesick Viennese waltzes in his work—"they were written by Emmerich, but there is also a lot of interesting atmospheric Hungarian music in it as well: they are the works of Imre Kálmán." The reviewer commented that the Hungarian translator, Andor Gábor, however, spiced the dialogues with ideas and good humor.[38] The text is parody at its best.

Perhaps the secret of the integrative power and world success of the operetta lies in this ambivalence of interpretation. It could be taken literally as a fairy tale: within the magical world of the stage the everyday laws of bourgeois reality are suspended. Or it could be perceived as a parody of the evils of militarism and bureaucracy, of all the faults of the Establishment. One could even discreetly buy the sheet music of the operetta—just as Gustav Mahler bought *The Merry Widow*—and enjoy playing and humming it in the privacy of one's home.[39]

This view may be supported by the worldwide success of *The Csárdás Princess* during World War I. It was first performed in Vienna in the autumn of 1915, a year later in Budapest, then in Paris, St. Petersburg, and Moscow in 1917. The operetta penetrated the trenches, the minefields, and all frontiers. A Viennese critic could write in 1917: "The whole world resounds with two things: the roar of the cannon and the success of *The Csárdás Princess*."[40]

The power of the operetta to effect social integration on both an internal and international level prevailed during World War I and World War II, between the wars, and in spite of the wars in our century. This genre is part of mass culture. Its standards may vary, but it opens the way to higher musical education. Surely this is what gives it its broad cultural and historical significance.[41]

Chapter Seven

SOCIAL MARGINALITY
AND CULTURAL CREATIVITY IN
VIENNA AND BUDAPEST
(1890–1914)

THE OVERTURE to a new age in Austria, the cultural era called "fin de siè-cle" was an odd and controversial book, *Beiträge zur Analyse der Empfin-dungen* (Contributions to the Analysis of Sensations), first published in Jena in 1886. The book's genesis stretches back into the early youth of its author, Ernst Mach. He might have been about fifteen, he later wrote, when "On a bright summer day in the open air, the world with my ego suddenly ap-peared to me as one coherent mass of sensations, only more coherent in the ego. Although the actual working out of this thought did not occur until a later period, yet this moment was decisive for my whole view."[1]

Mach's ideas on sensations matured in Graz during the mid-1860s when, stimulated by the impact of Gustav Fechner's concept of "psycho physics," he worked out the first draft of his "empiriocritical" views. But Fechner's negative criticism of those views discouraged Mach from publishing the manuscript; he set it aside for almost twenty years.[2] Only during the years of his rectorate at the University of Prague in the eighties, as he became dis-illusioned with rising national conflicts, did he feel stimulated to revise and finish this psycho-physico-philosophical work. The book greatly influenced the thinking and Weltanschauung of fin-de-siècle intellectuals, not only in Austria but in Central and Eastern Europe and even as far away as the United States.[3] Why did the "Analysis of Sensations" create such a sensa-tion? I believe that the younger generation of Austrian (and Central Euro-pean) intellectuals read into it their own philosophy of relativism and used it to bolster their own sentiments of decadence. They were particularly fas-cinated by an idea embodied in one of Mach's famous propositions: "Das Ich ist unrettbar" (the ego is irremediable). This proposition seemed to be a strong argument that both explained and lay down "psychophysical" foun-dations of their collective identity crisis.

Though this was not a misinterpretation, it was an overestimation of Mach's original idea. Taken in context, his position actually stresses the on-tological unity of the physical and psychic world and attacks theories de-fending an autonomous and separated existence of the *Individuum*: "We shall then no longer place so high a value upon the ego. . . . We shall then be willing to arrive at a freer and more enlightened view of life, which shall preclude the disregard of the other egos and the overestimation of our own."[4]

The re-imbedding of the ego into physical phenomena, a logical demand of his phenomenalism, expressed more of an ethical ideal than a philosophy of "the dissolution of the ego." (Characteristically enough, some American pragmatists cannot fully comprehend the term "unrettbar.") The English translation, "The ego must be given up," expresses Mach's real intention in my opinion.[5]

This short exegetical meditation can lead us to the heart of the problem of Mach's phenomenalism and its tremendous influence. Its virtue lay not only—or even primarily—in its oft-debated epistemological stand, in the philosophical reunification of the physical and psychic world. Rather it lay, in Albert Einstein's words, in Mach's "incorruptible independence of thinking," the consequent relativization of all our knowledge of the world and ourselves, including the relativization of appearance and reality and, above all, of human existence.[6] The cultural activities of Mach and his followers in philosophy, literature, and the arts suggest—and this suggestion has been put forth by a great many recent scholarly works—that it was Austria, particularly Vienna, which played a preeminent role in generating and propagating fin-de-siècle sentiments and modern twentieth-century Western culture. This becomes evident when we open our lens to include the entire European cultural panorama.

In the last two decades of the nineteenth century, the impending chronological end took the shape of an historical or cosmic end. People believed that they faced the end of a great creative age, one inexorably declining and moving toward ultimate destruction. Oscar Wilde captured this feeling in his novel "The Picture of Dorian Gray": "Fin de siècle," murmured Lord Henry. "Fin du globe," responded the hostess, Lady Marlborough. "I wish it were fin du globe," said Dorian. "Life is a great disappointment."[7] The French term "fin de siècle" appeared in drama, literature, and the arts, in the everyday conversation of the educated elite; in short, it came to be very much in vogue. A simple adverb of time became an adjective. It meant tiredness, strangeness, and degeneration; it also implied the sort of exhaustion and jangled nerves that easily grew into neurasthenia and neurosis. The simple adverb of time also became transformed into an adverb of condition. Fin de siècle would shortly be associated with decadence.[8] The word became a new definition of the human condition, at least in the vocabulary of the European cultural elite who claimed it was shorthand for modernity. "Nous acceptons sans sensibilité comme sans orgueil le terrible mot de decadence," wrote Paul Bourget in 1896.[9] The bold acceptance of decadence as a higher form of existence meant aristocratism, the enjoyment of splendor and beauty, intellectual excitement and exotic drugs, an exquisiteness of sorts.

The development of fin de siècle as a new sentiment of life and decadence as a new Weltanschauung had deep roots in late nineteenth-century science and art. However great and salutary the culture of the passing age, it provoked wide-ranging criticism from numerous scientists, philosophers, writers, and artists. It was the liberal-rational culture itself that provoked skepticism about the benefits of liberalism and the omnipotence of reason. To be sure, fin-de-siècle sentiments and decadence did often take the shape of poses, affectations, and mannerisms, but they were still based on widely held concerns about the harmful effects of liberalism and the unsolved problems of modern sciences.

If we mention, only by name, great Scandinavians like Ibsen and Munch or, in addition, figures like the Catalan architect Gaudi, the Anglo-Belgian painter Ensor, the Italian writer D'Annunzio, we can see that it was not the old Monarchy, nor even Vienna-centered Central Europe which was in the vanguard of cultural modernism. The cultural flourishing in Vienna and Budapest started just before the 1890s. Central European intellectuals were late not only in the sense of "late-borns" (Spätgeborene), as Hofmannsthal put it, but really cultural latecomers.[10] Nevertheless, their sentiments of decadence were the same. They were Hofmannsthal's few thousand men, scattered all over Europe, "the conscience of the generation." These men suffered from a permanent and mysterious neurosis; they were disappointed in escaping from life yet still infatuated with it. They, the priests of a new cult of Beauty, wrote brilliant essays, novels, and plays, despite leading enervating, decaying lives, always face to face with death.

Vienna was quite receptive to Western ideas. It was fertile soil for the growth of modernism and capable of nurturing a new and quite unique strain. Perhaps Central European modernism was, like its Western model, filled with a great deal of superficiality and affectation, but there was an essential difference between the two. In the West, with its great power and prosperous economy, the public did not regard decadence and decline as posing an imminent or even inevitable threat. In the Monarchy, however, decay and disintegration were historical menaces; with the rise of sentiments of decadence, social and national conflicts intensified and the symptoms of decline grew stronger and stronger. In the West, decadence was treated with humor; it was a perverse enjoyment of the autumnal smell of decay, not anxiety. In the Monarchy, decadence gained authenticity from history itself, impending doom cast a shadow on and was in turn incorporated into modernist culture.

Now we can better define our specific problems:

1. What was the actual contribution of the Austro-Hungarian Monarchy—primarily of Vienna and Budapest—to European modernist culture?

2. Was there a definable social background to or a beneficial impact of social factors on fin-de-siècle culture? Were the estrangement and marginality of the Central European cultural elite different from those of other Europeans?

Several approaches could be chosen to answer these problems. I have used a bifurcated method of analysis. First, I have studied some outstanding cultural pioneers, apostles of new theories and world views. These were Ernst Mach, Albert Einstein, Sigmund Freud, and Endre Ady, the Hungarian poet and writer. Second, I have studied almost two hundred scholars, writers, and artists from Austria and Hungary, all representatives of various branches of modern twentieth-century culture.

Ernst Mach's Phenomenalist Relativity

The boy of fifteen who experienced the flood of sensations described at the beginning of this paper might well have been suffering from a physical disability. Ernst Mach is said to have had disturbances of perception since the age of three. He had to cope with troubles in perception of perspective, causality, space, and time. He was physically weak, did not play sports, and lacked playmates. As a child, he often stayed at home in almost total seclusion. He failed his first year of high school. The Benedictine fathers dissuaded him from further studies, regarding him as completely untalented and unteachable. It was his father who instructed him at home for five years until he was fifteen. The father, Johann Nepomuk Mach, was himself rather odd: a discontented farmer, an unlucky entrepreneur, and a frustrated intellectual all in one.[11]

In the university years Mach's interest was focused on the sciences, mainly physics influenced by the noted Vienna school. Childhood seclusion and retarded intellectual development may explain this choice. "Lateness in psychological development, or resistance to socialization can have its scientific compensation"—as Einstein once said, speaking of Mach and thinking also of himself.[12] He proved most sensitive and successful in exploring problems in such areas "where physics, physiology, and psychology intersect."[13] He made rapid progress in the profession suited to his constitution. In 1865, at the age of twenty-seven, he was already university professor in Graz, and two years later he was in Prague, where his career spanned three decades.

Mach came into the cross-fire of a bitter struggle between the German and Czech national intelligentsia, especially during the stormy period that witnessed the separation of the university and the establishment of the Czech university. He did not side with any party, least of all with the newly emerging anti-Semitic trend. He remained a liberal unaffiliated to any party or group, feeling at home only in his laboratory and at his desk. It was during his Prague years that he wrote his finest works: "Grundlinien der Lehre von den Bewegungsempfindungen" (Outlines of the Theory of the Sensations of Motion, 1875), "Die Mechanik in ihrer Entwicklung historisch-kritisch dargestellt" (The Science of Mechanics: A Critical and Historical Account of Its Development, 1883), and "*Beiträge zur Analyse der Empfindungen*" (Contributions to the Analysis of Sensations). Most influential were the latter two. In "Mechanik," he acknowledged the fundamental achievements of the giants of the seventeenth century but severely criticized their "metaphysical obscurities," particularly Newton's third law and his postulates of absolute time, space, and motion, as physically meaningless. "*All* masses and all velocities, and consequently all forces are relative," he declared.[14] Mach suggested "the elimination of all propositions from which [it] cannot be deduced . . . that the motion of bodies be considered relative to all observable matter in the universe."[15] Similarly, he posited the principle of "the functional interdependence of every single body of the universe with every other one," that is, the elimination of the principle of causality that supposes the existence of outside forces behind and beyond such bodies.

Whereas in "Mechanik" Mach exhibits a strong positivistic relativism, in "Analyse" he shows an equally strong positivistic phenomenalism. He asserts in his fundamental thesis an echo of David Hume's proposition that "Nihil est in intellectu quod non fuerit in sensu": the notion that we receive all of our knowledge of the world through the perception of sensations. Physical objects, psychic reflections, and the ego are but various complexes of sensations (elements) interdependent on each other.

"Analyse" is no doubt the most influential and controversial, the most often interpreted and misinterpreted, of Mach's works. Its argument that the world is composed of coherent complexes of sensations—of which the ego, the individual psyche, is only one—represents a very unusual standpoint in the confrontation with both traditional idealism and materialism. Mach certainly disagreed with Kantian idealism. He denied the existence of any kind of "absolute," particularly the necessity or usefulness of the metaphysical construction "thing in itself" (*Ding an sich*). Mach's theory of the consubstantiality of the material and psychic world (both are complexes of sensations) eliminates the bewildering dualism of Kantian philosophy and leads to a monistic world view. This monism, though, is by no means some kind of materialism. Mach did not acknowledge any permanent substance (matter). Science will not suffer, he said, if the permanent and mutual interaction of the elements substitutes for a stiff and sterile "unknown something" (matter).

"To us investigators, the concept of 'soul' is irrelevant and a matter of laughter, but matter is an abstraction of exactly the same kind. . . . We know as much about soul as we do of matter. . . . What we represent to ourselves behind the experiences exists only in our understanding (*Vernunft*), and has for us the value of a *memoria technica,* that is, it serves but as the 'economy of thought.' "[16]

Mach went so far in this staunch positivistic phenomenalism as to refuse to acknowledge even the physical reality of atoms (electrons)—though he did admit to them as "working hypotheses"—and vehemently opposed the discoveries of Boltzmann, Lorentz, Planck, and Einstein's theory of relativity. Even his followers criticized his unbending positivism and agnosticism, which ultimately verged on solipsism and subjective idealism. Lenin regarded Mach's empiriocriticism as pernicious, since subjective idealism basically contradicts Marxist materialism. This judgment prevails even up to the recent writings of Marxist ideologists.[17]

Indeed, Mach's philosophy was by no means consistent. His overdone phenomenalism had a dangerous kinship with solipsism. Yet in spite of all the criticism, I would argue that Mach pioneered a completely new approach in examining and explaining our world. Mach recognized that the rapid development of science and radical social changes at the end of the nineteenth century challenged the validity of both the Newtonian world view and Kantian philosophical order, and even the existence of matter itself. Nineteenth-century science discovered "invisible light, inaudible sounds, unsmellable odors, intangible fields, and other phenomena transcending the unaided human senses."[18] These discoveries might have led scientists toward a new agnosticism, but they actually adumbrated new explanations of time, space, motion, matter, and physical phenomena. What Mach accomplished was one of the most remarkable efforts to elaborate a new approach to explanation.

I would also argue that such traditional categories as idealism and materialism, determinism and indeterminism are not properly applicable to Mach's philosophy. Despite some similarities, he cannot be stamped as a "subjective idealist." He did not dissolve the "objective" world, the universe, in the individual consciousness. On the contrary, he dissolved the ego in the universe, equalizing it with any other complex of sensations. For Mach, the question of whether matter exists or not was without any importance. He was interested in the problem of how, and in what connection our sensations function, rather than whether they exist at all. Similarly, the dichotomy between reality and appearance is meaningless in the Machian concept. As for the functional aspect, it makes no difference, he claims, whether we regard given things as contents of consciousness or physical objects. The old question of "whether the world is real or we are only dreaming it" makes absolutely no scientific sense. Even the most confused nightmare dream is a fact as well as any other. "Cognition and error flow out of the same source."[19]

I also disagree with those who have found an adequate philosophy of (artistic) Impressionism in Machian phenomenalism. Aside from the methodological problems of transferring terms of artistic styles to history or the sciences, I think Machian phenomenalism differs in its essence from Impressionism.

Mach states that color, tone, and warmth are the only existing qualities, but Impressionism does not accept color, tone, and warmth as genuine properties of objects. Unlike Machian phenomenalism, Impressionism attributes a specific role to the subjective perception of the observer. The fact that Viennese writers and artists who used Impressionistic language of expression were at the same time enthusiastic about Machian ideas is no evidence of the latter's Impressionistic character.

Machian phenomenalism, particularly its strict positivism, finally proved conservative and untenable for later developments in theoretical physics and philosophy. Still, it was Mach who first formulated a number of fundamental principles in disciplines ranging from modern physics to philosophy and the arts, including the relativity of all physical and psychic phenomena and the elimination of epistemological boundaries between reality and illusion (appearance). Both principles inspired fin-de-siècle modernism.

Ludwig Boltzmann

We must briefly recall another great Austrian physicist, Ludwig Boltzmann, because of—or despite—the fact that his career was strikingly different from Mach's. His scientific achievements probably surpass Mach's findings, and his life seemed happier, full of successes, compared to his colleague.[20] He enjoyed fame and a happy family life and was even awarded the title "Hofrat" (Court Counselor). Then, at the age of sixty-two, he unexpectedly committed suicide.

On closer inspection it is clear that Boltzmann was not a balanced personality. He often suffered from bouts of depression and anxiety neurosis. He also felt kinship with modern artistic endeavors: "In like manner, in art the Impressionist and Secessionist stand arrayed against the old schools of painting, and the Wagnerian school of music against the schools of the old classical masters. There is accordingly no occasion for surprise that theoretical physics does not form an exception to this general law."[21]

At this point we may refer to the general confusion of the Viennese cultural elite at around the end of the nineteenth century. Boltzmann was no exception but, rather, a typical case of such an identity crisis. He was born in a religiously mixed household: his father was Lutheran and his mother Catholic. The parents agreed that young Ludwig should be raised a Catholic as was proper for a loyal subject of the Monarchy. Boltzmann was, in fact, a devout Catholic and loyal Austrian citizen throughout his life. Nevertheless, he confessed many times to his attraction to Germany and admired Bismarck and Moltke. He was sympathetic to the Reich, even before he accepted a professorship at the University of Berlin. So he was an Austro-German, a liberal freethinker who liked and praised America. But in his resentment of rising conservatism and political intolerance he remained an old Austrian liberal. He kept clear of all forms of political activity. All political parties, he said, fought only for selfish material interests: it was left to men of art and knowledge to defend great ideals against everyday politics.[22] He deliberately withdrew into science from active political participation. Scholarship gave him a kind of identity, and his dedication to it was absolute and unconditional. Thus, when this last shred of a fading identity was destroyed, Boltzmann remained hopeless and defenseless.

His death occurred just before atomic physics vindicated his theory. It is certainly "one of the most tragic ironies of the history of science that Boltzmann ended his life just before the existence of atoms was finally established by experiments."[23]

And now let us examine the life and work of two paradigmatic geniuses, the founders of our view of the physical and psychic world.

Why Albert Einstein?

I apologize for this question on two accounts.

First, I apologize for including Einstein in a book on Vienna and Budapest. Born in Ulm, raised in Munich, student and resident in Zurich and Bern, what could possibly have attached him to the old Monarchy? One could, of course, enumerate some relatives, a friendly circle of colleagues, even mention his first wife, Mileva Maric, who was born in old Hungary. One could also refer to Einstein's professorship in Prague in 1911–1912 and the impact of both the city's strange atmosphere and his Jewish friends on his mental state. But I do not want to call on accidental relations to support my thesis. In investigating this problem—that of the correlation between social position and creativity—I will not restrict myself to Vienna and Budapest but rather plan to include parallels from the whole Central European region. I vote for late Austro-Hungarian citizenship for the late Albert Einstein.

Second, I must also apologize for the implication of my question: why was it precisely Albert Einstein who discovered the theory of relativity? At first glance, it seems to be a silly question, one to which an answer can quickly be provided: he was an extraordinary genius, greater than any of his peers. That is, he benefited from a period of heuristic *Sternstuden* (propitious hours). Yet I do not think that this answer is satisfactory. If so, the Sternstuden in physics lasted at least twenty years both before and after the turn of the century. These heuristic revelations did not in themselves suffice to solve any of the fundamental problems of modern physics.

In the physical sciences, a new epoch had unfolded with the theories on electrodynamics initiated by Maxwell. Since the old and new physical concepts did not harmonize, physics was stuck in a critical phase. All of the major new discoveries in thermodynamics and electromagnetism contradicted the Newtonian world view, which explained physical phenomena in terms of mechanics. However brilliant the application of mechanics in the theory of heat or optics might be, it did spawn some unresolved paradoxes, as fin-de-siècle physicists quickly found out. Physicists were particularly unable "to give a really satisfactory mechanical foundation for electromagnetic theory."[24]

The problems generated by the incompatibility between mechanics and electromagnetic theory attracted the attention of some of the age's greatest brains, men who had long known that Newton's third law (action-reaction equality) was somewhat untenable in the light of Maxwellian and post-Maxwellian achievements. Some physicists were skeptical of the existence of a stationary luminiferous "ether" implied by "absolute" space and time. These doubts were stimulated by the failure of the accurate and increasingly improving experiments of Albert Michelson and Edward Morley to prove the relative motion of the earth and the changing velocity of light related to the motion of the earth in the "ether." Explanations were born without eliminating the disturbing dualism of the physical world view that persisted at the time.

At the turn of the century, what physics needed was a man who had the courage and knowledge to go back to its philosophical foundations.

Why Albert Einstein? This is not the playful and speculative query of a cultural historian. Physicists and historians of science ask the same sorts of questions.[25] Precisely it was not—and is not—so obvious that Einstein was predestined by Providence to solve divine riddles about mass, motion, and energy. Einstein himself "used to say that the special theory of relativity was in the air when he discovered it, that Paul Langevin, for instance, might have done so as well."[26] And Boltzmann, Planck, Poincaré, and, indeed, Lorentz might have done so even earlier. If so, then what was the decisive factor? Einstein's superiority of talent? But how can we measure the greatness of a genius? By what criteria? By the achievement itself? But this would be a proper petitio principii, explaining something by the result we are first supposed to explain. Without discarding the imponderable qualities of this unique genius, I want to draw into the discussion Einstein's historical moment: his situation and life story.

The family was an average Jewish middle-class one, residing in Southern Germany and with a history of involvement in commerce on both the father's and the mother's side. Einstein's father was not very lucky in business. Ruined in Munich, Pavia, and Milan, he could not afford a very comfortable life for his family or educational support for his son. According to Einstein's recollections and the opinion of his biographers, he was a slow student who disliked severe Teutonic discipline, his boring education, and the barely hidden anti-Semitism of his Munich high school (the Liutpold Gymnasium). He may not have finished his education there, for we know that he did not take the final exam (Matura). Rather, he followed his parents to Italy. Instead of settling down with his parents, though, he chose to move to Switzerland and become a Swiss citizen.

I would suggest that his choice of Switzerland was the outcome of serious considerations. First, he decided to study science as early as the age of sixteen. As a high school student he wanted nothing less than to comprehend the universe. He chose physics because it "seemed most fundamental to understand-ing the latest advances in the most basic way."[27] I do not think it was mere ado-lescent fantasy when he dreamt of riding on top of a wave of light and asked, "What should I see then?" Young Einstein had probably already guessed that the basic problem of physics lay hidden in a beam of light. If one could follow, at the same speed, a beam of light with velocity c one would perceive it as a sta-tionary field of energy. "After ten years of meditation I found this principle [of relativity] in a paradox which I had got at when I was sixteen."[28]

Einstein's devotion to physics emerges unequivocally from his career; there is no need to prove it. I quote only an early letter to illustrate his intransigent desire to subordinate everything to his studies. In 1898, writing to his sister Maja, he noted:

> What taxed me most, of course, was the misfortune suffered by my poor parents, who had not had another lucky minute for many years. Furthermore, it hurt me deeply that as an adult I had to look on, inactively, unable to make the smallest move. I am nothing but a burden on my family. . . . It really would have been better if I had never lived. The one idea . . . that year in, year out, I should not allow my-self, even once, a satisfaction or diversion other than that which study affords me, is what keeps me going and sometimes has to shield me from despair.[29]

Einstein was also fully aware of the price of unconditional devotion to sci-ence. "The turning point of development for a person of my kind comes when the main interest gradually detaches itself from the momentary and personal, and turns into the pursuit of the mental comprehension of things."[30]

This ambition appeared very early and explicitly. He was eighteen, still a student in Zurich, when he wrote to his parents that "Strained mental work and the contemplation of God's nature are the angels that will guide me, rec-onciled, strengthened and relentlessly strong, through all the tribulations of this life."[31]

Akin to this devotion, independent thinking and a desire to avoid commit-ments were characteristics of the young Einstein. After a short period of child-hood religiosity, he became a radical freethinker, a strong autonomous person-ality. He was "a professed atheist and completely indifferent to all religious problems."[32] The term that fitted him best was "unaffiliated," an adjective he often used to describe himself in official documents.[33] This might be the main reason that he chose to live in Zurich, the free and tolerant city, the refuge of emigrants, homeless utopians, and autonomous intellectuals. Even in his later Jewish period, Einstein avoided Chassidic mysticism and uncritical accep-tance of Zionist politics.

Zurich was a remarkable city at the turn of the century, truly a place "where future revolutions were nurtured."[34] It lay at the crossroads of European revo-lutionary ferment. "Socialists, nihilists, Zionists, and sectarians of all sorts . . .

congregated in Zurich."[35] No doubt, the city made a strong impression on Einstein. Nevertheless, there is no evidence that he was involved in revolutionary movements; he was involved only in probing the secrets of physics and mathematics.

Contrary to his public image, Einstein was a busy student, the best in his class, and worked hard during his student years at the Polytechnic School of Zurich and, later, as a modest "technical expert" at the Federal Patent Office in Bern. He read and sometimes reviewed all the new papers on thermo- and electrodynamics. In addition, he educated himself in philosophy, being particularly fascinated with Hume and Mach. Although he dealt with various problems in physics ranging from capillarity to the "Determination of Molecular Dimensions" (the title of his 1902 doctoral dissertation), he found the exciting paradoxes of electrodynamic theories the most stimulating of all.

It would be a vast pretension on my part to attempt a lay interpretation of the theory of relativity. What I can offer, though, is a simple historical account of how a great and bold discovery was born and how one can follow it through Einstein's letters to his friends and his girlfriend and later wife, Mileva Maric. Einstein expressed serious doubts about the existence of "der Äther" at the end of the nineteenth century. In August 1899, he wrote a remarkable passage in a letter to Mileva:

> I am becoming ever more convinced that the electrodynamics of moving bodies, as it has manifested itself up to now, does not conform with reality, for it can be described far more simply. Introducing the term "ether" into electrical theories led to the idea of a medium, to whose movement one might refer, without, I think, anyone managing to attach physical meaning to this assertion.[36]

In April 1901, he reported a long conversation with his friend Michele Besso. They discussed the principle of separation of the light-ether from matter and a new way to define it.[37] And he wrote to another friend: "On the scientific side, I have had a couple of splendid ideas come into my head, which only need to hatch out properly. I am now certain that my theory of the attractive force of atoms can be extended to gases as well."[38]

Around the same time he noted to Mileva: "The idea recently came to me that when light is generated, a direct change of kinetic energy into light may take place due to the parallelism of the living force of molecules-absolute temperature-spectrum. Who knows when a tunnel can be built through this hard mountain."[39] At the end of the same year he wrote to Mileva of an important change in his unfolding theory: "I am working eagerly on an electrodynamics of moving bodies, which promises to make a fundamental treatise."[40]

Einstein's basic ideas of special relativity crystallized by 1905, the miraculous year when he published four famous papers. So what was Einstein's ultimate and revolutionary discovery, the one that finally resolved the internal paradoxes with which he had been grappling and which rendered a new paradigm of the perception of nature?

After ten years of strenuous reading, research, and contemplation, he arrived at the conclusion that some basic suppositions of classical (Newtonian) physics, corresponding to seventeenth-century philosophical foundations of mechanics, were impediments to a new, adequate, and unitary explanation of nature. In other words, the supposition of a stationary ether as the basis of reference of absolute space, time, and motion is neither experimentally provable nor theoretically necessary. Instead of attempting a new reinterpretation of the traditional wisdom and looking for the umpteenth explanation of the constancy of the velocity of light, he took his hypotheses to be axioms. He based his theory on two postulates. The first one asserted that the "same laws of electrodynamics and optics will be valid for all frames of reference for which the equations of mechanics hold good"—this is the principle of relativity. The second postulate stipulated that "light always moves with the same velocity in free space, regardless of the motion of the source."[41] "These two postulates suffice for the attainment of a simple and consistent theory of the electrodynamics of moving bodies based on Maxwell's theory for stationary bodies."[42] Metaphorically speaking, Einstein did not cut the Gordian knot of physics, but postulated that the rope originally had a knot, and then looked for how it might have functioned without the knot.

Einstein had to reconsider the physical meaning of time and space. Relying on Mach's philosophical suggestions and applying the Lorentz transformation equations, Einstein arrived at the revolutionary insight that there is no need for a general "absolute" time. His conclusion was similar to his insight that, having eliminated the stationary ether, "absolute" space is a superfluous supposition. "The inherent ambiguity of instantaneity . . . precludes any ability to establish absolute simultaneity."[43] (Greenwich Mean Time, for instance, is only a practical convention that facilitates orientation and does not correspond to the actual temporality of moving objects within different time zones.)

Somewhat later the outstanding mathematician Hermann Minkowski, fascinated by Einstein's theory, suggested that it be expressed in the geometric terms of four-dimensional space, where time and space are not only connected with but equal to each other. "Henceforth space by itself, and time by itself, are doomed to fade away into mere shadows, and only a kind of union of the two will preserve an independent reality."[44] Einstein immediately accepted Minkowski's contribution because it logically followed from the elimination of absolute space. Since space is nothing else than an electromagnetic field of moving bodies (electrons), field and motion—that is, space and time—have to be equivalent. Further developing his theory, Einstein discovered that gravitational fields, like electromagnetic ones, should only have a relative existence and that inertial mass is equal to gravitational mass. Gravitation is an immanent property of space and time. This way he extended the great idea of the equivalence of space and time first to mass and energy and then to inertia and gravity.

To be completely fair, we must point out that—among others—Poincaré and Lorentz got very close to the same discoveries. As a matter of fact, it was Poincaré who first introduced the term "principle of relativity" into science. He knew that "absolute" space and stationary ether did not exist, accepted the concept of multidimensional space, and suggested that the velocity of light might be taken as a new absolute constant. Nevertheless, he argued that "the electromagnetic ether was a pragmatic convention." "Whether the ether exists or not matters little," he declared, "let us leave [that] to the metaphysicians; what is essential for us is that everything happen as if it existed, and that this hypothesis is found to be suitable for the explanation of phenomena."[45]

As to Lorentz, he knew almost as much as Einstein and in many aspects preceded him. In her brilliant essay, Nancy Nersessian points out that Lorentz elaborated almost the same principles and got the same results as his younger colleague but did not derive the same consequences from them. "He always retained the aether frame as the primary reference system in which length, time, and the velocity of light would have their true value."[46] Nersessian's main argument is that Lorentz had a concept of scientific method different from Einstein's. "Einstein," she writes, "simply postulated what we have deduced, with some difficulty and not altogether satisfactorily, from the fundamental equations of the electromagnetic field. Lorentz consciously avoided *meta*-physical reflection. He considered such reflection to be outside the province of a scientist."[47]

Unlike Lorentz, Einstein went back to the bare foundations of mechanics and electromagnetism. He used precisely the epistemological analysis that Lorentz believed inappropriate for scientific enterprise.[48] He was convinced that "only the discovery of a universal formal principle could lead to assured results."[49] Nersessian concludes: "With hindsight we see that Einstein's approach was required in that problem situation and that his interpretation was needed for subsequent physics. There are certain scientific questions, particularly foundational, which do require critical epistemological analysis."[50]

After all these remarkable thoughts, the initial question remains: Why Albert Einstein? Why was it just he who raised the "critical epistemological questions"?

The renowned historian of science, Lewis Feuer, offers a very attractive sociopsychological explanation. According to him, Einstein belonged to the young, fin-de-siècle generation of intellectuals in revolt. Einstein, for instance, elaborated the special theory of relativity in the so-called "Olympia Academy," a friendly circle of Marxist and Machian revolutionaries who met in Zurich and Bern. The general theory was matured in Prague under the influence of the Jewish circle of Brod, Kafka, and others. To sum up Freur's argument, though inevitably simplifying his finely chiseled explanations: the special theory was "the sublimation of revolutionary emotion into physical theory" (as the title of one chapter reads), but the general theory bears the unmistakable marks of "Jewish cosmological-mystical thinking."

I am unwilling to correlate directly sociopolitical revolutionism and scientific innovation. Particularly I regard the connection between the Prague Jewish circle and Einstein's discovery as a misinterpretation. The facts of Einstein's life do not convince me of his social revolutionary inclinations. He was a lonely and slowly maturing person throughout his life, even after he had reached the pinnacle of his fame. Despite his circle of close friends and colleagues and the growing ranks of his admirers, he remained an isolated and lonely man. "I am a horse for a single harness, not cut out for tandem or teamwork. I have never belonged wholeheartedly to country or state, to my circle of friends, or even to my own family."[51] This confession is by no means inconsistent with Einstein's character. He really lacked (or discarded) any definite and strong national, religious, or class identity. He was born German and liked German culture but deeply resented vehement German nationalism and anti-Semitism. He often declared himself Jewish, but in spite of his sympathy to the cause, was never a political Zionist. He did not subordinate his devotion for truth to the interests of the movement, and for this Chaim Waizmann stamped him "mentally deranged," harmful, and "a great nuisance."[52] Einstein was born in a middle-class family but never enjoyed the comforts and privileges of middle-class life. During his student years, he lived in poverty and experienced various slights and humiliations until he found a second-rate job in Bern. Unlucky also in family life, Einstein was a typical marginal man living in a permanent state of marginality—a social, political, and professional marginality—even if, in the end, he emerged better off financially and world famous.

Certainly, Einstein once belonged wholeheartedly to a small, informal countercultural community, the Olympia Academy, of which he was the spiritus rector. What kind of group was the Academy? One of its founders, Maurice Solovine, a Jew from Romania, was the prototype of the marginalized man. Michele Besso, another founder, came from a respected Italian-Jewish family. His uncle was an ardent Garibaldist and his aunt a pioneer of the Italian fascist movement and later secretary of the women's organization of Mussolini's fascist party.[53] Besso became a Swiss citizen, a genuine cosmopolitan "free-floating intellectual," in the true Mannheimian sense. Einstein even numbered a true revolutionary among his close friends: Friedrich Adler, the son of the famous Austrian socialist leader. Through Adler, an Austro-Marxist and Machian, Einstein became acquainted with Marxism and revolutionary socialism.

The Olympia Academy was a remarkable club of "homeless" and marginalized intellectuals whose discontent found expression in nonconformism, in protest against the Establishment, and in sympathy with anti-Establishment political organizations. Perhaps this common discontent might be the very reason they looked for radical innovations in science and the arts.

I would suggest that Einstein's psychic constitution and social situation were responsible for his uncompromising and passionate quest. These nourished his inclination to raise fundamental questions that other professionals, contented members of the Establishment, did not dare to raise. Einstein's genius was a necessary but not sufficient condition of his epochal discoveries. Genius must coincide with a salutary historical situation; it must accede to the demands of the Zeitgeist. Albert Einstein, the German, Italian, Swiss, and American citizen, the emotional Jewish cosmopolitan, the man who belonged wholeheartedly only to the universe and not to any nation, country, macrocommunity, or a small group, could comprehend wholeheartedly the final law of relativity as the natural state of existence.

Despite his ordeals, Einstein was born in a Sternstunde, and his age still merits the name "belle époque" because it tolerated him.

And now it is time to return to Vienna for a true Viennese genius.

SIGMUND FREUD: SCHOLAR AND PROPHET

This title could have been similar to the previous one, and have read "Why Sigmund Freud?" because there are many parallels between the lives of the two men. I gave up my attempt at such symmetry, though, because Freud was more than merely a professional psychologist or cultural anthropologist. His life may be characterized by two basic features. First, he was blessed and cursed with an almost limitless ambition. As an adolescent, he dreamt of being a great man, a powerful politician, perhaps even minister; his idols were Hannibal and Cromwell. He characterized himself as a "conquistador" for whom science was just another province to conquer. Second, he inherited and cultivated two cultures, Jewish and Christian, neither fully accepting nor renouncing either of them.[54]

From Ernest Jones's lengthy biography (1953) to Peter Gay's most recent essay (1987), Freud's life and activity has received many different interpretations.[55] As is known, the extraordinarily gifted and ambitious young Jew was prevented from asserting his abilities either in politics, which he secretly yearned for, or in academic science, both by his family circumstances and his environment, consisting of aristocratic-liberal Austrians and anti-Semitic nationalistic Germans. He was compelled to become a physician, but instead of practising his profession he became the founder and prophet of a new school of psychology, a quasi religious sect. The motto taken from Virgil that Freud used to introduce his "Interpretation of Dreams"—Flectere si nequeo superos, Acheronta movebo! (If I cannot bend Heaven, I will move Hell)—is perhaps not only a metaphor of his method and discoveries, but also the epitome of his entire walk of life (see Figure 23).[56]

We know that as early as the 1880s he became interested in hysteria, one of the fashionable neuroses of the age. In Paris, he studied the elements of hypnotic cure with Charcot, and he learned the methods of "cathartic talking cure"

23. Sigmund Freud. Vienna, 1900s

and "free associations" from Josef Breuer in Vienna.[57] In the mid-1890s a deep human and professional crisis came about in his career, caused by anti-Semitism, slighting family problems, and professional failures. He overcame the crisis by his recognition of the relationship between suppressed sexual instinct, the subconscious, and dreams, by writing his "Interpretation of Dreams" and by laying the foundations of psychoanalysis. In that work he expounded the methodology of interpreting fears and desires that are suppressed in conscious life but break loose, usually in a distorted form, in dreams.

Taking separately the various elements of psychoanalysis, we may well wonder about their originality. The theory seems to be constructed out of already known elements. The existence of the unconscious had been well known for the past hundred years; the importance and symbols of sexuality were described by Bachofen and an Austrian scholar, Krafft-Ebing, who was an outstanding expert in sexual pathology. Childhood sexuality was a familiar phenomenon to priests and schoolmasters, and discovered in a scholarly fashion by Jules Michelet and Lucien Arreat. Both described the "incestuous" relationship of children to their parents, the Freudian "Oedipus complex." Before Freud, Nietzsche also wrote of the unconscious and the inhibition of instinct through simulation and sublimation. Explanations of dreams have also existed since the mid-nineteenth century (by, for example, Volkelt, Scherner, and Delage), even if they possessed less analytical and imaginative qualities than Freud's.[58]

Was Freud's theory really epochal and original or only a skillful compilation? Had the "Interpretation" been merely a coherent synthesis, it would still have been a great and original work, for a synthesis as a whole is always greater than the sum of its parts. The "Interpretation," however, was incomparably more than a popular compilation of sex secrets. The work and the analytical therapy that went into it, containing as it does the basic elements of Freud's observations, show him to be a theorizing genius.

Ignoring Freud's mistaken impression of the dream mechanism and his value judgments, the historical relevance of the "Interpretation" lies, first, in finding the actual via regia, the two-way route of interdependent communication between the conscious and unconscious; second, in discovering the unitary rules of the healthy and ill psyche, in other words, the sameness of normal and deviant sexual behavior, the basic mechanism of recollection and oblivion, anxiety and compensation. Third, in his work Freud was able to bridge the gap between Jewish and Christian culture and open the possibility of reconciling two different minds. In the next few decades, Freud set forth to legitimate psychoanalysis and extend its validity to the phenomena of everyday life and deviance, pathological cases, and the cultural history of mankind.

At this point, we should raise the question: why Sigmund Freud?

There are two comparable counterexamples before us, both contemporaries of Freud and pioneers of modern psychiatry.

Richard Freiherr von Krafft-Ebing was born in Germany in 1840 and came from a respectable old family of professionals and officials (his mother was a baroness). Graduated from the Heidelberg Medical School, his career soared straight upward. At the age of thirty-one he was appointed professor at Strassbourg University and shortly after was called to Graz, where he founded the chair for psychiatry. Succeeding Thomas Mexnert, he took over as director of the Psychiatric Clinic of Vienna. From the beginning, he was engaged in neurology and specialized in a new branch of the field: psychopathology. It was he who observed and described various cases of obsessional neurosis and first applied the terms "sadism" and "masochism" for specific sexual deviances.[59]

Although Krafft-Ebing presented startling cases of perverted sexuality, his lectures, papers, and manuals never provoked heated controversies or public outrage. He remained a highly respected scholar, staying always within the boundaries of science. Beyond some rather fair descriptive works, he had his own theory of childhood sexuality and aberrations caused by repression or frustration. He never attributed any general validity to these theories, however, either in history or everyday life. He was fifty when he was invited to Vienna, where he became the preeminent authority in his field. Not involved or interested in the intrigues of Viennese life and remaining far from politics, he was a level-headed, fair, always impartial scholar: just like his marble bust in the archway of Vienna University.[60]

Janet presents an even more striking comparison to Freud than Krafft-Ebing. Pierre Marie Félix Janet (1859–1947) was almost the same age as Freud but born in a somewhat different family. His great-grandfather, grandfather, and father were book dealers and publishers in Paris and, on his mother's side, many of his relatives were better-off entrepreneurs in Alsace. The family was devoutly Catholic and ardently patriotic, and therefore terribly affected by the loss of Alsace-Lorraine to Germany in 1871. Janet, who disliked his secluded father and, like Freud, loved his beautiful, domineering mother, survived a serious psychic depression as a young teenager. However, recovering at a famous high school, the École Normale Superieur, he became a brilliant scholar. He began his career as a high school teacher, philosopher, and, again like Freud, turned toward psychiatry only after some delay. He obtained the good graces of Charcot, becoming his disciple and—after graduating from the Sorbonne Medical School—succeeded him as the leading psychiatrist at Salpêtrière Hospital. From this point on his career was a triumph. Professor at the Collège de France and renowned authority in psychiatry, he was invited to teach or lecture by many of the world's leading universities and honored by most of the same. Janet even represented France at many scholarly meetings and negotiations.

Janet began his psychological investigation—like Freud—in the rewarding subjects of hysteria, phobias, and obsessions. He observed hundreds of cases, preparing and analyzing each with meticulous care. He elaborated a well-balanced theory of the causes of these illnesses, being careful not to exaggerate the unconscious, and made some very valuable contributions to analytical methods. He knew almost everything that Freud did by the end of the nineties, although his value judgments differed from those of the author of the "Interpretation." At the International Congress of Medicine in 1913, the psychiatric section organized a discussion of Freud's psychoanalysis. The first reviewer, Janet, claimed that he had first discovered the "cathartic cure," the traumatic origins of neuroses, and stated that Freud's theory was simply a modification of his own earlier concept. Second, Janet sharply criticized Freud's method of symbolic interpretation of dreams and his "overemphasis" of the sexual origins of neurosis. "He considered psychoanalysis a 'metaphysical' system."[61] In later years, he developed his discovery of "subconscious fixed ideas" into a systematic theory of psychic illnesses (*Les obsessions et la psychoasthénie*, 1903). Twenty years later he summed up all his findings in a monumental synthesis that included a new theory of the normal and abnormal mechanism of the psyche, ranging from primitive reflexive tendencies to complex rational activities.[62]

Now the more sensible question to ask is: why was Janet not Freud?[63] As in the case of the Einstein-Lorentz parallel, we cannot reduce this question to who was a greater "genius." A better answer can be found in the relationship of situation and character.

Janet was the embodiment of the ideal positivist scholar who did not accept anything but thoroughly monitored experiments and strict evidence. By birth, education, and voluntary identification, he had been integrated into the French social and cultural elite. His French and Catholic identity was never challenged. Enjoying a smooth and successful career, he never wanted to transcend the boundaries of elite society and top scholarship. He served and represented this society and this scholarship, and not the idea of the liberation of mankind.

Unlike Janet, Freud was an Austrian Jew who spent his whole life in in-between situations, between nations, religions, and social and cultural communications in this Danubian Babel of an empire. Freud's marginality can be explained by several major factors. First, at the peak of his adult years in the 1890s, he became frustrated in his academic career and identification with the Austro-German world. Academic, civic, and personal frustration intertwined to cause a serious psychosomatic crisis. Freud was not a lonely child and an asocial man by character, but he became a marginal man through the many traumas of his life and his social environment.

Second, Freud's marginality may be regarded as typical of the common situation (or fate?) of assimilated Jews in Central Europe. Jews in Russia or Romania lived separate and oppressed lives, though in close communities with a strong Jewish identity and an awareness of a divine mission. Reformed Jews in Central Europe, though, were in a different situation. They were partly assimilated, and many wanted to be fully integrated into their adopted nation. The great majority abandoned the strong Jewish ethnic-religious community in their quest for assimilation, but even they were usually only politically emancipated and not emotionally accepted as full citizens. These Jews were integrated in the economy and partly integrated in society, but remained "others" in intimate personal relations with most gentiles. This "otherness"—connected with discrimination and often humiliation—was the common denominator in fin-de-siècle Jewish life, particularly for the Central European Jewish intelligentsia.

As far as Freud is concerned, we have abundant material relating to his Jewish marginality from his childhood recollection of the humilation of his father to the decade-long official intransigence in granting him a professorship. Still the question remains: to what extent did Freud identify himself with the Jewish ethnic-religious community? There is no doubt that he was firmly indifferent to religious matters and felt but minimal affinity to the Jewish community. "Quite by the way, why did none of the devout create psychoanalysis? Why did one have to wait for a completely godless Jew?" Peter Gay proposes the answer that psychoanalysis could be developed only by an atheist, particularly by an Jewish atheist.[64] What Freud felt might be called an intellectual-cultural identification with Jewish tradition, with "this miraculous thing in common which . . . makes the Jew."[65] What he appreciated as Jewish tradition was exactly the opposite of ethnic or political Judaism. "Because I was a Jew I found myself free from many prejudices which restricted others in the use of their intellect;

and as a Jew I was prepared to join the opposition, and to do so without agreement with the 'compact majority.' "[66]

If we accept this statement as true, we must accept Jewish marginality as a special case of human marginality, a stage of independence and integrity that offers marginal men a sort of cognitive privilege.

Freud did not belong to any ethnic or social group. By birth and education he might have belonged, of course, to the Viennese middle class *(Bildungsbürgertum)*, but he resented identification with the bourgeoisie and the middle-class Establishment. "He himself was a product of bourgeois culture," writes a sensitive interpreter of Freud, "but he never espoused their cause as a ruling class and never associated himself with their interests. . . . He was bourgeois in his tastes and revolutionary in his vision, respectful of bourgeois conventions but profoundly revolutionary in his emulation of the ancient prophets. . . . Psychoanalysis was a product of this contradiction."[67]

The concept of "prophet" is key to understanding Freud. He was a scholar with an almost limitless imagination. He was a psychiatrist who did not shrink from involvement in philosophy and anthropology or vice versa; he applied philosophy, anthropology, and literature in his scholarship. He was a physician who wanted to heal not only individuals but mankind itself. He dared to extend the validity of his strictly scholarly findings in neurosis to the ancient and present history of mankind in works like *Totem and Taboo, The Future of an Illusion, Civilization and Its Discontents,* and, finally, *Moses and Monotheism.* These works all developed, and perhaps overdeveloped, various traumas caused by repressed sexual and aggressive instincts, wishes, and the Oedipus complex as examples of universal validity.

Finally, I would suggest that Freudian psychoanalysis was born from the lucky coincidence of the historical situation, the professional situation of psychiatry, and the exceptional character of a genius.

My examination may so far seem one-sided. I have presented mostly Austrian scientists and scholars. But how did artists and writers react to the new moods and menaces of a dramatically changing world in fin-de-siècle Budapest?

ENDRE ADY: POET AND PROPHET

Endre Ady, the great fin-de-siècle poet, came from the periphery. He was born in a remote village in northeastern Hungary, close to Transylvania, in 1877. His father came from the impoverished landed gentry (with a small estate of about 130 acres) and his mother from a family of Protestant ministers and teachers. Ady claimed that he had inherited an impressive family tree, if not a prosperous orchard. He bragged that his forefathers belonged to the tribe of Prince Árpád and were among the first settlers of Hungary. But, at any rate, he was the scion of poor, "sandaled" gentry, priests, and civil servants. He was born and raised in a borderland of different ethnic and religious communities, social groups, and beliefs. He veered away from the traditional path of his clerical and farming ancestors. Against his father's will, who wanted him to reestablish the family's reputation by becoming a high-ranking civil servant, he went into journalism.

This choice was not unusual among young déclassé gentry and did not necessarily imply a break with their noble origins. Ady, however, became a radical journalist, a social reformer opposed to anything that smacked of traditional political thinking or the social order of the Hungarian nobility. Shedding his ties to the nobility, Ady dropped out not only of politics but of the everyday life and mentality of the gentry. As a radical reformer, he was able to be intimate with middle-class intellectuals, most of Jewish origin, without being integrated into the rising bourgeoise. As a talented journalist, he lived amid political and cultural happenings, with colleagues, lovers, and enemies. Though in the thick of life, he always felt alone, wanting only to be loved and to belong somewhere.

Ady was not only a talented journalist but also a devoted one, dedicated to his profession and to progress. In a letter to his disappointed father, he tried to explain and justify his stand. "We are believers in and protagonists of radical democratic progress," he wrote in 1903, "We fight against the harmful oppressor: the obsolete feudal county-system. We are tired Olympian gods and ostracized, despised pariahs. . . . Often we are comedians. . . . Still we are the true fighters for a better life, for a more decent world, for progress, for light, and for that most ephemeral, wildest, and most beautiful, of all phantoms: for truth. We are the knights of the Holy spirit" (an allusion to a phrase invented by Heine).[68]

Ady and his radical compatriots fought against the pressing backwardness of Hungary, which had been caused by the prevailing remnants of the feudal past: chauvinism, clericalism, and the big estates and political rule of the latifundian aristocracy. In Ady's words, their foremost enemy was the "Hungarian Fallow" that reeked of death and was the graveyard of souls. Socially, "we live in prehistoric times," he wrote, our society is "immature, uncultured, superstitious and sick. In this country, only magnates, priests, and donkeys can exist. . . . We are oppressed and backward, we are beggars. . . . Our people will be lost, as Fate wishes to lose them." For him this fate had a name: "Class society, class state, gendarme." He was well informed of the Viennese Sezession and its slogan "Freedom to the arts," but he reinterpreted the meaning of Sezession (Art Nouveau) as freedom. "My Sezession," he declared, "is the freedom fight against [academic] pedantry."[69]

As a journalist, Ady incessantly stressed that the future of his country lay in reform. Democratic reform was an indispensable ingredient in saving and anchoring this unfortunate ferry / country which had been criss-crossing between two worlds, Asia and Europe, for centuries. "We have to be finished with feudal ranks, privileges, aristocracy, and the sweating capital at the same time. If we want to live, let us begin our lives. Let us solve our problems in a

Hungarian way, because there is little hope that the successors of Prussian Bebels or Slavic Bakunins will accomplish it for us."[70] What Hungary badly
needed was a radical, that is, structural change in order to catch up with modern Western civilization.

Judging only from what was said above, one might conclude that Ady, like
many of his fellow writers and artists, was completely immersed in politics
and active in public life, that he was a firm believer in a positivistic evolutionism. If so, this image must be corrected. Ady was deeply involved in public
life but always wanted to escape it; he was an evolutionist but always questioned the benefit of evolution; and he was a rationalist reformer but never
ceased to search for God and embrace metaphysics. Ady also went through es-
capist periods, accepting fin-de-siècle decadence and the Sezession in its original sense of Art Nouveau.

Fin-de-siècle intellectuals had three ways to secede: flight abroad, into the
self (psyche), or into love. For Ady, these ways converged in the summer of
1903. As he later recalled, "I worked for a newspaper, and wrote editorials,
and would most likely have perished . . . if someone had not come for me. . . .
[Then] she took me by the hand and we never stopped until we'd got to
Paris. . . . She wanted me to open my mouth. . . . [In Hungary] I felt life to be
miserable, and had long ceased to be at home here."[71] In Paris, Ady became acquainted with modernism as a literary trend and lifestyle. He was on the
Montparnasse when he finally awakened to his true calling as the chosen poet
of the new age.

Before 1905, Ady wrote a hundred rather poor poems, none of which would
have ensured his entrance to Parnassus. Coming back from Paris, he burst into
the Hungarian literary arena in the full armor of modernism and fought val-
iantly against lukewarm literature and poetry. He invented a unique poetic
language, with modern metaphors and striking symbols, which was barely ac-
cessible to purely rational minds but comprehensible to receptive spirits. He
expressed the typical decadent sentiments of modern life: the longing for ideal
beauty, exotic regions, the erotic with its close relationship to death (the identification of Eros with Thanatos, first substituting for and then defeating each
other), destructive love, and inspiring illness. Ady discovered his personal God
in decadence and enjoyed both sinning and repentance.

One may suspect, of course, that Ady emulated Western decadence (seen,
for example, in such lines as "I am kin of Death, I love vanishing love . . . ill
roses and fading women when they are still longing"). I would not deny the evidence for such suspicions, but would still emphasize the inadequacy of life
that flows through his gests and other poetry. Ady was really deadly ill, alco-
holic, persecuted, and banned by the country of the magnates, bishops, and
donkeys. He died at the age of forty-one, after a life spent incessantly wanting
to escape from Hungary. "At home I will be killed by nothing," he wrote his
lover, Léda. He felt a burning desire to go to Paris, he wanted to fly "from the
filth at home. . . . I'm going and that's all there is to it."[72] "I am living ill and

cheerless. In politics, everything is yet more topsy-turvy and hopeless than it ever was. . . . How I'm suffocating in Budapest, you know. . . . I don't even want to die here."[73] He was on the verge of suicide.

Nevertheless, he continued to live, remaining in Hungary. Why did he stay? What force bound him to the country and the politics? These are more interesting questions than those seeking the causes of his escapism and antipolitical revolt. Flight from public life, breaking with the establishment, homelessness, and nonaffiliation even with the organized opposition were general features of fin-de-siècle decadence and generational revolt. From Oscar Wilde to Joris-Karl Huysmans, from Proust to Hofmannsthal and Musil, almost all of the most creative writers and poets at the turn of the century were antipolitical "secessionists." According to Schorske's interpretation, even Freud's "Interpretation of Dreams" was a scholarly sublimation of his antipolitical revolt.[74] In the same way, we could almost regard Ady's first volumes (*New Poems* in 1906, *Blood and Gold* in 1907, and *On Elias's Cart* in 1908, for example) as a poetic (lyric) sublimation of his antipolitical revolt.

But only *almost*. In his programmatic lead poem in *New Verses,* he declares that he wants to burst into Hungary "with new poems for the new times." Even if banned by old Hungary, they will still be "new, victorious, and Magyar!"

Here we come across a specific feature of Hungarian (and perhaps eastern Central European) society and culture. Ady's first volumes were first met by a flood of attacks and a campaign of slander. The "feudal" Hungary of the magnates and gentry banned him, questioning and even denying his Magyar patriotism. Under the circumstances, official rejection should have so deepened his marginality as to lead him to final emigration, psychic seclusion, and the loss or loosening of his national identity. However, unlike Viennese creative intellectuals who had but a fading and weak Austrian national identity and patriotism, most of their Hungarian counterparts never had the faintest doubt or uncertainty about their national loyalty. Magyar identity was redundant. It could be shaken neither by slander nor bans. Ady responded to the campaigns against him by "banning" the society of the lords and squires. In doing so, he reinterpreted the prevailing idea of nation.

Instead of the nobility and "historical middle class," Ady held the simple workers, peasants, and professionals to be the nation. Only freedom and the rise of the people can rejuvenate the nation, he believed, and only a rejuvenated nation could realize social and democratic progress. This democratic idea of nation made Hungarian reconciliation with its neighbors a possibility. This idea was familiar to reformers, but Ady's form of expression was new and original. Seeking to express this yearning for democracy, Ady reached back to the seventeenth and eighteenth centuries, to the "kuruc" freedom fighters who were recruited from serfs, free soldiers, and peasants. Magyars associated them with a specific popular patriotism and the language of poetry; they were a perfect vehicle for his feelings. But it was Ady's genius that transformed the archaic metrical forms, rhythm, and structure of this poetry about the kurucs into the sophisticated form of fin-de-siècle Symbolism. (This creative modernization can be compared with Bartók's similar musical language reform.) Ady revived not only this poetic form but the names and personalities of some of the characteristically valiant kuruc soldiers, particularly the betrayed, defeated, and exiled ones who had lost everything except their loyalty to their country. As fascinating as the new aesthetic form might be, it was also attractive because it identified with the tragic fate of the people's history.

Ady was not alone in the fin-de-siècle literary revolution in Hungary. Outstanding writers, poets, and critics, all in the vanguard of modernism, gathered around him and the brilliant literary journal *Nyugat* (West). This generation of reformers emancipated arts and literature for the unprivileged people and identified them with the nation. They were able not only to reconcile the concept of the "historic" nation and the "unhistoric" people but also to bring the Hungarian nation ("Magyardom") into harmony with the rest of Europe and mankind.

Ady did not stand alone in his artistic aspirations. With respect to social status and constitution, the writer Gyula Krúdy, the painter Lajos Gulácsy, and the musician Béla Bartók stood close to him.

Like Ady, the former two came from impoverished gentry families. Bartók was from the traditional intelligentsia. All, however, fell out of the old social framework and all became modernists. Just like Ady, they too adopted the feeling of life and the means of expression of Art Nouveau and Symbolism. Generally speaking, they moved easily between appearance and dream, between imaginary existence and reality. Nevertheless, they always sharply distinguished Hungarian social reality from appearances. Although they were not involved in political activities, their art, their many deeds allied them with the camp of radical progress. This holds especially true during the First World War and the following years of revolution.

The synthesis of people and nation in Ady's poetry was accomplished in this period. In the dark years, illness, despair, and fear of the future took hold of him. He felt sure that mankind faced catastrophe and predicted the coming Magyar misfortune as the general fate of mankind. In his "Leading the Dead," he realized the absurdity of the world and foresaw the advent of an age when reason would lose control over the fate of small nations and creative intellectuals. One of his last dialogues between two kurucs reads:

> It's all the same, my friend, to me
> If wolves eat me, or the Devil,
> But surely we will be eaten.
>
> If a bear eats us, it's all the same.
> The sad, age-old thing is:
> It's matter of chance who eats me and you.[75]

What did Ady believe was left for creative and talented individuals? Only to preserve truth, humanism, and the arts, as a seed keeps life under the snow.

The individual cases described suggest that creativity and originality are the privilege of the marginal intelligentsia, an intelligentsia independent of political parties and ideologies. The historian must, however, handle the method of verification through individual examples with caution, and must view with suspicion the validity of his own conception based on such verification. He must pay attention to counterexamples. Reviewing the lives of creative talents in Vienna and Budapest, I found explicitly "establishment careers." Particularly conspicuous are the careers of architects, in comparison with the overwhelmingly deviating and marginalized careers of painters. (The difference seems to be obvious: architects are mainly dependent on patronage; painters, however, are freer to express their visions.)

Nonetheless, it is precisely at the turn of the century that we encounter irregular examples. Coming from an affluent middle-class family, the highly successful Vienna architect Otto Wagner or, in Budapest, Ödön Lechner, risked their careers by joining the Sezession. Both were indeed founding masters of Art Nouveau architecture. Their choice was not motivated by alienation and marginality but, rather, the recognized need to surpass "style architecture." Also guided by similar consideration was Gustav Klimt, the successful Ringstrasse painter, who left behind affluence and security for the artistic principles of the Sezession. With this countergroup may be ranked Josef Hoffmann, Josef Maria Olbrich, and Kolo Moser from Vienna, with Simon Hollósy, Aladár Árkay, and Béla Lajta from Budapest. The counterexamples are also underlined by Richard Strauss, who belonged to the establishment and who was not particular about his political contacts. His innovative talent may serve as a warning that marginality is not the precondition of creativity in every case. We therefore have to verify our theory on a broader sample, examining whether the correlation between creativity and marginality was at least a tendency.

Looking for the social backround of creativity, I felt in a crossfire between "marginalized" and "established" intellectuals. At this point, I put together a sample that included 70 Viennese and 130 Budapest intellectuals, representatives of one or another modernist group or trend.

For the Budapest sample, I selected individuals based on the type and intensity of their participation in various fin-de-siècle journals and reviews. With cultural areas for which this analysis was not applicable, I used standard works in the field, for example the most recent edition of *Magyar müvészet*.[76] This latter method also proved useful in examining the Viennese sample because the modernist movements in Vienna usually did not have lasting journals, with the exception of the Wiener Sezession's *Ver Sacrum*. Thus, I used some of the major recent works in Austrian cultural history, most from the last ten years.[77]

I also included some German-speaking writers from Prague who actually belonged to Austrian culture.

I set out to analyze the individuals' social and family background, ethnic and religious affiliation, profession, and how intensively they were marginalized or integrated in their society. I should explain here what I mean by the term "marginalized." American sociologists have tended to define marginality as racial or cultural "hybridization." As one declares, "The marginal man . . . is one whom fate has condemned to live in two, not merely different but antagonistic, cultures."[78] Marginal man has been regarded as nonintegrated but still nondeviant. He is usually an outsider, "more self-segregated than pushed out of society."[79] Edward Sagarin notes: "There are groups of people who are on the fringes of society . . . [who] are not seen as a threat to others and not labeled anti-social."[80] Sagarin here is speaking mostly of marginal groups, especially immigrants and other assimilates (Jews, for example). "Yet marginality can be highly individual, taking on the form of rebellious nonconformity."[81]

In this study, I concentrated on three major types of marginality. The first is the psychic or constitutional marginality manifested in asociability, communication problems, recurrent depressions, and neuroses. A typical case of psychic marginality was Ernst Mach; another example is Otto Weininger, the infamous misogynist, who committed suicide at the age of twenty-three.

The second type of marginality can be found in an individual or group that exists within or between other predominant groups. This could be called situational marginality. The third type is of a political nature. Some individuals or groups are not marginal by birth or situation, but become marginal by not conforming with or by segregating themselves from the Establishment. I would call this form oppositional marginality.

I accept Jerry Seigel's concept that although bohemians can be marginalized, "Bohemia" as a whole is not separate from bourgeois society. "Bohemian and bourgeois were—and are—parts of a single field: They imply, require and attract each other."[82] It was in the nineteenth century, Seigel suggests, that the modern bourgeoisie "assumed the position in society that allowed 'Bohemia' to take form as its reverse image and underside."[83] Still, the author admits that "Bohemia grew up where the borders of bourgeois existence were murky and uncertain. It was a space . . . where social margins and frontiers were probed and tested."[84] He points out that both the frontiers and residents of "Bohemia" changed during the nineteenth century, moving the region toward marginality and the avant garde. I would, however, stress that "Bohemia" was always receptive to marginal figures and many native Bohemians readily embraced marginalization.

Now let me briefly sum up the main results of my sample.

In the Hungarian sample, we find that 48 percent of the individuals are Jewish, 27 percent Catholic, and 25 percent Protestant. It also turns out that the modernist groups were mainly composed of impoverished lesser nobility (the majority officials and professionals), rising middle-class Jews, and assimilated Germans. In the Viennese sample, modernist groups have a different cast. The ratio of Jews was high, also 48 percent, but virtually all of the rest were German Christians (though, to be sure, many of these were converted Jews). Unlike the Hungarians, the overwhelming majority of creative intellectuals (about 80 percent) came from the ranks of the upper middle class, the loyal Austrian bureaucracy and professional class, out of the Besitzbürgertum and Bildungsbürgertum.

The results clearly show that the modernist trend was supported by a highly mobile bourgeoisie or, as in Vienna, by the members of the wealthy "second society." What is most striking is that, in Budapest, traditional social strata, including the declining nobility, participated to such a large extent. In contrast, the German "nationalist" middle class played an almost negligible role in the pursuit of modern scholarship, the formation of a modern world view, and the revolution in the arts.

SOCIAL MARGINALITY AND CULTURAL CREATIVITY

What does the sample tell us about the correlation between social (including ethnic) marginality and cultural creativity?

Carefully studying the lives and works of these individuals, I arrived at the conclusion that out of the Budapest sample we can classify about two-thirds (65 percent) and of the Viennese about three-quarters (74 percent) as marginalized men or outsiders by virtue of their social position of opposition to the values, ideals, and morals of the Establishment. In Budapest, marginality was found most frequently among poets, writers, painters, and musicians, and less often among scholars. In Vienna, scholars and writers were strongly overrepresented as marginal men, and artists were underrepresented.

In Budapest, marginal men came out of two distinct social strata: the intelligentsia of the rising bourgeois middle class and the declining gentry middle class. The influential group of positivist, middle-class sociologists, for instance, did not represent their class, as they detested its social conformism and political opportunism. Since the country's feudal remnants and backwardness still prevailed, their belief in a utopia of rational evolutionism was correct and realistic, and easily reconcilable with scientific and artistic modernism. Still, it was not this group which really represented modernism, probably because their utopia finally proved elusive. The most original and creative talents can be found in the ranks of the déclassé and marginalized gentry who joined the social reform and Art Nouveau movements. These individuals lived in a state of "multiple marginality" in Budapest, a kind of "symbiosis without integration" in the assimilated German and Jewish middle class. They had no hopes for a utopia, but accepted radical reforms in order to preserve Hungary and

Hungarian identity. They were simply fascinated by the artistic and moral values of contemporary modernism.

If we are looking for socially definable categories in Vienna, we face some difficult problems. Except for the Sezessionists, all the modernist groups were rather amorphous, without much organizational continuity or framework. Consider, for example, Das Junge Wien. It was an informal, friendly group of a few well-to-do literati who were social strangers to each other and were connected mainly by common aesthetic values and a hatred of everything academic, conventional, positivist, or naturalistic.[85] The permanent members of this group had different social backgrounds and positions, different religions and political affiliations. What they shared was a "multiple marginality," a growing alienation from the threatening reality of Vienna.

The financial state of the Viennese modernists was much better, and their general disposition—their general malaise—much worse than was the case with their Hungarian counterparts. They no longer had utopian visions or illusions of reform. They lacked even a strong national identity, unlike a Hungarian Ady or Bartók, a Polish Wyspianski, or a Czech Brezina, Janácek, or Hasek. Thus they arrived at a new perception of the existential problems of mankind. They could even be regarded as the forerunners of existentialist philosophy.

THE DISTINCTIVE ROLE OF AUSTRIA
AND THE JEWS OF THE MONARCHY

Finally, I have to answer, even if very briefly, two immanent questions. First, why Austria? Why did this backward Central European monarchy become one of the centers of scientific innovation and artistic modernism? It is impossible to reduce this complex phenomenon to a single reason. But keeping to the topic at hand, I will only try to explain one of the main reasons: the Habsburg Monarchy itself existed in "multiple marginality." The Empire was situated between East and West, with the semifeudal, noncapitalistic southeastern regions of Europe on one side and the Western industrialized countries and consolidated nation states on the other. The Empire was actually multinational, but supranational in its conception of the state and in the mentality of its ruling elite. The Empire was developing and prospering, and declining and disintegrating at the same time. The Empire was an acknowledged great power even in the last hours before its dissolution; it straddled the margin between existence and nonexistence. The Empire embodied marginality during this fin-de-siècle crisis.

The second question is: why mostly Jews? Why can one find so many Jewish creative talents in the fin-de-siècle cultural renewal?

This question is neither new nor surprising. We have a great many answers and explanations. But first let me quote a competent scholar and contemporary, the language philosopher Fritz Mauthner: "A Jew born in one of the

Slavic provinces of Austria is compelled to deal with linguistics. As a matter of fact he learned . . . to understand three languages at the same time [German, Czech, and Yiddish]." This is the reason why he, as a child, preferred to raise the crazy question "why does[n't] one name stand for one thing? Why is it this way in Czech, that way in German. . . . As a Jew in bilingual Bohemia, I was 'predestined' to pay attention to languages."[86] And, let me add, to raise axiomatic questions as well. Mauthner was unknown and unappreciated until well after his death, when posterity rediscovered his writings. He was born in Horitz, a small Czech city. His father was the owner of a middle-sized textile factory, his relatives were respectably middle class. Even in childhood he was shy and retiring, not suited for business. He went to high school in Prague, but he considered himself German-Bohemian. His love for Germany was, however, unreciprocated. He himself wrote, in a letter of 1906: "Liebloses Land, ich liebe Dich (Loveless land, I love you)." Never having gone to a university, he never received any academic degree. He occupied himself with journalism as well as belles lettres, but mostly philosophy, which was his hobby.

His work was never recognized and appreciated by anyone, except the other undiscovered genius, Ludwig Wittgenstein. He respected Jewish tradition, and his critique of language was developed "first and foremost in religious terms," but he rejected dogma and what he felt to be the lies of religion. He died in 1926 but, since there was no Jewish cemetery, he was buried among Lutherans. His epitaph reads: "Von Menschsein Erlöst" (Redeemed from Human Existence).[87]

Mauthner was a typical figure of Jewish marginality. There were many intellectuals in the old Monarchy who struggled in similar circumstances: assimilated Jews, good citizens and patriots who were nevertheless not fully integrated into gentile society. Gustav Mahler said of himself: "Triply homeless (*heimatlos*): as a Bohemian among Austrians, as Austrian among Germans, and a Jew among all nations of the world."[88]

Kafka many times complained of the "diabolic circles of alienation," as his biographer, Max Brod, reveals.[89] He was a stranger as a German speaker among Czechs, as a Jew among Germans, as a bourgeois among workers, and as an indifferent man among Jews. Similarly, in Munich, Jacob Wassermann wrote that he was totally an outsider there: "as literate, as German without social legitimation, as Jew without any allegiance."[90]

Still we do not have to think that multiple alienation was some sort of exclusively Jewish destiny. Rilke felt himself isolated and abandoned in his parents' house as well, and even more so in military school, from which he sought refuge in God and poetry. Robert Musil made a similar journey away from his own social class, from military school, and finally, from the Monarchy itself. This set of examples can be followed by a great many marginalized talents in Vienna, Prague, Cracow, and Budapest, as well.

And if we still regard the Jewish contribution to modern culture extraordinarily relevant, first we have to take social structure into consideration. The

Jews of Central Europe did not constitute an independent national group divided in the usual way along class and status lines. Instead, in the Monarchy the large majority were middle class, only a minority working class, making up one-third of the Jewish earning population. It is obvious that a group which is more than 60 percent middle class—with a quarter of these being intellectuals—can produce more writers, scientists, scholars, and artists than a society that is largely agrarian or made up mostly of workers and craftsmen.

One can argue that the Jewish lower middle class also sent more children to higher education and sacrificed more money for their higher education than the equivalent Christian stratum. This can perhaps be explained on the one hand by the high prestige of learning and knowledge within Jewish tradition, and on the other by the inequalities of opportunity for Jews even after emancipation. The various paths to upward mobility and social prominence such as public service, the army, and diplomacy remained closed to Jewish youth, who therefore thronged to the medical, legal, and other free professions.

However, all these arguments concern the unexpectedly large dimensions of the contribution, and do not approach the crux of the problem: what explains the great attraction of modernism for talented Jews? Perhaps this propensity could be explained as part of an inherited inclination toward radicalism, innovation, and other sociopsychological factors. I think that a valid answer to the question was given by the outstanding economist Thorstein Veblen. He argued that Jews had a disproportionately great share in the intellectual life of modern civilization. "They count particularly among the vanguard, the pioneers . . . and iconoclasts." Looking for an explanation, Veblen asserted that the first requirement for creative work in modern science is "a skeptical frame of mind." And it is just this skepticism that is the "situative property" of assimilated Jewish intellectuals. "[It is] only when the gifted Jew escapes from the cultural environment created and fed by the particular genius of his own people, only when he falls into the alien lines of gentile inquiry and becomes a naturalized, though hyphenate, citizen in the gentile republic of learning, that he comes into his own as a creative leader. . . . It is by loss of allegiance to the people of his origin, that he finds himself in the vanguard of modern inquiry."[91] In their prototypical marginal situation, Jewish intellectuals can arrive at a high level of "impartiality," that is, nonaffiliation. But they have had to pay for such immunity with the loss of the security and peace of mind "that is the birthright of the safe and sane quietist."

Starting from a different position, the well-known social psychologist, Kurt Lewin, acknowledges that assimilation to gentile society plunges Jewish intellectuals into marginality, generating psychic tensions and conflicts. These are socially and psychologically harmful, he argues, but may be beneficial for creative work.[92] The Hungarian writer and artist Anna Lesznai (she and her entire family were converted Jews) also characterized Hungarian Jews as highly marginalized individuals. She wrote in 1917 that to be an assimilated Jew does not mean to belong to a denomination or a religious community but to live in a steadily neurotic state of mind. Conversion may be destructive and stimulating at the same time.[93]

In sum, it may be said that at the time of the turn of the century the tendency toward marginalization of the creative intelligentsia surfaced in Europe. It may also be demonstrated that this tendency showed a certain correlation with new research trends, new ideas, and the scientific, literary, and artistic formulation of a new physical view of the world. Marginality and sensitivity, modernism and creativity were universal European experiences and the fate of modern life. In the case of Vienna, Budapest, and Prague a critical historical moment of epochal change coincided with a declining and marginal Empire. Within the Monarchy it coincided with declining Hungarian and Polish gentry intellectuals, and raising multiple-marginalized Jewish intellectuals and many other sensitive talents with a split consciousness and divided loyalty.

24. Francis Joseph with his great-nephew, Charles, the last
emperor of the Habsburg monarchy. Vienna, 1894

Chapter Eight

VOX POPULI: INTERCEPTED LETTERS
IN THE FIRST WORLD WAR

THE LETTERS recorded here are in themselves beautiful, eloquent, and moving; moreover, some eighty years later, they still have the power to provoke a sense of outrage in the reader. Over and above their inherent worth as human documents, they possess a particular value for the historian. Ethnographers, historians, and literary historians know only too well how few authentic sources exist from which we can experience at first hand the outlook, the thoughts and feelings, in short the mentality, of ordinary people; and more especially, from which we can experience such a mentality—of serfs, of poor peasants, and of workers—without any inevitably distorting meditation: in their own words and as a confession of their deepest feelings.

The vast majority of the people were unlettered at the end of the nineteenth century. The few among them who could read and write seldom had cause to put pen to paper. And even when they were obliged to write a letter (or, more likely, to dictate it to the scribe of the neighborhood) it was unlikely that it would have survived, since only the nobility—and only the wealthiest at that—together with prosperous burghers and the authorities were in a position to preserve their correspondence. It is not only historical accident therefore, nor solely the orientation of historians, that is responsible for the fact that in numerous published collections of letters vox populi is only very occasionally to be heard. It is also historically speaking highly understandable that the collection of serfs' letters published twenty years ago, are not letters in the true sense of the word, but rather petitions, complaints, or written formulations of legal claims, and thus in the main not composed by the serfs themselves but by students, priests, and such people as estate factors.[1] The true expression of vox populi in written form really only begins in the twentieth century, and even then is at first largely restricted to the framing of requests and similar matters.[2]

Of course, before simple people—peasants and workers—could even think about writing letters, the skills of reading and writing had to have become widespread. This only occurred following the institution of universal compulsory education in 1868, and even then only after a lag of decades, around the turn of the century. But before the peasant or his wife reached the point of actually writing a letter, an exceptional set of circumstances had to arise, involving the disturbance of time-hallowed rhythms of existence and the dissolution of the familiar patterns of family and social life: in short, the conditions resulting from the First World War. At the same time, the fact that these authentic letters of the people, the by-products of extraordinary social upheaval, have not been lost to us in the absence of family archives or such, is entirely due to a single phenomenon: namely, the all-embracing tutelage of the twentieth century's ubiquitous state bureaucracy. In order for letters deemed damaging to morale or suspect on other grounds to be subjected to an enormously painstaking scrutiny, and also for the suppressed parts to be conscientiously recorded, a sophisticated and pedantic application of censorship was required, itself the end product of a centuries-long tradition of bureaucracy that had reached its apotheosis under the Austro-Hungarian Monarchy. The letters printed here are to be found among the documentary material of the various censoring authorities in the Vienna and Budapest war archives.[3] As back-up material to the censors' reports on the mood of the populace, as well as sources on their information pools and their suggestions for further data-gathering activities, one finds hundreds of thousands of quotations and extracts from letters, but very few originals. In the Budapest war archive, however, several hundred original letters are available. From the latter I have selected the letters published here; in doing so I was not guided by any preformed concept but instead was concerned to exhibit typical examples.

THE LETTERS

1. István Szabó of Jánoshalma to his brother-in-law, Vince Kovács in Tula, March 11, 1917

"Dear Brother-in-law, I can report that here at home we are all in good health, and we all wish that you are too." He goes on to say that he himself is in the hospital, that some of their relatives are missing, and others are wounded. Everything is expensive, particularly labor, if indeed one can get any. His sister is also in a difficult situation, alone on the farm and without any help. "She wanted me to buy you out so that you could come home, but that would cost too much. The notaries here are so arrogant and greedy, they won't even write a letter for less than 5 or 6 hundred forints . . . a poor man has no rights, save one, namely, that poor as he is, he may go to the front."

2. Mrs. Kiss from Békés to her husband in Grosseto, Italy, April 16, 1917

"My dear, beloved husband, in God's name. I wish that these few lines find you in the same good health as they find me." Things are not too bad with her; she worries only that her husband might have married someone else while in captivity, as many of the prisoners do. She has been pondering a lot whether he had done the same; he could perhaps deny her. But not everyone has such thoughts, and "I could never bear to do such a thing, because one can only truly love one person, my dear, good husband."

3. Ernő Sallay from Győr to his elder brother, György Sallay in Sulmona, Italy, April 18, 1917

He reassures his brother that he has had good news. Soon they can expect great changes "because the belly will decide, ours and other people's."

4. Mrs. Koza from Galgamácsa to her husband in Vittoria, Italy, April 20, 1917

"Praised be the sacred name of Jesus Christ, now and in all eternity, amen; I send you my greetings from afar, I wish in dear God's name, that these few lines from me find you in good health in that far off land. We are both well, thank God, and lack for nothing, only sad that you have been stolen from us and are so far away; my heart is almost bursting with worry and grief, because I cannot even speak to you in letters, because you write to me my dear, faithful husband, that you have received no letters from me, although I write you three times a week. Yet you write that months go by without your receiving a letter from me. Life is misery, I don't know what I can do, when I write to you, the letters are drowned with my tears, often I cannot see them for the tears in my eyes, because I also have had no letter from you for ages. Between February and the 20th of April I have had no letter from you; you write you are no longer in Padua and I should have sent you some bacon and something for Easter; but I sent them to you on February 2nd, when I took a 3 kilo packet to the post with things inside worth 25 forints; but I can no longer hope that you received it, because I sent it to Padua; since you're no longer there, ask Jóska Pesti if he knows anything about your packet.

"My dear husband I know you would be overjoyed to receive it, because you could gorge yourself with the food in it for several days. Inside there were bacon, pancakes, nuts, your prayer book, tobacco, two bath towels, two small hand towels, something to read, all packed in a box and sewed up with the best linen; well, someone will enjoy it. I would send you what little remains also, my dear, true, husband, because I know how much you would like it, if you had it, but when I send you something and you don't receive it, it will be eaten by somebody else, because nobody tries to trace a lost parcel, especially if it belongs to the poor; I feel sorry about the old cloth, not to mention the food; we also buy everything by the kilo, one can't live otherwise, except by scrimping and sparing. So I would send you packets if you were going to get them, and also money, but if you never get it I'm only helping somebody else, and we desperately need everything we have; if I was only a little bird, I would fly to you, oh so much I would like to give you, and could bring to you; but I am not a bird, and cannot fly to you, I can only grieve and offer you my heart; you should close it up in your own, in the very depths of your heart, where no one can tear it away, my dear true husband, for my heart knows only you, beats only for you, by

night and by day, in my every act, I think continually of you, where you might
be in the wide world, or where you languish in that foreign land, and whether I will
ever see you again or never, because my grieving orphaned heart is full of sorrow
that you have been away from me for three years; here at home are many soldiers released from service, the rich and fortunate, those who could buy themselves out of a
soldier's fate, who cheat the many widows and orphans here at home, and at least
have something to lose, but the poor have nothing, and can grieve only for what they
do not have. I do not know how you are, my dear, but here the prisoners are well
treated, I would thank God if you are also well treated, but I have no way of know-
ing, my good, true husband. I embrace and kiss you, and so does little Örzsike, and
my mother and father also greet you and we wish you good health in God's name,
God be with you and with us."

5. *An unknown writer from Temesvár to Béla Fixmer in Padua, May 3, 1917*

The letter begins with a short report on the suspension of work on May 1. The
shops were closed, and in the inner city there was a demonstration, "because we
want peace, justice, and bread, and that you poor sufferers [at the front] should return home, . . . we are often hungry, because there is so little bread. I fear that there
will soon be an explosion, because of the hunger, God help us all, for I don't know
where it will all end."

6. *Mrs. Böthi of Gomba to her husband in Rouen, May 7, 1917*

She reports to her husband that their relations and acquaintances are either at the
front, in captivity, or here at home living out their lives as cripples. "Géza is a prisoner of war, Imre is a cripple, Magda's husband is missing, our neighbor, Gyula,
was twice wounded, Pali is at the front. Only a few survived." Among your friends
some have survived, some are no longer here, most are at the front, if not killed.
"Only the rich are at home, because they are all deaf and blind, it's only their sack
of money that can see . . . those who can do so amass money; the poor are all away"
at the front. She apologizes that she cannot write more often; what with the children, the cattle, and the sowing there are many worries and much work.

7. *Julia Mogyoródi from Mór to her brother Sándor Mogyoródi in Alfieri, Italy (postmarked May 8, 1917)*

Soon she will visit the woman who writes letters for her and bring the children
home. If the war is not over by the end of the year, they will all die. Starvation is
threatening the people, for weeks one can get no flour, for three to four weeks at a
time. "One only dares to look at it; if one eats from it, it very soon vanishes, and
then we'll have only the sun to look at." Everything is rationed, but ration cards can
only be gotten with great difficulty. "First one has to go to the local administration
for the ration cards, where one is ruthlessly pushed about, and from early in the
morning until midday is made to run from one office to another, until with enormous difficulty one is able to get a card; then one is jostled by the gendarmes' bayo-
nets from midday to evening in front of the shop door, until at last one can get in;

but then there is no flour left and one goes home empty-handed. And it will be a week before there is again something available." The situation is desperate, but one has to trust in God.

8. Mrs. Vida from Feketegyarmat to her brother Mihály Erdős in Padua, May 14, 1917

"I send my letter to a foreign land, in the hope it will reach my dear, imprisoned brother." One has not enough hours in the day, everyone runs after food, prices are impossible. A servant gets two kilos of flour for ten days "which might be all right if it was wheat flour, but it is often only a third wheat and the rest maize, although many would be happy if there were only maize pancakes," and many have no bread at all. Women, men, old people, and children stay in their houses with nothing to eat for a whole week and can't work. "May the dear God have mercy on them and send the prisoners home."

9. Erzsébet Murányi from Istenmezeje to her husband Mátyás Ludwig in Cassino, Italy, May 21, 1917

She complains that she has had no letter from her husband, and that he seems not to have had hers. She was therefore overjoyed with one she did receive, but her joy was mixed with tears, she wept for the beautiful day when God will bring them together again, if it ever comes. She has to bear a heavy fate, while a woman can't undertake men's work. The beef fetches a good price, but she is afraid to sell it, since one can't get anything with the money. "If we work, it is bad, and if we don't work it is also bad; if we work and have something for our pains, then it is taken away from us; but if we don't work, we don't have anything to eat." Hitherto there has been no actual starvation, but there is little flour, little bread, and the future is completely uncertain. "Oh, I have so much to endure, what can I do, what will become of me?" The five orphans only cry all day, they miss their father terribly, they only speak about what he will bring, will it be sugar, apples, or cakes?

10. Mrs. Szöllősi from Hajduszováta to her husband in Padua, June 15, 1917

She complains of the high prices and the food shortages. The little children are crying "because for a week there was no bread in the house, and when I go in tears to the magistrate, he tells me we should eat the air, such people should be thrown out of office, it is an evil shame how a poor woman is treated here." The wheat was taken from the village, and one can't get food at any price; nor can one keep cattle any more, "we will all die of hunger."

11. Mrs. Orosz from Nagybajcs to her husband in Arezzano, July 20, 1917

She can report nothing new, the war seems to be never-ending. The masters were "clever enough to stumble into war" to the ruination of the entire nation, and with the result that those at home starve; "but they are not clever enough to make peace; that will have to be left to the socialists."

12. Mrs. Rákóczi of Mezōgyán to her husband in Vilabate, Italy, September 9, 1917.

The high prices are impossible, the cow has had to be sold because there is no feed, but she has given up trying to cope with everything, "life is no longer life, but sheer misery. . . . Weeping we fall asleep, and weeping we get up in the morning; as we eat we are still weeping, as we think over our life, we think why doesn't the earth simply open up and swallow the millions of poor, so that only the masters and bosses remain? I know that would soon put an end to the war. The bosses are all at home, the dear God should hang another war around their necks if they aren't yet satiated with the bloodshed."

13. Mrs. Piti from Szentes to her husband in Siena, September 20, 1917

She misses her husband terribly, the only comfort for her would be a few lines from him, since "my very life is in your hands, when I get some dear lines from you I feel better, but when I get none, life is unbearable, and I at once remember how much I care about you; but it's all the same whether I die here or somewhere else." Since it makes no difference where one dies, she is sorry she didn't go to war with her husband. She need only think how "two true hearts are torn apart by the evils of the world," to break out in grief. My husband "has lost both his feet . . . yet he has to endure it and get around with crutches." Meanwhile we have to endure the piggish behavior of the villains who have bought exemption, the many fake invalids."

She has come to the conclusion that "God himself is no more than a villain, not to mention his people, who are capable of anything from robbery to murder."

14. Károly Tóth from Csepel to his sons in Vittoria, September 30, 1917

The war will only end "when the great have had their fun and the profiteers have filled their pockets . . . and there is no one left to send to the front, then will it perhaps come to an end."

15. Mrs. F. Gy. to her husband in Orvieto, October 21, 1917

"My beloved, golden-hearted, good husband, thank the dear Lord that we are well, as we hope with all our hearts you are also, my dear, good husband, you should know that I have kept all your letters, and have answered them all, but I don't know where these letters were intercepted. I don't understand why the letters are not delivered, my dear, good husband; in many letters I have already written about my circumstances, in what misery I find myself, and all that has happened; but now I can't hold out any longer, the dear God has laid this burden upon me, my dear, good husband, I shall describe how it happened, my dear husband, when I was digging the beets in autumn, the farmer persuaded me to this wicked life, he constantly urged me to do it with him, and I as a young wife, listened to his urgings, because he told me that I could then have what I wanted for the cattle, and I listened to him once, and was made miserable by it, but my dear husband, you know very well that I must always be running after the cattle, so that at least we still have something when you return, and I didn't do it because I am a bad woman, or perhaps a whore, but because I tried so hard to do everything for the best and now I am so unhappy. I have a daughter from the farmer, Jula had her baptized, your God-daughter, the dear God placed also this burden on me, and now what can I do? Forgive me, my dear, good man, write to me whether, when with God's help you come home, you will forgive me, and if not, then write to tell me that, too; but in any case write me what you propose to do and only then will I think about what is to become of us. (I enclose a picture of the little girl.) Now I am going to sleep with the children, the two little girls, the dear God will provide for us if you will not, and anyway it's all the same to me, it's not only me the dear God robbed of my senses; the same thing has happened to many who were older than me; and yet I can't say that I did it because I was bad, because I wasn't an evil woman, thank God! This was the fate prepared for me, so do not be angry with me, my dear, good husband, and forgive me. We all greet you and send you kisses, myself and the little girls; because of the worry I am not in the best of health."

16. Jan Strba from Pozsony to his comrades imprisoned in Russia, January 20, 1918

A deserter, who is held in the barracks at Pozsony, describes the pitiful story of his escape from Russian captivity, and his arrest on his return home. Although he had already been caught and beaten in Russia, he escaped again, to come back and serve his fatherland. "And what did my fatherland give me, stupid ox that I am? My reward is prison and persecution." He thinks that the comrades in Russia have a better lot and more freedom. "Home is simply where there is freedom."

17. Sándor Kaskó to his father Dániel Kaskó in Nagykövesd, from Troick, Russia, May 15, 1918

The Hungarian prisoner-of-war informs his parents that he has joined the Red Army. That was simply his duty, since "even if I once took up weapons on behalf of the capitalists and the bosses, now I would not deserve to go on living if I stood by like a coward, while our brothers defended freedom." The workers are his brothers, the enemy are the capitalists, the lords and kings. They set the poor at each other's throats, but now the same weapons will be used against them. The revolution was caused by the oppression and desperation of the people. Many tried to escape from captivity, but were driven back at the Austro-Hungarian frontier. Thus, thousands of ordinary soldiers had joined the Red Army. Soon they would march on Hungary, to free the laboring classes from the yoke of the bosses. He is well and receives 150 roubles per month, not, of course, for nothing, but in return for military service.

18. Angela Krenki in Vienna to her husband Leopold Krenki in Ekaterionoslaw, February 1, 1918

"Dear husband of mine!

"I greet you with all my heart, and have to say that I have no news of your parents and brothers and sisters, because I still have not been in contact and when you come back I shall be interested to see whether you come to me or [them]. Your brother is in the field and no longer in Völlersdorf, Resie and Poldi have gone away again.

"I have been frantically knitting, what else can I do because everything's expensive, one can't get anything and everybody goes so hungry our very skins begin to crack. In Vienna everyone hopes for peace soon, my darling, if there's really a God he should see how we suffer here, one could well believe the dead had risen when one sees what hunger has done to people, and indeed how I eat a scrap of bread myself, I'm not at all surprised when I read that someone or other has done this or that, because every woman has a bad conscience when she sees her child wasting away, at the court adults get $^1/_2$ liter of milk and we only $^1/_4$ liter for children daily and weekly $^1/_2$ kilo of flour, 6 decagrams of dripping, $1^1/_2$ kilos of potatoes, and that's all for a child that one day will have to earn its daily bread, and half of the potatoes must be thrown out, the soldiers have said they won't shoot at us if the general strike comes, because we're hungry, and they would give in, but the Hungarians and Bosnians said it not the Germans, and even if the order comes we have had enough and we want peace.

"Your faithful Wubie and Burlie greet you and send you kisses."

19. *Maria Schlosser of Schwaderbach, Groslitz, to her husband in Italy, March 13, 1917*

"If death does not free us from the world, we poor people will have to slaughter our children like pigs, so that we have something to eat and our children have peace, because they are whimpering from the time they wake in the morning and there is nothing to be done. The Lord God should send 1,000 cannons against us and destroy us, for no one cares about the poor. In the end we shall have to eat the earth itself, or the better quality dung like the guard dogs. We want to break down everything that stands in our way, if we are not better provided for, that is our ultimate goal."

20. *Maria Sedláčkova of Reznovice to her husband Ludvig Sedlacek, imprisoned in Russia, January 19, 1918*

"But I do not know whether we will see each other again, since we are treated here like slaves; the mayor's arrogance is insupportable, and he fiddles the food handouts, which is not surprising since his one aim is to avoid conscription. I don't know if he can, but he apparently claims that he has the right to beat us, and there have in fact been cases of this."

21. *The citizens of the District of Fojnica to the Emperor. Slav. Brod. November 15, 1917*

"In our district of Fojnica the people have been completely neglected; not enough assistance or food is available for the distressed poor; also there is no one we can turn to with our problems, since all requests are contemptuously rejected. We have been deprived of our sons and breadwinners, but the officials are merciless with us and tolerate no petitions.

"Your Majesty! There is here great injustice and many people are sickening and dying of hunger and all suffer the greatest misery. The officials have requisitioned all the grain and potatoes from the peasants, and there is none for us, and we get only what comes from Hungary. In our area there would have been sufficient stocks of grain to last two years and more. They have taken it all for their own personal needs over two years. They give the cattle barley and corn and we, the poor people, are desperate for bread, and hunger, although the situation could be avoided. They traded and are still trading with our grain; thus they sell a kilo for 6 crowns, and a kilo of potatoes for 3 or 4. In our district the bosses eat and drink with our people and take bribes from the poor. The following persons are concerned:

"In the local council, Stojic, Dujmusic, and Koscica. Then the merchants Serkija and Cunkovic. They sell grain at 6 to 10 crowns a kilo, and are hoarding the grain. In autumn the council ordered that the grain could be sold at dearer prices. The profits from this they divided among themselves. A certain Derwis Effendi, the notary public, satisfied all the needs of his Turks and for us Catholics there was no one to speak a word. A third man, a stranger from Visoko, sells grain, potatoes, smoked meat, dripping, and cheese from our district to other councils, and nothing is left for us. He bribes the council and shares the proceeds with them. He buys from the peasants at high prices and sells it at double what he payed. The Turks control us and everything is done to please them. Also the merchants and mayor have become profiteers during the war—Niko Ilicic, Marian Dragicevic. They know nothing of the war. They have everything they need. They have gold and silver illegally hoarded, as well as copper at 4 crowns a kilo, all the best bits sought out and kept by them. There are also plenty of Turks who have bribed the council, in order to avoid the call-up. In this distress and misery we beseech Your Majesty most humbly to give us other officals and other people who could alleviate the lot of the Catholics here. When we complain to the council the answer is always the same, we are to be silent, we can perish for all they care, and they threaten us with the front, while they themselves have no fear of being sent there, but will continue to grind the faces of the poor, so that they can stuff themselves and get drunk, while the youth and the people waste away from hunger. We are forbidden to write petitions, and if one lands up with the government in error, it is sent back to the local authorities, and those who framed it are punished. We are given only 4 kilos of corn, and sometimes there is nothing for 2 to 3 days and so the people waste away and starve. The officials treat us as if we were the guilty ones as if we had made no sacrifices for the fatherland. But it is not we who are hoarding gold, silver, and copper, and all manner of valuables; we have sent our sons and breadwinners for the defense of our fatherland and Your Majesty. We were not sorry for it. But what makes us miserable is that the officials have no insight and no human feelings for us, since they torture us with hunger and high prices, and allow no representations, and forbid all petitions. We poor people receive no charitable assistance during the war, those whose relatives are in the armed forces receive 30 heller per day for a child, 40 heller for adults; that is for food and clothing; if one can bribe Messrs. Koscic and Stojic, however, one can get better financial support, but the poor cannot afford it, and our children sometimes go 10 days without bread. We humbly beseech Your Majesty that an uncorrupt administrator should be sent, to rescue the people from hunger and to report honestly to Your Majesty on our plight. We throw ourselves on the bountiful mercy of Your Majesty in the hope that we may enjoy Your Majesty's gracious assistance. Our poverty and distress is impossible to describe in words, neither can we describe the misery caused to us by officials and the council. We hope for help and mercy from on high, that we may be given bread and something to cover our nakedness.

"We humbly beg Your Majesty, out of your bountiful grace and mercy, to visit our much neglected region, and to appoint better officials and councillors, so that our grain will no longer be taken from us. We beseech Your Majesty that we also should be granted our rights, because we Bosnians suffer most under the officials, who hold us in contempt. We humbly beseech Your Majesty to hear our humble requests, and not to send back our petition, for then our requests will not be heard and we will be even more harshly persecuted. Thus we most humbly beseech Your Majesty to listen to our request and abide in this hope with the wish that Almighty God may grant Your Majesty good health and the well-being and strength for the governance of the great Monarchy.

"We humbly bow before Your Majesty as Your Majesty's most loyal subjects—the abandoned, poor people, citizens and workers of the District of Fojnica."

Postscript

"Life is a misery and harsh sufferings are laid upon us. Now those who have been so long at home should be sent to the front. They have not even seen the front, and we have tolerated enough. Therefore we ask that they should come home who have fought for so long, in place of those who were so long at home, such as the clerks and magistrates."

22. *Mathias A. Mieskoci from Tjumen, Russia, to his sister in Chicago, June 24, 1917*

"My dear sister, dear brother-in-law,

"I would be inexpressibly happy to get the first news of you. My wife already informed me last year that she can send a detailed letter to me via you, for which however I have waited in vain. Probably you don't correspond with her any more. You cannot do so with your compatriots in Hungary. I also receive hardly any news from there. Soon it will be three years, and I don't know how my loved ones are faring, whether they are in good health, what their financial situation is, who has died in our family, who is still a slave-worker of the merciless aristocratic government, and so on. . . .

"You certainly read the newspaper. Now we are certain that we will not return to the same order of things. After the Russian revolution it will no longer be possible for the Magyars to oppress us. We must become free, even if only partly. Now the whole world knows our plight and looks to our future. Naturally, we must show ourselves worthy of liberty, we must be prepared to earn it, we must demonstrate that

we value it, that it is dearer to us than life itself. You know that in Russia we already
have an entire brigade of volunteer Czechs and Slovaks, and 20–30,000 have joined
the reserve. . . . I am one of these. I have fought a lot, I have thought a lot about my
beloved children and my dear wife, yet I am now convinced that if my children will
have the opportunity to learn in a purely Slovak environment, and if they are free, it
is worth the sacrifice of my life. Unfortunately there is a great lack of self-confidence
amongst us Slovaks. The great majority have been so infected by the stink of "Magyarization" that it is very easy to terrorize them. The Russian socialists also put obstacles in the way of our movement, in that they do not recognize any national strivings
or feelings; but it may nonetheless be possible to make a break-through with Masa-
ryk's help—who is here at the moment, with his staff, and who with his shadow National Assembly uses every means to realize our ideal. One-third of all members of
the National Assembly should be protagonists for Slovakia. Thus, by the way, it
came about that I was elected to the prisoners' commission. We must indeed be very
few when the cup passes to us, who are scarcely competent and at home do only the
detailed work of nationbuilding. Naturally I devote my entire energies to this, in the
hope of being of some use to our sacred cause. I do not know when they will call on
me; I will certainly be in Petrograd. Simply to go there will involve some sacrifice, because there the inflation is horrendous. I also don't know what will happen with my
clothes. I have one suit from home. From there I will write to you. . . .

"I send you all my very best wishes and kiss you all.

Your Mathias"

*23. Erich Keiter from Hadjesdinskij Sawod, Perm, to Ulle Pelikan in Vienna,
November 26, 1917*

"You should not throw this post card into the wastepaper basket unread, like the
others! . . . Yesterday was a great day for me! We were able to hold the first great
mass meeting of the prisoners in Narodni Dom [House of the People]. A huge hall,
and a vast number of people—wherefore? Czech and Romanian officers wanted to
seduce our people back to the front . . . . Colossal success for our side—speeches in
5 languages—I was the convener and gave the German speech—faultless discipline!
Just think: the Romanian officer was arrested by the Soviet [the current peace party]
and thrown out. The people whom he had recruited we took back."

• • •

The letters are of an intimate nature, a number of them written by wives to
husbands in captivity. Their honesty and truthfulness is to some degree cir-
cumscribed by an element of self-censorship in order to get past the official
censor—this, however, becoming less evident as time goes on. The letter
writer was generally aware, especially when the letter was destined to be sent
abroad, that his or her letter would be checked by the authorities. As the end of
the war approached, however, this constraint was gradually loosened, as was

the control of the state generally, and waves of bitterness and anger burst over the dykes of censorship. The letters I have chosen can therefore be seen as honest and undistorted expressions of the mood and attitudes of the people.

The reflection in the letters of concrete reality, of worries and longings, is in no way politically oriented, and no political consciousness as such is evident in them. The picture that they give hardly corresponds to the over-simplified historical analysis of a fictive representative "mood of the people"—which is in any case often the product of retrospective projection onto the period of the consequences of later events. The letters speak not of loyalty to the Monarch, but of loyalty to the spouse; and not of love of the fatherland but rather of a yearning for brotherhood and peace. The great events of national and international politics seldom find an echo here, and if they do it is muffled and obscure; in contrast, the daily troubles and burdens of wartime poverty are vividly present, and it is these which then give rise to a limited prespective on the events of "world politics." From the great majority of the letters it is all but impossible to extract principles or ideas. By the same token, the yearnings and emotions, which ripen to convictious under the impact of the clash between fateful events and personal experience in 1918, stand out all the more clearly, as in the penultimate letter; or, as in the final letter, are transformed into a revolutionary form of consciousness and mode of behavior.

The historian cannot be satisfied, however, with the effect created by the unique atmosphere of these letters. He is impelled by the nature of his business to pose the question: where and how have barely literate peasant women and workers, used to heavy physical labor but not to pen and paper, been able to acquire the skills of letter writing; from where did they take the necessary formulas, the traditional or individual motifs, the power of poetic expression for their loves and fears?

THE FORMULAS

A glance at these letters makes it instantly apparent that the form of address, the greeting, the inquiry after health, and the ending all go back to traditional formulas and rules, with only minor variations. The form of address is the same whether the writer is of bourgeois, peasant, or working-class origin: dear, beloved, my dear. Only in a few cases does the unrestrainable love of a wife lead to a piling up of terms of affection: "My dearly beloved, good and loving dearest husband." The form of address is almost always followed by the greeting: wishes for good health and happiness are either simply bestowed or offered with God's help and blessing. This is followed by the customary formula describing the writer's state of health and that of the family that has remained at home.

These phrases are so rigidly adhered to that they may even be followed by a recital of illnesses. "Here at home we are all in good health. . . . I am in the hospital . . . Paul has passed on . . . your wife is not too well" (no. 1).

Such formulaic greetings spring from an ancient tradition. In Europe they originated with the Greeks and Romans. The transformation of a wish for good health into a greeting (*salutatio*) was sanctioned by the best authorities, such as Cicero and Pliny (*salutem mittit*), and so taken over during the Middle Ages; the same applied to the repetition of good wishes at the close of a letter, the simple *vale*.[4] Of course, the greetings and farewells of antiquity were "Christianized" in the Middle Ages: wishes for health and happiness were accompanied by diverse references to God and God's blessing. In this the greeting took on a religious complexion; especially in letters between clerics, they became an opportunity for the manifestation of individual piety. At the same time, the form of medieval letters was more rigid: strict rules governed every aspect of them. Inevitably this implied a high degree of uniformity, since a medieval letter was either a certificate of some kind, conferring, confirming or suspending legal rights; or alternatively a work of art that replaced the language of everyday speech with rhetorical and artistic forms.[5] Private letters (*missilis*) themselves appear as semi-official to our eyes, since they were mainly exchanged between high dignitaries or official personages.

At the end of the eleventh century Albericus Classinensis was the first person to systematize the rules for letter writing.[6] From that time on, forms of address and greetings were most precisely laid down, particular regard being given to the social rank of the addressee; the same was true of the transition to the material part of the letter, the way in which a request (the usual case), communication, or direction should be introduced, and finally the requisite form for the close and compliments. The correctly written letter demonstrated at once, in the form of address and greeting adopted, the exact social relationship (and thereby any difference in rank) between sender and addressee. The beginning was also to imply the general nature of the letter's content, the specific details of which should then be presented in a rational manner, supported by logical argument. Exhortations to follow rules of this kind may be found in *Libellus de dictamine,* the scholastic masterpiece of Jean de Limoges (1208–1218), the abbot of Zirc, which was well known in Hungary, although not actually written there.[7] These strict rules forced letters into a straitjacket, compressed their contents within it, and endowed them with certain typical features; since they were made to conform to a pattern, they afforded no opportunities for private and informal correspondence displaying individual traits of character or expression.

It was Humanism that freed the letter, as it did also thought and art generally, from the rigidities of epistolary practice. In Hungary, however, it had little observable influence; whether this was due to the cult of classical Latin or the tendency to turn letters into a literary genre is not clear. Whatever the reason, letter writing did not succeed in meeting the functional claims that would today be demanded of it. Only with respect to more lively description of daily happenings are humanistic influences evident.[8] In this area also it was the Reformation that brought about change: after a number of sporadic and half-

hearted attempts, the end of the fifteenth century saw correspondence beginning to be carried on in the vernacular, this being a direct result of the Reformation; this practice, so far from being dispensed within the Counter-
Reformation, was in fact encouraged by it and indeed developed further.

The Reformation and Counter-Reformation were responsible for casting in
stone the epistolary forms and address, greeting, and leave taking that had
been inherited from the Middle Ages, and had therefore originally been bor-
rowed from Latin and Christianized.[9] In the form of address adopted even in
the most intimate family letters, the appropriate formalities for each social or
family relationship were observed, while in the servile petitions of serfs the attention paid to niceties of rank was of course even more assiduous. Greetings
and farewells, and above all inquiries after the health of the addressee, together with a long list of good wishes and a report on the well-being of the letter writer, became ever more long-winded and not infrequently took up the
greater part of the letter. Letters of the sixteenth and seventeenth centuries
written by adherents of all confessions exhibited a rich embroidery of religious
platitudes and were in general impregnated with a biblical tone and manner.[10]

"In honor and duty I am grateful to the Lord God to know that your Grace
is in health. Through God's grace all of us here are at peace. . . . God preserve
your Grace in happiness and bring you to us in health," wrote Anna Paxy to
her husband in 1550.[11] "I trust that the Almighty Lord will grant your Grace
good health, long life, and the happy fulfillment of your wishes. My beloved
husband, your Grace's letter was given to me, from which I understand that
your Grace enjoys good health, which I hope with all my heart; thank the Lord
I am also well. . . . May Almighty God keep your Grace in health and grant us
that we may soon see each other in good health"; so wrote Susanna Forgách to
her spouse in 1596.[12] "My dear son . . . in God's name I wish you all that is
good. I received your letter that my heart so desired . . . and understand from
that, that your Grace, with my beloved daughter, has arrived in Gács in good
health. . . . I trust that my letter finds you both in good health"; so Kata Mári-
ássy greeted her children in 1709.[13]

The Counter-Reformation competed with the Reformation in the popular-
ization of formulaic religious expressions. In the middle of the sixteenth century the Council of Trent formulated important resolutions concerning the
teaching of Catholic doctrine. As a result of the council's deliberations, in 1566
the so-called Roman Catechism appeared, an abbreviated form of which was
taught in the vernacular in every Catholic school. The opening sentence of this
catechism laid down the Catholic form of greeting: "Praised be Jesus Christ,"
to which, as a result of Jesuit influence, the words "and Mary" were subsequently added.[14] The impact of this "Catholic" greeting is evident also in the
letters of the sixteenth and seventeenth centuries,[15] principally in correspondence between priests, monks, and pious laymen, either in the shortened form,
"Jesus + Mary,"[16] or in longer expressions: "Praised be the name of the Lord in

eternity."[17] A fine example of the Baroque embroidery of letters of the period is that of Kata Zrinyi's letter to her husband: "Till death do us part, in honor and duty to your Grace, the sweet lord of my captured heart; in the name of God, our Lord and Father, I wish you every inexpressible good for body and soul; and that he, the Almighty, may grant your Grace many years of life by my side, let us pray to his Holy Majesty in honor of his holy name and of our salvation." After this lengthy introduction the writer comes to the substance of her letter. In two lines she tells her husband that the sleigh has been sent to fetch him. Then follows the close: "With this I offer your Grace my honor and duty till death us do part and my love from a pure heart flowing. May God, the Lord, soon bring your Grace, my dear and sweet lord, in good health home to me, and God grant, that I may see your Grace, my blessed and beloved good lord, in the same good health and happy peace, as already seems so long a time ago, and may the Lord of Heaven and Earth preserve us for the sake of his blessed and beloved son. Amen."[18] The pious love—or rather the Baroque bombast of its expression—of this lady for her husband is indeed remarkable, when one considers he was due home in a day or two.

The serfs' letters of the time also adopt the above-mentioned greeting and leave-taking formulas. This is hardly surprising in view of the fact that the letters would have been written by the same people who tutored the noble lords and ladies or, indeed, learned from them. These serfs' letters begin almost without exception with a submissive form of address and the customary greeting ("We wish your Lordship in the name of God all that is good").[19] In the seventeenth century, the formulas used in serfs' letters also made greater use of religious bombast. "We wish your Grace in God's name and for the sake of his holy son everything good for soul and body, and a long and happy life ever after for your Grace's whole family"; so wrote the serfs of Fehértó in 1641 to the castellan at Sárospatak.[20] The dignified formulations remained the same whether one was complaining of accidents and the blows of fate, or whether one was threatening riot and rebellion. If the lords do not set some imprisoned comrades free, we will "raze the entire village to His Majesty's ground and go to where we can find protection. . . . The Lord preserve your Grace in good health and grant him a long and happy life"; so wrote the inhabitants of Látrány in 1674.[21]

The same formulas are found in a serf's family letter which, unlike most such, was somehow preserved through time: "May God bless you with all that is good, my dear wife. Thank the Lord, I am well and I wish in God's name that you also should be well"; so wrote a serf named Vassilj Málas from Celna in 1749.[22]

These quotations may serve as orientation points for the greetings and farewells of the First World War letters, the sources for whose forms lie deep in the past. They even increase our knowledge of them. In the Middle Ages and the early modern period, *missilis* follows immediately after *salutatio*, and con-

firms receipt of the last letter, from which the recipient "abstracts" that his relation or acquaintance is in good health, which in turn is a matter of satisfaction to himself. Sometimes the letter writer, instead of confirming receipt of a
letter after the *salutatio,* complains that in fact none has arrived. One also
often encounters this formula: "I received the letter and abstracted its contents," as well as greetings such as "Praise be" and other similar religious
phrases; or the wish for the very "best" of health or for "fresh" health. The
rhymed ending may well be of a later date: "Here my letter has an end. May
God his grace the reader send" (in nos. 2, 8, 14). These lines probably date to
the end of the eighteenth or the beginning of the nineteenth centuries and were
perhaps composed in some college, and subsequently spread around the villages by homecoming students, then passed on through generations of students or the local versifiers to the authors of these letters.[23]

The leave taking itself is simpler, representing a return to the spoken language: with expressions of love, kisses, greetings, and so on, or "God be with
you." There are also examples, however, where love breaks through the traditional barriers, as if the writer was unable to bring her letter to a close, and
heaps up every possible greetings formula: "I remain your devoted admirer
and lover. I embrace and kiss you a thousand times. . . . God bring you to me,
servus, pa-pa, my love" (no. 2). The "servus" probably came from the everyday speech of the beginning of the century, and the rather odd-sounding "pa-
pa" was most likely taken over from the villages by the bourgeoisie of Pest,
transmitted via the serving girls and nannies (nos. 2, 11, 15).

The sources of the traditional formulas and stereotypes can also be identified with more or less certainty. It remains unclear, however, how the poor village populations actually learned these formulas and their correct use. It can
hardly have been from family tradition, since in the childhood of the authors
of these letters literacy was uncommon among the peasants, which was why
the local scribe was entrusted with such letters as had to be written. Thus the
question arises, through what channels and by what means of communication
was the art of letter writing conveyed to them?

MODEL LETTERS AND LETTER-WRITING GUIDES

The obvious answer to this question, namely, that these people learned something of letter-writing in school, is certainly not without foundation. In the
schools at the end of the previous century model letters were to be found in the
textbooks used by the fourth classes, as well as by the two so-called "repetition" classes, the fifth and the sixth.[24] However, the letters published here are
in no way like these school models. The latter were partly used to inculcate
into ten-year-olds how parents should be greeted or how one should convey information to absent relatives or friends; they were used didactically to assist
the assimilation of learning or to realize specific pedagogic goals. Partly, also,

the model letters followed in style and structure the correspondence of the contemporary educated classes in slightly simplified form: a short form of address without a formulaic greeting, and immediately thereafter the matter of the letter—in the style of a piece of homework for the fourth class. Even the Catholic textbooks are sparing with references to God's blessings.[25] It is remarkable, however, that these textbooks contained many rhymed greetings, popular expressions, and folk songs, in the manner of popular almanacs, but left out many practical aspects of correspondence, apparently taking the view that such were simply not necessary for a peasant.[26] Thus the school actually supplied our letter writers very little of their skills, and those which the child did learn were certainly long since forgotten by the adult.

Another likely supposition is that the correspondence manuals of the day served as models for the letter writers. Here one may imagine that the morale-boosting "Feldbriefe" had considerable impact. This series was designed to promote—and indeed influence—correspondence between simple soldiers and members of their families, and huge editions of it were sent to the front, as well as being distributed at home through the good offices of the parish priests. These model letters suggested for the "warriors," for their families, and for the village community spontaneous and homely thoughts—all of them, of course, of a patriotic and Christian hue—while at the same time beginning them with the "message of the fatherland."[27]

In these wordy ten- to fifteen-page models, the "warrior" explained to his wife, children, and relations, with great philosophical, historical, and political expertise, that our land was forced to fight this war by our barbarous enemies, "who wished to wipe the thousand-year-old Hungary from the face of the earth and to place the yoke of slavery on her people, that sought only justice." In such a situation complaints were uncalled for. One should suffer with patience "as also the rich suffer in silence." And when it was a question of defending "Christian culture," a true Hungarian woman did not complain, but entered lustily into the fight, as once did Katica Dobó and Ilona Zrinyi.[28] Warriors, too, were to be aware of the importance of their historic mission. At night in their dreams, they would be visited by "Árpád with his panther-skin shoulder-slung, Botond with his war antlers, Lehel with the horn, and all the other heroes." Then the warrior, who shortly before was still trudging behind his plough, would feel one thing, and one thing alone: "I also am become a hero among heroes."[29] No deep philological analysis is required to see that this ubiquitous series had an impact on letters written by ordinary souls, both in terms of content and of style.

It might also be supposed that the influence of the numerous and extremely popular manuals for love letters left their mark on the letters of their day. These cheap booklets were surely popular with the serving girls in the city, and also circulated in the villages through markets and fairs. However, a glance at one such manual yields disappointingly little, although they were all intended "for every eventuality in life." Everything, of course, is to be found set out very precisely in its pages: model letters for making an acquaintance, with a request for a meeting or for an intimate relationship; confessions of love as well as answers to newspaper advertisements and letters; letters of refusal and those designed to break off a relationship; commemorative verses for post cards, and so on.[30] The authors can hardly be accused of neglecting, in the composition of these models, the "war, imprisonment, and the husbands and wives who tremble for each other's well-being." Quite apart from that, the letter writers could definitely have used this manual, if it had employed their own kind of words, habitual expressions, and mode of thinking.

Yet what could they do with flowery formulations such as: "The pen quivers in my trembling hand, as I set these lines down. . . . Your words are still ringing in my ears. . . . I can still see before me the slender figure, like a fairy floating by me."[31] And the fairy's answer: "I tried to hide and to stifle that first spring flowering of my heart, which wove such lovely wreaths around us when we met."[32]

This saccharine Biedermeier romanticism was a common feature of the many letter manuals published from the middle of the nineteenth century onward. The later manuals, with titles like "Family Secretary," "The Lady's Secretaire," and so on, were in many respects really useful and practical, and reflected the rational spirit of the Enlightenment. They taught the fundamentals of grammar, the characteristics of the individual genres of the letter, the thematic and formal requisites of each genre, and presented a logical system of model letters of every type and for every purpose—greetings, requests, reports, condolence, recommendations, reminders, admonitions, apology, introductions, declarations of love, marriage proposals, commercial letters, official letters, and so on.[33] The style adopted in most of the letters in this selection— with the exception of the love letters—was concise and unornamented. After a simple form of address (Dear Parents, Dear Friend, etc.), they come straight to the point, leaving out formulary greetings and apostrophes to the Deity.

Most of these manuals were compiled for the middle layers and the populace, if one includes in the term populace the "craftsmen, merchants, and traders,"[34] or—the proclaimed target audience for Mihály Stancsics's "Letters for All Occasions"—scholars and students, respectable citizens, and artisans.[35]

The respected authors modeled their work on earlier Hungarian or foreign letter-writing manuals. Thus Elek Farkas, the "author" of the much reprinted *New Family Secretary*,[36] plagiarized Stancsics's work, and both writers drew heavily on a compilation published in German and Hungarian by a certain János Kis,[37] who for his part candidly admitted that he had incorporated in his book all of the *The Rules of Letter Writing* by the celebrated Professor of Kassa, András Vályi.[38]

Naturally Vályi himself drew on a German source, as did Kilián Fémer, the author of a work described by the professor, with some justification, as a worthless compilation, cobbled together from standard works, the most important source for it being C. F. Gellert.[39] Gellert had transplanted French manuals to German soil, in order to demonstrate that "German too is a suitable means of expression for courtesy and wit."[40] The original models were therefore French, among them the popular work by C. Rollin written in the 1730s, *De la manière d'enseigner et d'étudier les belles-lettres*.[41] This in turn was based on yet earlier compilations, such as Richelet's "Selection of the Most Elegant French Letters" from the end of the seventeenth century and Vaumorière's manual "for every rank and theme," which also served as a model for Kelemen Mikes, as he whiled away the lonely hours of his exile at Rodosto with the composition of his literary epistles.[42]

Mikes brings us back to the end of the seventeenth century, to the letter writers of the Rákóczi period, the Károlyis, Telekis, Rádays, and Révays—almost as if the threads of the tradition were joined together at this point and its continuity was made manifest. In reality these threads do not come together. Mikes did not continue the tradition of the Hungarian *missilis* of the sixteenth and seventeenth centuries, but instead followed the French example, which, with the Enlightenment, brought to a close the tendencies of the antique and Renaissance epistle. And at this point we must again take up the threads of our survey of letters.

The Enlightenment broke with the traditions of the Middle Ages in the field of correspondence, as in other fields. The letter became on the one hand a beautiful artifact (belles lettres) and thus an artistic genre in its own right,[43] and on the other, a normal means of communication between private persons or in business. In the first instance, personal and purposeful communication was subordinated to artistic expression of ideas, thoughts, and moods; in the second, functional statement drove out the traditional formulas of pious wishes, and all the orotund ornament of the Baroque. From the end of the eighteenth century onward, a similar division appears in Hungarian letters: one type of letter was crystalized into a literary genre, this tendency pervading also the private correspondence of artists, educated people, and intellectuals. By contrast, the business letter also gained currency, and to this we owe many types of private communication of requests, thanks, and recommendation. Love letters, nearly a century before the age of Romanticism, incorporated features of both types.

The letters of ordinary people in the First World War cannot be placed in either of the above categories, either in terms of style or of content. The question therefore again arises how this tradition of correspondence of gentlemen and serfs was preserved from the Middle Ages, or rather from the sixteenth and seventeenth centuries, and who communicated it to the ordinary folk of the twentieth century? We may begin searching for the answer in the activity of András Vályi, a disciple of the renewer of the language of the Enlightenment, Kazinczy, and an enthusiastic propagator of the "national school." In the spirit of the Enlightenment, Vályi equated the necessity of instruction in the mother tongue with the common good: only in the mother tongue was it possible to inculcate the fundamentals of education in the "simple inhabitants of the fatherland," the majority of the people, and thus to educate them to "become members of a human society that stood on its own feet."[44] Vályi also led the struggle to introduce clarity and comprehensibility in his model letters. He attacked "bombast and obscurity" and considered it absurd for someone to lard his letter with "superfluous ornament," while also judging the "expressions of joy for good health" as supererogatory, since these were only appropriate "if one was writing to someone who was ill."[45] He allowed of only one exception to his strictures—and this on rational grounds. His model letter for the populace began with the greeting "God bless you with all good things," continued with "God, our Holy Majesty, visited a great suffering upon your son" and ended with the formula "I recommend you and your whole household to God's grace." Vályi appended the following note to this model: "In general it is the dominies and village notaries who will be required to compose such letters. It would be inappropriate to write them in the foregoing mode, in the case of a poor uneducated peasant of low birth communicating with some one at the same social level." (He is referring to the preceding models in concise French style.) "Such letters must be written in the same way as the warmhearted peasant himself actually speaks."[46]

From this comment, which sometimes also appears in the manuals of the nineteenth century, it may be inferred that the peasants "of low birth" rigidly stuck to the traditional style of letter with its greetings and leave takings with God's blessing. A rare and ceremonial act, like writing a letter, had to be carried out with all due attention to the traditional proprieties. The comment also affords us a further insight into the modus operandi of teachers and conveyors of the art of letter writing.

The Teachers and Conveyors of the Art

Not only were the formulas of letters rooted in tradition but so also was the process of having a letter written. Andreas Vályi mentions the dominies and village notaries; in general the composition and ventilation of the serfs' complaints, requests, and reports fell to the students, the parish priests, the magistrates, and the lawyers.[47] This tradition continued in the nineteenth century—in the main it was the teachers and the local intelligentsia, together with students visiting home, who rendered assistance. Later, there would be among the relatives or acquaintances a reasonably educated person with a fine handwriting, who "specialized" in letter writing, and was thereby just as well known, and just as much in demand in the village, as the woman who dispensed herbs. There are examples of this in the letters published here. A peasant woman reassures her husband that she has had a letter written by a village teacher and has indeed been to Petervásár expressly to have it written by Mrs. Szabó, whose writing skills are known everywhere (no. 9). Not infrequently, one comes across letters in which only the signature belongs to the sender; the text, complete with his or her own personal best wishes, has been entirely composed by the local correspondence "specialist."

On the basis of the available data, those who passed on tradition, the teachers and the creators of rules, formulas, models, and themes, can be divided into three groups. At the time of the First World War, the clerics in the villages still had great influence. The events and festivities of local holidays still took place under the aegis of the priest in the church, or of the teacher in the school strictly within the context of religious instruction. (In 1900 80 percent of schools were still church-run, and only 10 percent were run by the state; the other 10 percent of community schools were also mostly under church control.)[48] This strong church influence is the main reason why the century of the Enlightenment left the village tradition of letter writing untouched and why, indeed, the tradition of the sixteenth and seventeenth centuries was continued unbroken.

The communicators of secular influence were probably the successors of the traditionally mobile students: those who studied in the city, at a university or gymnasium, the students and scholars who visited home from time to time, as well as the analogous village intellectuals. It is likely that they were active in the composition of love letters, in the transmission of old Hungarian love songs (virágének, "flower-songs"), in coining love phrases and inventing rhymes for the rhymed greetings and leave takings.

The third group is constituted by the local correspondence "specialists." In the age of Dualism, the notaries, and even more the magistrates, were such great potentates that they would never have concerned themselves with writing letters for poor people, employees, and servants. The "specialists" were mostly drawn from the ranks of the literate peasants, the village chroniclers and popular versifiers. Their job was to compose letters with the exactly prescribed manner of address, and with an elegant form, using the customary and appropriate language—or, in other words, to add the technical niceties to the dictated message. The general form and nature of the letter was therefore governed by the preferences and taste of the peasants themselves, as inherited with unbroken continuity from the seventeenth century, and as learned from the handed-down formulas of their own teachers and forefathers. And these same formulas were subsequently adopted by the clients of the letter writers, when they finally began to write for themselves.

In the case of workers' letters it would not be very easy—and also not very informative—to unearth their original sources and models. In 1910, 85 percent of the urban population of Hungary, 93 percent of the inhabitants of Budapest, and more than 80 percent of industrial workers could read and write. If a worker had to put pen to paper, he generally wrote his letter unaided; but if he did need help, he could easily get advice and assistance from the people among whom he lived or at his work place. Individual phrases, forms, or expressions could be lifted from his reading, above all from the newspapers.

The Themes

The main themes of the letters concern the details and worries of everyday life, the fates of families and individuals, wishes and fears with regard to these, but above all and repeatedly, war and peace. In this respect there is a marked difference between village and peasant letters and those of workers in the cities, even when similar feelings, wishes, or thoughts are being expressed.

A well-known theme of the letters is, of course, love, yearning, and fidelity. The tone of the utterances is always sad and full of complaint. In the letters of the peasant women can be seen the stirrings of love, and the solemnity of its avowal—indeed, they sometimes achieve a marvelously graphic form of expression. The joy over the letter just received "was mixed with weeping; when will the dear and merciful God allow that lovely day to dawn, when will we see each other again? Or will we indeed ever see each other again?" (no. 9). "When I write to you, the letters are drowned with my tears, often I cannot see them for the tears" (no. 4). Yearning and fear are sometimes given expression through poetry or folk song: "If I was only a little bird, and could fly to you, there is so much I would like to give you, if I could bring it all with me; but as I am not a bird, and cannot fly to you, I can only grieve and offer you my heart; you should close it up in your own, in the very depths of your heart, where no one can tear it away . . . for my heart . . . beats only for you, by night and by day, in my every act, I think continually of you" (no. 4). I am waiting, ever waiting for the letter "because that is my only comfort, my very life is in your hands, when I get some dear lines from you I feel better, but when I get none, life is unbearable, and I at once remember how much I care about you; but it's all the same whether I die here or somewhere else" (no. 13).

In these lines it is easy to detect the echo of Hungarian love songs or folk songs. One recognizes the traces of a Hungarian love song from the eighteenth century: "Fly to my lap, as to a beautiful garden / Build your nest here, as on a lovely meadow"; or the verses from the song of the exiled kuruc warriors: "My heart is lonely without you / Like the dove without its mate / I have no love save yours / I yearn for you ever more and more."[49] In the fear for the beloved there is often a touch of jealousy: "Perhaps you will even marry again there" . . . you could deny me. Then the letter writer answers her own fears: "But not everyone has such thoughts, and I could never bear to do such a thing, because one can only truly love one person" (no. 2). A similar question and answer occurs in Krisztina Barkoczy's letter to her husband, Sándor Károlyi, in 1698. "From your letter I know, my sweetheart, what sort of lodgings you have and that there are many ladies there. But I dislike it that the cavaliers often spend a night here and even sometimes try to court me."[50]

A rare example of the admission of love and "sin," combined with genuine faithfulness, is the letter from a young woman from Perkáta (no. 15). She knows full well that her lapse was a shameful deed, but desperation and inexperience were responsible for it. The cattle had to be fed and the seducer, a well-to-do peasant, offered her feed: "You know very well that I must always be running after the cattle, so that at least we still have something when you return, and I didn't do it because I am a bad woman, or perhaps a whore, but because I tried so hard to do everything for the best and now I am so unhappy . . . so do not be angry with me, my dear, good husband, and forgive me." Such a situation was not unusual during the war; hundreds of letters, as well as censors' reports, contain references to "war children." A woman even writes quite candidly: "There was nobody to give me a few kisses"—and so she chose one of the prisoners of war.[51]

Another recurrent theme is the increasing difficulty of the living conditions with terrifyingly high prices driving people into poverty. This is described in peasants' letters, both generally and in specifics, in both cases knowledgeably and in detail. People are continually in quest of locations "where there is something one can buy. But first one has to go to the local administration for ration cards," then there is nothing to buy in the store, "and it will be a week before there is again something available" (no. 7).

The same theme occurs elsewhere, not chronologically described but in a sort of free-association description: "We are all continually running after food . . . because one searches in vain for something to buy, mainly food, which one then doesn't get. From the administration one gets something, but a servant is given only two kilos for ten days, which might be all right if it was wheat flour, but it is often only a third wheat and the rest maize, although many would be happy if there were only maize pancakes," but those with nothing at all can't replace them with anything (no. 8). "I'm not at all surprised when I read that someone or other has done this or that, because every woman has a bad conscience when she sees her child wasting away"; so writes one poor woman from Vienna (no. 18).

The letters are often equally precise, indeed dry and detailed in their approach, when they deal with human beings and their fates. Géza is a war prisoner, Imre a cripple, Magda's husband is missing, Gyula from the neighborhood was twice wounded, Pali and Karcsi are at the front, "very few there are who have not been killed since then. Elek Bicskeji died at home" (no. 6). Here are to be found names and events, a bleak and precise stock taking without obituary. It is the muted and factual description of injustice and poverty that one researcher into serfs' letters described as "the pathos of realism."[52] This pathos is not engendered by florid language and exclamation, but by the rhythm of the description, the grim flow of facts progressively intensifying the underlying pattern of thought.

Some of the peasants' letters content themselves with a recital of troubles and complaints; the majority however, spill over into subdued anger, social dissatisfaction, and indignation in the face of injustice.[53] The contrasting of the life of the rich and the plight of the poor is here conspicuous and tangible. This is not simply a standard formula, like the daily worries about work and money; such things have now been elevated from a recurrent, if resigned, complaint to a fixed point of their existence. This phenomenon will be returned to in another context: here we are concerned with its various manifestations high-lighted as a result of the war.

Again and again one reads that only the poor suffer in the war, while the rich do not even notice it. The rich "at least have something to lose, but the poor have nothing" (no. 4). "In this country the poor man has no rights; the only thing he has is the duty, poor as he is, to fight at the front" (no. 1). "Our poor children weep for a scrap of bread . . . when I go in tears to the magistrate, he tells me we should eat the air . . . it is an evil shame how a poor woman is treated here" (no. 10). There is general indignation with regard to those who have been excused from military service, the shirkers and parasites. "Only the rich are at home, because they are all deaf and blind, it's only their sacks of money that can see" (no. 6). "Here at home are many soldiers released from service, the rich and fortunate, those who could buy themselves out of a soldier's fate" (no. 4). "My [husband] has lost both his feet . . . yet he must endure it and get around with crutches," but we have to tolerate "the piggish behavior of the villains who have bought exemption, the many fake invalids" (no. 13).

An interesting and new theme is the popular assessment of the causes and prospects of the war. For the very backward, the war is punishment of God: "This [desolation] was necessary for many, because the people had become very degenerate."[54] Closely related to this sort of attitude is the frequently recurring note of messianism. In every corner of the Monarchy at this time prophets appeared who announced the end of the world.[55] Equally often, one encounters the confident prediction that the merciful God will intervene and put an end to the slaughter, bring home the prisoners, and instill some sense into the governments of all nations concerned (nos. 6, 7, 8, 15). Less crude is the view that "soon mankind will be fed up with all this; it is not the providential intervention of God, but the will of merciless men, who rejoice in the shedding of much blood."[56] This perception leads to the rebellious idea that God himself is on the side of the masters, and is indeed "no more than a villain" (no. 13).

Now and then one even encounters seditious threats and despairing curses. An oft-recurring theme is that of an irrevocable self-destruction that would necessarily bring the war to an end: "Life is no longer life, but sheer misery. . . . Weeping we fall asleep, and weeping we get up in the morning; as we eat we are still weeping, as we think over our life, we think why doesn't the earth simply open up and swallow the millions of poor, so that only the masters and bosses remain? I know that would soon put an end to the war" (no. 12). This attitude is everywhere to be found, in every nation of the Monarchy. Mrs. Karolina Horvath from Rohonc writes to her husband: "Our poor children suffer so, as soon as a child is born it should be immediately strangled, so that the emperor gets no soldiers."[57] Maria Schlosser, writing from Bohemia, is no less embittered: "If death does not free us from the world, we poor people will have to slaughter our children like pigs, so that we have something to eat and our children have peace" (no. 19).

Peasant letters whose senders expect peace to be achieved by any kind of political action or revolutionary movement are something of a rarity: The masters "were clever enough to stumble into war, which reduces the nation to ruin and starves the population at home; but they are not clever enough to make peace: that will have to be left to the socialists" are the sentiments of one letter—the greeting of which, incidentally, retains the invocation of Christ's name (no. 11). It does, however, seem to be a spontaneous outburst of rage.

Here the distinguishing features of workers' letters become conspicuous. These also report objectively and precisely about prices and poverty, and also in them anger takes a drily impassioned and rhythmic form: "When the great have had their fun and the profiteers have filled their pockets and our sufferings are exhausted" then will "this comedy" come to an end (no. 14). Yet the workers' letters are generally shorter (most of them only postcards), clearer and more concrete. The causes of war and poverty are concisely presented, and the sentence structure itself tends less toward statements of general evils, such as "there were robberies," "it has been carried off," "the cattle are driven away," and so forth. In these letters it is "the *comrades*" who strike, "*we*" who demonstrate, "because we want peace, justice, and bread and that you poor sufferers should return home" (no. 5). The government hinders the peace, the capitalists are bloodsuckers. What appears in the peasants' letters as self-destruction culminating in an apocalyptic scenario of general collapse, in the workers' letters takes on the far more concrete form of a general strike—especially in the letters between January and February of 1918.

Actual historical events and turning points are reflected more often and more distinctly in the workers' letters.[58] After the Russian revolution of 1917, even the expression "wind from the east" appears more frequently. The October revolution left its mark on the majority of the letters, not least in the renewed hopes for peace. These, however, are often rather vague and can only be understood as a fact of the general peasant mentality. Apparently it is the felt solidarity of the people, influenced by rumors of revolutionary change, that leads to the statement: "But the Russian is just waiting until the Germans also turn against us; then he will join on our side and let fly at the Germans." A Slovak peasant woman had heard that around the middle of January a big change should have come. "The German Emperor sent a letter to the Russian Czar asking if he wanted peace." The Russian Czar said he did, providing the areas occupied by the Germans were evacuated. "Our lot wanted to grant him that, but the Germans did not, saying that if they'd held on thus far, they would hold on to the end."[59] We would certainly give in, wrote Mrs. Krenki from Vienna, "and so would the Hungarians and the Bosnians . . . they have all had enough" and "want peace," but the Germans do not (no. 18).

In almost all the workers' letters the Russian revolution engenders a note of optimism; the strike in Vienna and Budapest in January 1918 is seen as a strike for peace, and often the thought is voiced that the real struggle is not that of the war aims, but that against the war.[60] Often there are apocalyptic or rousing slogans: "we live in the great times," "the solution is: now or never," "we must be socialists"; repeatedly one comes across the Social-Democratic vocabulary: "the revolution to save the world," "the disinherited workers of the world," and so on.[61] The motivations of the movement are repeatedly discussed: "The workers will not tolerate what is going on, and therefore they agitate for a revolution at home" and all want peace.[62] Prime Minister Tisza and his supporters stand in the way of peace, "they are happy with the situation . . . they have all comforts for themselves and would have them even if the war lasted forever; but it is pointless to talk about such things; war teaches the people how to arrange things better in the future."[63] And yet another telling sign of the times: the most graphic manifestation of the general strike was that the trams didn't run, the newspapers didn't appear, and there was no electricity. Everyday life was completely thrown out of gear.

A process of consciousness raising similar to that stimulated by the influence of the socialist movement was provided by the experiences of soldiers at the front or in captivity, especially after the October revolution. Examples of this may be found in letters no. 16 and 17, almost certainly written by soldiers of peasant origin. The fateful and decisive experiences of contemporary prisoners of war are encountered both in the form of first-hand narrative, but also in the form of word-of-mouth transmission: the "fatherland" welcomed home its "sons"—who had undergone all manner of trials and suffering—at best with suspicion and defensive measures; at worst with imprisonment or even the firing squad. The treachery of the "fatherland" thus released the simple soldiers from the oath of loyalty they had sworn to the king. Thus home was simply the place where there was freedom (no. 16). The author of the next letter followed the same path as the prisoners of war, who became internationalists. He is already a conscious revolutionary, neither complaining nor boasting, and at the same time as the attempts to console his parents, he also tries to stimulate them to rebellion. He took up arms originally in the interests of the bosses, but "now I would not deserve to go on living if I stood by like a coward, while our brothers defended freedom." This was the argument from morality. Neither the Russian nor the Serb was the enemy—if they were workers, then they too were brothers; the enemy was the capitalists, the barons, the princes, all the bosses. This was the argument from politics. They should not worry about him: thousands and tens of thousands were gathering under the red banner, the workers of the world were with him. This was the argument from personal conviction. The brief reference to 150 roubles a month, which naturally was not given as charity and without strings, appears chiefly as reassurance, in deference to the peasant's traditional concern with practicalities (no. 17). The last two letters, composed in a Russian prison camp, show vividly the consciousness-raising and polarizing effect of the Russian revolution (nos. 22, 23).

The Structure of the Letters

After the analysis of the contents of the letters, we must turn our attention to their typical structural features and organization. Generally speaking, two types of letter are involved.

The structural scheme of the peasant's letters may be broken down into the following:

Form of Address.   This is usually short, with one, occassionally more attributes, quoting either the Christian name of the addressee or the family relationship. Sometimes it is not present at all at the beginning of the letter, and only after the greeting is the relationship between sender and addressee made clear in the text.

Greeting.   Sometimes this takes the form of an invocation ("praised be") or of verse ("to a foreign land I send my letter"); good wishes, inquiry after the health of the addressee, and expressions of hope that all is well with him are usually combined with it.

Confirmation of Letter Received and Reference to Same.   The recipient confirms receipt of an earlier letter and makes appropriate reference to it, or complains that no letter has arrived and that the addressee persistently fails to write. Often the confirmation of receipt is joined together with the wishes for good health.

The Substance of the Letter.   Although the information, reports, and requests in the letters are multifarious, they tend to exhibit two typical characteristics. First, there is almost always a report on the troubles of daily life, the condition of the peasant economy, and the prospects for the harvest; also the high prices and the prevailing injustice, as well as a detailed description of the packets and sums of money sent to the addressee, all of this rounded off with an emphatic avowal of love and fidelity. The second main characteristic to be observed is that the topics and themes appear in fragmented form in the letters—they are not the result of a logically thought-through concept but are rather produced through a process of the association of ideas. When talking of the food parcel, the letter writer naturally falls into a discussion of the high prices, and then of poverty, and from the topic of poverty arise remarks about the arrogance of the well-to-do and the bosses; desperation is associated with humanity, and the latter with the suffering of the children, and of the beloved husband far

away; then follows the protestation of love and fidelity. The order of these hap-
hazardly arranged themes can vary considerably, with this or that topic constantly recurring at different places in the letter. For example, see no. 4: complaint over the grossly neglected correspondence; detailed description of the
package being sent; life at home is also hard; if she were a bird, she would fly to
her man; at home, on the other hand, are the many well-to-do who are excused
from military service; how are things with her captured husband? Or no. 11:
confirmation of receipt of a letter; a pity that her husband does not work as a
laborer with a peasant; at home the prisoners are well treated; in the packet is
a whole piece of "moldy salami"; the socialists will have to make peace; she
has taken a second lodger for the sake of her reputation in the village; there are
many who are excused from military service; war is a dirty business.

Farewell.   Usually this consists of a short repetition of the good wishes, the
invocation of God's blessing, and the affirmation that the addressee is eagerly
awaited at home, to which is attached a customary form of greeting.

It will already be clear that these letters share many characteristics with
those of the sixteenth and seventeenth centuries. The similarities are all the
more evident when one looks at the structural analysis made by a nineteenth-
century researcher—the only one so far in this field—of the epistolary style of
women's letters in the sixteenth and seventeenth centuries.[64] His model was as
follows: 1. form of address: exact citation of rank and relationship; 2. greetings
formula: invocation—greeting in God's name; 3. expression of good wishes,
report on writer's own state of health and inquiry into that of the addressee;
4. confirmation of receipt of a letter, complaints about nonarrival or the late
arrival of one; 5. the substance of the letter; 6. leave taking: short recapitula-
tion of points 2 and 3, together with the appropriate salutation.

It becomes clear that the structural scheme is identical in the two cases, with
the single insignificant difference that the form of address and the farewell between persons of the same rank or members of the same family became simpler
and more colloquial with the passing of time. Not only the structure, however,
but also the associative handling of the ideas in the substantive part, and the
sort of problems touched upon, show striking similarities. In the letter from
Krisztina Barkóczy previously quoted there are several not entirely logical di-
gressions from the main theme: first come references to health and children,
then to the debtors, who do not want to pay up; then a description of problems
on the estate; then a sudden leap to nobles who here fled the country and the
damage caused by the game on the Weinberg; then a warning to her homecoming husband about bandits on the way; and finally the already quoted dig
about her husband being surrounded by women, and the reminder of her own
faithfulness.[65] All these topics, of course, have an intuitive, if not logical, relationship to each other.

A peasant's letter from the middle of the eighteenth century also supplies
ideal material for comparison. After the traditional form of greeting, it goes

on: "I send with this man two pairs of boots, one for my daughter Nastasi, the other for my son Andris. Give me a report on how the autumn sowing has gone, and how many cows have calved. . . . I sent a pair of boots to Lõrinc Simon for ploughing, tell me if he really uses them for that. . . . I am making boots for you as well, but they aren't ready yet, so I can't send them. . . . You send me no message whatsoever, I don't know why you don't write. I gave a twenty to Gyurka Szabó, so that he should plough the fallow land by the stream . . . if it's raining, stop him from ploughing."[66]

The similarity in structure can of course he explained by the similarities in the situation. In the sixteenth and seventeenth centuries the men were often far from home on war service, and the wives had to bear the burden of all the family and financial problems.[67] In their correspondence, the reports, anxious solicitude, affection, and requests for advice are jumbled together in exactly the same way as in the First World War letters. Wars and separation from home, however, existed earlier—have existed, indeed, from time immemorial. To attribute similarities solely to the common aspects of the situation of the letter writers would therefore be a superficial interpretation, all the more so since the First World War letters do not represent a return to earlier forms but the continuation of a tradition of almost three hundred years in their formulas, themes, and mode of expression.

Looked at simply in terms of "genre," the cause of this permanence may be explained as follows: for the nobility and bourgeoisie and the educated layer of society in general, the letter at the end of the eighteenth century had become either a literary artefact or a personal and quotidian means for swapping information and expressing ideas. For the common people, and especially for the peasants, it remained what it had been in the social conditions of the seventeenth century: an exceptional necessity adopted when circumstances compelled the transmission of an urgent message. Structurally, the difference could be expressed thus: the traditional type of letter that went back to the sixteenth and seventeenth centuries was unstructured in its main content, though framed within traditional rules governing its external form; its matter was expressed by a progressive association of ideas, rather than by logical discourse. By contrast, letters that had pretensions to literary value, or the related individualized letters of the bourgeois epoch, were stamped with the personality, taste, and mood of their authors. They were formed in a manner of their choosing and given an appropriate internal coherence.

As far as social history is concerned, the structural continuity of the peasants' letters can be traced back to the fact that the characteristic pattern of peasant life, even in the twentieth century, rendered individualised communication and regular correspondence neither necessary nor, indeed, possible. When some urgent necessity compelled a village inhabitant to write a letter, he found the model for its form and structure ready to hand in the traditions and customs that continued to regulate the most important aspects of the still intact village community.

The workers' letters have a simpler, clearer organization, just as they are more succint. The almost universal short form of address, with only one attribute, is followed by the greeting—an expression of good wishes—in which religious invocations are seldom to be found. The substance of the letter is also shorter, generally restricted to one or two themes. The examples here can be regarded as typical, where the letter begins with the harshness of current living conditions and the misery engendered by war, and progresses to a greater or lesser degree of anger and dissidence.

Workers' letters are thus structurally to be distinguished from those of the peasants, although this does not place them in the same category as the letters of the educated classes. They are also primarily messages that convey what is for the sender important news or requests; in no sense are they literary artefacts that seek to transmit ideas or thoughts. Their structure comes closest to that of the "report" type of letter in the manuals at the turn of the century, although there is no evidence that the workers either knew or made use of such manuals. It is far more likely that they learned letter writing from their surroundings and their acquaintances and applied to it, almost instinctively, the rational manner of proceeding that had also come to govern their professional activity.

Hungarian correspondence in general up to the eighteenth century, and the letters of the people up to the present day, did not and have not become a literary form or a means for transmitting literary values. From the point of view of literary history, that is a regrettable failure. A scholar who has studied the genre profoundly laments the backwardness of the Hungarian letters in comparison with the level of perfection the genre achieved in France.[68] What is a loss for literature, however, is perhaps a gain for social history. These traditional letters, stimulated usually by specific events—whether from aristocratic ladies or from peasant women—are emotionally genuine, richly informative with regard to the conditions of daily life, and give a more authentic picture of the mind and character of the sender than would more literary letters. In this respect a remark by Gyula Illyés is extremely pertinent: "The letter, and especially the love letter, is not a literary genre; and is all the less successful in achieving its aim, the more it is regarded as such."[69] In other words its "success" depends precisely on its genuineness and spontaneity, and thus its ability to reflect the mentality of the sender.

THE BASIC CATEGORIES OF POPULAR THOUGHT

The letters reprinted here represent only a modest selection from those available. Together with the several thousand similar letters and extracts that are extant, they can, however, supply the fundamental materials for the description of permanent categories of the popular mentality, something that would be impossible without prior analysis of their content and structure. A basic topic for ordinary people, always revealing about the way they looked at the world, is that of subsistence and work. In the peasant mentality, the preservation of the natural order and the continuity of cultivation occupy a central position. In thousands of letters confiscated by the censor or in those allowed through, the men at the front inquire after the state of the weather, the work in the fields, the harvest, the condition of the cattle, the daily and exceptional problems of agriculture—and those at home conscientiously answer all their questions.

The peasants' letters complain primarily not simply about hunger and poverty, but about the problems of cultivation, the high prices with the concomitant scarcity of goods, and requisitions by the government. Labor is very expensive if one can get it at all (no. 1). "All work is carried out too late, and jobs like hoeing and mowing and bringing in the harvest begin to pile up, and we're pushed to get them all done" (no. 6). "I offered the oat everywhere, but no one wanted it . . . because seed was very expensive and I couldn't buy it on my own" (no. 9).

"I have so much to endure, what can I do, what will become of me?" (no. 9). "There are even some who have been unable to feed their cattle for a month, although they have the land, but one can't by anything even with large sums" (no. 10). "Nevertheless I am on the point of selling the cow, for I can get no feed for her; and even a pair of shoes costs 40 forints, who can survive in such conditions?" (no. 12).

The continuation of cultivation and the maintenance of the property were hard problems for the women, especially when there was nobody to help them. Those sad two years were a very long time for those who "are dependent for everything on somebody else, for a man's work is too much for the women. . . . If we work, it is bad, and if we don't work, it is also bad; if we work and have something for our pains, then it is taken away from us; but if we don't work, we don't have anything to eat" (no. 9). In the peasant's hierarchy of values, continuing to cultivate of the land easily took precedence over marital fidelity; even an illegitimate child can be forgiven, if that was the price for rescuing the cattle. One of the horrors of war for peasants of all nationalities was that it disrupted the traditional economic order of agriculture and threatened its continuance. Peace was thus synonymous with the restoration of the old natural order of things.

In the letters of the urban and village proletariat and the have-nots, subsistence and work manifest themselves as social questions. Even with more work one earns ever less, one hungers, one is constantly running after food. The industrialist or the estate owner is an exploiter, but so is the government, and the authorities are unconcerned about the people. Subsistence is reduced to a minimum. "We are often hungry, because there is so little bread" (no. 5); "we lack everything, above all bread, which is the most important."[70] "In the end we will have to eat the earth itself, or the better quality dung, like the guard dogs" (no. 19). A great change has to come "because the belly will decide, ours and other people's" (no. 3). The war threatens the worker in the very fundamentals of his existence. Peace is thus the same as life itself.

Another basic category of popular thought was the contrast between rich and poor. Here, "poverty" and "wealth" embodied not only a difference in financial circumstances, but also one of social position. A rich man was always the "master." The category of master or boss had as many subsidiary rungs and elevations as a tower reaching to the sky. At the lowest level were the notaries and at the top the princes, the counts, sometimes even the king, and occasionally even God is counted in. There were two Gods, however: that of the rich, whose wealth was composed entirely of the money made by the starving poor; and that of the poor, "who died at the front. Now only the rich man's God lives on."[71]

This instinctive division of society into classes of rich and poor is of very early origin. In this respect the popular letters, despite the similarities of formulas, themes, and structure, are sharply differentiated from the aristocracy's and the nobility's letters of the sixteenth to the seventeenth century, and show a direct lineage from the letters of the serfs. A conscious contrasting of rich and poor is already evident in the sixteenth century, in the attitudes of the populace conscripted for the crusade of 1514 (which, in fact disintegrated into a peasants' revolt). To them, the poor (*minores, pauperi*) were the true "chosen people" of God; the powerful (*potentes*) and the lords (*domini*), on the other hand, were just as heathen as the Turks.[72] Recurrent formulas of the serfs' letters are, typically, phrases such as "we, who have been downtrodden," or "we miserable serfs"; and the accusation against the lords and masters of whatsoever rank or station is ever-present.

The letters published here show very clearly that the contrast between rich and poor was also very much in the front of the minds of the masses and a fundamental ingredient of popular attitudes during the First World War. It should be added that about half the letters confiscated by the censor were unacceptable because of complaints about the level of subsistence, and another quarter because of seditious "incitements" against the rich, the bosses, and the authorities.[73] According to the censor's reports on the mood of the country, there are frequent references to obscene inequalities and crying injustices even in letters that were not officially objected to.[74] As has been remarked, the poor people were most embittered about the requisitions, the inadequate distribution of food, and the privileges of the rich.

In the course of the war, the contrast between rich and poor increasingly became the central preoccupation of the popular mentality. The degree of intensity of this perception varied according to environment, social standing, and education, as well as chronologically. In the early years of the war, the most backward layers of the peasantry regarded inequalities of wealth, oppression, and suffering as a natural dispensation, ordained from on high: "here the poor have none to hear them," "the poor were created for suffering." As time went on and conditions worsened, the tone grew sharper, the complaints turning into threats and even curses, even if this ran the risk of God's punishment. "The bosses are all at home, the dear God should hang another war around their necks if they are still not satiated with the bloodshed, all without exception should be proscribed who have still not had enough of all this" (no. 12). In this curse and the imagining of a war that would devastate the rich as well, the bitterness of the peasants' revolt is already apparent. "If our heart is also full of bitterness, we must continually pretend that all is for the best, and who knows how long the great lords want it like this?"[75] In the autumn of 1917 the complaints in the villages crystalized into a general dissatisfaction, but in the towns and cities into a political movement. In the course of 1918 in the villages, the vision of world destruction and the last judgment gained currency; but in the towns and cities the impulse was driving toward a general strike and general revolution.

This ripening process, proceeding at a different tempo and at different levels, but everywhere ineluctable, was not confined to Hungary. It was international in the same way as the polarization between rich and poor was everywhere a fundamental aspect of popular social attitudes. Maria Sedláčkova, writing from Bohemia, denounces the boss class with a specific instance of abuse: ". . . since we are treated here like slaves; . . . the mayor . . . apparently claims that he has the right to beat us, and there have in fact been cases of this" (no. 20). Similarly, Mrs. Stefankova in Slovakia: "Here there is huge inflation, not to mention the villainy of the bosses, always massive and unbridled as it is."[76] The Romanian Maria Bucsa writes that "in war only the poor are in the thick of it, while the bosses get out of it in their thousands. . . . The sons of the rich escape a certain death, but the poor are killed and their little children are orphaned."[77] Similar sentiments against the "villainy of the bosses" are expressed by Hungarian peasant women, but also Mrs. Hauser, a Swabian from Budaörs, would like to turn the social pyramid on its head: "The barons, princes, counts, the kings, and the emperor have no idea of poverty; if they had, they would long ago have put an end to this grinding toil. . . . These great lords should once do the work of a peasant and eat at his table."[78] A particularly savage outburst was occasioned by the misuse by the authorities of the Bosnians' petition to the emperor (no. 21).

Among the workers, also, this fundamental way of perceiving society was widespread. "*Socialism* seems to be gaining ground among the working classes" is the comment of the Viennese censor in 1918. "And here it must be emphasized that there are no *national* differences observable in the mood of the senders." One letter, said to be typical, even contains the sentence "Here too the plebeians are uniting against the patricians, and soon blood will begin to flow."[79]

Plebeians against patricians, workers against capitalists, the people against their masters. In the course of four years these basic categories of popular attitude underwent fundamental change. The war disrupted the natural and social order, and destroyed its rhythm of production; it made even a minimal level of existence precarious, accentuated the contrast between rich and poor through new and savage injustices, and provoked to rebellion even those who had been resigned to the traditional oppression of the social order in time of peace. War decimated harvests and men alike, and sowed only the seeds of hatred.

The seeds of hatred ripened apace in the mass consciousness through the summer of 1918.

NOTES

Introductory Reflections on Cultural History

1. To illustrate this, let me mention some more important works of cultural history to appear in the last quarter century: W. Johnston, *The Austrian Mind* (1972), A. Janik and S. Toulmin, *Wittgenstein's Vienna* (1973), W. McGrath, *Dionysian Art and Populist Politics in Austria* (1974), F. Ender, *Das k. u. k. Wien* (1977), F. Morton, *A Nervous Splendor. Vienna 1888–1918* (1981), C. Schorske, *Fin-de-Siècle Vienna: Politics and Culture* (1980), *Experiment Weltuntergang: Wien um 1900*, edited by W. Hofmann (1981), P. Vergo, *Art in Vienna 1898–1918* (1981), M. Rosenblit, *The Jews in Vienna 1867–1914* (1983), E. Godoli and F. Borsi, *Wiener Bauten der Jahrhundertwende* (1985), K. Varnedoe, *Vienna 1900. Art–Architecture–Design* (1986), P. Berner, F. Brix, and W. Mantl, *Wien um 1900* (1986), S. Beller, *Vienna and the Jews 1867–1938: A Cultural History* (1989), H. Segel, *The Vienna Coffeehouse Wits 1890–1938* (1993), *Kreatives Milieu. Wien um 1900*, edited by F. Brix and A. Janik (1993).

2. I can mention the book by John Lukacs, *Budapest 1900: A Historical Portrait of a City and Its Culture* (1988), although this comes more into the category of an impressionistic literary essay. Judit Frigyesi, *Béla Bartók and Turn-of-the-Century Budapest* (1998) is in the press.

3. The last pages of this foreword and some of the essays in this book were written at the Institute for Advanced Study in Princeton, where I was a fellow in 1986–1987. In this English edition, published by Princeton University Press, I would like to express heartfelt gratitude for the stimulating scholarly environment and the exceptional opportunity to work that the Institute provided.

Chapter One
Urbanization and Civilization

1. For the connections between the city's development and urbanization see David Landes, *The Cambridge Economic History*, vol. 6/2 (Cambridge, 1965); and *The New Cambridge Modern History*, vol. 13, companion volume edited by Peter Burke (London-Cambridge, 1980), 75–79, 99–105. A standard work for European city development is Lewis Mumford, *The City in History* (New York, 1961); a basic work of the Chicago school of city sociology is R. E. Park, E. W. Burgess, and R. McKenzie, *The City* (Chicago, 1925). A useful book for comparisons with American cities is Arthur Meier Schlesinger, *The Rise of the City 1878–1898* (New York, 1975). Informative for European models is Leonardo Benevolo, *Storia delle citta* (History of the City) (Rome-Bari, 1975), and by the same author, *La Citta nella Storia d'Europa* (The City in the History of Europe) (Rome-Bari, 1993). A basic work on Vienna is Hans Bobek and Elisabeth Lichtenberger, *Wien* (Vienna-Cologne, 1978). Among Hungarian works, I would mention Ferenc Erdei, *A magyar város* (The Hungarian City) (Budapest, 1974), and the important manual *Budapest története* (The History of Budapest), vols. 1–4, edited by László Gerevich (Budapest, 1975–1980).

2. Max Weber, *The Protestant Ethic and the Spirit of Capitalism*, translated by Talcott Parsons (London, 1971), 21–22; *Wohnen im Wandel*, edited by Lutz Niethammer (Wuppertal, 1979), 15–17.

3. Elisabeth Lichtenberger, *Die Wiener Altstadt* (Vienna, 1977), 13–14, 105–10.

4. Lajos Nagy, *Budapest története a török kiűzésétől a márciusi forradalomig* (The History of Budapest from the Driving out of the Turks until the March Revolution [1686–1848]), vol. 3 of the *Budapest története,* edited by László Gerevich (Budapest, 1975), 127–32, 143–49.

5. *Historisch-Statistische Übersicht von Wien*, edited by Felix Olegnik, part 1: *Mitteilungen aus Statistik und Verwaltung der Stadt Wien* (Vienna, 1956), 1:21–22.

6. Ibid., 22–23.

7. Erwin Schmidt, *Die Geschichte der Stadt Wien* (Vienna-Munich, 1978), 58. The kuruc forces (from the Latin *crux*) were freedom fighters against the Habsburgs at the end of the seventeenth and the beginning of the eighteenth centuries.

8. Mihály Pásztor, "A százötven éves Lipótváros" (The Hundred-and-Fifty-Year-Old Lipótváros), *Statisztikai Közlemények* (Statistical Publications) 93/4 (Budapest, 1940), 18–22.

9. Nagy, *Budapest története* 3:373–75, 382, 384–88.

10. Pásztor, "A százötven éves Lipótváros," 39–44.

11. Ibid., 75–84; Nagy, *Budapest története* 3:258–63.

12. Heinrich Habel, *Zur Sozialgeschichte und Typologie des Münchener Privathauses. Münchener Fassaden. Bürgerhäuser des Historismus und des Jugenstils* (Munich, 1974), 15; similar problems are dealt with in Renate Watner-Rieger, "Geschichte der Architektur in Wien. Vom Klassizismus bis zur Sezession," in *Geschichte der Stadt Wien*, new edition, vol. 7/3 (Vienna, 1973), 174.

13. Wagner-Rieger, *Zur Sozialgeschichte und Typologie des Münchener Privathauses*, 83–84.

14. On the Hungarian developments, see *Magyar művészet 1800–1945* (Hungarian Art 1800–1945), edited by Anna Zádor (Budapest, 1958), 26, 52–56.

15. Wagner-Rieger, *Zur Sozialgeschichte und Typologie des Münchener Privathauses*, 174.

16. Bobek and Lichtenberger, *Wien*, 212–14; particularly interesting is table 1, between pp. 216 and 217.

17. On the origins and the history of the term "Biedermeier," see Georg Himmelheber, *Biedermeier butorok* (Biedermeier Furniture) (Budapest, 1982), 10–12; Willi Geismeier, *Biedermeier* (Leipzig, 1982), 25–32; Günther Böhmer, *Die Welt des Biedermeier* (Munich, 1968), 8–13; Niethammer, *Wohnen im Wandel*, 18.

18. Himmelheber, *Biedermeier bútorok*, 31–35.

19. Lichtenberger, *Die Wiener Altstadt*, 14–15, 201–2; Bobek and Lichtenberger, *Wien*, 76–77.

20. *Historisch-Statistische Übersicht von Wien*, 59, 81; *Die städtebauliche Entwicklung Wiens bis 1955*, edited by Wolfgang Maier (Vienna, 1978); *Wien am Anfang des 20. Jahrhunderts*, edited by Paul Korta (Vienna, 1905–1906), vol. 1.

21. Quoted by Carl E. Schorske, *Fin-de-Siècle Vienna: Politics and Culture* (New York, 1980), 31–32.

22. Elisabeth Lichtenberger, *Wirtschaftsfunktion und Sozialstruktur der Wiener Ringstrasse* (Graz, 1970). See the tables between pp. 49 and 60.

23. Camillo Sitte, *Der Städtebau nach seinen künstlerischen Grundsätzen* (Vienna, 1922), 2–10, 90–92; Otto Wagner, *Moderne Architektur* (Vienna, 1895). A contemporary polemic with C. Sitte may be found in Schorske, *Fin-de-Siècle Vienna*, 62–68, 71–74, 83–85.

24. *Budapest Székesfőváros Statisztikai Hivatalának Közleményei* (Publications of the Statistical Office of the Capital City Budapest), vol. 53 (Budapest, 1924), 6–7, 16–17, 20–22.

25. *Az 1869-ik évi április 20-ára hirdetett országgyűlés képviselőházának naplója* (The Journals of the House of Representatives of the Parliament Convened to April 20 of the Year 1869) (Pest, 1870), 368–82; László Siklóssy, *Hogyan épült Budapest? A Fővárosi Közmunkák Tanácsa története* (How Was Budapest Built up? The History of the Board of Public Works of the Capital City) (Budapest, 1931), 42–43, 92–94, 135–38, 143–46.

26. Siklóssy, *Hogyan épült Budapest?*, 69–74.

27. Ibid., 220–54; Rezső Ruisz, *A Nagykörút* (The Great Boulevard) (Budapest, 1960); Lajos Schmall, *Buda-Pest utcái és terei* (Streets and Squares of Buda-Pest) (Budapest, 1906), 85–103; Jenő Rados, *Budapest városépítésének története* (History of the Architecture of Budapest) (Budapest, 1926), 25–28; Gábor Preisich, *Budapest városépítészetének története a kiegyezéstől a Tanácsköztársaságig* (History of the Architecture of Budapest from the Compromise [1867] to the Hungarian Soviet Republic [1919]), vol. 2 (Budapest, 1964), 65–70.

28. Béla Borsos, Alajos Sódor, and Mihály Zádor, *Budapest építészettörténete, városképei és műemlékei* (The History of Budapest's Architecture, Its Cityscapes and Monuments) (Budapest, 1959), 76–111; Pál Granasztói, *Budapest egy építész szemével* (Budapest through the Eyes of an Architect) (Budapest, 1971), 67–69, 87, 117; Siklóssy, *Hogyan épült Budapest?*, 173–75; György Spira and Károly Vörös, "Budapest története a márciusi forradalomtól az őszirózsás forradalomig" (The History of Budapest from the March Revolution [1848] to the Aster Revolution [1918]), in *Budapest története* (The History of Budapest), edited by László Gerevich, vol. 4 (Budapest, 1978), 198–99.

29. Wagner-Rieger, *Zur Sozialgeschichte und Typologie des Münchener Privathauses*, 134–36.

30. Nikolaus Pevsner, *A modern formatervezés úttörői* (Pioneers of Modern Design, from William Morris to Walter Gropius) (Budapest, 1977), 115–45. The third edition of the English original was published in London, 1960.

31. Wagner-Rieger, *Zur Sozialgeschichte und Typologie des Münchener Privathauses*, 187.

32. Budapest Főváros Ingatlanrendezési Hivatala. Tervtár (Real Estate Registration Office of the Capital City Budapest, Collection of Plans, cited hereafter as Coll. of Plans), nos. 29 246, 29 248, 29 250, 29 303, 29 304, 29 305, 29 306, 29 307, 29 334. I also used the Register of Names and Addresses from 1883–1884 (cited hereafter as Register).

33. Compiled from the Register.

34. Gábor Gyáni, "Egy lipótvárosi lakóház lakói a huszas évek elején" (The Residents of an Apartment House in the Lipótváros at the Beginning of the 1920s), in *Budapest* (journal), 1978, no 9.

35. Coll. of Plans, 29 248.

36. *Die Wiener Ringstrasse*, edited by Renate Wagner-Rieger, vol. 5 (Vienna, 1975),

266; Hannes Stekl, "Die Entstehung bürgerlicher Wohnkultur," in *Beitrage zur historischen Sozialkunde* (July-September 1979), 53; Coll. of Plans, 29 248.

37. Budapest Főváros Levéltára (Archive of the Capital City Budapest), Papers of Gusztáv Frölich from 1891, 4:1, 411b.

38. Coll. of Plans, 28 325.

39. Calculated on the basis of the *Budapest Székesfőváros Statisztikai és Közigazgatási Évkönyve* (Statistical and Administrative Yearbook of the Capital City Budapest), vol. 9, 1909–1912 (Budapest, 1914).

40. Bobeck and Lichtenberger, *Wien*, 238.

41. Ibid., 47, 238, 307, 351.

42. Ibid., 212–16.

43. Ibid., 48–57; Eugen von Philippovich, *Wiener Wohnungsverhältnisse* (Berlin, 1894); and by the same author, *München und seine Bauten* (Munich, 1912), and *München 1869–1958. Aufbruch der modernen Kunst* (Munich, 1958); Neumüller, "Das münchener Wohnhaus von 1870 bis zum Ausbruch des ersten Weltkrieges," in *Das Wohnungswesen der Stadt München*, edited by Albert Gut (Munich, 1926); Karl Erdmannsdorfer, *Das Bürgerhaus in München* (Tübingen, 1972).

44. *Magyarország története 1890–1918* (The History of Hungary 1890–1918), edited by Péter Hanák (Budapest, 1978), 468–69; Bobek and Lichtenberger, *Wien*, 91–92; Stekl, "Die Entstehung bürgerlicher Wohnkultur," 55–56. It turns out from the quoted sources that almost half of the middle-class families had or rented a three-room apartment.

45. Niethammer, *Wohnen im Wandel*, 8, 19–22, 30–40.

46. Béla Borsody-Bevilaqua and Béla Mázsai, *Pest-budai kávéházak* (Cafés of Pest-Buda), 2 vols. (Budapest, 1935); Vilmos Balla, *A Kávéforrás. Régi pesti kávéházak legendái* (The Coffee-Spring. Legends of Old Pester Cafés) (Budapest, 1927); Imre Gundel and Judit Harmat, *A vendéglátás emlékei* (Records of the Catering Trade) (Budapest, 1982), 185–246; Lajos Halás, *Az Országos Kaszinó ötvo: en éves története* (Fifty Years of the Country Casino) (Budapest, 1923); János Bognár, *Három évtized egy úri kaszinó életéből* (Three Decades in the Life of a Gentleman's Club) (Budapest, 1927).

47. An informative case study is Zoltán Tóth, "Polgárosodás és hagyományőrzés a századfordulói Szekszárd anyagi életviszonyaiban" (Civilization and Traditionalism in the Material Life Conditions of the Town Szekszárd at the Turn of the Century), *Ethnografia*, 1982, no. 2.

48. Budapest Főváros Levéltára (Archive of the Capital City Budapest), Hercog Papers, 4: 1, 411b.

49. Ibid., Golberger Papers.

50. *Új országgyűlési almanach 1887–1892* (New Almanac of the Parliament), edited by Albert Sturm (Budapest, 1988), 209.

51. Papers of Gusztáv Frölich, 4:1, 411b.

52. Mária Visi Lakatos, "Das Leben in einer Pécser Bürgerfamilie," in *Bürgerliche Wohnkultur des Fin de Siècle in Ungarn*, edited by Péter Hanák (Vienna-Cologne-Weimar, 1994), 167–93.

53. Gábor Gyáni, "Bürgerliches Heim und Interieur in Budapest," ibid., 45–88; Péter Hanák, "Ein Miethaus am Budapester Ring," ibid., 141–66.

54. Schorske, *Fin-de-Siècle Vienna*, 62–71; Wagner, *Moderne Architekture*, 20–22,

36–41; Hans Dieter Hellige, "Generationskonflikt. Selbsthass und die Entstehung anti-kapitalistischer Positionem im Judentum," in *Geschichte und Gesellschaft*, 1979, no. 4, 476–518.

55. Schorske, *Fin-de-Siécle Vienna*, xxvi–xxix, 5–19, 212–25.

56. Pevsner, *A modern formatervezés úttörői*, 20–29; Jürgen Joedicke, *Modern épí-tészettörténet* (History of Modern Architecture) (Budapest, 1961), 25–30, 38–53.

57. Pevsner, *A modern formatervezés úttörői*, 50–60.

58. Schorske, *Fin-de-Siècle Vienna*, 63.

59. Wagner, *Modern Architekture*, 66–70. In this chapter Wagner laid down the famous formula: "Artis sola domina necessitas."

60. Quoted by Joedicke in *Modern építészettörténet*, 27.

61. "A new structure, new materials, new human tasks and views always implemented changes of forms. Great social changes have created new styles." Otto Wagner, *Zur Baukunst unserer Zeit*, 4th ed. (Vienna, 1914), 17; Schorske, *Fin-de-Siècle Vienna*, 83.

62. Heinz Geretsegger and Max Peintzner, *Otto Wagner 1841–1918* (Munich, 1980), 29.

63. Wolfgang E. Knabbe, *Gesellschaftsveränderung durch Lebensreform. Strukturmerkmale einer sozialreformatorischen Bewegung in Deutschland der Industrialisierungsperiuode* (Göttingen, 1974), 88–111, 167–72; *Das Wilhelminische Bildungbürgertóum. Zur Sozialgeschichte seiner Ideen*, edited by Klaus Vondung (Göttingen, 1976), 28–33.

64. Hendrik Petrus Berlage, *Gedanken über den Stil in der Baukunst* (Leipzig, 1905), quoted by Lajos Pók, *A szecesszió* (The Secession) (Budapest, 1972), 250–53.

65. Henry van de Velde, *Vom neuen Stil* (Leipzig, 1907), quoted by Pók, *A szecesszió*, 229.

66. Hans Wichmann, *Aufbruch zum neuen Wohnen* (Basel-Stuttgart, 1978), 64–68; *Kunst und Alltag um 1900*, edited by Eckhard Siepmann (Berlin, 1978).

67. Wichmann, *Aufbruch zum neuen Wohnen*, 61.

68. Ibid., 44.

69. *Magyar művészet 1890–1919* (Hungarian Art 1890–1919), edited by Lajos Németh (Budapest, 1981), 94.

70. Ibid., 103.

71. Tibor Bakonyi and Mihály Kubinszky, *Lechner Ödön* (Ödön Lechner) (Budapest, 1981), 35–36, 40.

72. Lajos Fülep, *A művészet forradalmától a nagy forradalomig* (From the Revolution of Art to the Great Revolution) (Budapest, 1974), 289.

73. Németh, *Magyar művészet*, 374–76.

74. Ibid., 377–79; Ilona Rév, *Építészet és enteriör a magyar századfordulón* (Architecture and Interiors in Hungary at the Turn of the Century) (Budapest, 1983), 126–28.

75. Ferenc Vámos, *Lajta Béla* (Béla Lajta) (Budapest, 1970), 205–12.

76. Eszter Gábor, Ildiko Nagy, and Ilona Sármány, "A budapesti Schiffer-villa. Egy késő szecessziós villa rekonstrukciója" (The Schiffer Villa in Budapest. Reconstruction of a Villa from the Late Secession), in *Művészettörténeti értesítő* (Bulletin of Art History), 1982, no. 2, 78.

77. Ibid., 78–79, 83–85.

CHAPTER TWO
THE IMAGE OF THE GERMANS AND THE JEWS

1. Völkertafel—Steiermark, early eighteenth century. "Kurze Beschreibung der in Europa befindliche Völker und ihren Eigenschaften." Museum für Volkskunde, Vienna.

2. *A magyar irodalom története* (The History of Hungarian Literature), edited by Klaniczay Tibor, vol. 2 (Budapest, 1964), 282–304.

3. *Magyarország képekben. Statisztikai és történeti, föld és népismereti gyűjtemény* (Hungary in Pictures. Statistical, Historical, Geographical, and Ethnographic Collection), edited by Imre Vachot (Pest, 1846; reprint, Budapest, 1984). The quoted passage from Elek Fényesis on pp. 7–8.

4. Tamás Dersi, *Századvégi üzenet. Sajtótörténeti tanulmányok* (Message from the End of the Century. Studies on Press History) (Budapest, 1975), 7–12. See also Géza Buzinkay, *Borsszem Jankó és társai. Magyar élclapok és karikatúrák a XIX. század második felében* (Jankó Borsszem and His Fellows. Hungarian Comic Papers and Cartoons in the Second Half of the Nineteenth Century) (Budapest, 1983), 6, 36.

5. *Das Dicke Busch-Buch*, edited by Wolfgang Teichmann (Berlin, 1982).

6. Buzinkay, *Borsszem Jankó*, 17.

7. Ibid., 20.

8. *Herkó Páter*, September 2, 1894. Interpretation of the comic paper may be found in Dersi, *Századvégi üzenet*, 63–74.

9. The illustration is in *Borsszem Jankó*, October 14, 1894, 11. See also Dersi, *Századvégi üzenet*, 16–18, and Buzinkay, *Borsszem Jankó*, 28, 37, 68.

10. *Herkó Páter*, July 1, 1895, 9.

11. Ibid., July 29, 1894; November 11, 1894; December 9, 1894; July 1, 1895.

12. Ibid., October 7, 1894: "The gentry does not perish."

13. *Borsszem Jankó*, May 27, 1894: "The arguings of Tobias Kraxelhuber, house owner from Preschpurg."

14. Ibid., July 15, 1894: "The meditations of Solomon Seiffensteiner."

15. For group dynamics and group identity, a basic work is Kurt Lewin, *Resolving Social Conflicts* (New York, 1948; Hungarian ed., Budapest, 1975), 272–75, 327–36. Another standard work I used was Gordon W. Allport, *The Nature of Prejudice* (Reading, Mass., 1954; Hungarian translation, *Az előítélet*, Budapest, 1977). See also Paul A. Hare, *Handbook of Small Group Research* (New York, 1982), and Maurice L. Farber, *The Problem of National Character. A Methodological Analysis* (New York, 1963), 80–87. A useful handbook is Peter R. Hofstätter, *Gruppendynamik. Die Kritik der Massenpsychologie* (Rohwolt, 1957).

16. An instructive volume of essays is *Előítéletek és csoportközi viszonyok* (Prejudices and Intergroup Relations), edited by György Csepeli (Budapest, 1980). I particularly appreciate the editor's introduction and the paper of Henri Tajfel, "Intergroup Behavior: Social Comparison and Social Change" (Ann Arbor, 1974). See also Tajfel, "The Roots of Prejudice" in *Psychology and Race*, edited by Peter Watson (Harmondsworth, 1973), and Barbara Wilska-Duszynska, "Rozwazania o nature stereotypow etnicznych" (Considerations on the Nature of Ethnic Stereotypes), *Studia Socjologiczne* 1971, no. 3.

17. Allport, *The Nature of Prejudice*, 67.

18. Emil Niederhauser, *Nemzeti megújulási mozgalmak Kelet-Európában* (Movements of the National Renaissance in East Europe) (Budapest, 1977), 227–45, and *Problèmes de la conscience historique dans les mouvements de renaissance nationale en Europe orientale*, Acta Historica Academiae Scientiarum Hungaricae, 1972, 39–71.

19. Jenő Szűcs, *Nemzet és történelem* (Nation and History) (Budapest, 1974), 83–101. See also *A Dunánál. Történelmi figyelő* (Along the Danube. Historical Review), edited by Péter Hanák (Budapest, 1982), 44–57.

20. Ferenc Erdei, *A magyar társadalom a két világháború között* (Hungarian Society in the Interwar Period) in *Erdei Ferenc összegyűjtött művei* (Complete Works of F. Erdei) (Budapest, 1980), 316–21. See also Péter Hanák, "Nemesi virtus—polgáre-rény" (Gentleman's Virtue and Bourgeois Ethics), *Kortárs*, October 1983, 1, 600.

21. The poem by Lőrinc Orczy is quoted and interpreted by Zs. Pál Pach, "Üzleti szellem és magyar nemzeti jellem" (Business Spirit and Hungarian National Character), *Történelmi szemle* (Historical Review), 1982, no. 3, 393.

22. Quoted by László Németh, *Kisebbségben* (In the Minority) (Budapest, 1938), 13.

23. Jakab Pólya, *A pesti polgári kereskedelmi testület és a budapesti nagykereskedők és nagyiparosok társulata története* (The History of the Commercial Society of Pest and the Association of Wholesalers and Industrialists of Budapest) (Budapest, 1896), 108–9.

24. Allport, *The Nature of Prejudice*, 30.

25. Pach, "Üzleti szellem," 397–401. See also Hanák, "Nemesi virtus," 1, 595–97.

26. *Politisches Archiv des Auswärtigen Amtes* (Bonn) Fond Österreich, no. 92–1, vol. 12. Below to Hohenlohe, June 20, 1900.

27. Zsolt Beöthy, *A magyar irodalom kistükre* (Small Mirror of Hungarian Literature) (Budapest, 1896). A representative volume of essays is *Mi a magyar?* (What Is the Hungarian?), edited by Gyula Szekfü (Budapest, 1939).

28. Károly Pekár, *A magyar nemzeti szépről. A magyar géniusz esztétikája* (Of Hungarian National Beauty. The Aesthetics of the Hungarian Genius) (Budapest, 1906).

29. Quoted by László Benczédy, "A magyar rendi nemzettudat sajátosságai a 16–17. században" (Characteristics of the National Mind of the Hungarian Estates in the Sixteenth and Seventeenth Centuries) in *Nemzetiség a feudalizmus korában* (Nationality in the Age of Feudalism) (Budapest, 1972), 126.

30. An appropriate cartoon is in *Borsszem Jankó*, July 26, 1885.

31. Ferenc Herczeg, *Történelmi regények. A hét sváb* (Historical Novels. The Seven Svabians) (Budapest, 1983), 425.

32. Ibid., 424, 425–27.

33. Sándor Kiss, "Zsidó fajiság—magyar fajiság" (Jewish Racial Spirit—Hungarian Racial Spirit), *Cél*, 1918, nos. 1–2, pp. 6–11, 30–31.

34. Gyula Szekfü, *Három nemzedék* (Three Generations) (Budapest, 1938), 340–41.

35. "A zsidókérdés Magyarországon" (The Jewish Question in Hungary), *Huszadik század* (Twentieth Century) 2 (1917) (referred to hereafter as "Jewish Question"), 59.

36. Miklós Bartha, *Kazár földön* (On the Land of the Khazars) (Budapest, 1938), 78.

37. Mihály Kolosváry-Borcsa, *A zsidókérdés magyarországi irodalma. A zsidóság szerepe a magyar szellemi életben* (Hungarian Literature on the Jewish Question. The Role of the Jews in Hungarian Cultural Life) (Budapest, 1943), 15.

38. Ibid., 16–17. See also Andor Szörényi, "Zsidó fajiság, zsidó lélek" (Jewish Racial Spirit, Jewish Mind), *Egyedül vagyunk* (We Are Alone), February-March 1939, 3.

39. János Vajda, "Polgárosodás" (Embourgeoisement), in *Vajda János Összes művei* (Complete Works of János Vajda) (Budapest, 1949), 1,124–25. See also Mihály Mester, "Magyar kereskedelem"(Hungarian Commerce), *Magyar szemle* (Hungarian Review), April 28, 1895.

40. Szörényi, "Zsidó fajiság," 5–6, 18–22.

41. "Jewish Question," 118.

42. Ibid., 127.

43. Wilska-Duczynska, "Rozwazania o nature," 104; Allport, *The Nature of Prejudice*, 531–32.

44. Allport, *The Nature of Prejudice*, 287.

45. "Jewish Question," 59.

46. Ibid., 135.

47. Szörényi, "Zsidó fajiság," 15.

48. "Jewish Question," 122–23, 127–28.

49. Rich documentation may be found in the review of the neoconservative agrarian groups, *Magyar gazdák szemléje* (Review of the Hungarian Landlords); see "Szabadság és egyenlőség (Liberty and Equality), vol. 1 (1897), 3, 7; and Károlyi Sándor, "A mozgó töke egynémely hatásáról" (About Some Effects of Mobile Capital," ibid., 328.

50. Péter Hanák, *Ungarn in der Donaumonarchie* (Vienna-Munich-Budapest, 1984), 305–10.

51. Zoltán Bosnyák, *Az idegen vér* (The Alien Blood) (Budapest, 1938), 8.

52. Werner Sombart, *Die Juden und das Wirtschaftsleben* (Leipzig, 1911), 198–202, 250–96.

53. "Jewish Question," 46.

54. Ibid.

55. Ibid., 105–6.

56. Kurt Lewin, "Psycho-Sociological Problems of a Minority Group: Self-Hatred among Jews," in *Resolving Social Conflicts* (New York, 1949).

57. "Jewish Question," 108.

58. Allport, *The Nature of Prejudice*, 189.

59. *A magyarság néprajza* (Hungarian Ethnography), vol. 1, edited by Zsigmond Bátky, István Győrffy, and Károly Viski (Budapest, 1941). See also Eszter Kisbán, "A kenyér a táplálkozási struktúrában" (Bread in the Food Structure), in *Népi kultúra—népi társadalom* (Popular Culture—Popular Society), vol. 4 (Budapest, 1970).

60. Andrásfalvy Bertalan, *Néprajzi jellegzetességek az északmecseki bányavidék gazdasági életében* (Ethnographic Characteristics in the Economic Life of the North Mecsek Mine Region), Dunántúli Tudományos Gyűjtemény, Transdanubian Scientific Collection, Series Historica, vol. 6. (Budapest, 1972), 126–27.

61. *Csoportdinamika, Válogatás Kurt Lewin Műveiből* (Group Dynamics. Selected Works of Kurt Lewin), Introduction by Ferenc Mérei (Budapest, 1975), 48–49. See also Allport, *The Nature of Prejudice*, 69–70, 83–85, 93–102, 185–89.

62. Sándor Kiss, "Zsidó fajiság," 16–17; see also Hanák, "Nemesi virtus," 1,597–1,600.

63. *Ignotus válogatott írásai* (The Selected Writings of Ignotus), edited by Aladár Komlós (Budapest, 1969), 616–18.

64. Allport, *The Nature of Prejudice*, 482–86, 526–29. See also Ottó Komoly, *Cionista életszemlélet* (Zionist View of Life) (Kolozsvár, 1942), 15.

CHAPTER THREE
THE GARDEN AND THE WORKSHOP

1. This view was expressed in István Király, *Ady Endre*, vol. 1 (Budapest, 1979), 471, and László Mátrai, *Alapját vesztett felépítmény* (A Structure with Its Foundation Lost) (Budapest, 1976).

2. Hermann Bahr, *Austriaca* (Berlin, 1911), 33.

3. Stefan Zweig, *Die Welt von gestern. Die Erinnerungen eines Europäers* (Hungarian edition, Budapest, 1981), 13–14.

4. Carl E. Schorske, *Fin-de-Siècle Vienna. Politics and Culture* (New York, 1980), xxvi–xxvii, xxix, 8–10.

5. Joseph Redlich, *Das österreichische Staats- und Reichsproblem*, vol. 1/1 (Leipzig, 1920), 38–55; Péter Hanák, "Osztrák állampatriotizmus a hódító nacionalizmus korában" (Austrian State Patriotism in the Age of Conquering Nationalism), *Világosság* (Daylight), March 1978, 151–57.

6. Peter Urbanitcsh, "Die Deutschen in Österreich," in *Die Habsburgermonarchie 1848–1918*, edited by Adam Wandruszka and Peter Urbanitsch, vol. 3/1 (Vienna, 1980), 47–56, 71–73, 124–53; Marscha L. Rosenblit, *The Jews of Vienna 1867–1914. Assimilation and Identity* (Albany, N.Y., 1983), 13–45, 127–46; Ernst Bruckmüller, *Socialgeschichte Österreichs* (Vienna-Munich, 1985), 319–21, 329–33, 395–98.

7. For the text of the Act of December 1867 see Edmund Bernatzik, *Die österreichischen Verfassungsgesetze* (Vienna, 1911), 422–27; Gerald Stourz, "Die Gleichberechtigung der Volkstämme als Verfassungsprinzip 1848–1918," in *Die Habsburgermonarchie*, vol. 3/2, 1, 011; Gerald Stourz, "Die österreichische Verfassung von 1867," in *Österreich in Geschichte und Literatur* 12 (1968); Éva Somogyi, *A birodalmi centralizációtól a dualizmusig* (From the Empire's Centralization to Dualism) (Budapest, 1976), 213–14.

8. *Grillparzers Gespräche und die Characteristiken seiner Persönlichkeit durch die Zeitgenossen*, edited by August Sauer, vol. 15 (Vienna, 1910), 110.

9. *Grillparzers politisches Vermächtnis*, edited by Hugo Hofmannsthal (Leipzig, 1917), 48.

10. Péter Hanák, "Látszólagosság és viszonylagosság a századforduló Monarchiájában" (Appearance and Relativeness in the Monarchy at the Turn of the Century), *Világosság* 4 (1979), 217–18.

11. *Das wilhelminische Bildungsbürgertum. Zur Sozialgeschichte seiner Ideen*, edited by Klaus Vondung (Göttingen, 1976), 29–31.

12. Friedrich Heer, *Der Kampf um die österreichische Identität* (Vienna-Cologne-Graz, 1981), 262–80. The phenomenon is elucidated by Hermann Bahr's comment, "It comes to pass that the middle class fails to succeed in incorporating its own intellectuals into the middle-class order, and in its midst the number of the disillusioned . . . who are

tormented by the dream of a higher heroic life challenging to the whole man, increases. Of these disillusioned and dream-drunk members of the middle class, some go into the proletariat which sets about destroying the middle class world in order to replace it with a human one. Other of these disillusioned or dream-drunk ones . . . see in art that life of the whole man denied them in the reductions of the middle-class world order." Quoted in J. William McGrath, *Dionysian Art and Populist Politics in Austria* (New Haven-London, 1974), 85; also quoted here is the view of the historian Heinrich Friedjung, pp. 206–7. See also Carl E. Schorske, *Fin-de-Siècle Vienna*, xxv–xxviii, 8–10, and Schorske, "Generational Tension and Cultural Change: Reflections on the Case of Vienna, " in *Daedalus,* Autumn 1978, 114–15.

13. Zoltán Horváth, *A magyar századforduló. A második reformnemzedék története (1896–1914)* (Turn-of-the-Century Hungary. The History of the Second Reform Generation [1896–1914] (Budapest, 1961), 114–18; *Ignotus válogatott írásai* (The Selected Writings of Ignotus), edited by Aladár Komlós (Budapest, 1969), 11–12, 615–21.

14. *A Hét. Politikai és irodalmi szemle, 1890–1899* (The Week. Political and Literary Review, 1890–1899), selections edited by Anna Fábri and Ágota Steinert. 2 vols. (Budapest, 1978), 1:5.

15. Michael Worbs, *Nervenkunst. Literatur und Psychoanalyse in Wien der Jahrhundertwende* (Frankfurt a. M., 1983), 48.

16. For the relationship between literature and neurotic experiences, see ibid., 57; for a comment by Karl Kraus, see ibid., 190.

17. *Stefan George és Hugo von Hofmannsthal versei* (The Poems of Stefan George and Hugo von Hofmannsthal), selected by Endre Szabó (Budapest, 1981).

18. *Rainer Maria Rilke versei* (The Poems of Rainer Maria Rilke), selected by Endre Szabó (Budapest, 1983), 42–43.

19. Leopold Adrian-Werburg, *Der Garten der Erkenntnis* (Vienna, 1985), quoted in Carl E. Schorske, *Fin-de-Siècle Vienna,* 306–11.

20. Hermann Broch, *Hofmannsthal und seine Zeit,* postscript by Hannah Arendt (Munich, 1964); Werner Volke, *Hugo v. Hofmannsthal* (Hamburg, 1969), 175.

21. *George és Hofmannsthal versei,* "Old Vienna—Prologue," 194–97.

22. Arthur Schnitzler, *Der grüne Kakadu. Gesammelte Werke in Einzelausgaben. Das dramatische Werk,* vol. 3 (Frankfurt a. M., 1978), 33.

23. *George és Hofmannsthal versei,* 185; William Shakespeare, *The Tempest,* act 4, sc. 1, lines 156–57.

24. Sigmund Freud, *Traumdeutung* (Leipzig-Vienna, 1911), 103.

25. Schorske, *Fin-de-Siècle Vienna,* 140–41.

26. Marian Bisanz-Prakken, "Programmatik und subjective Aussage im Werk von Gustav Klimt, 2 in *Traum und Wirklichkeit. Wien, 1870–1930* (Vienna, 1984), 112–13. An essential work for a philosophical and cultural-historical interpretation of Klimt is Christian M. Nebehay, *Gustav Klimt. Dokumentation* (Vienna, 1969).

27. Rainer Maria Rilke, "Schluss-Stück," in *Gedichte,* 4th ed. (Leipzig, 1986), 40.

28. Rainer Maria Rilke, *Das Stundenbuch* (Frankfurt a. M., 1976), 94.

29. Ibid.

30. Ibid., 95.

31. Rainer Maria Rilke, *Malte Laurids Brigge feljegyzései* (The Notebook of Malte

Laurids Brigge), Hungarian translation and introduction essay by Ambrus Bor (Budapest, n.d.), 6.

32. Hugo von Hofmannsthal, *Gedichte und lyrische Dramen. Gesammelte Werke,* edited by Herbert Steiner (Hamburg, 1952), 219. The same thought is expressed even more profoundly in Hofmannsthal's short story "Märchen der 672. Nacht." The protagonist, an antiquities dealer, again senses the nothingness of beauty, and he cannot get rid of the thought that death is always present. See Hugo von Hofmannsthal, "Das Märchen der 672. Nacht" in *Ausgewählte Werke in Zwei Bänden,* edited by Rudolf Hirsch (Frankfurt a. M., 1957), 2:10.

33. *George és Hofmannsthal versei,* 187.

34. "In the bleakness of agony there are wonderous, delusive moments when everything is more beautiful than ever before. . . . You lose quite a lot when one day you feel strong and healthy. Because there are so many kinds of death, but only one kind of health, " says Anatol in *Agony.* See *Gesammelte Werke in Einzelausgaben. Das dramatische Werk,* vol. 1 (Frankfurt a. M., 1987).

35. András Batta, *Richard Strauss* (Hungarian edition, Budapest, 1981), 159–65. The author points out that most Catholic countries refused to perform the *Salome* in the 1900s.

36. Schnitzler, *Gesammelte Werke. Das dramatische Werk,* vol. 4 (Frankfurt a. M., 1979), 147–48.

37. Hofmannsthal, "Grossmutter und Enkel," in *Gedichte und lyrische Dramen,* 33–34.

38. Hubert Lengauer, "Auf 'Leben' und 'Tod.' Askese und Pompe funebre bei Hofmannsthal." Paper for the conference "Ornament und Askese" (1985), 9.

39. Hofmannsthal, *Gesammelte Werke in 10 Einzelbänden,* vol. 3 *Dramen* (Frankfurt a. M., 1979–1980), 352. Quoted in Lengauer, "Auf 'Leben' und 'Tod,' " 2.

40. Hugo von Hofmannsthal, "Lord Chandos levele" (A letter from Lord Chandos), in *A szecesszió* (The Secession), edited with an introductory essay by Lajos Pók (Budapest, 1972), 323–25.

41. "Miért adunk ki folyóiratot?" (Why Do We Publish a Journal?) in *Ver Sacrum* 1(1898); see. *A szecesszió,* 362–67.

42. Hermann Bahr, "A szecesszióhoz" (To the Secession), in *Ver Sacrum* 1(1898); see *A szecesszió,* 369–70.

43. "Miért adunk ki folyóiratot?", 367.

44. Harry Zohn, *Karl Kraus* (New York, 1971), 125.

45. Ibid., a quote from the journal *Fackelo* no. 194 (1906), 11.

46. William M. Johnston, *The Austrian Mind. An Intellectual and Social History, 1848–1938* (Berkeley and Los Angeles, 1972), 202–6, 212, 216, 223, 316, 402.

47. Gerhart Baumann, *Franz Grillparzer* (Freiburg-Vienna, 1954), 169.

48. *Kulturprofil der Jahrhundertwende. Essays von Hermann Bahr,* edited by Heinz Kindermann (Vienna, 1962), 153.

49. Kristóf Nyíri, *A Monarchia szellemi életéről* (On Intellectual Life in the Monarchy) (Budapest, 1980).

50. Albert Einstein, "A relativitáselméletről. Egy londoni beszéd" (On the Theory of Relativity. A London Speech), in *Válogatott tanulmányok* (Selected Essays), edited by Robert Tőrös (Budapest, 1971), 241–42, 275.

51. Karl Kraus, *Untergang der Welt durch schwarze Magie* (Vienna-Leipzig, 1922), 418; see also Hermann Broch, *Hofmannsthal und seine Zeit* (Munich, 1964), 89, 166.

52. *A Hét*, 1:5–6.

53. Bernát Alexander, "Irodalmi bajok" (Literary Ills), ibid., 2.

54. Zsigmond Justh, "Báró Mednyánszky Lászlóról" (About Baron Laszlo Mednyánszky), ibid., 56.

55. Sándor Bródy, ibid., 61–62.

56. Endre Ady, "A hétről" (On 'A Hét'), in *Ady Endre összes prózai művei* (Endre Ady's Collected Prose, hereafter AEÖPM), vol. 1 (Budapest, 1955), 125.

57. "Lechner Ödön," in *A Hét* 1:498–99.

58. *Magyar művészet 1890–1919* (Hungarian Art 1890–1919), edited by Lajos Németh (Budapest, 1981), 262–66.

59. Bálint Magyar, *A Vígszínház története. Alapítástól az államosításig 1896–1949* (The History of the Comic Theater. From Its Founding to Its Nationalization 1896–1949) (Budapest, 1979).

60. Ferenc Katona and Tibor Dénes, *A Thália története* (The History of the Thalia Theater) (Budapest, 1954), 175.

61. Tamás Kóbor, "A délibábok hőse" (The Hero of Mirages), in *A Hét* 1:391.

62. Ignotus, "Bródy Sándor," in *Ignotus válogatott írásai*, 348.

63. Dezső Szomory, "Séta a temetőben" (A Stroll in the Graveyard), in *A Hét* 1:110–13.

64. István Bársony, "Halálos Szerelem," ibid., 380–82.

65. Zoltán Ambrus, "Pókháló kisasszony" (Spiderweb Lady), ibid., 393–99.

66. *Babits Mihály összes versei* (The Collected Poems of Mihály Babits) (Budapest, n.d.) 54, 79.

67. Dezső Kosztolányi, "Alföld," in *Kosztolányi Dezső összegyüjtött versei* (The Collected Poems of Dezső Kosztolányi) (Budapest, 1943), 11.

68. Endre Ady, "Societas leonina," in AEÖPM, vol. 3 (Budapest, 1964), 192.

69. Endre Ady, "Bilek," ibid., vol. 4 (Budapest, 1964), 132–33.

70. *Bródy Sándor válogatott drámái* (The Selected Dramas of Sándor Bródy) (Budapest, 1957), 104, 147–48.

71. Endre Ady, "Az Ige veszedelme" (The Danger of the Word), in AEÖPM, vol. 7 (Budapest, 1968), 32.

72. "Ismeretlen Korvin-kódex margójára" (To the Margin of an Unknown Corvin Codex), ibid., 16–17.

73. Endre Ady, "Bilek," ibid., 4:132–33. See also Chapter Five below.

74. Mihály Babits, "In Horatium" in *Babits Mihály összes versei*, 1.

75. Ignotus, "A magyar kultúra és a nemzetiségek" (Hungarian Culture and the Nationalities), in *Nyugat* (West) 1908.

76. Endre Ady, "A muszáj-Herkules" (The You-Must-Hercules), in *Ady Endre összes versei* (Endre Ady's Collected Poems) (Budapest, n.d.), 1:245.

77. György Rába, *Babits Mihály* (Budapest, 1983), 15–16.

78. *Ady Endre válogatott levelei* (Endre Ady's Selected Letters) (Budapest, 1956), Ady to Léda, September 30, 1903, 53; Ady to Bódog Somló, December 18, 1903, 91.

79. Péter Hanák, "A Szent Lélek lovagjától az Új Versekig" (From the Poem "The Knights of the Holy Soul" to the "New Poems"), in *"Akarom: tisztán lássatok." Tudományos ülésszak Ady Endre születésének 100. évfordulójára* ("I want that you see

clearly." Conference for the 100th Anniversary of Endre Ady's Birth), edited by Edit Csáky (Budapest, 1980), 42.

80. Mihály Babits, "Ady Endrének" (To Endre Ady), in *Babits Mihály összes versei*, 151.

81. Dezső Kosztolányi, "Pipacsos, alföldi út, forró délután" (Road in the Great Plain with Poppie on a Hot Afternoon), in *Kosztolányi Dezső összegyűjtött művei*, 134.

82. *Magyarország története 1890–1918* (The History of Hungry 1890–1918), edited by Péter Hanák (Budapest, 1978), 734.

83. Endre Ady, "Az utolsó kuruc" (The Last Kuruc), in *Ady Endre összes versei*, 1:416.

84. Károly Kristóf, *Beszélgetések Bartók Bélával* (Conversations with Bela Bartok) (Budapest, 1957), 8.; József Újfalussy, *Bartók Béla* (2nd ed., Budapest, 1970), 72–74.

85. Dezső Malonyai, *A magyar nép művészete* (The Art of the Hungarian People), vols. 1–5 (Budapest, 1907–1923).

86. Ferenc Vámos, *Lajta Béla* (Budapest, 1970); Tibor Bakonyi and Mihály Kubinszky, *Lechner Ödön* (Budapest, 1981).

87. Ede Thoroczkay Wigand's article in *Magyar művészet* (Hungarian Art), 364–68; Károly Kós, ibid., 373–79.

88. Ibid.

89. József Újfalussy, ibid., 76–77; Ernő Lendvai, *Bartók költői világa* (Bartók's Poetic World) (Budapest, 1971), 23–58.

90. Endre Ady, "A fajtám sorsa" (The Fate of My Kind), in *Ady Endre összes versei*, 2:34; "Beteg századokért lakolva" (Expiating for Sick Centuries), ibid., 1:679.

91. Mihály Babits, "Óda a bűnhöz" (Ode to Sin), in *Babits Mihály összes versei*, 4.

92. György Rába, *Babits Mihály*, 33–34.

93. Dezső Kosztolányi, "Párbeszéd magammal" (Dialog with Myself), in *Kosztolányi Dezső összegyűjtött művei*, 125.

94. Dezső Kosztolányi, "Régi szerelmes levele" (Old Love Letter), ibid., 151.

95. Endre Ady, "A menekülő Élet" (Life Fleeing), in *Ady Endre összes versei*, 232–33.

96. Mihály Babits, "Esti Kérdés" (Evening Question), in *Babits Mihály összes versei*, 66–67.

97. Ágnes Nemes Nagy, *A hegyi költő* (The Mountain Poet) (Budapest, 1984), 46–47.

98. Gyula Krúdy (pseudonym "Rezeda"), "A műhelyből" (From the Workshop), in *Krúdy világa* (Krúdy's World), edited by Áron Tóbiás (Budapest, 1964), 114.

99. Ernő Szép, "Szinbádról" (On Sindbad), in *Krúdy világa*, 127.

100. Endre Ady, "Krúdy Gyula könyve (Gyula Krúdy's Book), in AEÖPM, vol. 11 (Budapest, 1982), 34.

101. Mihály Czine, "Krúdy Gyula," in *A magyar irodalom története 1905-tól 1919-ig* (The history of Hungarian Literature from 1905 to 1919), edited by Miklós Szabolcsi (Budapest, 1962), 371.

102. *Magyar művészet*, 409.

103. Béla Szíj, *Gulácsy* (Budapest, 1979), 28–31; Judit Szabadi, *A magyar szecesszió művészete* (The Art of the Hungarian Secession) (Budapest, 1979), 63–67.

104. Szíj, *Gulácsy*, 124.

105. Ibid., 166.

106. Ibid., 188.

107. Lajos Németh, *Csontváry*, 2nd ed. (Budapest, 1970).

108. Géza Csáth, *A varázsló halála* (The Death of the Magician), edited by Endre Illés (Budapest, 1982); Géza Csáth, *The Magician's Garden and Other Stories*, edited by Marianne D. Birnbaum, translated by Joscha Kessler and Charlotte Rogers (New York, 1980).

109. Schorske, *Fin-de-Siècle Vienna*, 323.

110. See note 40, *A szecesszió*, 324.

111. Gustav Janouch, *Beszélgetések Kafkával* (Conversations with Kafka) (Budapest, 1972), 83.

112. Schorske, *Fin-de-Siècle Vienna*, 135–38.

113. Robert Musil, *Die Verwirrungen des Zöglings Törless* (Hamburg, 1978), 25.

114. Ibid., 46–47.

115. Karl Kraus, *Die letzen Tage der Menschheit*. 2nd ed. (Vienna-Leipzig, 1922), 492–97.

116. Oszkár Jászi's Correspondence. Archive of the National Széchenyi Library, Budapest. Ady to Jászi, October, 1914.

117. Ibid., November 4, 1914, and December 10, 1914.

118. "Kurucok így beszélnek" (A Kuruc Speaks Like This), in *Ady Endre összes versei*, 389.

CHAPTER FOUR

THE ALIENATION OF DEATH IN BUDAPEST AND VIENNA

1. Historical writing in Austria and Hungary has not concerned itself with the historical meaning of death, although its specific subject is the passage of time and mortality. The theme of death in a historical-anthropological interpretation has been discovered by French historians and is presented in such excellent historical works as Edgar Morin, *L'homme et la mort devant l'histoire* (Paris, 1961); Philippe Ariès, *L'homme devant la mort* (Paris, 1977), a model work; Pierre Chaunu, *La mort à Paris* (Paris, 1978); and M. Vovelle, *La mort et l'Occident de 1300 à nos jours* (Paris, 1983). See also the useful collection of essays in *Man's Concern with Death* (New York-London, 1969).

2. Jolán Antónia Fehér, *Budapest székesfőváros temetőinek története* (The History of the Cemeteries of the Capital of Budapest) (Budapest, 1933), 71–72; *Zur Geschichte der Bestattungswesen in Wien: 75, Jahre städtische Bestattung* (Vienna, 1982); Hans Bobek and Elizabeth Lichenberger, *Wien* (Vienna-Cologne, 1978), 236–37; Lajos Nagy, *Budapest története a török kiűzésétől a márciusi forradalomig* (The History of Budapest from the Expulsion of the Turks to the March Revolution, 1948), 3; *Budapest története*, edited by Domokos Kosáry (Budapest, 1975), 272–75.

3. Fehér, *Budapest székesfőváros temetőinek története*, 72–88; Walter Obermaier "'Die schöne Leich': Tod, Begrabnis und Totengedanken in Wien," in *"Die schöne Leich": Exhibition Catalog* (Vienna, 1986), 12–16.

4. "A fővárosi köztemető szabályzata" ("Statutes of the Public Cemetery of Budapest") in *Fővárosi Közlöny* (Municipal Ordinances of Budapest) (Budapest, 1882); "Szabályzat a temetőkről ("Statute of the Cemeteries"), ibid., 34.

5. Ibid., 633–36.

6. *Magyar Törvénytár: Corpus Iuris Hungarici, Az 1875–1876. Évi törvények.* (Collection of Laws 1875–1876.) (Budapest, 1896).

7. *A halottkémi szolgálat kézikönyve* (Coroner's Manual) (Budapest, 1887). See also the enlarged edition: *A halottkémlés kézikönyve* (Funeral Cult) (Budapest, 1910).

8. "I cannot deny that burials in Pest are accompanied by great expenses, that widows and orphans . . . usually spend almost the entire relicted fortune for a decent burial of the deceased spouse or parents." Quoted in József Patacsich, *Szabad Királyi Pest városának leírása* (Description of the Royal Free City of Pest) (Pest, 1831), 69. The same view is expressed in Franz Schams, *Vollständige Beschreibung der Königlichen Freystadt Pest in Ungarn* (Pest, 1821).

9. *Fővárosi Közlöny* 5:4 (Budapest, 1901), 641–42 and Béla Szántó, "A temetkezés és a kötelező ravatalozás" (The Funeral and the Obligatory Laying Out) in *Városi Szemle* (Urban Review) 1–2 (1911), 790–91, 805.

10. Ibid., 802–3. On the shame of the "gratis funeral" see *Fővárosi Közlöny* (Budapest, December 1920).

11. Szántó, "A temetkezés és a kötelező ravatalozás," 801; and Zoltán Xantus, "A budapesti temetkezések történetéből" (Out of the History of Burials in Budapest) in *Városgazdasági tájékoztató* (Information on the City Management) 1 (1981), 81.

12. "*Die schöne Leich,*" item 104, a receipt of the Vienna City Council.

13. "It is well known that burials settled at public expense are so bleak, so divergent from the existent funeral customs that only deceased persons without relatives get buried at public expense. He who has nothing but a pillow will be buried otherwise." Quoted in Szántó, " A temetkezés és a kötelező ravatalozás," 803.

14. Ibid., 789.

15. Ibid., 788–89. The same issue can be found in *Budapesti hírlap* (Budapest Journal), May 16, 1913.

16. A detailed list of the prices of coffins and the expenses of the bier can be found in Szántó, "A temetkezés és a kötelező ravatalozás," 790, 804.

17. A price list of Catholic funerals is contained ibid., 805.

18. "Amidst the troubles of life the workers of Budapest cry out in pain against the outrages of the undertaker-hyenas," wrote Béla Szántó in "A kötelező ravatalozás" (The Obligatory Laying Out) in *Szocializmus*, 1911–1912, 566. He noted that the leftist press sharply attacked the "usurers of death" after one or another scandal, but it was all in vain (ibid., 570).

19. Xantus, "A budapesti temetkezések történetéből," 80–81.

20. Gyula Pikler, "Az 1911: évi budapesti lakásszámlálás főbb eredményei" (Main Issues of the Apartment Census in Budapest in 1911) in *Városi Szemle* 1–2 (1911).

21. Kálmán Végh, *A holtak iránti kegyelet hajdan és most* (Reverence the Dead Then and Now) (Budapest, 1891), 94–98; *Temetkezési kézikönyv lelkészek és kántorok számára* (Funeral Manual for Priests and Cantors) (Esztergom, 1911), 1; Bárkányi, "Budapesti Katolikus temetési szertartás leírása" (Description of the Catholic Funeral Rite in Budapest) in *Halottkultusz* (Funeral Culture), edited by Mihály Hoppal and László Novák (Budapest, 1982), 377–80.

22. Végh, *A holtak iránti kegyelet hajdan és most*, 92.

23. László Ravasz, *Agenda—a református egyházi liturgia* (Agenda—The Liturgy of the Reformed Church) (Budapest, 1929), 377–80.

24. Nátán Halász, *A Kegyelet forrása. Zsidó temetkezési és gyászszokások* (The Source of Piety. Jewish Funeral and Mourning Customs) (Budapest, 1902), 10–14.

25. Zsuzsa Szarvas, "Ortodox zsidó temetkezési és gyászszokások" (Orthodox

Jewish Funeral and Mourning Customs) in *Halottkultusz*, edited by Mihály Hoppal and László Novák (Budapest, 1982), 388–89. See also József Farkas, *Hitéletünk szertartásai és szokásai* (Rites and Customs of Our Religion) (Budapest, 1941); and Sándor Scheiber, *Folklor es tárgytörténet* (Folklore and History of Objects), 2 vols. (Budapest, 1974).

26. Wolfgang Krabbe, *Gesellschaftsveränderung durch Lebensreform* (Göttingen, 1974), 78–94.

27. Carl E. Schorske, *Fin-de-Siècle Vienna. Politics and Culture* (New York, 1979), 8–10, 19–20. Péter Hanák, "A kert és a műhely" (The Garden and the Workshop) in *Új hold évkönyv* (Yearbook of the New Moon) (Budapest, 1986), 217.

28. Excerpt from Jean-Paul Sartre, "Das Sein und das Nichts" in *Der Tod in der Moderne*, edited by Hans Ebeling (Königstein: Syndicat, 1984), 81–82.

29. Rainer Maria Rilke, *Selected Poems*, translated by Albert E. Fleming. (2nd ed., New York-Toronto, 1986), 88.

30. Ibid., 56.

31. Rainer Maria Rilke, *The Notebook of Malte Laurids Brigge*, introduction by Stephen Spender (New York, 1984), 9–10.

32. Arthur Schnitzler, *Professor Bernhardi, Gesammelte Werke: Das dramatische Werk*, vol. 6 (Frankfurt a. M., 1979), 147–48.

33. Schorske, *Fin-de-Siècle Vienna,* 240–42.

34. Ignotus, "Bródy Sándor," in *Ignotus válogatott írásai* (The Selected Writings of Ignotus), edited by Aladár Komlós (Budapest, 1969), 348.

35. István Király, *Ady Endre* (Budapest, 1970); György Rába, *Babits Mihály* (Budapest, 1982); Béla Szíj, *Gulácsy* (Budapest, 1979); Géza Csáth, *The Magician's Garden and Other Stories*, edited by Marianne D. Birnbaum, translated by Joscha Kessler and Charlotte Rogers (New York, 1980); A. Tóbiás, *Krúdy világa* (Krúdy's World) (Budapest, 1964).

CHAPTER FIVE
THE START OF ENDRE ADY'S LITERARY CAREER

1. For this interpretation of the line, see I. Király, *Ady Endre,* vol. 1 (Budapest, 1970), 214–15.

2. "Szecesszió" (Art Nouveau), in *Ady Endre összes prózai művei* (Endre Ady's Collected Prose, cited below as AEÖPM) (Budapest, 1966), 1:119–20.

3. "A hódító szép" (Conquering Beauty), ibid., 358.

4. "Monna Vanna igazsága" (Monna Vanna's Truth), ibid., 4:29.

5. "A tűz márciusa" (The Fire's March), in *Ady Endre összes versei* (Endre Ady's Collected Poems) (Budapest, n.d.), 245.

6. AEÖPM, 4:17. Cf. "Ideális őrületek" (Ideal Lunacies).

7. Quoted by J. Varga, *Ady és kora* (Ady and His Age) (Budapest, 1977), 85.

8. "Ujságírók és színészek" (Journalists and Actors), AEÖPM, 1:397.

9. "A hétről" (About the Week), ibid., 125.

10. "Prohászka és vidéke" (Prohászka and His World), ibid., 4:24.

11. Let me make just one more methodological comment. Although it helps the researcher to have all of Ady's articles collected in book form, it hinders his understanding of these writings not to see them in their original environment, not to read them in the spirit of the overall trend of the entire newspaper. That is why it is necessary, at

times, to go back to the original sources, in our case, to the *Nagyváradi Napló* (Nagyvárad Daily). It is only in this context that we can make sense of the political trend of a number of Ady's articles; he had, at times, to adapt himself to the political line, tactics, and propaganda of the paper for a while—as, for instance, in the case of most of the articles praising the two Tiszas or Dezső Bánffy.

12. To name only the most important: see J. Dóczy and Gy. Földessy, editors, *Ady-múzeum* (Ady Museum), vols. 1–2 (Budapest, 1924); Gy. Bölöni, *Az igazi Ady* (The Real Ady) (Paris, 1934); L. Bóka, *Ady Endre pályakezdése* (The Early Years of Endre Ady's Career) (Budapest, 1955); N. Hegedűs, *Ady Endre nagyváradi napjai* (Endre Ady's Days in Nagyvárad) (Budapest, 1957); E. Vezér, *Ady Endre* (Budapest, 1969); M. Kovalovszky, *Emlékezések Ady Endréről* (Recollections of Endre Ady), vol. 2 (Budapest, 1974); and J. Varga, *Ady és kora* (Ady and His Age) (Budapest, 1977).

13. "Egy lövés után" (After a Shot), AEÖPM, 1:83.

14. "Várad és Debrecen" (Várad and Debrecen), ibid., 3:125. Hungarian freedom fighters of the seventeenth and eighteenth centuries were called "kuruc," a word derived from *crux,* cross. The term came simply to mean the opponents of the 1867 Compromise.

15. "Rátót államférfia" (The Statesman of Rátót), ibid., 1:189–90. The Széll government was from February 1899 to June 1903.

16. "A magyar városok" (The Hungarian Towns), "A zsíros város" (The Greasy Town), ibid., 3:120.

17. "Zsidók és hugenották" (Jews and Huguenots), ibid., 76.

18. "Várad és Debrecen," ibid., 125.

19. "István király országa" (King Stephen's Country), ibid., 128. The "casino" is the National Casino (or gentelman's club), called the Magnate's Casino.

20. "A társadalmi viszonyok" (Social Relations), ibid., 56–57.

21. "Mely ápol és eltakar" (Which Gives You Care and Shelter), ibid., 169–70.

22. "Societas leonina," ibid., 192–93.

23. "Egy nagy vagyon átka" (The Curse of a Great Fortune), ibid., 4:8–9.

24. "Marseillaise," ibid., 3:123.

25. "Nostra res agitur," ibid., 4:26–27. Dózsa was the leader of the great peasant revolt in 1514.

26. "Az új program" (The New Program), ibid., 33–34.

27. "A szépnek sorsa" (The Fate of Beauty), ibid., 44.

28. "Levél az apámhoz" (Letter to My Father), ibid., 45. The term "knight of the Holy Spirit" Ady adopted from Heinc.

29. Ibid., 46.

30. "Akik nem tanulnak" (Those Who Don't Learn), ibid., 30.

31. "Mi lesz hamvazó szerdán?" (What Will Happen on Ash Wednesday?), ibid., 40–41.

32. "A hétről" (About the Week), ibid., 54.

33. "Ábel páter misézik (Father Abel Says Mass), ibid., 136.

34. "Itthon vagyok" (I'm Home), ibid., 184.

35. "A hétről," ibid., 53.

36. Ibid., 79.

37. "Nevezetes május" (Famous May), ibid., 82. *Ex lex* denotes a state without a budget accepted by the legislature.

38. "Döntés a Somló-ügyben" (Decision in the Somló Affair), ibid., 106.

39. "Merénylet a nagyváradi jogakadémián" (An Attempted Murder at the Law School of Nagyvárad), ibid., 97.

40. Quoted by Vezér, *Ady Endre*, 67.

41. "A börtön filozófiája" (Prison Philosophy), AEÖPM, 4:107.

42. "Bilek," ibid., 132–33.

43. Vezér, *Ady Endre*, 84.

44. L. Bóka's comment is quoted by Varga, *Ady és kora*, 107.

45. Király, *Ady Endre*, 1:397.

46. Bilek, AEÖPM, 4:132.

47. "Földindulás" (Earthquake), ibid., 7:84.

48. Király, *Ady Endre*, 397.

49. E. Ady, *Vallomások és tanulmányok* (Confessions and Studies), vol. 1, *Biography* (Budapest, 1944), 14.

50. "Iró a könyvéről" (The Author about His Book), AEÖPM, 7:111.

51. "Lázban ég a világ" (The World Is in a Fever), ibid., 4:152–53.

52. Ady to Léda, September 30, 1903, in *Ady Endre Válogatott Levelei* (Endre Ady's Selected Letters, cited hereafter as AEVL) (Budapest, 1956), 53.

53. Ady to Berta Brüll, November 26, 1903, ibid., 73.

54. Ady to Bódog Somló, December 18, 1903, ibid., 91.

55. "Protestálunk" (We Protest), AEÖPM, 4:175. István Tisza, minister-president from November 1903, was a mainstay of the Liberal party.

56. The question was first put by R. Musil in his great novel, *The Man without Qualities* (New York, 1965), 1:177.

57. The image is Rilke's: Rainer Maria Rilke, *Malte Laurids Brigge feljegyzései* (The Notebook of Malte Laurids Brigge) (Budapest, n.d.), xi.

58. "Még egyszer" (Once More), AEÖPM, 4:161.

59. Ady wrote "A vár fehér asszonya" (The White Woman of the Castle) in July of 1905, but he put it in his volume entitled *Uj versek* (New Poems), published in 1906.

60. Ady to Berta Brüll, January 11, 1905, AEVL, 114.

61. Ady to Léda, November 30, 1905, ibid., 133.

62. "Egy könyv és egy ember" (A Book and a Man), AEÖPM, 6:60.

63. "A moszkvai rekviem" (Moscow Requiem), ibid., 65.

64. "Veér Judit rózsája" (Veér Judit's Rose), ibid., 51.

65. "Péntek esti levél" (Friday Evening Letter), ibid., 112.

66. "A nacionalizmus alkonya" (The Twilight of Nationalism), ibid., 117–19.

67. "A hazafiság reviziója" (The Revision of Patriotism), ibid., 205.

68. "A béka kuruttyol . . ." (The Frog Sings), ibid., 39.

69. "Jókai szobra" (Jókai's Statue), ibid., 73.

70. "Egy kis ügy és egy nagy ügy" (A Small Affair and a Big Affair), ibid., 199.

71. "Bródy Sándor tragédiája" (Sándor Bródy's Tragedy), ibid., 201.

72. "Egy vándorgyűlés" (A Congress), ibid., 261.

73. The origins of the study have deep roots in Ady's journalism. We shall refer only to some of the articles: "Menjünk vissza Ázsiába" (Let's Go Back to Asia), ibid., 2:373–74; "A kúltura ígéretei" (The Promises of Culture), "Nemzeti főváros" (A National Capital), "A magyar városok" and "Várad és Debrecen" (The Hungarian Town and Várad and Debrecen), ibid., 3:114–26; "Egy könyv és egy ember" (A Book and a Man) ibid., 6:58–60; "Jókai szobra" (Jókai's Statue), ibid., 72–74. Of Wesselényi he wrote,

He was no Christ, "just in his sufferings. In the success of his crucifixion, no" (ibid., 89). Of Csokonai he wrote, "How Magyar you were, how Magyar. Ah, how painfully Magyar. The best of the Magyar kind. . . . Of the agonizing, of the sensitive kind. Of the kind that has empathy for the whole world, for every thought, for every emotion. For all this, he suffered bitterly" (ibid., 170). In connection with Sándor Bródy's suicide, he wrote the following: "Hungarian society's great swing to the West was but the swinging of a pendulum. It was a great comedown for many souls, for the sons of the new Hungary, her impatient, forward-pushing sons" (ibid., 201).

74. "Ismeretlen Korvin-kódex margójára" (To the Margin of an Unknown Corvin Codex), ibid., 7:19–22.

75. Legend has it that it was at Pusztaszer that the chiefs of the conquering Magyar tribes made their compact sealed in blood. Pusztaszer became the symbol of genteel Hungary.

76. St. Gerhardt (Gellért), missionary and bishop, was martyred by the pagan Magyar tribesmen in the early eleventh century.

77. "Ismeretlen Korvin-kódex margójára," 16–18.

78. "Az ige veszedelme" (The Danger of the Word), ibid., 31–32.

79. Ady to Léda, October 23, 1903, AEVL, 127.

80. Ady to Léda, no date (1905), ibid., 128.

81. Ady to Léda, November 30, 1905, ibid., 133.

82. Ady to Léda, December 13, 1905, ibid., 134.

83. Ady to Léda, mid-December 1905, ibid., 135.

84. B. Révész, *Ady trilógiája* (Ady's Trilogy) (Budapest, 1935), 14–15.

85. The "and yet" moral was first explicated by Király, *Ady Endre*, 1:198–216.

86. "A fajok cirkuszában" (In the Circus of the Races), in *Ady Endre összes versei*, 200.

87. "A márciusi naphoz" (To the March Sun), ibid., 198.

88. "Két meggyőződésű emberek" (Men of Two Minds), *Nyugat* (West), August 1, 1911.

89. "Véres panorámák tavaszán" (Spring of Bloody Sights), in *Ady Endre összes versei*, 359.

90. "Kurucok így beszélnek" (A Kuruc Speaks Like This), ibid., 389.

CHAPTER SIX
THE CULTURAL ROLE OF THE VIENNA-BUDAPEST OPERETTA

1. It is not by chance that an outstanding monographer of the operetta regarded his work as a kind of "cultural history": Bernard Grun, *Kulturgeschichte der Operette* (Munich, 1961); see also Martin Lichstfuss, *Operette im Ausverkauf* (Vienna-Cologne, 1989); and Otto Schneiderei, *Paul Lincke und die Erststehung der Berliner Operette* (Berlin, 1989).

2. Bernard Grun, *Kulturgeschichte der Operette*, 75–80.

3. Ibid., 105–6, 115ff; see also Paul Bekker, *Jacques Offenbach* (Berlin, 1909).

4. Otto Brusatti and Wilhelm Deutschmann, eds., *Die Wiener Operette*, Katalog der 91, Sonderausstellung des Historischen Museums der Stadt Wien (Vienna, 1985), 25.

5. Ibid., 31; see also Franz Hadamowsky and Otto Heinz, *Die Wiener Operette* (Vienna, 1947).

6. With regard to Strauss's oeuvre, see Ignaz Schnitzer, *Meister Johann* (Vienna, 1920); Ernst Decsey, *Johann Strauss* (Stuttgart, 1922); and György Sándor Gál and Vilmos Somogyi, *Mesél a bécsi erdő* (The Wienerwald Talks) (Budapest, 1972).

7. The meeting is depicted in Schnitzer, *Meister Johann,* in Gál and Somogyi, *Mesél a bécsi erdő,* 533–37, and in H. E. Jacob, *A régi Budapest* (The Old Budapest) (Budapest, 1938), 261–66.

8. Gál and Somogyi, *Mesél a bécsi erdő,* 538–39.

9. Jacob, *A régi Budapest,* 266; Schnitzer, *Meister Johann.*

10. "Mit den ersten vier Takten klingt der Akkord der Ungarnwelt, beginnt das Mollreich der Synkopen, beginnt das Czimballhafte, Rhapsodische, wozu als Gegensatz das Wienertum tritt." See Decsey, *Johann Strauss.*

11. It was the novelist Jókai who recommended the unknown recruiting music to Strauss.

12. Jacob, *A régi Budapest,* 269–70.

13. Adolf Bassaraba, "Schweinzuchter mit gräfischer Krone," *Wochenschau,* October 24, 1965.

14. *Pesti hírlap* (Pest Journal), October 25, 1885, 7, and March 27, 1886, 7; *Pesti napló* (Pest Daily), October 27, 1885 and March 27, 1886; and *Vasárnapi újság* (Sunday Gazette), April 25, 1886.

15. *Ország-világ* (Country and World), April 3, 1886, 228.

16. *Borsszem Jankó* (Johnny the Pepper), November 1, 1885. Cartoon on page 1, text on page 8.

17. *Vasárnapi újság,* November 15, 1885, 742.

18. The *Extrablatt,* quoted by Grun in *Kulturgeschichte der Operette,* 232.

19. Hermann Broch, *Hofmannsthal und seine Zeit* (Munich, 1964), 57.

20. Gál and Somogyi, *Mesél a bécsi erdő,* 542–43.

21. Alma Mahler Werfel, *Mein Leben* (Frankfurt, 1960), 149.

22. Grun, *Kulturgeschichte der Operette,* 323–24. See also Curt Riess, "Als die Witwen noch lustig waren," *Du. Kulturelle Monatschrift,* April 1963, 84–86.

23. Erzsébet Vezér, *Ady Endre publicisztikai írásai* (Publicist Writings of Endre Ady), vol. 1 (Budapest, 1977), 414.

24. Gyula Juhász, "Az Operett," *Nagyvárad,* July 1, 1909.

25. Grun, *Kulturgeschichte der Operette,* 333–41; Ernst Decsey, *Franz Lehár* (Vienna, 1924); Hadamowsky and Otte, *Die Wiener Operette.*

26. Péter Molnár Gál, "A víg özvegy" (The Merry Widow), *Mozgó Világ* (Moving World), April 1988, 110–16. I appreciate the kind support of Professor Moritz Csáky, Graz, Vienna, who allowed me to read his manuscript on the Viennese operetta.

27. Curt Riess, "Als die Witwen noch lustig waren" (When the Widows Still Were Merry) in *Du. Kulturelle Monatschrift,* vol. 23, 84–86.

28. Grun, *Kulturgeschichte der Operette,* 349.

29. With regard to this unique piece of Hungarian operetta based on folklore, see János Bókay, *Egy Rózsaszál szebben beszél . . .* (One Rose Speaks More Sweetly . . .) (Budapest, 1978).

30. István Takács, "A csárdáskirálynő—Egykor és most" (The Csárdás Princess—Once and Now), in *Színház* (Theater) 13.5 (May 1980), 19.

31. Julius Bistron, *Emmerich Kálmán* (Vienna, 1932); Rudolf Oesterreicher, *Emmerich Kálmán* (Vienna, 1954); Róbert Rátonyi, *Operett.* 1 (Budapest, 1984), 160–71.

32. Grun, *Kulturgeschichte der Operette*, 386–87.

33. The libretto of the play, *Színházi élet* (Theater Life) 6.15 (April 1917), 1.

34. Rátonyi, *Operett*. 1:216–17.

35. *Színházi élet* 6.15 (April 1917), 6–8.

36. Ibid., 5.40 (1916).

37. *Budapesti Hírlap*, November 4, 1916.

38. *Pesti Hírlap*, November 4, 1916.

39. Alma Mahler Werfel, *And the Bridge Is Love* (New York, 1958), 32.

40. Rátonyi, *Operett*. 1.220.

41. I would like to refer the reader to the archives of the Hungarian Institute for Theater, where I found valuable data relating to the librettos, performances, and reviews of operettas discussed in this chapter.

CHAPTER SEVEN
SOCIAL MARGINALITY AND CULTURAL CREATIVITY

1. Ernst Mach, *Analysis of Sensations* (New York, 1959), 30.

2. T. John Blackmore, *Ernst Mach. His Life, Work, and Influence* (Berkeley and Los Angeles, 1972), 25, 63.

3. Ibid., 117–20, 127, 184–89, 214–17, 247–59. See also Peter Kampits, *Zwischen Schein und Wirklichkeit. Eine kleine Geschichte der österreichischer Philosophie* (Vienna, 1984), 122–24; and Lloyd S. Swenson, Jr., *Genesis of Relativity* (Houston, 1979), 154–55. For Nietzsche's impact on Mach, see Leszek Kolakowski, *The Alienation of Reason* (Garden City, N.Y., 1968), 105.

4. Mach, *Analysis of Sensations*, 29; idem, *Erkenntnis und Irrtum* (Leipzig, 1917), 9; Blackmore, *Ernst Mach*, 35–36.

5. Lewis S. Feuer, *Einstein and the Generation of Science* (New Brunswick, N.J., 1982), 37.

6. Ibid., 43–44; Albert Einstein, "Autobiographical Notes," in P. A. Schlipp, *Albert Einstein: Philosopher-Scientist* (New York, 1949), 21.

7. Wolfdietrich Rasch, "Fin de siècle als Ende und Neubeginn," in Roger Bauer, ed., *Fin de siècle. Zu Literatur und Kunst der Jahrhundertwende* (Frankfurt a. M., 1977), 32 and passim; original in English. Also see Oscar Wilde, *Picture of Dorian Gray*, edited by Isobel Murray (Oxford, 1974).

8. Fritz Schalk, "Fin de siècle," in Bauer, *Fin de siècle*, 3.

9. Ibid., 5. "We accept without sensitivity and without pride the terrible word, decadence."

10. "Gabriele D'Annunzio," in Hugo v. Hofmannsthal, *Gesammelte Werke,* vol. 1, *Prosa* (Frankfurt a. M., 1950), 170–72.

11. Blackmore, *Ernst Mach*, 6–10.

12. Quoted by Feuer, *Einstein and the Generation of Science*, 29. Einstein added: "In Mach's case, every one of his unusual emphases or contributions to scientific method was founded on some childhood experience."

13. *Dictionary of Scientific Biography*, edited by Charles Coulston Gillispie, vol. 8, edited by J. H. Lane and P. J. Macquer (New York, 1973), 598.

14. Ernst Mach, *The Science of Mechanics. A Critical and Historical Account of Its Development* (6th ed. from 9th German ed., LaSalle, Ill., 1960), 279.

15. Swenson, *Genesis of Relativity*, 282.

16. Ernst Mach, *Die Geschichte und die Wurzel des Satzes von der Erhaltung der Arbeit* (Leipzig, 1909), 25, 31; Kristóf Nyíri, *A Monarchia szellemi életéről. Filozófiatörténeti tanulmányok* (On the Intellectual Life of the Monarchy. Essays on the History of Philosophy) (Budapest, 1980), 89.

17. Albert Fuchs, *Geistige Strömungen in Österreich* (2nd ed., Vienna, 1978), 202–4; Manfred Diersch, *Empirokritizismus und Impressionismus. Über Beziehungen zwischen Philosophie, Aesthetik und Literatur um 1900 in Wien* (Berlin, 1977), 6.

18. Swenson, *Genesis of Relativity*, 3.

19. Quoted by Diersch, *Empirokritizismus und Impressionismus*, 29.

20. Feuer, *Einstein and the Generation of Science*, 335; *Dictionary of Scientific Biography*, 2 (New York, 1973), 261–66.

21. Ludwig Boltzmann, "The Recent Development of Method in Theoretical Physics," in *The Monist* 2, quoted by Feuer, *Einstein and the Generation of Science*, 336.

22. *Neue Österreichische Biographie*, vol. 2 (Vienna, 1925), 137; Engelbert Broda, *Ludwig Boltzmann. Mensch, Physiker, Philosoph* (Vienna, 1955), 26–28.

23. *Dictionary of Scientific Biography*, 2:267.

24. Ibid., vol. 4 (New York, 1971), 313.

25. Recently the question was raised by Nancy J. Nersessian in her article, "Why Wasn't Lorentz Einstein?" in *Centaurs* 29 (1986).

26. Feuer, *Einstein and the Generation of Science*, xiii.

27. Swenson, *Genesis of Relativity*, 2.

28. Einstein, "Autobiographical Notes," 3–6.

29. John Stachel, ed., *The Collected Papers of Albert Einstein*, vol. 1 (Princeton, 1987), 211.

30. Ibid., xxxviii; see also Einstein, "Autobiographical Notes," 6.

31. Stachel, ed., *The Collected Papers of Albert Einstein*, pp. 55–56.

32. Ibid.

33. Carl Selig, *Albert Einstein. A Documentary Biography* (London, 1956), 113.

34. Feuer, *Einstein and the Generation of Science*, 14.

35. Swenson, *Genesis of Relativity*, 149.

36. Stachel., ed., *The Collected Papers of Albert Einstein*, p. 226.

37. Ibid., 285.

38. Ibid., 290, letter to Marcel Grossmann, April 1901.

39. Ibid., 294–95, letter to Mileva Maric, April 30, 1901.

40. Ibid., 325, letter to Mileva Maric, December 12, 1901.

41. Wolfgang Pauli, *Theory of Relativity* (New York, 1958), 5.

42. *The Principle of Relativity* (New York: Dover and Methuen, 1923), 38.

43. Swenson, *Genesis of Relativity*, 175.

44. Hermann Minkowski, "Space and Time," in *The Principle of Relativity*.

45. Swenson, *Genesis of Relativity*, 164.

46. Nersessian, "Why Wasn't Lorentz Einstein?" 205.

47. Ibid., 207. That is why Einstein called him "the greatest and noblest man of our time." Albert Einstein, *The World as I See It* (New York, 1934), 250.

48. Nersessian, "Why Wasn't Lorentz Einstein?" 228.

49. Einstein, "Autobiographical Notes," 53.

50. Nersessian, "Why Wasn't Lorentz Einstein?" 233.

51. P. A. Schilpp, *Albert Einstein, Philosopher-Scientist* (New York, 1949), 4.

52. Feuer, *Einstein and the Generation of Science*, 28.

53. Ibid., 40.

54. Marthe Robert, *From Oedipus to Moses. Freud's Jewish Identity* (Garden City, N.Y., 1976), 15ff.

55. Ernest Jones, *The Life and Work of Sigmund Freud* (New York, 1961); Peter Gay, *A Godless Jew. Freud, Atheism, and the Making of Psychoanalysis* (New Haven, 1987).

56. Carl E. Schorske, "Politics and Patricide in Freud's Interpretation of Dreams," in *Fin-de-Siècle Vienna. Politics and Culture* (New York, 1979), 200.

57. Henri F. Ellenberger, *The Discovery of the Unconscious. The History and Evolution of Dynamic Psychiatry* (New York, 1970), 444.

58. Ibid., 493.

59. Richard v. Krafft-Ebing, *Pathologia Sexualis* (Vienna, 1986).

60. Erna Laski, *Die Wiener medizinische Schule* (Vienna, 1965), 381–86; *Neue Deutsche Biographie* 10:649–50.

61. Ellenbeger, *The Discovery of the Unconscious*, 344.

62. Ibid., 345. Janet's synthesis, *Les medicationes psychologiques*, appeared in 1919.

63. One can see the judgment of the *Encyclopedia Britannica* (1973 edition) in the relative length of the articles on the two scholars. It published 29 lines about Janet and 127 lines about Freud, as well as 260 lines dealing with Freudian psychoanalysis.

64. Gay, *A Godless Jew*, 37. In this book Gay modified his stand explained in his earlier book, *Freud, Jews, and Other Germans* (New York, 1978).

65. Robert, *From Oedipus to Moses*, 35.

66. Sigmund Freud, *Standard Edition of the Complete Psychological Works of Sigmund Freud*, edited by James Strachey. 24 vols. (1953–1974) 20:274.

67. Robert, *From Oedipus to Moses*, 49.

68. "Levél az apámhoz," in *Ady Endre prózai művei* (Endre Ady's Collected Prose), vol. 4 (Budapest, 1964), 45.

69. Ibid., vol. 1 (Budapest, 1966), 192–93.

70. Ibid., 4:26–27.

71. Endre Ady, *Vallomások és tanulmányok* (Confessions and Studies), vol. 1, Biography (Budapest, 1944), 14; Ady, "Iró a könyvéről" (The Author about His Book), in *Ady Endra prózai művei*, 7:111.

72. *Ady Endre válogatott levelei* (Selected Letters of Endre Ady) (Budapest, 1956), 53, 91.

73. Ibid., 133–35.

74. Schorske, *Fin-de-Siècle Vienna*, 196–98.

75. "Kurucok így beszélnek" (A Kuruc Speaks Like This), in *Ady Endry összes versei* (Endre Ady's Collected Poems), 389.

76. Lajos Németh, ed., *Magyar művészet 1890–1918* (Hungarian Art 1890–1918) (Budapest, 1981).

77. Schorske, *Fin-de-Siècle Vienna*; William M. Johnston, *The Austrian Mind* (Berkeley and Los Angeles, 1972); Allan Janik and Stephan Toulmin, *Wittgenstein's Vienna* (New York, 1973); Peter Berner, Emil Brix, and Wolfgang Mantl, eds., *Wien um*

236   NOTES TO CHAPTER SEVEN

1900. Aufbruch in die Moderne (Vienna, 1986); *Traum und Wirklichkeit. Wien 1870–1930*, exhibition catalog (Vienna, 1985); James Leggio, ed., *Vienna 1900. Art, Architecture, and Design*, catalogue, Museum of Modern Art (New York, 1986); Ákos Moravánszky, *Építészet az Osztrák-Magyar Monarchiában 1867–1918* (Architecture in the Austro-Hungarian Monarchy 1867–1918) (Budapest, 1988).

78. Everett V. Stonequist, *The Marginal Man* (New York, 1961), 15.

79. Edward Sagarin, *Deviants and Deviance* (New York, 1975), 34.

80. Ibid., 35.

81. Ibid., 37.

82. Jerrold Seigel, *Bohemian Paris* (New York, 1986), 5.

83. Ibid., 25.

84. Ibid., 11.

85. Michael Worbs, *Nervenkunst. Literatur und Psychoanalysis in Wien der Jahrhundertwende* (Frankfurt a. M., 1983); Jens Rieckmann, *Aufbruch in die Moderne. Die Anfange des Jungen Wien* (Frankfurt a. M., 1986).

86. Fritz Mauther, *Sprache und Leben*, edited by Gershon Weiler (Salzburg-Vienna, 1986), 5–6.

87. Ibid., 7–8, 31–38.

88. Kurt Blaukopf, *Gustav Mahler oder der Zeitgenosse der Zukunft* (Munich-Vienna-Zurich, 1969), 20.

89. Related remarks of Kafka can be found in Max Brod, *Franz Kafka. Eine Biographie* (New York, 1946), 95, 105, 113–14, 210–12; Brod, *Über Franz Kafka* (Frankfurt a. M., 1966).

90. Jakob Wassermann, *Men Weg als Deutscher und Jude* (Berlin, 1921), 73. Quoted by Hans Dieter Hellige, "Generationskonflikt, Selbsthass und die Entstehung antikapitalistischer Positionen im Judentum," in *Geschichte und Gesellschaft 5* (1979), 491.

91. Thorstein Veblen, "The Intellectual Pre-eminence of Jews in Modern Europe," in *The Portable Veblen,* edited by Max Lerner (New York, 1948), 472–74.

92. Kurt Lewin, "Self-Hatred among Jews," in *Resolving Social Conflicts* (New York, 1948), 186–200.

93. Lesznai's comment on the discussion is in "On the Jewish Question in Hungary," in *Huszadik század* (Twentieth Century), vol. 1(1917), 105.

CHAPTER EIGHT
VOX POPULI

1. *Jobbágylevelek* (Letters of Serfs), edited by Éva H. Balázs (Budapest, 1951).

2. *Parasztsors—parasztgond 1919–1944* (Fate of Peasants—Cares of Peasants 1919–1944), edited by Dezső Kiss (Budapest, 1960).

3. The letters can be found as follows: Letters 1–10 and 12, Hadtörténeti Levéltár, Első világháborús gyűjtemény (Archive of War History, Collection from World War I), Zensurkommission für Korrespondenzen an Kriegsgefangene in Budapest, no. 4447; letter 16, ibid., no. 4448. Letters 11, 13–15, K.u.K. Zensurstelle Budapest, no. 4442. Brief 17, Archive of War History, Vienna, Armeeoberkommanda (AOK) GZNB, Abteilung fasc. E. 5942, no. 12, 110; Abteilung D. Res. fasc. 5905; Abteilung E. fasc. 5939, nos.

11,173, 10,811, 10,991, 11,021, and Res. no. 5050. If the letters quoted in the text can be found under these numbers, the reference will not be repeated.

4. Pál Mikó, *Női magyar levélstilus a 17. században* (The Style of Letters of Hungarian Women in the Seventeenth Century) (Székelyudvarhely, 1896), 1. László Makkai and László Mezei, *Árpád-kori és Anjou-kori levelek, XI–XIV. század* (Letters from the Age of the Árpad Dynasty and the Anjou Dynasty, Eleventh to Fourteenth Centuries) (Budapest, 1960), 10.

5. Ibid., 8–9, 11–12, 21–23.

6. Ibid., 37–39.

7. Ibid.

8. Lajos Hopp, "Le genre épistolaire Hongrois et ses rapports Européens," in *Littérature Hongroise—littérature Européenne* (Budapest, 1964), 196–98.

9. Mikó, *Női magyar levélstílus,* 9–11, 22–25.

10. József Gulyás, *Levélíró magyarok* (Corresponding Hungarians) (Sárospatak, 1926), 6.

11. Farkas Deák, *Magyar hölgyek levelei. 1515–1700* (Letters of Hungarian Ladies. 1515–1700) (Budapest, 1879), 13.

12. Ibid., 141–42.

13. Ibid., 373–74.

14. I express my appreciation to Dr. Győző Kenéz for this valuable information.

15. For example, the letter of the Monk Josa from 1551 in Deák, *Magyar hölgyek levelei,* 16.

16. Ibid. See also the letters of Anna Franciska Csáky, 268–90; of Éva Kapi, 319; and of Judit Perényi, 357.

17. From the letters of Mária Forgács, ibid., 115. See also Mikó, *Női magyar levélstílus,* 11.

18. The date of this letter is 1512, in Deák, *Magyar hölgyek levelei,* 67–68.

19. Sándor Eckhardt, "A legrégibb parasztlevelek nyelve és stilusa" (Language and Style of the Oldest Peasant Letters) in *Magyar Nyelvőr* (Hungarian Language Guardian) 2–3 (1950), 114.

20. Balázs, *Jobbágylevelek,* 81. Similar forms can be found in letters no. 42, 44, 46, 47.

21. Ibid., 98–102. Cf. Eckhardt, "A legrégibb parasztlevelek nyelve," 121.

22. Balázs, *Jobbágylevelek,* 186.

23. Lajos Takács, "Népi verselők, hírversírók" (Popular Rhymesters, Writers of News-Poems), in *Ethnographia* 1–2 (1951), 15, 24–25; Vilmos Gyenis, "Emlékirat és parasztkrónika" (Memoirs and the Peasant Chronicle), in *Irodalomtörténeti Közlemények* (Publications of Literary History) 2 (1965).

24. See for example Mátyás Vass, *Népiskolai olvasókönyv a leányiskolák IV. osztálya számára* (Textbook for Elementary Schools for Girls) (Szeged, 1883).

25. Ignác Bárány, *Ötödik olvasókönyv a katholikus népiskolák ötödik és hatodik osztálya számára* (Fifth Textbook for 5–6th Class of Catholic Elementary Schools) (2nd ed., Budapest, 1881).

26. A widespread and popular calendar, for example, was Vilmos Méhner, ed., *Magyar gazda naptára* (Calendar of Hungarian Farmers), or the *Kis házi naptár* (Little Home-Calendar) or the *Kincses kalendárium* (Thesaurus Calendar).

27. The "Feldbriefe" series was published by the publishing house Leben (Life) in Budapest in 1914–1915. Single pieces in the series were: "Brief des Kämpfers an seine Frau," "Brief des Kämpfers an seine Mutter," "Brief des Kämpfers en seine Kinder," "Brief des Kämpfers an sein Dorf," "An diekämfenden Helden," and so on.

28. Kálmán Kertész, "A harcos levele feleségéhez" (Letter of the Soldier to His Wife) in Feldbriefe series, 6–8.

29. Dr. Kálmán Radványi, "A harcos levele édesanyjához" (Letter of the Soldier to His Mother) in Feldbriefe series, 4–51.

30. Dr. Dénes Bálint, *Szerelmi levelező* (Love Correspondence) (Budapest, 1916); Dezső Kovács, *Szerelmi levelező* (Love Correspondence) (Budapest, n.d.); Géza Ilosvai, *Legkitűnőbb és legelső eredeti magyar szerelmi levelező jeles magyar irók által összeállítva* (The Best and First Original Hungarian Love Correspondence Edited by Renowned Hungarian Writers) (Budapest, n.d.); *Legujabb hölgyek titkára* (Newest Secretary for Ladies) (Budapest, 1889).

31. Bálint, *Szerelmi levelező*, 12, 19.

32. Kovács, *Szerelmi levelező*, 15.

33. *Legújabb hölgyek titkára*; Béla Csongor, *Legújabb és legteljesebb levelezőkőnyv mindenki számára* (Newest and Complete Correspondence for Everybody) (Budapest, n.d.); Sándor Verőczi, *Legújabb levelezőkönyv a magyar nép számára* (Newest Correspondence for the Hungarian People) (Pest, 1871).

34. Verőczi, *Legújabb levelezőkönyv*, Preface.

35. Mihál Stancsics, *Minden alkalmi köszöntések* (Letters for All Occasions) (Pest, 1841).

36. Elek Farkas, *Legújabb házi titoknok. Mindennemű családi és kereskedői levelek* (Newest Family Secretary. All Kinds of Family and Business Letters) (Pest, 1856).

37. [János Kis], *Legújabb magyar és német levelező könyv* (Newest Hungarian and German Correspondence) (2nd ed., Pest, 1815).

38. K. András Vályi, *A 'norma és a' levél író* (The Norm and the Correspondence) (Kassa, 1789).

39. Kilian Fémer, *Mindennapi közönséges és barátságos levelek, a levél írásban gyakorlatlanoknak kedvekért és hasznokért követésre való például kibotsáttattanak* (Everyday Usual and Friendly Letters for Illiterates as Examples to Follow) (Pozsony-Kassa, 1786). Kilian Fémer was a pseudonym, the anagram of Ephraim Klein, who was a Lutheran priest in Kassa (now Košice).

40. Christian Fürchtegott Gellert, *Briefe nebst einer praktischen Abhandlung von dem guten Geschmacke in Briefen* (Leipzig, 1858), 4.

41. Charles Rollin, *De la manière d'enseigner et d'étudier les belles-lettres, par rapport à l'esprit et au coeur*, vols. 1–4 (Amsterdam, 1736).

42. *Mikes Kelemen törökországi levelek és misszilis levelek* (Kelemen Mikes, Letters from Turkey), edited by Lajos Hopp (Budapest, 1966). On p. 400 he quotes the French writer Richelet, *Recueil des plus belles lettres sur toutes sortes de sujets, avec des avies sur la manière de les écrire, et des réponses sur chaque espèce de lettres* (Paris, 1690).

43. Explained by Hopp, *Le genre épistolaire Hongrois*, 202–7.

44. Vályi, *A 'norma és a' levél író*. Dedication to Ferenc Kazinczy, the head of the Hungarian literary reform movement.

45. Ibid., 108–9.

46. Ibid., 122–23.

47. Balázs, *Jobbágylevelek, 3*; Eckhardt, "A legrégibb parasztlevelek nyelve és stílusa," 114.

48. *Magyar statisztikai évkönyv. Új folyan* (Hungarian Statistical Yearbook. New Series) 10 (Budapest, 1903), 346.

49. Quoted in Géza Lampérth, *Régi magyar levelesláda* (Old Hungarian Letters) (Budapest, 1923), 22, 28.

50. *Adassék a levél . . . Régi és új magyar szerelmes levelek 1528–1938* (Should Be Given This Letter . . . Old and New Hungarian Love Letters 1528–1938), edited by Farkas Ferenc Bisztrai (Budapest, 1938).

51. Letter of M. Z. to a woman from Nagykáta, on March 26, 1917.

52. Eckhardt, "A legrégibb parasztlevelek nyelve és stílusa," 119.

53. Some of the most frequent complaints in our letters were protests against the ever-higher cost of living and the pressing requisitions. One repeatedly comes across such phrases as "If this goes on, we all will starve," or "We work too much and . . . eat too little." This motif became a stereotype also used by persons who did not suffer from hunger. György Szmódits wrote to his son on March 21, 1917: "We are deprived of our basic food, we hardly eat sufficient meals. . . . Therefore I had to buy one cow from uncle Jóska, so now we have three cows and some swans and piglets."

54. Letter of Mrs. Tatár on June 20, 1917.

55. For example, the letters of Mrs. Tóth from Medina and Mrs. Keczeli from Keszü, both in September 1917.

56. Letter of Mrs. Papp, peasant from Mezőberény, June 12, 1917.

57. Letter of Mrs. Karolina Horvath, November 27, 1917 (in German).

58. Frau Gábor, "Az oroszországi forradalmi mozgalmak visszhangja a magyar dolgozók hadifoglyokhoz írt leveleiben" (The Echo of the Russian Revolutionary Movements in the Letters of Hungarian Workers to War Prisoners) in *Párttörténeti Közlemények* (Publications of the Party History), 2 (Budapest, 1958).

59. Letter of Mrs. Erzsébet Tomovics, peasant from Kisvicsáp, January 17, 1918.

60. Péter Hanák, "Die Volksmeinung während des letzten Kriegsjahres in "Österreich-Ungarn," in *Die Auflösung des Habsburgerreiches*, edited by Richard Georg Plaschka and Karlheinz Mack (Vienna, 1970), 60–66. A high percentage of the letters from January and February 1918 welcomed and supported the general strike that broke out in January.

61. Letter of Mr. Sándor Csörsz, April 28, 1917.

62. Letter of Mr. József Bíró, worker of Erzsébetfalva, January 19, 1918; quoted in Gábor, "Az oroszországi forradalmi mozgalmak visszhangja," 143–44.

63. Letter of Mr. Antal Schneider, worker of Soroksár, January 29, 1918.

64. Mikó, *Női magyar levélstílus*, 32–34.

65. Bisztrai, ed., *Adassék a levél*.

66. Balázs, *Jobbágylevelek*, 186–87. Letter of Vaszilij Málas, serf from Celna, to his wife, May 18, 1749.

67. Cf. Mikó, *Női magyar levélstílus*, 29, and Lampérth, *Régi magyar levelesláda*, 93–94.

68. Hopp, *Le genre épistolaire Hongrois*, 210–11.

69. Bisztrai, ed., *Adassék a levél*, introduction by Gyula Illyés, 2.

70. Letter of Mrs. Rédei, peasant from Nagymajlát, August 18, 1917.

71. Letter of Ambrus József Kis, February 4, 1918, and of an unknown peasant woman from Zsámbok, December 31, 1917.

72. Jenő Szűcs, "Dózsa parasztháborújának ideológiája" (The Ideology of the Dózsa-Peasant War), in *Valóság* (Reality), 1972, 24–27.

73. The Censorship office compiled a comprehensive report of the general atmosphere each month. The reports summarized the number of confiscated letters and the proportion of the main causes of objection. See, for example, the report of the Budapest Zensur Office from April 1917, no. 4447; for Austria: AOK, GZNB, Abteilung D. Res. fasc. 5931. 8080. In July 1918 there were just eighty of the "reproachable" letters; out of these one-third belonged to the so-called "hunger letters." Ibid., fasc. 5915. 5174.

74. See the report on the general atmosphere from January until April 1918, no. 4448. For Austria: AOK, GZNB. Abteilung D. Res. fasc. 5912. 4940, 4986; fasc. 5913. 5030, 5059.

75. Letter of Mrs. Papp, June 12, 1917, and note 56 above.

76. Letter of Mrs. Stefankova from Galgóc on May 23, 1917.

77. Letter of Mrs. Maria Bucsa from Borzás, August 1917.

78. Letter of Mrs. Hauser, April 4, 1917 (in German).

79. Archive of War History, AOK. GZNB, Abteilung D. Res. fasc. 5913, 5030, Annex no. 28 to the monthly report of February 1918.

INDEX

absolutism, 65–66, 122

Act LIII/1868 (Hungarian), 99

Adler, Friedrich, 160

Ady, Endre, xv, xvii, 79, 82, 86–87, 108, 110–34, 166–71; "and yet" morality, 133–34; "Bilek," 118–20; *Blood and Gold*, 125; "Danger of the Word," 130; escapism, 128–30, 168–69; health, 130; intellectual formation, 110–12; as journalist, 110–11, 125–26, 167; "Leading the Dead," 170; letters, 116–17, 121, 125, 167–69; marginality, 169; *New Poems*, 124–25, 132, 169; "Nostra res agitur," 116; "Notes on an Unknown Corvin Codex," 110; in Paris, 124–25; as poet, 117, 119–22, 124–25, 130–32, 168-70; political activity, 113, 125–27, 132–34; political disillusionment, 122–23; political program, 114–17; quoted, 78, 80–81, 84, 89–90, 92, 96, 112, 114–22, 125–30, 133–34, 141, 167–70, 230–31n.73; "Short Walk," 118; "To the Margin of an Unknown Corvin Codex," 129; "Twilight of Nationalism," 127; *Újversek*, 86; "Vision in the Fens," 119–21; and World War I, 134

aesthetics: of death, 106–9; expressionist, of Austrian avant garde, 95

Agai, Adolf, 48

Agonie (Schnitzler), 74

agrarianism, 114

Alexander, Bernát, 77

alienation: of death, 98–109. *See also* marginality

Allegro barbaro (Bartók), 88

Anatol (Schnitzler), 68-69

Andreas-Salome, Lou, 123

Andrian-Werburg, Leopold, 68

antifeudalism: of Ady, 111, 114–17; in Budapest operetta, 143–44

antinaturalism, literary, 68

anti-Semitism: Austrian, 65; Einstein's experience of, 155; Hungarian, 48–49, 55–60

apartment buildings: in Budapest, 15–19; functional divisions, 17; open- corridor style, 21–22; social divisions, 17–18; and urbanization, 6–8

apartments: functional divisions, 24; size, 22, 103; three-room, 22, 216n.44

Arany, János, 53

Arany, László, quoted, 78

architects, 37, 39; in Budapest, 6, 12; and historical revivalism, 14- 15; Hungarian, 41–43; Sezession, 32–35

architecture: Art Nouveau, 171; of Budapest, 20–21; folk, 40–41; Hungarian, 87; monastic, 7, 21; national tradition in, 39; of Pest, 6–7; revival, 6–7, 32; styles of, 35; of Vienna, 10–12. *See also names of styles*

aristocracy: Austrian, 65–66; modernism and, 173–74

aristocracy, Hungarian: Ady family, 110–12; "genealogical" mentality, 108; and national self-image, 52–54; satire of, 145

Árkay, Aladár, 171

arrangement, of middle-class home, 22–30

art: industrial, 75; as reality, 70

Art Nouveau, 170; Ady and, 111, 120, 123–24; in architecture, 171; use of term, 123–24; Viennese, 107. *See also* Sezession

assimilation: in Austria, 65; of Germans, 48, 50, 53; in Hungary, 66; of Jews, 48, 50, 53, 56–57, 59, 165, 176–77; linguistic, 50; as threat, 57

Attaché, L' (Meilhac), 141–42

Austrian Museum of Ethnography, 44

Austrians, Hungarian image of, 54

avant garde: Austrian, 94–97; Hungarian, 86–91

Az ópiumszívó álma (Gulácsy), 93–94

Babits, Mihály, 82–83, 87, 108; *Darutörpeharc*, 84; *Esti kérdés*, 90; "Fekete ország," 79; quoted, 79–80, 82, 84, 89–90; "Szimbólumok," 79–80

backwardness, cultural, as Hungarian self-perception, 77–80, 88, 108, 128–29, 167

Bahr, Hermann, 67, 75–76; quoted, 75, 221–22n.12

Barkóczy, Krisztina, 206

Baroque: in architecture, 7; in Vienna, xix; Viennese theater and, 69